THE PLAYS OF LORD BYRON
Critical Essays

LIVERPOOL ENGLISH TEXTS AND STUDIES
General editors: JONATHAN BATE and BERNARD BEATTY

This long-established series has a primary emphasis on close reading, critical exegesis and textual scholarship. Studies of a wide range of works are included, although the list has particular strengths in the Renaissance, and in Romanticism and its continuations.

A full list of titles available in this series can be obtained from Liverpool University Press.

THE PLAYS OF LORD BYRON

Critical Essays

EDITED BY

ROBERT GLECKNER
Duke University, North Carolina

and

BERNARD BEATTY
University of Liverpool

LIVERPOOL UNIVERSITY PRESS

First published 1997 by
LIVERPOOL UNIVERSITY PRESS
Senate House, Abercromby Square, Liverpool L69 3BX

British Library Cataloguing-in-Publication Data
A British Library CIP Record is available for this book
ISBN   0-85323-881-2 *cased*
          0-85323-891-X *paper*

Typeset by BBR, Sheffield
Printed and bound in the European Union by
Page Bros (Norwich) Ltd, UK

Contents

Acknowledgements

The editors and publisher wish to thank the following for their permission to reproduce copyright material:

David Eggenschweiler, 'Byron's *Cain* and the Antimythological Myth', *Modern Language Quarterly*, XXXVII (1976), pp. 324–38, reprinted by permission of Duke University Press.

A. B. England, 'Byron's *Marino Faliero* and the Force of Individual Agency', *Keats–Shelley Journal*, XXXIX (1990), pp. 95–122, reprinted by permission of the Keats–Shelley Association of America, Inc. and the editor of the journal.

David V. Erdman, 'Byron's Stage Fright: The History of His Ambition and Fear of Writing for the Stage', *English Literary History*, VI (1939), pp. 219–43, copyright 1939 by The Johns Hopkins University Press, reprinted by permission of the publisher.

Caroline Franklin, excerpt from *Byron's Heroines*, copyright Caroline Franklin 1992, reprinted by permission of Oxford University Press.

Wolf Z. Hirst, 'Byron's Lapse into Orthodoxy: An Unorthodox Reading of *Cain*', *Keats–Shelley Journal*, XXIX (1980), pp. 152–72, reprinted by permission of the Keats–Shelley Association of America, Inc. and the editor of the journal.

Malcolm Kelsall, excerpt from *Byron's Politics* (Hemel Hempstead: Harvester, 1987), pp. 82–118, copyright Malcolm Kelsall, reprinted by permission of the author.

G. Wilson Knight, excerpts from *The Burning Oracle* (Oxford: Oxford University Press, 1939), pp. 225–42, 243–60, copyright Routledge: International Thomson Publishing Services, reprinted by permission of Routledge.

Peter J. Manning, excerpts from *Byron and His Fictions* (Detroit: Wayne State University Press, 1978), pp. 136–45, 159–70, copyright 1978 by Wayne State University Press, reprinted by permission of the author and the publisher.

Jerome J. McGann, excerpts from *Fiery Dust: Byron's Poetic Development* (Chicago: University of Chicago Press, 1968), pp. 205–06, 215–27, 262–66, copyright 1969 by University of Chicago Press, reprinted by permission of the author and the publisher.

Daniel M. McVeigh, '"In Caines Cynne": Byron and the Mark of Cain', *Modern Language Quarterly*, XLIII (1982), pp. 337–50, reprinted by permission of Duke University Press.

Alan Richardson, excerpts from *A Mental Theater: Poetic Drama and Consciousness in the Romantic Age* (University Park: Pennsylvania State University Press, 1988), pp. 84–99, 201, copyright 1988 by Pennsylvania State University Press, reproduced by permission of the publisher.

Charles E. Robinson, 'The Devil as Doppelgänger in *The Deformed Transformed*: the Sources and Meaning of Byron's Unfinished Drama', *Bulletin of the New York Public Library*, LXXIV (1970), pp. 177–202, reprinted by permission of the New York Public Library.

Murray Roston, excerpt from *Biblical Drama in England* (Evanston: Northwestern University Press, 1969), pp. 212–15, copyright 1969 by Northwestern University Press, reprinted by permission of the publisher.

Daniel P. Watkins, 'The Ideological Dimensions of Byron's *The Deformed Transformed*', *Criticism*, XXV (1983), pp. 27–39, copyright 1983 by Wayne State University Press, reprinted by permission of the author and publisher.

Susan J. Wolfson, '"A Problem Few Dare Imitate": Sardanapalus and Effeminate Character', *English Literary History*, LVIII (1991), pp. 867–97, copyright 1991 by The Johns Hopkins University Press, reprinted by permission of the author and publisher.

The editors also gratefully acknowledge the efforts of Julie Rainford (Liverpool University Press), Chris Reed and Carol Fellingham Webb in preparing the text for publication.

Introduction

This collection brings together in a single volume a number of the best twentieth-century essays on Byron's dramas, in our judgement, together with comprehensive bibliographies of all recent writings on each of them. We have deliberately included some well-known and foundational essays as well as writings which are very recent or more difficult to obtain, for we wish the collection to be as representative and yet as varied and useful as possible to those interested in Byron as a dramatist. Since, earlier in this century, Samuel Chew methodically and G. Wilson Knight more flamboyantly examined Byron's plays as though they were worth attention but were not receiving it, many more books and articles have appeared to build on or argue with the pioneering efforts of Chew and Knight, as well as those of a few others. In part, this increase in attention is due to a renewed and far more sustained effort to critically study and evaluate Romantic and Gothic drama generally. This volume, therefore, may serve not only as a critical tool in relation to Byron studies but also as an illustration of the momentum and varied directions of criticism itself over the last fifty years. During that time, Byron's reputation has steadily gained, or regained, its stature and along the way his own relation to drama, to the contemporary theatre, and to dramatic tradition was often deliberately considered in and for itself, without regard for its pertinence to the study of his other poetic enterprises. But in relatively recent years, attention to his dramas has played a real part in the revaluation of Byron's entire *oeuvre*, thereby helping to restore the whole Byron to view, to take him seriously as a thinker, and to respect his energetic concern with new as well as traditional forms.

Our intention to represent this movement accurately ran

into some predictable difficulties. There are, for example, substantially more essays on *Sardanapalus* or *Cain*, many of them very fine, than on *Werner* or *Heaven and Earth*. Our selection reflects this weighting, and we are fully cognizant of the omission of some very good criticism on the first two of these plays, but at the same time we wanted to include material on all his plays. The obvious exception to this rule is *Manfred* and the reasons for excepting may be equally obvious: it is virtually central in all thorough critical studies of Byron as a poet and it has attracted a large body of journal articles devoted solely to it. Perhaps, indeed, it deserves a collection of its own (as *Don Juan*, for example, has) but in any case we may take some comfort from the fact that Byron himself sub-titled the play 'A Dramatic Poem'. Needless to say, our particular exclusions of certain essays or book chapters devoted to one or more of the plays are at least debatable, but in such a volume as this space is always at a premium and had we tried to include all the critical work we regarded as first-rate, our desired balance between the book's different sections would have been severely skewed. Reading through the considerable material now available on Byron's dramas is daunting but not depressing. If the selections we offer in the first instance, from books and journals alike, reflect to some extent our own tastes, that is perhaps inevitable, but we have quite deliberately eschewed any attempt to represent or balance different critical approaches or to pursue any critical agenda or stance with which we are in special sympathy. We have tried, in other words, to present some of the best and most provocative of what has been thought and written about Byron as dramatist.

A collection of this kind is most useful, we think, if it is extensive in range and its selections substantially uncut. Ours is certainly the former and largely the latter, although here and there we have had to prune both text and notes, especially in longer essays, in order to permit us to include as many essays as possible. There are a few silent omissions and adjustments of an unimportant kind, but all significant omissions are signalled by ellipses and are, in our judgement, of material which does not relate directly to the plays themselves. In some cases the authors themselves have revised or updated previously published work specifically to fit our editorial intentions. In the case of older essays, although we have corrected obvious errors and standardized references, we have normally preserved the format and original form of textual citations since it would be anomalous to use the standard McGann edition of Byron's poetry for all quotations when the essayists themselves did not have that version of Byron's text available to them.

The volume begins with David Erdman's vigorous account of 'Byron's Stage Fright', and is followed by a bibliography of material concerned broadly with Byron's relation to the stage. Thereafter there is a bibliography at the end of each section containing all recent writings on the play with which the section is concerned. In this way, we have tried to make the volume as comprehensively useful as possible to the reader, student and scholar of Byron's remarkable theatre, as well as to the company of other Byronists and the students of the Romantic era at large.

Byron's Stage Fright: the History of his Ambition and Fear of Writing for the Stage

DAVID V. ERDMAN

> I composed it actually with a *horror* of the stage, and with a view to render even the thought of it impracticable, knowing the zeal of my friends that I should try that for which I have an invincible repugnance, viz. a representation.
>
> (Byron to Murray, of *Manfred*, 9 March 1817)[1]

> Unless I could beat them all, it would be nothing...
>
> (Byron to Kinnaird, 31 March 1817)[2]

Why did Byron write plays 'to reform the stage'—and then violently protest against their being staged? None of Byron's major biographers has asked this question, although it affords an excellent opportunity to probe into the core of Byron's paradoxical psychology. Most critics who have considered the matter at all have either begun with the axiom or ended with the conclusion that Byron's dramas are closet dramas, never intended for the stage. [...] The obvious contradiction between Byron's professed aim to reform the English stage and his vociferously professed intention to keep his own plays off the English stage has been lightly dismissed even by the two critics who have taken some pains to document Byron's 'horror of the stage'. Samuel Chew notes without further comment that the failure of Byron's 'plays' was 'a *contretemps* that mortified him notwithstanding his repeated declarations that they were not intended for the theatre.'[3]

William J. Calvert, after quoting page upon page of Byron's protests—apparently not sensing that they add up to perhaps 'too much'—casually remarks: 'How he expected to found a tradition of the theatre by the means of unactable plays he never made clear.'[4]

I believe it will be nearer the truth of the matter to say that far from considering his own plays unactable, Byron only feared they might be. That he did protest too much, that he really yearned for dramatic success—the visible and audible applause of an audience mad for the great lines of a Byronic protagonist, a Marino, a Sardanapalus, or a Tiberius in the person (why not?) of Kean—like a moth for a flame, should be as clear a biographical fact as that, unlike a moth, conscious and fearful that the flame might burn him, Byron angrily refused to make the 'experiment for applause'[5] which representation would constitute. It is time that a bit of modern psychological understanding were applied to what has remained until now a merely curious 'Byronic paradox'. Byron's attitude towards his dramas is a significant clue to his behaviour generally and to his artistic behaviour in particular.

This contradiction—Byron's desire and terror of dramatic fame—is like the many other Byronic contradictions that have been so often described and so seldom explained without the aid of metaphysics;[6] it can be cleared up only when we look upon the paradoxical statements and actions of Byron as complementary *symptoms* of a single drive of behaviour, a drive towards a goal of imagined superiority or a position of maximum attention, desired as compensation for an intense feeling of inferiority and insecurity, which itself was based on his abused lameness, his relative social isolation before schooltime, and his insecure position as only child under the alternating tyranny and indulgence of 'Mrs. Byron *furiosa*' (*LJ*, I, 101).

His mother's 'violent' and 'capricious' treatment of a sensitively intelligent child developed in the young Byron such a hunger for kind attention and such a terror of condemnation, that he formed a paradoxical life-plan to cope with a paradoxical situation:[7] one had to expose oneself to gain attention; so Byron did what he found most attention-getting, he gave his 'ravenous ego', to use the language of Gamaliel Bradford, all the 'brilliant and varied assertion'[8] in verse and prose and voice that he was able to give it. But exposure courted rebuff and the possible failure of one's experiments for applause; so at the same time Byron's mind made an elaborate fortification against ridicule, against failure in any public undertaking. Not to expose himself at all would have been to stand no chance of attention, no chance of proving his superiority. Failure would have been bitter *just because* he wanted so much to succeed. [...]

Towards his poetry, Byron found convenient the pose of the aristocrat and the Dandy, an affectation of indifference to cover his anxious desire for the public's approbation. But also, by way of fighting a trivial battle to save his deeper defences, he was, as he confessed, 'a good deal of an author in *amour propre* and *noli me tangere*' (*LJ*, IV, 182). He made a great fuss about such *tours de force* as modernizing Horace or translating Pulci and Dante 'line for line' into '*cramp* English' (*LJ*, IV, 405, 419). These were noble feats, like swimming the Hellespont, to be bragged about with impunity. On the other hand, his concern for original works, such as his first play or, to take an earlier example, the first *Childe Harold* cantos ... was too personal, and their fame was too precarious, for any but a nervous silence on the part of the fearful author.

Here again, in the matter of Byron's attitude towards *Childe Harold*, criticism has been obtuse. It is as absurd to repeat as fact that Byron did not recognize merit in the poem that was to make him famous overnight, as it was ill-advised of Hobhouse to deny Dallas's story of Byron's hesitant release of the manuscript. The 'Hints from Horace', dashed off in a day or two, was easy for him to entrust to his somewhat officious cousin and to any publisher he might find.[9] But the *Childe* was Byron's first big poem,[10] representing five months' protracted effort carried on so secretly that companion Hobhouse hadn't suspected for weeks. [...] It was only with a careful show of nonchalance that he let the manuscript into Dallas's hands.

Once *Childe Harold* was out of the bag and the praise of friends had given it social existence, the author grew bolder, began protesting that printer Cawthorne did not 'stand high enough in the trade' to be given this job. And then Byron's concern took various forms of touchiness in the struggle for anonymity, the fury at Murray's showing the *Childe* to Gifford, Byron's critical pagod, and the melting when praise was Gifford's judgement.[11] The indifference and the touchiness were Byron's lines of defence. If the public had damned the poem, Byron could have blamed Dallas for pushing it, Murray for not keeping it anonymous, and, inconsistently, he could have maintained that he hadn't thought much of it from the start. We can imagine what would have happened if we consider the intensity with which Byron scolded his 'meddling friends' when the representation of his play, *Marino Faliero*, was reported damned. The difference between the publishing of *Childe Harold* and the representation of *Marino Faliero* is that the first succeeded and Byron's defences were not needed, whereas the second failed and the record is crowded with Byron's disclaimers. In reviewing the history of Byron and his dramas, both Chew and Calvert array only the documents of protest;[12] the evidences of Byron's desire to capture the English stage are equally necessary to complete the picture, for his protests are rooted in his desire. From his boyhood on, Byron was a passionate theatre-goer, a spectator easily, and often deeply, moved. And as with anything that fascinated him, Byron could not rest in a simply passive part; periodically throughout his life he hovered on the threshold of active participation in the theatre, now planning 'to get up a play', now trying his hand as a playwright. The longer he stayed on the threshold, unfortunately, the stronger a case he developed of what may be called a playwright's stage fright. The passionateness of his interest reverberated in his denials.

To bring out clearly the extent and duration of this interest, I shall first survey briefly what is known of Byron's career as an actor and then examine chronologically the rôle he played as a protesting playwright.

During the Harrow speech-days Byron had his first taste of the sweets of applause when he declaimed his favourite dramatic selections. His debut was with a passage *'ex Virgilio'* in 1804; in 1805 he recited Young's Zanga in June, Lear in July. In his poetic account of his life at Harrow[13] the applause he received from this 'acting' is the high point: when he recited the part of Zanga, 'with spectators surrounded', 'to swell my young pride, such applauses resounded,/ I fancied that Mossop himself was outshone...' and as Lear, 'fired by loud plaudits and self-adulation,/ I regarded myself as a Garrick revived.' In 1806 he acted 'in some private theatricals at Southwell', again, as he remembered long afterward, 'with great applause'.[14] The plea of his 'Prologue' on this occasion— for one 'who hopes, yet almost dreads, to meet your praise'[15] —although conventional, fits patly into the Byronic pattern of hunger for applause surrounded by a strong defence of fear. In 1808 Byron decided

> to get up a play here [at Newstead]; the hall will constitute a most admirable theatre. I have settled the *dram. pers.*, and can do without ladies, as I have some young friends who will make tolerable substitutes. (*LJ*, I, 189)

It is interesting to note that 'the play we have fixed on ... will be the *Revenge*', for this is the play that contains the part of Zanga in which Byron 'outshone Mossop' three years earlier. He wanted now to relive that triumph with a full company.

The rest of Byron's 'acting career' consisted of some 'masquing' and an occasional private recitation of blank verse to a worshipful group of friends. To these should be added his two speeches in the House of Lords, which he considered 'a little theatrical' (*LJ*, II, 105). In 1814 '"us Youth" of Watier's Club' gave a Masquerade 'to Wellington and Co.', which Byron remembered as a bright spot in his life as a Dandy (*LJ*, V, 444, 423). The next year, when he was on the managing committee of the Drury Lane Theatre, the same Masquerade was put on the stage by the professional actors; Byron saw a chance to get the feel of an audience from the real Stage:

> Douglas Kinnaird, and one or two others with myself, put on Masques, and went *on* the Stage amongst the 'οἱ πολλοί' to see the effect of a theatre from the Stage. It is very grand. (*LJ*, V, 445)

A lord could of course go no further. But Byron impressed Ticknor with his perfect imitations of the Drury Lane stars, and he convinced Medwin, years later at Pisa, that he 'perhaps ... would have made the finest actor in the world.' The occasion for Medwin's observation was the result of another sudden decision of Byron's to get up a play, this time *Othello*:

> Lord Byron was to be Iago. Orders were to be given for the fitting ... rehearsals of a few scenes took place.... All at once a difficulty arose about a Desdemona, and the Guiccioli put her veto on our theatricals.[16]

This is Byron's last stage record. Throughout his life he retained the attitude of an amateur actor. His fascination with the rôle of the great actor—Garrick and Mossop then, or Kean and Kemble now—pervaded the drama of his own life and inspired much of his playwriting.[17]

In 1812 the theatre called to Lord Byron, the newly fashionable poet, to write an address for the opening of the new Drury Lane. His response is a symbol of his neurotic dread of competition. When the managers asked him to enter the contest which they had arranged to obtain an opening address, Byron curtly refused. When they offered to reject all the entries they had received in favour of whatever Lord Byron would be good enough to write, he accepted the task and then sweated blood over it for a month, polishing and repolishing, and wishing he 'had known months ago' (*LJ*, II, 150). He had never taken so much pains with anything. Writing not only to order but for stage recitation was disturbing; the symptoms of his stage fright appeared.

As for the writing of plays, the occasional hesitant efforts before 1815 are known only by hearsay; Byron seems to have given them all the fate of his first play, *Ulric and Ilvina*, an early—perhaps even his first—literary effort, which he wrote at the age of thirteen and had 'sense enough to burn'.[18] The 'comedy of Goldoni's ... one scene', which he translated in 1811, is not extant. A year after the 'Drury Lane Address' he wrote some scenes of a comedy, but burnt them. Playwriting was 'difficult'—perhaps tragedy would not be so hard.[19] The career of a playwright, because it was a possible career for Byron, was terrifying to consider. 'Conscious insecurity', says the psychologist, 'produces stage fright: stage fright previews the failure and one suffers it in advance, to avoid experiencing it in its actual and full seriousness.'[20] [...]

In all his criticism of the contemporary stage, Byron's own theatrical ambitions may be detected beneath the accents of the disinterested patriotic critic. In *English Bards and Scotch Reviewers*, in 'Hints from Horace', and in the 'Address' the main theme was always the crying need for a new and reformed drama. Here was the chance, he seemed to say, for 'some genuine bard' to mount a vacant throne at one leap. Byron, like some shy swimmer fearful of entering the water, first called upon all his friends to venture what he, obviously, would rather like to do himself. In *English Bards* he had exhorted Sheridan to

> Give, as thy last memorial to the age,
> One classic drama, and reform the stage.[21]

And in 1814 he wrote to Moore, 'As it is fitting there should be good plays, now and then, besides Shakespeare's, I wish you or Campbell would write one' (*LJ*, III, 81); then he admitted his own trepidations: 'The rest of "us youth" have not heart enough.' But everyone else saw Byron as the logical 'genuine bard' for tragedy. He was immensely flattered by the petitions, especially from Kemble (in January) and Jeffrey (in August), that he write a tragedy, but he was also naturally made more fearful: 'I wish I could,' he said in January, 'but I find my scribbling mood subsiding.' 'I wish I had a talent for the drama,' he confided to his Journal, 20 February, on the eve of an introduction to Kean the day after seeing Kean as Richard; 'I would write a tragedy *now*. But no,—it is gone' (*LJ*, III, 126, 16; II, 387).

Nevertheless, at the year's end he found himself on the managing committee of Drury Lane, closer than ever to the 'strutters and fretters', and, as he later admitted, he entered with 'some idea of writing for the house myself' (*LJ*, II, 230; Medwin I, 90–91).

He told Medwin he had soon given up the idea rather than be a slave to public taste. But, after all, the public was the only source of applause. Moreover, if Medwin has quoted him accurately, Byron was obscuring the causal sequence of events when he seemed to suggest that contact with the realities of the theatre had discouraged him from 'writing for the house': indeed it was *after* he had been on the committee a year, during which time he had read his share of some 'five hundred Drury Lane offerings' (*LJ*, IV, 31) and had had a chance to see what trash could succeed and that there was no good work to be found either produced or rejected, that he began, apparently encouraged by the dearth of good dramas, to write a first draft of *Werner* which would have been by contemporary canons a Legitimate tragedy, with stage directions so explicit and prominent as clearly to reveal his purpose.[22]

It was 'Lady Byron's farce' (*LJ*, V, 391), the Separation, and not any sudden discovery of the depravity of English stage tastes, that interrupted Byron's career as a playwright. Abandoning *Werner*, he wrote nothing more, outside of a personal stanza or two, in England.

Before this dramatic attempt of his own, Byron was busy as committeeman trying to find a good play to make 'the Drama be where she hath been'.[23] His view of the ripeness of the time and his own 'wish' to exploit it stand out in a letter he wrote to Coleridge in March 1815:

> If I may be permitted, I should suggest that there never was such an opening for tragedy. In Kean [first London appearance January 1814], there is an actor worthy of expressing the thoughts of the characters which you have every power of embodying .... We have had nothing to be mentioned in the same breath with *Remorse* [Coleridge's poetic drama, successful in 1813] for very many years; and I should think that the reception of that play was sufficient to encourage the highest hopes of author and audience. (*LJ*, III, 191–92)

Each of these encouragements Byron was anxious, we may surmise, to apply to himself. [...] Ideals of a new 'classic drama' had been forming in Byron's mind for some time,[24] but in *Werner* he was ready to meet his audience half way, with a tragedy free of the traditional rant and horrors, but still more Gothic than Greek. Later, perhaps, he might lead his audience to higher forms....

Then England slapped him in the face, just as his 'amiable Mamma' had often done after she had been most indulgent; and Byron left, mortified and defiant. The beginning of his play, inadvertently or not, was left behind.

From this point Chew dates 'Byron's thorough opposition to the stage' as a 'part of his increasing dislike of all things English' (p. 36). And in a sense Chew may be right. Byron had been allowing himself to adjust to the demands of English society, with his conventional marriage, his *Hebrew Melodies*, and all that, in spite of his own anti-social fears. In spite of trepidations he had begun at last a tragedy for the English stage. The recoil from society's rebuff was violent, and when Byron turned again to drama (but notice that he did return to drama, and fairly soon at that)[25] he made, in *Manfred*, no *Werner*-like concessions to stage tastes; he took, as it were, the typical horror play and condensed it into one defiant soliloquy, rendering it, he hoped, '*quite impossible* for the stage'.[26]

His latent stage fright now burst forth, and he came out with the explanation that his 'intercourse with D Lane' had given him 'the greatest contempt' for the stage, or as he put it again more honestly, 'an invincible repugnance' for 'a representation' (*LJ*, IV, 55, 71–72). In his reasoning after the event, he seems to have allowed the pain of the Separation to colour surrounding experiences, for we have seen that *before* the shock of ostracism his 'contempt' for the stage-as-it-was merely served to spur him to write a good drama to reform that stage. Chew may be right as to *Manfred*, and I am in doubt whether to consider Byron's attitude here purely one of fright and defiance or to look beneath that for a somewhat conscious step towards the uncompromisingly classic drama that he was to produce later as a threat to bring down the English house and revive its jaded tastes. However that may be, what Byron next *did* was to dig in for a protracted 'struggle for the more regular drama'. Most critics have simply taken Byron's word for it that this was to be done with unactable plays in a 'mental theatre'.[27]

Let us recapitulate the situation in 1817. Byron had been driven from England by what was the opposite of applause, the hisses of a hypocritical morality. All the greater became the need for his ego to find some importance, some security.

But his goal of superiority was now shifting significantly into a less childish, more socially useful alignment. He had written for fame and had put himself painfully at the public's mercy. Now he would cater no longer to degenerate tastes but would write stuff so good that the public would have to like it. If they were pleased, it would be that 'they chose to be so'; but if 'the Bulgars' should *not* like what he wrote, he would take another line, for he *'would be read'*.[28]

Two points are important here: first, he did not stop writing for the English public; his hunger for fame went not out but deeper—he needed the warmth of applause, but, once burnt, he would keep more carefully aloof from 'the stove of society' (*LJ*, VI, 33). Second, he did not stop writing drama. With full knowledge that the Drury Lane people were eager for a 'stage-worthy' play from him and might be expected, if he wrote one, to put it on, he turned from the ambiguous 'dramatic poem' of *Manfred* to start work on definite, 'regular' tragic plays, owing something to Alfieri perhaps, yet not, like his, mere 'dialogues' but unmistakable five-act 'Tragedies'.[29] Byron would, of course, object to their being produced. Thus he would, by writing good plays, stand a chance of filling the still-vacant 'opening for tragedy'; he would also, by every conscious effort to forestall action, barricade himself against the 'calamity' of failure at 'the mercies of an audience'.[30] Byron was probably as well aware as [Chew] that in the English theatre 'taste was improved to an extent which made the presentation even of Byron's dramas a matter of financial speculation despite his own vigorous opposition' (*Dramas*, p. 12).

If we admit the possibility of disguised intentions, it is difficult or rather impossible to determine what Byron's conscious intentions were with regard to his 'regular tragedies'; but his unconscious desire for real stage applause is unmistakable. For instance, in his letter of 3 February 1817, to Douglas Kinnaird, who had just 'had a row' and left the Drury Lane Committee, the wish of Byron's heart is very thinly disguised in jest:

> Sooner or later you will have your revenge, and so
> shall I (in other matters) ... and by Nemesis! you
> shall build a new Drury—... and *I will write you a*
> *tragedy* which shall reduce your pounds to shillings;
> besides, for my own particular injuries (*while this*
> *play is representing* with much *applause*), ordaining a
> proscription to which that of Sylla shall be a comic
> opera.... In the meantime ... 'il faut cultiver notre
> jardin.'[31]

Byron at this point did not just 'happen' to be dreaming of
playwriting; on the contrary, he was most probably already
active ransacking Venice for materials on the specific subject
of Doge Faliero—for he wrote to Murray three weeks later
asking for some English material only after he had 'searched
all their histories' in vain (*LJ*, IV, 58). The proposal to
Kinnaird, though veiled in jest, was a sort of hidden allusion to
activity in progress: 'I mean', he told Murray, 'to write a
tragedy upon the subject.' [...]

Furthermore, when Douglas Kinnaird, familiar from long
acquaintance with Byron's defensive banter, read this letter, he
sensed so clearly the underlying wish that he implored Byron
(it appears) to make good his threat; for Byron in his next
letter, still saying nothing of Faliero, protested: 'As to tragedy,
I may try one day, but *never* for the *stage*' [Byron's italics].
The rest of this second letter strikingly documents my diagnosis of Byron's hypersensitiveness to failure and his refusal
to enter competition:

> Don't you see, I have no luck there? My two
> addresses were not liked, and my committeeship did
> but get me into scrapes; no—no, I shall not tempt
> the Fates that way—besides, I should risk more than
> I could gain.... *Unless I could beat them all, it would*
> *be nothing*; and who could do that?[32]

The last clause betrays him, for Byron had been claiming in all his criticism of the stage that anybody could beat the best contemporary playwrights.

Another two and a half years rolled by before his first tragedy was written, but all the while that Byron was pondering over his *Faliero* ('four years ... I have meditated this work')[33] and busy with other projects, he kept a watchful eye on the English stage. In June 1817, he heard that Maturin's *Manuel* had failed. 'I 'gin to fear, or to hope, that Sotheby, after all, is to be the Æschylus of the age' (*LJ*, IV, 136–39)— that would mean the rule of mediocrity; he was almost glad to see it, for it bore out his own fears, proved him right. 'The more I see of the stage,' he continued, 'the less I would wish to have anything to do with it'; yet he was mightily concerned to see better plays attempted; he hoped Maturin would 'try again'.

Next March the *Fazio* of Milman, whom Byron considered to have 'dramatic power' and good '*material* for tragedy',[34] was 'brought out ... with great and deserved success at Covent Garden: that's a good sign. I tried ... to have it done at Drury Lane, but was overruled....'[35] It was a 'good sign' to one secretly anxious to reform the stage.

On 9 April 1820, Byron wrote a bickering and noisy letter to Murray about several pieces of 'trash' sent within the last month and about Italian Conversazioni and Lawyers, and then modestly slipped into a postscript the laconic information, 'I have begun a tragedy on the subject of Marino Faliero, the Doge of Venice' (*LJ*, V, 7). Another line a month later announced advance 'into the second act' and revealed the qualms and misgivings with which the playwright was proceeding: 'my present feeling is so little encouraging on such matters...' (*LJ*, V, 24–25). [...] By the end of August Byron had sent the finished play to Murray and was meekly waiting to find out 'what your parlour boarders will think'[36] of it. So far there had been no mention of its not being written for the stage.[37] [...]

Murray's response was apparently rather guarded and certainly not enthusiastic; it elicited the reply:

> I *have* '*put my Soul* into the tragedy' (as you *if* it) [apparently Murray hoped he had not]; but you know that there are damned souls as well as tragedies. (*LJ*, V, 67; Byron's italics)

Byron had still made no disclaimer of stage ambitions, although the negative response from Murray may have been the deciding straw. Definite protest did not come, however, for another month, and then apparently in answer to some word of Murray's indicating that that gentleman had assumed the play *was* to be staged:

> I thought that I had told you long ago, that it *never* was intended nor written with any view to the Stage. ... It is too long and regular for your stage. (*LJ*, V, 81)

Byron was bringing up his defences now. [...] Even while saying his aim was not the stage, however, Byron was careful to call *Marino* to the attention of his theatre friend, Douglas Kinnaird.[38]

At any rate, this weak protest did not impress Murray. [...] Murray proceeded to allow Elliston of Drury Lane to take the proof-sheets to the actors as fast as they came off the press (*LJ*, V, 226n.), so that representation and publication would be timed close together. Undoubtedly this was the best way to carry out Byron's hidden desire in the face of his open protests. But meanwhile Murray's lack of warmth had set in motion the defensive machinery of Byron's stage fright. It operated quietly at first. When Murray complained that the speeches in *Marino* were too long, Byron replied with 'True, but I wrote for the *Closet*' (*LJ*, V, 90)—an illegitimate excuse, to use the word with its dramatic connotation, and 'Your *old* dramatists ... are long enough too, God knows'—a legitimate one.

Three months of silence followed, and then a letter revealing how the cool or negative criticism of Murray and others ('many people')[39] had eaten into the heart of Byron's confidence, and how he, having carefully never committed himself to any high opinion of his four-year labour, was now ready to retreat ('I am not at all clear') and belittle his play with the term 'Sketch':

> I think him [Barry Cornwall, whose *Mirandola* had just been noticed] very likely to produce a good tragedy, if he keep to a natural style, and not play tricks to form Harlequinades for an audience.... You will laugh, and say, 'Why don't *you* do so?' I have, you see, tried a Sketch in *Marino Faliero*; but many people think my talent '*essentially undramatic*,' and I am not at all clear that they are not right. If *Marino Faliero* don't fall, in the perusal [Murray had not yet committed himself], I shall, perhaps, try again (but not for the stage).... (*LJ*, V, 217–18)

The ambiguity of the last line allows the interpretation that *Marino was* written for the stage.

Murray's opinion that the play might not be popular did not reach Byron till February. Meanwhile in mid-January news reached him through the Italian papers that an English theatre was going to act his play, and all his defensive guns were swung into position—but not all of them were fired. He asked Murray 'to *protest* stoutly and *publicly* (if it be necessary), against any attempt to bring the tragedy on *any stage*' (*LJ*, V, 221, Byron's italics). The tremendous moment was approaching when *his* play might be 'representing with much applause'—or might be suffering that 'palpable and immediate' 'calamity' of 'the trampling of an ... audience on a production which, be it good or bad, has been a mental labour to the writer',[40] and his 'horror' was asserting itself. He had done what was necessary to expose himself to the 'opening for tragedy' which might make him king of a new drama. [...] Now he would make sure not to 'be exposed to the insolences of an audience, without a remonstrance' (*LJ*, V, 221). He framed a public protest for Murray to use; he 'wrote a letter to the Lord Chamberlain to request him to prevent the theatres'; and he began an open letter to Perry, editor of the *Morning Chronicle*—but in the middle of this he 'stopt short'.[41] May we imagine Lord Byron dashing off this protest against the 'pollution' of being 'dragged forth as a Gladiator in the theatrical arena', hesitating with a doubt whether to risk having protested too much, deciding to let the case rest? Or did the letter merely 'happen' not to be finished and sent? The goal of such behaviour normally 'happens' to remain unconscious to the individual.[42] It is worth noting, however, that at first Byron 'even prohibited the *publication* of the Tragedy' (*LJ*, V, 231), and then hastened to withdraw this order—which might effectively have stopped the plans to act it.

The protests, at any rate, stopped, and little more was heard from Byron on that score for almost four months, while back in London, not unknown to Byron,[43] his wilful well-wishers were busy with casting and production of the play, Elliston dickering with the Lord Chancellor to withhold his injunction, rushing copy from the press to the green room; and on 25 April, four days after publication, *Marino Faliero* was represented at Drury Lane Theatre.

Byron's last protest (10 May) before hearing of the production touches yet another side of his aspirations: neither Kemble nor Kean, his favourite actors, was in England that year—who else could act the Doge? Here again the veil is lifted for a moment and we see the difference between what Byron hoped and what he dreaded. If Elliston insisted on acting the drama anyway, said Byron, 'Surely *he* might have the grace to wait for Kean's return before he attempted it.' Byron hastened to cover up this revelation by insisting that '*even then, I* should be as much against the attempt as ever'.[44]

If Kean *had* played the Doge—or, a safer if, if Byron's

Sardanapalus had been the first of his plays to be tried on the stage, a play which had a first run of almost two months [twenty-two performances] in 1834—we may imagine how Byron's wrath would have melted after the first successful month and a few packets of congratulatory mail (remember how praise melted his fears about *Childe Harold*). But now news reached him that the failure which his ego had dreaded from the beginning was now *realized* in the fate of *Marino*, and his fury knew no bounds.

> A Milan paper states that the play has been represented and universally condemned. (*LJ*, V, 285)

> What I feel ... is an immense rage. (*LJ*, V, 288)

> I was kept for *four* days ... in the *belief* that the *tragedy* had been acted and 'unanimously hissed'; and this with the addition that '*I* had brought it upon the stage.' ... At present I am, luckily, calmer than I used to be, and yet I would not pass those four days over again for—I know not what. (*LJ*, V, 290)

So much did his feeling of security, of superiority, depend on the success of what he dared not even admit to himself was an 'experiment for applause'. The great Poet who scoffed at Keats for being killed by a review came on several occasions much nearer than Keats to such a fate.

Byron now could only hope that Murray 'and my other friends will have at least published my different protests' (*LJ*, V, 285). The face-saving precautions were now most important, for they made the failure *not his own fault* at all, as he was quick to point out. Fatalism was now serving its psychological purpose:

> All this is vexatious enough, and seems a sort of dramatic Calvinism—predestined damnation without a sinner's own fault. I took all the pains poor mortal

could to prevent this inevitable catastrophe. (*LJ*, V, 286)

Poor Byron in this case had been needlessly pained, for the Milan papers had lied as to the extent of the 'catastrophe'. And when Byron found out after the terrible four days that 'it was *not* hissed, but is continued to be acted, in spite of Author, publisher, and the Lord Chancellor's injunction', he had a moment of pride as keen as his 'vexation' had been (*LJ*, V, 288).

This is the climactic picture of Lord Byron, Author of Legitimate plays, and it is a pity that *Marino* did not go on much longer than the four days he thought it was being hissed. Apparently all the information that reached him for a month or so was the news that it 'continued to be acted'. Eventually the correct story must have reached him, that the play was acted seven times, to poor houses, and finally folded up (*LJ*, V, 227n.2). But for a while his guard was down. He wrote letters to Moore and to Hoppner asking them to have the success version put in the papers of Paris and Milan and Venice: 'If the play had been condemned, [he gloated,] the injunction would have been *superfluous* against the continuation of the representation' (*LJ*, V, 288).

His note was now: 'If we succeed, well: if not, previous to any future publication, we will request a *promise* not to be acted.' 'I have now written nearly *three* acts of another [*Sardanapalus*]' (*LJ*, V, 281).

Six days later—his work was flourishing under the stimulation of success—he could boast, writing again to Hoppner:

> I care nothing for *their criticism*, but the matter of fact. I have written *four* acts of another tragedy, so you see they *can't* bully me. (*LJ*, V, 296)

Even a month later Byron believed *Marino* 'is still continued to be performed'. He insisted, of course, that the new play was also '*not for* the stage, any more than the other was intended for it—' (*LJ*, V, 304) but it is curious how closely his hopes for his subsequent 'regular tragedies' depended on the fate of *Marino*:

> I am quite ignorant [29 June] how far *the Doge* did or did not succeed: your first letters seemed to say yes—your last nothing.... It is proper that you should apprize me of this, because I am in the *third* act of a *third* drama [*The Two Foscari*]; and if I have nothing to expect but coldness from the public ... it were better to break off in time ... *if* I am trying an impracticable experiment, it is better to say so at once.[45]

Here we have probably the most conclusive single bit of evidence that *all three* of Byron's classic dramas were written with at least a secret 'eye to the Stage'. *Sardanapalus* was sped to a finish and *The Two Foscari* was penned in extreme and confident haste during the few weeks that Byron was in the belief that *Marino Faliero* was acting successfully!

The rest of the record bears out this conclusion. When *Sardanapalus* was begun, *Cain* had been 'pondered' as 'something in the style of Manfred, but in five *acts*', and also 'Francesca of Rimini, in five acts; and ... Tiberius.'[46] When *Cain* was actually written (16 July to 9 September 1821) Byron did not trouble to give it the Legitimate five-act form; by 23 August he knew *Marino* had not succeeded (*LJ*, V, 347). The Bulgars had rendered their verdict. Francesca and Tiberius were left in the inkwell.

In the very wording of his confession of the failure of *Marino*—'no reform ever succeeded at first'—Byron admitted that his hope *had* been to reform the stage with *Marino*. Although he protested that he would continue trying 'to make a *regular* English drama, no matter whether for the Stage or not', actually he abandoned the 'regular' form, thus further admitting that his hope to reform the stage had been to reform it by writing for it.

The three 'regular tragedies' are to all appearances Legitimate plays, except for the denials of 'the Author'. *Cain* and
Heaven and Earth, written after the failure of *Marino* was
known to Byron, are more obviously designed for 'a mental
theatre'. Nevertheless Byron's hidden urge to reach the stage
was amazingly persistent, for in that same year he reverted to
his early Gothic drama, *Werner*, abandoning his ideals of
dramatic reform, but also in practice if not theory abandoning
the 'mental theatre', producing what not only was calculated
to suit the degraded tastes of the contemporary audience, but
did suit them, being acted many times between 1826 and
1860.[47]

The motive behind this about-face is expressed clearly in a
letter of 20 September 1821, in which, after a defiant dying
hope that his 'new dramas ... will in time find favour'—he has
just been 'mortified that Gifford don't take to' them—Byron
breaks down with the pathetic declaration:

> For that matter—
>   'Nay, if thou'lt mouth,
>   I'll rant as well as thou'—
> would not be difficult, as I think I have shown in my
> younger productions [the Oriental Tales]—*not
> dramatic ones*, to be sure. (*LJ*, V, 372)

If Byron did not descend to ranting in *Werner*, he at least
supplied all the 'irregular' attractions of the most popular
current melodrama. To the very end and even while pandering
to 'an ignorant audience', Byron reiterated his disclaimer:

> I am sorry you think *Werner* even *approaching* to any
> fitness for the stage, which, with my notion upon it,
> is very far from present object. (*LJ*, VI, 31)

For his ego this stand was, of course, more necessary now
than ever. Unfortunately no one had the temerity to venture
another Byron play on the stage in his lifetime.

It is interesting to note that Byron's last fling at amateur dramatics, the rehearsal of *Othello* described above, occurred at about the time of the composition of *Werner*. In the general context, such action indicates, I believe, the stage-consciousness of Byron at this period.

There remains to be considered the sophistry with which Byron rationalized the failure of his plays into a proof of his superiority as a playwright. This process may be seen most curiously presented in a mutilated page of manuscript once intended to conclude the Preface to *Werner*, 1822.[48] Here Byron achieves the position that not only his own plays but all plays of any worth ever written have been not 'generically intended for the stage'. It follows that his own motive for writing drama differs in no essential way from the motives of all great dramatists, and that the matter of stage presentation is immaterial if not actually a spot upon one's record. This position is arrived at by the following argument:

Byron denies that *all dramatic* writing is for the stage.
    a. Forty-nine out of fifty plays are much read but never acted.
    b. The greatest dramatists are all among those whose plays are never or almost never acted. (Shakespeare might appear to be an exception, but his plays as staged are not the real Shakespeare but 'Tate, Cibber, and Thompson under his name'.)
    ∴ The stage does not belong to playwrights. Q.E.D.
Ergo: Byron wishes to class himself with *them* at least by coinciding with them in the matter of *not* being produced. ('I am far from attempting to raise myself to a level with the least of these names—I only wish to be [exempted] from a stage which is not theirs.')
P.S.: See Charles Lamb to the effect that the plays of Shakespeare are not calculated for the stage. This may be applied a 'hundredfold to those of others'.[49]

Thus Byron, by a full circle of sophistry, ranges himself with the dramatists of all time, with Ford, Marlowe, Webster, all whose plays are never acted but 'may be read'. In other words, he insists that his plays are as good *plays* as any.[50]

The reality of Byron's dramatic aspirations is, I think, clear—whether revealed in elaborate rationalizations such as that discussed above, or in a simple naked remark such as this reported by Medwin: 'If he [Kemble] had acted "Marino Faliero," its fate would have been very different' (Medwin, I, 144). And we may be sure that if *Marino* had succeeded on the stage, Byron would have taken to the rôle of the Great Playwright as though that were in the natural course of things, and the critics would have easily understood his earlier stage fright for what it was. As Byron himself put it, 'If we succeed, well.' Since, however, the play failed, the critics have taken Byron's word for it that he had never wanted to see it succeed, and they have completely overlooked the fact, which I have been at pains to make evident, that Byron wrote the second and third of his 'regular classic tragedies' in a bright period of two months or so when he was under the mistaken impression that his first tragedy was having a successful run 'in spite of Author, publisher, and the Lord Chancellor's injunction'.

NOTES

1. *The Works of Lord Byron: Letters and Journals*, ed. R. E. Prothero (London: John Murray, 1898–1901), IV, 71–72, hereafter referred to as *LJ*, vol. and page(s).

2. *Lord Byron's Correspondence*, ed. John Murray (London: John Murray, 1922), II, 43–44, hereafter referred to as *Correspondence*.

3. Chew, *Byron in England*, p. 117. Chew forgets that only one of Byron's plays was tried on the stage while he lived.

4. Calvert, *Byron: Romantic Paradox*, p. 169.

5. See *LJ*, V, 223, 278, 257.

6. Charles du Bos is an exception among critics in asserting that Byron's behaviour is completely understandable—*Byron and the Need of Fatality*, p. 16. Peter Quennell employs some psychological understanding on the level of discussion of symptoms such as Byron's homosexual tendency, but he makes no effort to get beneath symptoms nor to bring

together his various surmises into a single analysis—*Byron: The Years of Fame.*

7. See Adler, *Individual Psychology*, p. 36, on the apparent dualism of tactics of behaviour leading to one object, on the ability to 'draw from two contradictory lines to reach [an] ideal situation of imagined superiority.'

8. Bradford, 'The Glory of Sin', p. 227—an unramified but fairly just psychological analysis of Byron.

9. Byron probably did not think much of 'Hints from Horace' when he first gave it to Dallas. It was only in March 1820, when Byron was taking up the cudgel for Pope, that he had serious 'thoughts of publishing the "Hints..." if Hobhouse can rummage them out of my papers' (*LJ*, IV, 425). Hobhouse thought they were good (see *Correspondence*, II, 154), but Murray delayed until, after six laconic requests, he sent an incomplete copy in January 1821. Only after Byron found Murray deaf to five more simple requests to send the rest and to publish did Byron exclaim that *he* looked upon the 'Hints' and the Pulci translation, which Murray was also trying to dodge, as 'by far the best things of my doing: *you* will not think so ... but I know that they will *not* be popular, so don't be afraid—publish them together' (*LJ*, V, 255). After this forlorn cry nothing more was ever said of the 'Hints'.

10. The 'Hints' was a continuation of his *English Bards* style; the *Childe* was a 'new line'. Throughout his career Byron was nervous about new ventures. See his letter to Moore, 28 February 1817, on the anxiety of going to press: 'And this is your month of going to press—by the body of Diana! ... I feel as anxious ... as if it were myself coming out in a work of humour, which would, you know, be the antipodes of all my previous publications' (*LJ*, IV, 62).

11. *The Works of Lord Byron: Poetry*, rev. edn, ed. Ernest Hartley Coleridge (London, 1898–1904), II, x–xi, hereafter referred to as *Poetry*.

12. They do present, of course, Byron's interest in the stage up to the writing of the first draft of *Werner*. But both critics accept as 'sincere' his denial of any stage hopes for the three 'regular' tragedies. Here Calvert fails to apply the wisdom of his own advice that 'It is impossible not to take Byron seriously, and it is disastrous to take him literally', *Romantic Paradox*, p. 67.

13. 'On a Distant View ... of Harrow on the Hill', 1806.

14. *LJ*, V, 445; *Detached Thoughts*, 1821.

15. 'An Occasional Prologue', 1806. Byron 'enacted "Penruddock" in the "Wheel of Fortune," and "Tristram Fickle" in Allingham's farce of "the Weathercock," for three nights (the duration of our compact) ...' (*LJ*, V, 445). The 'Prologue' asks applause for 'not one poor trembler only'—but the *one* is very evidently in mind.

16. Medwin, *Conversations*, I, 141–42, hereafter cited as Medwin.

17. Calvert, *Romantic Paradox*, points out that 'The interest in the individual actor dominates all his plays, with the sole exception of *Heaven and Earth*; one character *possesses the attention of the audience*, if not throughout the play, at least for the duration of a scene' (p. 155). My italics. The index of Byron's works is rich in references to Kean and Kemble.

18. *Poetry*, V, 338.

19. 'A comedy I take to be the most difficult of compositions, more so than tragedy' (*LJ*, II, 373).

20. Wexberg, *The Psychology of Sex*, p. 92.

21. In *English Bards*, ll. 687 ff., he exhorts 'some genuine bard ... to drive this pestilence from the land', i.e. the degenerate amusements of opera and ballet and gaming. In the context he is calling for a moral satire; 'E'en I', he ventures, 'must raise my voice.' But the positive reform called for is a better drama. 'Good plays are scarce,' he wrote in a verse letter to Hodgson of 13 September 1811 (*LJ*, II, 34). Here clearly 'classic drama' was to be written *for the stage*. Only later, when he himself was writing classic dramas to reform the stage, did Byron's stage fright lead him to double back his logic and insist that 'classic' qualities were a cause of unfitness for the stage and that he was writing for 'a mental theatre'.

22. Noted by E. H. Coleridge, *Poetry*, V, 326, and confirmed by Chew, *The Dramas of Lord Byron*, p. 35. Contrast Byron's own assertion, in the Preface to *Marino Faliero* (1820), that 'even during the time of being one of the committee of one of the theatres, I never made the attempt [to write a stage-worthy play], and never will.' Among the things that a later Byron would no doubt have gladly forgotten were (a) that he had while on the committee begun *Werner*, and (b) that in *English Bards* he had scoffed at a playwright forced to 'live in prologues, though his dramas die', and had suggested sarcastically that Lord Carlisle, whose plays were spurned by theatre-managers, could laugh at their judgement, 'And case his volumes in congenial calf.' Byron's attitude with regard to his later tragedies became dangerously similar to that he here had attributed to Carlisle.

23. 'Drury Lane Address', l. 24.

24. See Chew, *The Dramas of Lord Byron*, p. 32.

25. *Manfred*, begun September 1816, was entitled finally 'a dramatic poem'. As he was writing to Murray about it, Byron referred to it as a 'drama' or 'play', but when it was about to be published he ordered Murray to 'call it "a poem," for it is *no drama*.' (*LJ*, IV, 100), 9 April 1817.

26. *LJ*, IV, 55. Yet *Manfred* has had a stage history of five productions, the first running sixteen days in 1834 (*Poetry*, IV, 78).

27. The first phrase comes from a later period (*Correspondence*, II, 201); *LJ*, V, 347.

28. *LJ*, IV, 285, in reference to *Don Juan* I and II. To Moore in June 1818 he wrote, 'I won't quarrel with the public, however, for the "Bulgars" are generally right, and if I do miss now, I may hit another time;—and so the "gods give us joy"' in reference to *Childe Harold*, IV. See *LJ*, IV, 237 and *Don Juan*, X, 28.

29. Byron, writing to Murray, is careful to distinguish his own plays from works that are not quite plays: 'The Italians have as yet *no tragedy*— Alfieri's are political dialogues, except *Mirra*' (*LJ*, V, 64).

30. In the Preface to *Marino Faliero* Byron reveals most plainly his sensitivity to applause: 'I cannot conceive any man of irritable feeling putting himself at the mercies of an audience. The sneering reader, and the loud critic, and the tart review, are scattered and distant calamities; but the trampling of an intelligent or of an ignorant audience ... is a palpable and immediate grievance....'

31. *Correspondence*, II, 34–35. My italics.

32. *Ibid*. My italics.

33. Preface to *Marino Faliero*.

34. *Ibid*.

35. *LJ*, IV, 210. *Fazio* was staged without the author's consent. Might Byron have been aware of this fact?

36. *LJ*, V, 51, 57, 53–54.

37. The letter in which Byron opens the question of publication and terms of 'the tragedy' and demands a 'speedy' judgement contains no mention (*LJ*, V, 44). Nor does the letter of 17 July in which the MS is described and Byron expresses the hope it will please (*LJ*, V, 52–55).

38. A few days after the protest to Murray, Byron wrote to Kinnaird: 'I sent Murray a tragedy (written *not* for the stage), read it if you can' (*Correspondence*, II, 156). Byron thought of Kinnaird as 'a fine fellow, and my zealous friend and ally, also a very good judge of dramatic effect ...' (*LJ*, II, 198).

39. There were, however, a few crumbs of praise: 'Foscolo thinks the tragedy very good Venetian, and Gifford says it is sterling English' (*Correspondence*, II, 158).

40. Byron's Preface to *Marino Faliero*.

41. *LJ*, V, 221, 180. The last is dated 22 January but was never sent to Perry. It was sent on 2 March to Murray with the explanation, 'Of course you need not send it; but it explains to you my feelings on the subject.' From the tenor of this note it appears that Byron expected Murray to let the representation proceed and his own protests to have no practical effect.

42. See Adler, *Individual Psychology*, p. 12. 'It so "happens" that [the goal of one's actions] remains in the unconscious, so that [one] may believe

that an *implacable fate* and not a long prepared and long meditated plan for which he alone is responsible, is at work.'

43. 'It seems', wrote Byron to Moore, 22 January, 'that the managers, assuming a *right* over published poetry, are determined to enact [*Marino*] whether I will or no' (*LJ*, V, 230). And see *LJ*, V, 256 to Murray: 'You say that "there is nothing to fear, let them do what they please;" that is to say, that you would see me damned with great tranquility.' This is the only protest between 21 January and 10 May unless the apology of 16 February for *Marino*'s threatened unpopularity be counted (*LJ*, V, 243).

44. *LJ*, V, 278 (Byron's emphasis). See also *LJ*, V, 223 to Murray, where on first hearing of the threat Byron cries, 'the play is *not for acting*: Kemble or Kean could *read* it, but where are they?' And see *Correspondence*, II, 198.

45. *LJ*, V, 313, 29 June, to Murray. Byron was still in ignorance 6 July, when he wrote to Hobhouse: 'I have sent to England a tragedy [*Sardanapalus*] a month ago, and I am in the *fifth* act of another [*The Two Foscari*]. Murray has not acknowledged its arrival' (*Correspondence*, II, 176).

46. *LJ*, V, 189; Byron's diary, 28 January 1821.

47. T. H. Vail Motter notes in Byron's disclaimer of stage aims for *Werner* a 'decided change in tone from the defiance of the previous year. ... Hope sprang eternal, and Byron would dearly have loved a success in drama, dearly bought after so much failure and vilification'—'Byron's *Werner* Re-estimated', p. 247.

48. Printed in *Poetry*, V, 338–39.

49. I have paraphrased and methodized Byron's argument. Here he has not kept the logic of Lamb, whose statement was that 'the plays of Shakespeare are *less* calculated for performance on a stage than those of almost any other dramatist whatever'.

50. A corollary to this announcement is Byron's statement, of about the same date, to Medwin, that 'Poetry' has nothing to do with or in a play (Medwin, I, 94). Byron was referring to Lamb only for the nonce and would by no means have subscribed to his evaluation of a play for its Poetry.

EDITORS' BIBLIOGRAPHICAL NOTE

So splendidly has Erdman covered the ground of Byron's seemingly para-doxical attitudes towards the staging of his plays that even where one might expect to find continuing discussion and debate about that history there is little in the way of even addenda. Most recent critical books on the plays implicitly or explicitly defer to Erdman's analysis—although Richard

Lansdown, in his *Byron's Historical Dramas*, has a fine chapter on the history, politics, and general functioning of, as well as Byron's involvement with, the Theatre Royal, Drury Lane. More typical is Richardson's *A Mental Theater*, in which, even in its two chapters on *Cain* and *Heaven and Earth*, the issue of Byron's attitudes and the relative stageworthiness of 'mental theater' dramas are referred to only obliquely. In this same category also are Hoagwood's *Byron's Dialectic,* although he devotes over fifty pages to *Cain*; Cox, *In the Shadows of Romance,* which has a section on Byron's 'Mysteries and Histories'; and Corbett, *Byron and Tragedy.*

Other books and essays that at least touch seriously on the matter, if only indirectly in the context of discussions of actual productions of Byron's plays and the nature of 'mental theatre' and closet drama, are:

Barker, 'The First English Performance', pp. 342–44.

Biggs, 'Notes on Performing *Sardanapalus*', pp. 378–85.

Carlson, 'A Theatre of Remorse', pp. 176–212.

Cave, 'Romantic Drama in Performance', pp. 79–104.

Corbett, 'Lugging Byron Out of the Library', pp. 361–72 (on a recent Yale production).

Damico, 'The Stage History of *Werner*', pp. 63–81.

Howell, *Byron Tonight*, and '*Sardanapalus*', pp. 42–53 (on Kean's performance in June 1853 at the Royal Princess's Theatre in London).

Magarshack, *Stanislavsky*—on Stanislavsky's staging of *Cain*.

Manning, 'Edmund Kean and Byron's Plays', pp. 188–206.

Richards and Thomson, eds, *Nineteenth Century British Theatre.*

Shilstone, 'Byron's "Mental Theatre"', pp. 187–99.

Taborski, *Byron and the Theatre*, and 'Byron's Theatre: Private Spleen, or Cosmic Revolt: Theatrical Solutions—Stanislavsky to Grotowski', pp. 356–79.

Venice Preserved

MALCOLM KELSALL

'In the first year of Freedom's second dawn/ Died George the Third.' The Liberal risings in Italy, Spain and Portugal of 1820 were followed by the insurrection in Greece in 1821. In 1822 Castlereagh committed suicide. That has been seen as the beginning of the 'age of reform'.[1] Henry Brougham welcomed the address from the throne of February 1823 as 'the signal for exultation to England'. It is the period of Byron's involvement with the Carbonari in Italy, and the Hellenes:

> The king-times are fast finishing. There will be blood shed like water, and tears like mist; but the peoples will conquer in the end. I shall not live to see it, but I foresee it.[2]

Byron's was not the prophecy of Cassandra. Revolution at home and abroad to many Britons seemed inevitable: Canning, Cobbett, Carlile, Queen Caroline, Hobhouse, Keats, Shelley, Southey, Wellington, Wooler, Wordsworth. The philosophical issue of 'resistance' was about to become practical. Against this background Byron composed his two Whig tragedies on Venetian history: *Marino Faliero* and *The Two Foscari*.

The first of these was written early in 1820 and completed a fortnight after the Carbonari rising at Nola (2 July). In Britain the immediate political events involve Peterloo (August 1819), the Cato Street conspiracy (February 1820) and the return of Queen Caroline (June 1820); the prosecution from Byron's circle of Burdett, Cartwright and Hobhouse. After the failure of the Carbonari Byron wrote *The Two Foscari* in June 1821. The plays convey a historical message for the times by analogy

33

rather than by allegory. (Byron specifically rejected the kind of party political reading which had been made earlier of *Venice Preserved* or *Cato*. In vain. The audience of *Marino Faliero* interpreted even the censored text as local politics.)[3] The two Venetian tragedies show one of the great republican states famous to history, and traditionally likened to Britain, locked in a constitutional impasse. Good order is corrupted; decline seems inevitable leading to the euthanasia of the constitution, corruption and extinction. In this situation revolution was provoked by misgovernment—as it was to be in France or England. Byron's essay to Southey on *The Two Foscari* makes the explicit connection. [...]

> I look upon [convulsion] as inevitable, though no revolutionist: I wish to see the English constitution restored, and not destroyed. Born an aristocrat, and naturally one by temper, with the greater part of my present property in the funds, what have *I* to gain by a revolution? ... But that a revolution is inevitable, I repeat. The government may exult over the repression of petty tumults; these are but the receding waves repulsed and broken for a moment on the shore, while the great tide is still rolling on and gaining ground with every breaker.

This is ambivalent. Seen as a great movement in European history 'freedom'—in the *Childe Harold* sense—is a natural force, a 'great tide' which impels revolution, and which the writer supports. But seen in a local context—revolution in England—the writer fears for himself as an aristocrat. The split shows even more clearly in the letter to Augusta, 2 January 1820, in which Byron claims he wants to get out of Europe entirely to 'preserve my independence'. He will fight only if the loss of his fortune no longer enables him to remain 'aloof' from events in England: 'but ... how I despise and abhor all these men, and all these things ... how reluctantly I contemplate being called upon to act with or against any of the parties.'

It is difficult to reconcile this distaste for revolution in England with the familiar romantic image of Byron as armed Carbonaro and Hellene. But Fox had been against the Wilkite mobs at home, and yet palliated the excesses of Jacobinism abroad as provoked by the Bourbons and the Allies. What was local and what was distant might be judged in different ways. It was much easier for Byron (and his gentlemen friends) in Italy to act as liberal Carbonari than to associate with radicals like Hunt and Cobbett at home. In Italy (and Greece) politics could be 'simplified' to a 'detestation' of government. 'Austrians Out' ('Turks Out') is a slogan which does not demand much thought. [...] The expectation of a Bentinck, Charles Kelsall or Lord Holland was that the peninsula would adopt a constitutional government.[4] But at home the issues, because better known, appeared far more complex and dangerous. Britain was threatened with the destruction of the present social order in its entirety.

Hence Byron's comment on Peterloo in relation to the Neapolitan resurgents is carefully balanced:

> An Englishman, a friend to liberty ... Having already, not long since, been an ocular witness of the despotism of the Barbarians in the States occupied by them in Italy ... sees, with the enthusiasm natural to a cultivated man [*ben nato*] the glorious determination of the Neapolitans to assert their well-won independence. As a member of the English House of Peers, he would be a traitor to the principles which placed the reigning family of England on the throne, if he were not grateful for the noble lesson so lately given to people and to kings, I think ... that if the Manchester Yeomanry had cut down *Hunt only*—they would have done their duty ... they committed *murder* both in what they did—and what

they did *not* do,—in butchering the weak instead of
piercing the wicked, in assailing the seduced instead
of the seducer—in punishing the poor starving
populace, instead of that pampered and dinnered
blackguard who is only less contemptible than his
predecessor *Orator Henley* because he is more
mischievous.—What I say thus—I say as publicly as
you please—if to praise such fellows be the price of
popularity—I spit upon it, as I would in their faces.[5]

As a Whig aristocrat in the tradition of 1688 he is the enemy
of the unjust power of the Crown (at home or in Europe)
and a 'friend of the people'. But as a gentleman and a man of
civilization, he is also the enemy of barbarians, whether they
are the troops of Austrian imperialism or democratic demagogues like Hunt. [...] Faced with 'a choice of evils with
Castlereagh', he concludes, 'a Gentleman Scoundrel is always
preferable to a vulgar'.[6]

The same distinction separates Byron, stockpiling arms for
the Carbonari in Italy, from the Cato Street conspirators at
home who would have killed the Cabinet. Both events are
immediate contexts for Marino Faliero's abortive conspiracy. In
Italy Byron was following, in principle, Erskine's argument, to
keep a firearm in the house to resist tyranny. The Liberty
League in America and Grattan's Irish Volunteers followed the
same principle. The American republic and the Irish Parliament
were established by revolutionary force. (The comparison of
Grattan with Castlereagh must await *Don Juan*.) Cato Street
sought to follow the same tradition. The very name 'Cato'
recalled Addison's Whig tragedy and republican opposition to
tyranny. Ings, on the scaffold, sang 'Give me Liberty or Give
me Death' to the huzzas of the crowd, and Brunt's final words
were an attack on the military government which ran the
country. The crowd asked God to bless him, and shouted
'murder' at the execution of each victim. Those who expected
'inevitable' revolution would have had their fears confirmed.

But, as with Peterloo, Byron's reaction to Cato Street was to close ranks with his own order. Thistlewood was merely a criminal. 'Desperate fools' he called the conspirators:

> if they had killed poor Harrowby—in whose house I have been five hundred times—at dinners and parties—his wife is one of 'the Exquisites'—and t'other fellows—what end would it have answered? ... but really if these sort of awkward butchers are to get the upper hand—*I* for one will declare *off*, I have always been ... a well-wisher to and voter for reform in Parliament—but 'such fellows as these will never go to the Gallows with any credit'.[7]

So much, then, for the ode on the frame-breakers Bill, and the 'Song for the Luddites'. His mind turns instead to the ill-effects of the Terror in France, and to 'Scoundrels' such as Hunt and Cobbett (ignorant of Tacitus, he remarks!). Revolutions are not made 'with rose-water', but if they are not made by gentlemen, Byron wants no part. 'Radical' was not a word in his vocabulary, he told Hobhouse, and he defined the new term pejoratively as 'uprooting', and a 'low imitation of the Jacobins'.[8]

Two references to the revolution in France at this time are particularly revealing:

> I am convinced—that Robespierre was a Child—and Marat a quaker in comparison of what they would be [Hunt and Cobbett] could they throttle their way to power.

> I can understand and enter into the feelings of Mirabeau and La Fayette—but I have no sympathy with Robespierre—and Marat—whom I look upon as in no respect worse than those two English ruffians.[9]

From Lord Liverpool this would seem Tory 'alarmism', from a

'Friend of Freedom' it is evidence of the way the mind is imprisoned by historical analogy. The Terror in France put back the case for constitutional reform in England half a century. 'In these times', wrote Lord John Russell, 'love of liberty is too generally supposed to be allied with rash innovation, impiety, and anarchy.'[10] What Byron had failed to see (from distant Italy) is the attempt of Hunt and the men and women of Manchester to break out of the vicious cycle in which mob murder and military murder continually provoked one another; to use the legal powers of the Bill of Rights to peacefully petition for the redress of wrongs.[11]

Instead, what Byron understands, more naturally, are the feelings of Le Comte Mirabeau and Le Marquis de La Fayette. One can only speculate what he imagined those feelings might be, but the dilemma of both men was that of the aristocrat in a popular revolution. [...] Le Comte Mirabeau is a Byronic figure: libertine, duellist, enemy of despotism who joined the *tiers état* proclaiming 'In all countries, in all times, the Aristocrats have implacably pursued every friend of the people'—witness the Gracchi ('history hath but *one* page'). Yet, with patrician imperturbability, he defended the absolute veto of the Crown because he feared more the tyranny of 600 irresponsible senators. Belonging neither to the Court nor to the Jacobins, he was none the less the supporter of the queen. After his death his bust was removed from the hall of the Jacobins—an act of the same symbolic significance as the veiling of Faliero's portrait.[12]

This is merely imaginative speculation. But Byron's empathy is with aristocratic revolutionaries (and men who failed) and not with the radicals—the Clodius and Milo of the times, demagogues who seduce and mislead the people.[13] Hence the importance of the Queen Caroline affair for Byron and the Whigs, for here was an issue in which 'gentlemen', on a surge of popular protest, might emerge in their traditional role as leaders of 'the people'. It was the allusion of *Marino Faliero* to this affair which caused the play to be cheered in the theatre. This sordid, and intrinsically insignificant, issue of the queen's honour has a contemporary and symbolic significance as important as that of Peterloo or the Carbonari in shaping the context in which the Venetian tragedies were conceived and in which they speak.

The affair seemed to confirm the further advance of the expected revolution. Such was the rhetoric of the press whether radical or establishment. [...] In fact, what Caroline enabled the opposition to effect was a massive expression of support for the ideal of monarchy (embodied symbolically in the queen) at the same time as attacking corruption (in the person of the king). Hundreds of loyal addresses from 'the people' (including the radicals) reached Caroline, often expressed in the traditional language of chivalry. Whig adherents of the queen—Erskine, Fitzwilliam, Grey, Lansdowne—were celebrated, and the attachment of people to the party was enhanced, claimed Lord John Russell. A famous passage reappeared likening Caroline to Marie Antoinette:

> Little did I dream that I should have lived to see disasters fallen upon her in a nation of gallant men, in a nation of men of honour, and of cavaliers. I thought ten thousand swords must have leaped from their scabbards to avenge even a look that threatened her with insult ....

But '"The age of chivalry" was not gone; the "glory of Europe was [not] extinguished forever",' the press commented. Caroline was saved from a corrupt king by a loyal people, and was herself the leader of revolution. Typical of the blend of monarchical and revolutionary imagery is Cruikshank's transparency design on the queen's success, in which Britannia holds in her left hand the Liberty tree as her spear, but her shield bears the image of the queen and rests upon a printing press. The motto would have delighted the heart of Wilkes or Erskine, for it celebrates 'the Victory obtained by the Press for the Liberties of the People'.[14]

It is extraordinary to realize that this affair drove Peterloo out of the forefront of debate, that it should have a revolutionary significance equivalent to that of the emergence of Liberalism. Caroline, the individual, was, of course, quite inadequate to carry the weight of symbolic suggestion with which the chivalry of a 'return to Camelot' invested her, and was soon forgotten. Byron laughed at her as a 'tragedy quean'. Yet he recognized the significance of the agitation. Her acquittal 'will prevent a revolution—though it may *hasten* a *reform*'. If it were to lead to the Whigs assuming office 'as is probable' (hope springs eternal!) then help would come to the Italian patriots.[15] The matter speaks to him directly in a way the agitation of Hunt or Thistlewood did not because personal relations are involved. Caroline had entertained him as her guest; since it is an affair of honour his hand searches for his duelling pistols (Brougham was in their sights).[16]

This matter is the contemporary analogy—and was recognized as such—for the strange motivation of the revolutionary plot of Doge Faliero: the insulted honour of Angiolina his wife. In Angiolina, and in Marina also (in *The Two Foscari*), Byron has created types of chaste, honourable, nobleblooded womankind for whom properly 'ten thousand swords' might be inspired. The idealization of art supplies types which the particular matter of contemporary history did not offer—the symbolic significance of the name 'Marina' in a sea-borne empire is obvious—perhaps too obvious. [...]

But the Caroline affair is another instance of how, in a patrician society, principles of politics and matters of family honour are intimately involved, and how large issues thus may arise from small causes. [...] Thus the revolutionary issue of whether Caroline's name should go in the Prayer Book has a major place in the list of minor causes of political upheaval which Byron emphasizes in the Preface to *Marino Faliero*:

> a basin of water spilt on Mrs. Masham's gown
> deprived the Duke of Marlborough of his command,

and led to the inglorious peace of Utrecht— ...
Louis XIV was plunged into the most desolating
wars, because his minister was nettled at his finding
fault with a window, and wished to give him another
occupation— ... Helen lost Troy— ... Lucretia
expelled the Tarquins from Rome— ... Cava brought
the Moors to Spain ... an insulted husband led the
Gauls to Clusium, and thence to Rome—a single
verse of Frederick II of Prussia on the Abbé de
Bernis, and a jest on Madame de Pompadour, led to
the battle of Rosbach ....

The emphasis of this contextual introduction has been
rather on contemporary events in England which find their
historical analogy in the Venetian tragedies, than on Byron's
conspiratorial association with the Carbonari. [...] But it is not
possible to see the Venetian plays as advancing contemporary
nationalism or liberalism. Marino's prophecy is not of the
establishment of an Italian state; it concerns the further
decline of the sea-borne empire (cf. Britain). His rebellion is
not against an external power, but against the corruption of
his class. The two Foscari refuse even to act against that
corruption. Rienzi might have offered a hero indicative of 'the
struggle of the people against tyrannous government',[17] if the
poet did not object to a tavern-keeper's son. But Byron's
heroes are not builders of nations. The issue they face is that
of resistance against the corruption of their own class:
whether the law of the state, made by their fellow patrician
rulers of the state, should be broken if it is misused, or obeyed
because without law there is no state. It is the dilemma of
tyranny against anarchy once more, the problem of constitutional Whiggery in the 1680s, of the revolutionary Whig of the
1790s and of Byron's own day when confronted with 'Tory'
courts backed by yeomanry sabres.

The two plays form a mutually commenting pair. The first
has attracted more attention, for its revolutionary subject

matter is more dramatically exciting, and it corresponds to certain popular stereotypes of Byronism because of the violent reaction of Faliero to corruption and his assumption of the role of the leader of the people in the cause of freedom. The 'ardent love of liberty and hatred of oppression' he shows derives from the tradition of resistance—the pervasiveness of that rhetoric may be shown by the fact that the 'revolutionary' phrase just employed was Henry Brougham's of his grandmother![18] But the tragic outcome of Faliero's resistance is indicative that there is something perverted, though noble, in the lengths to which he carries his action (beyond the 'prudential' boundary). The Aristotelian form of the drama suggests a fatal flaw. That flaw may not be merely Faliero's exaggerated and rash sense of family honour. Possibly it is in the very nature of violent resistance itself.

The Two Foscari takes the opposite case. It is a tragedy, as Jeffrey described it, of 'passive obedience and non-resistance'.[19] Resistance had only been justified in 1688 when the very Constitution was in danger, Burnet had argued. The normal, 'prudential' pathway was to use the law to uphold the state, and to reform the law to redress the constitution. Wilkes escaped from the mob of his supporters and insisted on going to prison; Erskine told the mob to desist and he would free those charged with constructive treason by process of law. In the crisis of the Princess Charlotte in 1814 (proleptic of Queen Caroline) when she told Brougham she would throw herself on 'the people' for protection, the great Whig lawyer (defender of Hunt, champion of the slaves) admitted that if she did, 'the people' would pull down Carlton House and 'blood will flow'; but he warned her, 'Through the rest of your life you will never escape the odium which, in this country, always attends those who by breaking the law occasion such calamities.'[20] She must obey the law, and the Regent. So, in Byron, the family of the Foscari honourably and legalistically follow the constitutional authorities of Venice, and in so doing expressly draw a series of contrasts with Doge Faliero.

But the outcome is equally tragic. Neither resistance, nor obedience, offers a way forward. Taken together the two plays are indicative of a total impasse producing, in Venice, decline and eventual extinction. What moral might that offer for Britain?

This impasse is a problem for the patrician. It is not the kind of issue which Hunt or Cobbett contemplates. For them the way forward was 'universal suffrage'—i.e. 'absolute democracy'. We have argued that Byron's window on the world is that of his class, that 'Byronism' is not a phenomenon separable from time, place, social position. These plays, in the context of 1819–21, raise the class issue as a major theme. [...] The issue of what it was to be a gentleman is not the usual way in which the Venetian plays are approached, but in large measure it is what the plays seek to voice. *Stemmata quid faciunt?* asked the bitter republican Juvenal: what does a noble pedigree do for a man? [...] His education, his family connections, his inherited place in the state fit him for a particular rôle in government, and shape his mind with a sense of historical destiny. [...] Marina, in *The Two Foscari*, speaks of her *stemmata*, and to personal 'qualities' joins the issue of breeding:

> We say the 'generous steed' to express the purity
> Of his high blood ...
> And why not say as soon the '*generous man*'?
> If race be aught, it is in qualities
> More than in years; and mine, which is as old
> As yours, is better in its product ...
> ... get you back, and pore
> Upon your genealogic tree's most green
> Of leaves and most mature of fruits ....
>
> (III.i.290–301)

She is rebuking the villain Loredano, and the comment is authoritative, for her (invented) allegorical name indicates that she speaks as the voice of the bride of the Adriatic and

Venice's traditions. Given the emphatic masculine composition of the patrician order, the rebuke is more cutting coming
from a woman. Loredano is degenerate, and the Latinate use
of *generosus* (of noble or eminent birth) distinguishes the
language of one of classical education from plebeian discourse
and understanding.

As for the 'honour' of one's 'house', it is the very cause of
the action of *Marino Faliero*. It would be an exercise of
pedantry to list from both Venetian plays all the phrases
linking house, name, family, birth, with honour, reputation,
fame: typical are Faliero's references to the 'deep dishonour of
our house', 'Their pure high blood, their blazon-roll of
glories,/ Their mighty name dishonoured', and his invocation
of the spirit of his sires, 'Your fame, your name, all mingled up
in mine'; then, in *The Two Foscari*, the praise of the 'heroes' of
'the great house of Foscari', the Doge's rejection of pity as
unworthy of 'my name', his lament that 'I have seen our house
dishonoured'.[21]

This is the language of 'the age of chivalry'. The qualities
which bestow honour on the men of generous houses are
success in war and political service (and in their womenfolk,
chastity, fecundity, obedience). Both plays particularly emphasize the military actions of the male protagonists in expanding
the empire of Venice and repulsing her enemies. Byron,
judging the historical record in his Preface, wrote of Faliero as
'a man of talents and of courage':

> I find him commander-in chief of the land forces at
> the siege of Zara, where he beat the King of
> Hungary and his army of eighty thousand men,
> killing eight thousand men, and keeping the
> besieged at the same time in check; an exploit to
> which I know none similar in history, except that of
> Caesar at Alesia, and of Prince Eugene at Belgrade.

As with Bonaparte in *Childe Harold*, classical typology places
the great man in the list of captains: Caesar, Eugene, Faliero.

The Roman analogy is invoked again concerning Doge Foscari's 'Thirty-four years of nearly ceaseless warfare' (II.i.14):

> The Romans (and we ape them) gave a crown
> To him who took a city ....   (IV.i.312–13)

And Marina reminds the Doge too of the Spartans:

>   these did not weep
> Their boys who died in battle ....   (II.i.74–75)

Byron may be recalling also the famous scene in Addison's *Cato* in which the hero rejoices at the death of a son—these classic, imperial types are the rôle-models for a patrician hero.

Another classic duty of the great man was to be the patron of his clients, establishing mutual dependency within a hierarchical structure—a tradition of which Burke writes (of the Whigs) in telling of their 'long possession of government; vast property; obligations of favour given and received; connections of office; ties of blood, of alliance, of friendship...'.[22] Faliero, preparing the insurrection, says that around him

>   will be drawn out in arms
> My nephew and the clients of our house ....
>   (III.ii.255–56)

and noble Lioni, appealing to the responsibility of 'poor plebeian Bertram' reminds him that he is his friend and

>   the only son
> Of him who was a friend unto thy father,
> So that our good-will is a heritage
> We should bequeath to our posterity.   (IV.i.249–52)

Faliero carries the relation of patron to client to a feudal extreme. Like Worcester or Hotspur, when he rises against the authority of the state, he looks for support to 'my own fief', to 'our retainers', the 'vassals' of his district, the 'serfs of my country' who will 'do the bidding of their lord' (IV.ii.1 f.).

This is not a window for looking into politics which one

would usually expect in the times of Paine, Hunt, Cobbett. It recalls rather Burke's chivalric admiration for the 'antient opinions and rules of life'. But there is danger in quoting Burke too frequently lest he sound an isolated and eccentric voice. He is not. Consider the great Whig polemicist Junius attacking the corrupt Ministry of his day. The conceptual vocabulary, like Byron's, reminds the great lords of the 'house' from which they come, their 'ancestors', their 'illustrious name and great property' and the proper paternal attitude of a friend of the people. [...] Consider Godwin's Falkland, who is likewise motivated by name and fame: 'He believed that nothing was so well calculated to make men delicate, gallant and humane, as a temper perpetually alive to the sentiments of birth and honour.'[23] The examples of Burke, Junius and Godwin are particularly pertinent to *Marino Faliero* for they are describing an order, and its value, which they see in danger of extinction. [...]

These parallels suggest that if we are to understand Regency politics it is just as important to turn to Plutarch or Polybius as it is to Paine: that is to say, to those writers who formed the thought of men of generous breed—'the antient opinions and rules of life'. The political typology of Byron's Venetian plays, indeed, might readily serve as a basis for instruction in the ideals of classical antiquity as moralized for an aristocracy by birth (or learning). It will suffice to list *passim* some of the historical names from *Marino Faliero* and comment laconically on the pertinence to the times of a few. Julius Caesar we have already seen here; with Caesar, his assassin, Marcus Junius Brutus, who 'died in giving/ Rome liberty, but left a deathless lesson' (his ancestor, Lucius Junius, is the archetype for Doge Foscari's sacrifice of his son); with Brutus, Cassius; the Gracchi (violent friends of the Roman people); Manlius, called a traitor, but rather one who 'sought but to reform what he revived'; Gelon (conqueror of the Carthaginians, ruler of Syracuse, known as father of his people and patron of liberty); Timoleon (tyrannicide, who killed his own brother in the cause, law-giver who lived as a private man though chief influence in the state); Thrasybulus (the general who expelled from Athens the 30 tyrants, but would accept no recompense beyond a crown of olive twigs). Most important of all is Agis, sovereign of Sparta, who sought to restore the Constitution of Lycurgus, but who was killed by the magistrates (the Ephori). This is the type with whom Faliero climactically chooses to identify himself at his death:

> there's not a history
> But shows a thousand crowned conspirators
> *Against* the people; but to set them free,
> One Sovereign only died, and one is dying ...
> The King of Sparta, and the Doge of Venice—
> Agis and Faliero! (V.iii.16 f.)

In making the connection Byron may not only be drawing attention to history, but to another of those Italian patriot writers who had a major role to play in the politics of *Childe Harold*: Alfieri—one who showed 'a hatred approaching to madness against every species of tyranny'.[24] The allusion is both to Plutarch, and Alfieri's neoclassical tragedy *Agide* (1786). (The same writer's *Bruto Primo* was dedicated to George Washington.)

The use of these traditional paradigms is a formidable check to radical innovation by tending to reimpose old patterns upon historical events: to return to the archetype rather than to make things new. It is the theme of the return of liberty on classic models again, or the restoration of the principles of the state—revolution in the sense of turning back the cycle of history. The ideal which *Marino Faliero* especially evokes is *tyrannicidium*: kill Julius Caesar and the Roman republic will be restored. It is a simplistic solution to political problems, for in its basic form it necessitates identifying tyranny with an individual—Caesar or Castlereagh—so that the particular violent act can achieve the widest possible purgation. [...]

The literary text, however, is more complex and one cannot read the tragedies directly in the simplistic way. The very number of the historical types suggests an uncertainty where to place the emphasis. [...] The problem for Faliero is that he cannot identify his target as a corrupt individual to be cut off. It is an entire class of society which is to be exterminated, and it is his own: the corrupted *aristoi*. Nor has he an entirely 'new order' of things which he wishes to impose, and which the radical revolutionary might claim necessitates the 'uprooting' which a massive revolutionary movement seeks to enact. That phrase quoted of Manlius, that he 'sought but to reform what he revived' (IV.ii.304), is straightforward Whig: the Constitution must be returned to its pure principles by reforming policies. The policy of the archetype Agis was to bring back the ancient code of laws of Lycurgus, not to make up a theoretical new system. As a man of great authority, like Faliero, his aim was to use 'true sovereignty' to establish 'freedom'. Thus, although the usual simplistic vocabulary of 'tyranny/ freedom' is frequently employed, the dramatic situation is not conceived in the straightforward manner such terms imply.

The attempt by Faliero to explain his position to the conspirators reads very strangely, and one must consider not only what he says, but the dramatic inappropriateness of the utterance.

> Our private wrongs have sprung from public vices,
> In this—I cannot call it commonwealth,
> Nor kingdom, which hath neither prince nor people,
> But all the sins of the old Spartan state,
> Without its virtues—temperance and valour.
> The Lords of Lacedaemon were true soldiers,
> But ours are Sybarites, while we are Helots,
> Of whom I am the lowest, most enslaved; ...
>   You are met
> To overthrow this monster of a State,
> This mockery of a Government, this spectre,

Which must be exorcised with blood,—and then
We will renew the times of Truth and Justice,
Condensing in a fair free commonwealth
Not rash equality but equal rights,
Proportioned like the columns to the temple
Giving and taking strength reciprocal,
And making firm the whole with grace and beauty,
So that no part could be removed without
Infringement of the general symmetry.
In operating this great change, I claim
To be one of you—if you trust in me;
If not, strike home,—my life is compromised,
And I would rather fall by freemen's hands
Than live another day to act the tyrant
As delegate of tyrants: such I am not,
And never have been— (III.ii.154–82)

In addressing 'the people' Faliero at once adopts the language of classicism. [...] The implication of the play is that the conspirators, though of lower order, share a common education, that they are members of what Hobhouse called in the Westminster election of 1819 the 'respectable classes'. The constitutional structure of the Spartan state (likened to Venice) is tripartite: 'prince' (Agis); 'lords' (whose magistrates, the Ephori, check the power of the prince); 'people'. Faliero (and Byron) sees Sparta, therefore, as analogous to the usual three-fold model embodied in Rome, Britain, America, that 'division of the whole legislative power into three estates' (Junius, 39). The fault of Sparta was that the austere military caste which embodied the virtues of the state—temperance and valour—reduced the people to slavery (helots). So, in Venice, the tripartite order has become unbalanced: its sovereign is a slave to a degenerate aristocracy just as much as the people are. The cause is the old, familiar, luxury which saps and destroys all constitutions. Hence the use of the word 'sybarite'. Venice is monstrous; something out of the true nature of political order.

Hence Faliero's definition of a 'fair free commonwealth' as one in which rights are:

> Proportioned like the columns to the temple,
> Giving and taking strength reciprocal,
> And making firm the whole with grace and beauty
> So that no part could be removed without
> Infringement of the general symmetry ....

The image of 'strength reciprocal' is in some ways preferable to the common notion of 'balance'—for the idea of checks and balances implies both the constant wavering into imbalance as one element becomes dominant and threatens (in Fox's word) to become 'absolute', and also a constant state of 'class warfare' as the balance is restored. Faliero's ideal derives from writers like Polybius who explained the extraordinary success of the Roman people in their heroic ability to resolve their internal contests and dissensions in patriotic purpose. It is appropriate therefore that the architectural image Faliero uses is of a classical building: a temple with columns. Any visitor to Washington may at once see on the Capitol that classic idea in architectural icon, and may read the words of Jefferson inscribed in stone declaring 'eternal hostility against every form of tyranny'.

This description reduces Faliero's speech to a rehearsal of commonplaces. It is not as easy as that. The commonplaces, to the ear of this critic, do not have the assurance and force manifested, for example, by the American founding fathers. Faliero leans heavily on the aesthetic of his description—words like 'grace', 'beauty', 'symmetry' show him like Burke aware of the poetry of politics—and he loads his discourse with words everyone would wish to associate with their cause: 'fair', 'free', 'right', 'truth', 'justice'. But the extensive use of these big, noble words is covering up the lack of any precision in the argument. It is like the use of 'Freedom' in *Childe*

Harold, except that the context is different. Faliero is in a pragmatic situation. He is about to stage a *coup d'état*. Who is going to be killed? What happens tomorrow? Those questions demand immediate, practical answers.

Nowhere is the imprecision better embodied in the rhetoric than in the extraordinary wobble of the line: 'Not rash equality but equal rights'. Is there not a strong potential for contradiction in the claim that equality is not equality, or, if that is too abrupt a division, that right equality is not rash equality? It is a shuffle, and the kind of shuffle an aristocratic monarch is likely to make leading a proletarian rising. He offers equal status, and denies it. [...] What Faliero does not recommend is hierarchical authority based on responsibilities and duties which might be more appropriate to his house and rank. The line is so tantalizing in its implications, however, that, at the risk of overreading, a little more will be suggested.

In a Whig context that word 'rights' is linked with ideas such as the Bill of Rights, the Declaration of Rights—rights, that is, as codified by law, and expressed, in a phrase already familiar, by 'equal laws'. Such a concept of right subsists with distinctions of rank and property. [...] Clearly this separates a revolution like that of 1688, or even 1789, from Jacobinical 'levelling'. 'All men have equal rights, but not to equal things', wrote Burke in the classic rejection of egalitarianism in the *Reflections*, and he listed as rights equal laws, the right to preserve the fruits of one's own industry, the right of inheritance, and the right to nourish one's own children.

Something of this kind, probably, Byron means by 'equal laws' in the 'Ode from the French' (which laments the corruption of revolution), and also by Faliero's preference for 'equal rights' to 'rash equality'. Democracy would be a tyranny of blackguards, a dictatorship of the proletariat. [...] Drawing the line, however, is not easy. This exposition of the context of Faliero's expressions should not smooth over the points of stress. On the contrary, the imprecise generalities of his speech, the inappropriateness of this kind of oratory as an appeal to the people, the potential contradictions in the notion of equality: these things are signs of unease.

What is the place of the people in this? Faliero is described as a 'liberal', one who recognizes the rights of man, and a friend of the people. Israel Bertuccio describes him:

> his mind is liberal,
> He sees and feels the people are oppressed,
> And shares their sufferings.   (II.ii.174–76)

When he appears to the people they at once recognize him as their proper leader, so that his 'sovereignty' is not imposed from above but arises spontaneously as an expression of the general will to 'purify' the 'corrupted commonwealth'. It is an odd thing how easily this process of recognition of the natural leader occurs (the real life Carbonari in Naples, Byron noted, were far less successful!),[25] and then how much alarm is engendered in Faliero that this has happened at all. [...]

The sufferings of the oppressed are carefully held at arms length. The specific complaint for which Israel Bertuccio seeks redress is that noble Barbaro has hit him on the face and drawn blood 'dishonourably'. Israel has the same code of values as the Doge himself (whose honour has been insulted), and is therefore a complainant within the aristocratic system. It is the same kind of conception which later leads 'honourable' Bertram as a client to turn to his patron when he betrays the revolution.

The pressure of Byron's model, Otway, operates here, for the motives in *Venice Preserved* are likewise personalized among members of the same class. Otway had to tread carefully in the political miasma of the 1680s. Byron too is writing in a highly charged political situation, but one must recognize that to a large extent form determines content. The decorum of the neoclassical tragic drama demands a 'high' style which of necessity excludes alternative discourses—including 'the voice of the people' who would use a different form of expression, and thus, different arguments. This is readily obvious by comparing *Marino Faliero* with *Henry IV*. Byron, by preferring the neoclassical to the Shakespearian mode, has excluded that variety of style which is so typical of Shakespeare, and thus the variety of voices competing in dialectical debate. Falstaff's speech 'What's honour?' is an obvious example. Shakespeare creates the dramatic illusion that the people can speak for themselves. They do not, and they cannot, in *Marino Faliero*. In this respect, 'the people' in Byron's tragedy are in the same position as the Luddites in the House of Lords debates. The oratory of the leaders of state operates over an immense void of silence.

Thus 'the people' are seen from a height and from afar, and treated with brevity. Indeed, the text needs to be scanned for references to them![26] The issue of their disfranchisement is raised by the Doge: the people 'are nothing in the state, and in/ The city worse than nothing'. The matter is raised, and disappears. Israel offers the Doge a list of 'wrongs' under whose 'strong conception' the people groan: the foreign troops are in arrears of pay; the people are taxed for the war against Genoa, which is fought with 'plebeian blood'; the class has suffered sexual 'oppression, or pollution' from the patricians. These matters also disappear. [...] When, at long last, the citizens eventually appear at the end of *Marino Faliero* after the execution, their function is brief and choric:

> *Third Citizen.* Then they have murdered him who
>   would have freed us.
> *Fourth Citizen.* He was a kind man to the commons
>   ever.   (V.iv.21–22)

This is very similar to the function of *Il Popolo* (thus the speech prefix) in Alfieri's *Agide* who comment on the greatness of the protagonist, but do not save him. A chorus does not participate in the action. [...]

Between Alfieri's eighteenth-century tragedy and Byron's lies the French Revolution, and a clear indication of the dangers of democratic insurrection. What Faliero is about to unleash is the Terror. No sooner has he committed himself to revolution than he becomes a prey to doubt and riddled with guilt. This is the main theme of the action. To describe this merely as typical of the 'Byronic hero' is to subsume it into vague typology. There are specific political reasons (belonging to Byron's epoch also) why Faliero feels guilty. To be a 'Friend of the People' was commonly represented as a noble end for nobility. But who are 'the people'?:

> At midnight, by the church Saints John and Paul,
> Where sleep my noble fathers, I repair—
> To what? to hold a council in the dark
> With common ruffians leagued to ruin states!
>
> (I.ii.579–82)

The comparison between 'noble fathers' and 'common ruffians' is pointed. The revolutionaries are 'malcontents' he thinks, and then, by implication, 'scoundrels':

> I cannot stoop—that is, I am not fit
> To lead a band of—patriots.   (III.ii.220–21)

The anachronistic allusion is obvious to anyone well-read in eighteenth-century English literature. The pause places irony on the word 'patriot', and the emphasis will recall Johnson's definition of 'patriotism'. It is 'the last refuge of a scoundrel'. Others in the play are more direct. The armed Signor of the Night speaks of 'the bloodhound mob', and noble Lioni refers to those 'discontented ruffians/ And desperate libertines who brawl in taverns ...' (IV.i.227–28). [...] Thus the Doge is unable to exclude from his feelings a sense of mutual relationship between himself and his fellow patricians. The Terror will be directed at those who were his friends, or whose fathers were his friends:

> I loved them, they
> Requited honourably my regards;

We served and fought; we smiled and wept in
　　concert; ...
We made alliances of blood and marriage;
We grew in years and honours fairly ... (III.ii.319 f.)

The key words here are 'blood', 'honour' and 'alliance', and
the Doge distinguishes himself from Israel (the plebeian
Gracchus and popular tribune): 'You never broke their bread,
nor shared their salt.' That heartfelt expression of the Doge's
is not dissimilar from Byron's reaction to the Cato Street
conspiracy. He was horrified at the attempt to assassinate his
political opponent Harrowby. Had they not dined together
hundreds of times? There is an empathy within the patrician
order which the poet understands from experience, and
which, therefore, he makes the Doge feel keenly. This is the
tragic dilemma of Faliero. At the climactic moment of the
play, when the bell rings too late for insurrection, and the
tramp of martial feet Faliero hears is not that of the rebel
forces but of the state's own soldiers, then the issue which he
debates is the justification of terror, and the desperate tone of
the soliloquy, its twists and suppressions, indicate how little
he has truly convinced himself:

> 　　　　And you, ye blue-sea waves! ...
> Now thou must wear an unmixed crimson; no
> Barbaric blood can reconcile us now
> Unto that horrible incarnadine,
> But friend or foe will roll in civic slaughter.
> And have I lived to fourscore years for this?
> I, who was named Preserver of the City? ...
> But this day, black within the calendar,
> Shall be succeeded by a bright millennium.
> Doge Dandolo survived to ninety summers
> To vanquish empires, and refuse their crown;
> I will resign a crown, and make the State
> Renew its freedom—but oh! by what means?
> The noble end must justify them—What

> Are a few drops of human blood? 'tis false,
> The blood of tyrants is not human; they
> Like to incarnate Molochs, feed on ours,
> Until 'tis time to give them to the tombs
> Which they have made so populous.—Oh World!
> Oh Men! What are ye, and our best designs,
> That we must work by crime to punish crime? ...
> I must not ponder this.   (IV.ii.141 f.)

Byron's defects as a dramatic poet make criticism more than usually difficult. To claim that this argument is 'unconvincing' may be a comment more on the uncertainty of the writing than of Faliero's mind. It *sounds*, however, as if he is trying to convince himself about his policy, and failing. The echo of *Macbeth*—the sea 'incarnadine'—suggests the immense potential of evil to spread its stain everywhere. The counter-claim, that there will be but 'a few drops of human blood' may be the equivalent of Lady Macbeth's 'a little water clears us of this deed'—it is a statement necessary for the murderer to make, but untrue and not necessarily believed by the speaker. It necessitates a further distancing of the bloodshed—'the blood of tyrants is not human'—a statement in utter contradiction to everything Faliero has said earlier about the ties of blood which bind him to those whose bread and salt he has shared. It is, of course, a common strategy to dehumanize one's enemy; as non-human they cannot therefore claim 'equal rights' to life, liberty and the pursuit of happiness. But he does not sound as if he is convincing himself, and even less a potential audience. That question, 'must we work by crime to punish crime?', is *not* answered by the assumption that the end justified the means. It is much closer to the question in *Childe Harold*, 'Can tyrants but by tyrants conquered be?'. Of course Faliero is eager to demonstrate that, as a friend of equal rights, it is not he but his enemies who are wrong, but the new order he is offering is now no more than a form of words: 'a bright millennium'. There is not a single pragmatic proposal surviving in the speech—except the requirement to kill. The extinction of the patrician order in 'civic slaughter' *must* produce freedom. This view is utterly naive, and there is no reason to suppose from the text that it is anything more than the wish-fulfilment of an old man whose mind, he will soon admit, has become unhinged. Dagolino early in the play has indicated the likely extent of the terror. He was indifferent if 'thousands' should be exterminated. It is 'The spirit of this Aristocracy/ Which must be rooted out' (III.ii.40–41). The historical analogy is quite clear. Like Mirabeau or La Fayette, for the noblest of reasons Faliero is committing himself to a disastrous course of action.

Faliero is enabled to preserve the nobility of his intention—to free the state from the corruption of its dominant aristocracy—only because the idea never issues in the execution of thousands. The betrayal of the conspiracy in many respects is more honourable than the (insulted) honour of the Doge and Israel Bertuccio. Bertram goes to Lioni for the best of motives. As a loyal 'client' to his 'patron' he wishes to save the life of this noble patrician. Nor is there anything to suggest that Lioni is unworthy of his regard. His concern for the state's safety as much as his own indicates his patriotism. In particular he shows the sensitivity and culture which belonged to a refined order of men. The over-long soliloquy in which he reflects upon Venice in the moonlight, her beauty and decadence, has often been noted as dramatically inappropriate. One of its functions, however, is to establish Lioni as a man of feeling, which is part of his true breeding, as much as his concern for his responsibilities to those beneath him who were his father's friends and to his own class. After Faliero and Angiolina, Lioni is the most conspicuous example of a patrician and a senator in the play, and he is admirable. It is impossible to claim the whole order is corrupt when it contains such quality, and if that aristocracy were extirpated it would carry with it all that sense of patriarchal responsibility and all that fine feeling which Lioni embodies. In short, we are told aristocracy is corrupt, we are shown in Lioni (and Angiolina) types of its excellence.

The play is structured, therefore, upon paradoxes and contradictions. The resolution to which it moves is Faliero's prophetic curse. Since it was written after the extinction of the Venetian republic, in this, at least, the Doge can speak the 'truth' about future times. Unlike Agide he does not offer the consolation to posterity that the nobility of his death will ensure that the greatness of his ideals will be fulfilled some time in the future:

> Maturo è omai, credete a me matur
> E il cangiamento: il ciel non vuol ch'io 'l vegga:
> Ma vuol ch'ei segua.   (IV.iii.292–94)

For the 1780s Agide's words have a prophetic upbeat. It is the equivalent of Byron's 'the king-times are fast finishing ... I shall not live to see it, but I foresee it', and may have inspired Byron's expression. Both are greatly different from the curse on Venice and its degenerate aristocracy:

> Yes, the hours
> Are silently engendering of the day,
> When she, who built 'gainst Attila a bulwark,
> Shall yield, and bloodlessly and basely yield
> Unto a bastard Attila. [Bonaparte]   (V.iii.45–49)

Agide dies involved with his incorruptible virtue, rejecting even his family with the austerity of a Socrates or a Lucius Junius Brutus: 'i cittadini sono:/ Di un giusto re figli primieri' (V.ii.44–45). Faliero's sententious summary of his position is: 'I am not innocent—but are these guiltless?' (V.iii.40). His crime has been against criminals. The line is obviously intended as a moral summary, and leaves the play locked in the basic contradiction which had produced its tragic outcome. In a corrupt state revolution itself corrupts: crime punishes crime. The name and fame of ideal virtue were the consolation of Sparta's king in his tragic failure. For Faliero there follows

in history the obliteration of his image and his ill-repute to
posterity.

[...]

The tragedy of *The Two Foscari* arises from the rejection of
'resistance' as a principle of state and the acceptance of the
paramountcy of law. Jeffrey, in calling this 'passive obedience',
would make the Foscari Tories and the Venetian regime
in some sense a historical parallel to the Stuarts. But that
avoids the dilemma Byron presents, for the Venetian state is
not operating by arbitrary prerogative. Jacopo Foscari is
condemned by due process of known law over which Doge
Foscari properly presides. The 'ideal' form of that tragedy is
the story of Lucius Junius Brutus, where the father has to
condemn the sons because the state and its laws are superior
to the ties of family. The Doge repeatedly in the last scene of
the play draws attention to his rejection of the revolutionary
cause adopted by 'attainted' Faliero and refuses to curse the
state. Faliero was executed at the Giant's Staircase as a traitor:
the Doge Foscari resolves to walk down the same staircase as a
private citizen divested of sovereignty. 'Resistance' was criminal in Faliero. Legality is Foscari's prudential choice.

Like Faliero, Foscari expresses his conception of the ideal
state. It is that in which he is chief 'citizen' of the 'whole
republic' and of the 'general will'. In another context this
might be the vocabulary of 'Jacobinism' (*citoyen, volunté
générale*), but it is here effectively colonized by the patrician
order. As chief of the legislature (the state's sovereign) it is
Foscari's duty to obey the state's laws (Erskine or Brougham
would agree). His view is put with the highest idealism:

                              in all things
    I have observed the strictest reverence;
    Not for the laws alone, ... but ...
    I have observed with veneration, like
    A priest's for the High Altar, even unto

> The sacrifice of my own blood and quiet,
> Safety, and all save honour, the decrees,
> The health, the pride, and welfare of the State.
> (II.i.248 ff.)

The key scene for a political reading of the play is the debate between Marina (Jacopo's wife) and the Doge at the end of the second act. Marina's allegorical name and idealized rôle give her utterances authority. The Doge's patriotism is misguided, she exclaims. The state which he serves is now in the hands of an oligarchy whose code of laws is more than Draconian. Such a government is a traitor to the constitution, not Jacopo. The oligarchs are tyrants. (Compare Hobhouse in *Examiner* 631 on 'the Oligarchical Conspiracy, which has ruined England, which can maintain its usurped power only by our perpetual enslavement, and which we must, therefore, determine to annihilate if we determine to be free'.)

> The Country is the traitress, which thrusts forth
> Her best and bravest from her. Tyranny
> Is far the worst of treasons. Dost thou deem
> None rebels except subjects? The Prince who
> Neglects or violates his trust is more
> A brigand than the robber-chief.   (II.i.386–91)

The awkwardness of Byron's theatrical writing as usual makes critical assessment of the dramatic function of this difficult, but it sounds as if part of a casuistical debate rather than an expression of character, although as Jacopo's wife Marina has motivation 'in character' for arguing like this. One might compare the tone and function of Angelo and Isabella debating justice and mercy in *Measure for Measure*. There is a morality-play feel to the language. The function of Marina's casuistry here is to identify the patrician order as an oligarchical tyranny. Once establish the word 'tyranny' as a correct description of the government, then the traditional appeal to tyrannicide might be made: it is a 'right' of 'slaves' to achieve 'freedom' by 'resistance'.

The Doge is given longer to reply, and that reply returns repeatedly to the word 'law':

> I found the law: I did not make it. Were I
> A subject, still I might find parts and portions
> Fit for amendment; but as Prince, I never
> Would change, for the sake of my house, the charter
> Left by our fathers.   (II.i.395–99)

This is liberal constitutionalism. The law may be used to amend the law—that is the right of the subject. The Doge, as supreme magistrate, is in the position of a judge. His function must be to apply the rule of law such as is given to him. It would be utterly corrupt to alter it unilaterally for family concern. That is what it means to be a 'citizen'.

> If we had not for many centuries
> Had thousands of such citizens, and shall,
> I trust, have still such, Venice were no city.
>   (II.i.415–17)

Unlike Faliero, who cursed a degenerate state, Doge Foscari sees himself as one citizen only in a great tradition stretching before and after.

Like Agide, therefore, his example must stand as a type of ideal state service. He says that had he as many sons as he had years he would have given them all for the state (though not without feeling). [...] Doge Faliero is spoken of as a 'stoic of the state' and as showing 'more than Roman fortitude'. He claims that under her laws

Venice

> Has risen to what she is—a state to rival
> In deeds and days, and sway, and let me add,
> In glory (for we have had Roman spirits
> Amongst us), all that history has bequeathed

Of Rome and Carthage in their best times, when
The people swayed by Senates.   (II.i.400–06)

His ultimate message to Jacopo is brief: 'That he obey/ the
laws' (II.i.435–36). The Doge's arguments in reply to Marina
are—to the ear of this reader—as abstract as her own. The
appeal is to an idealized concept of classical antiquity on
which the great man of modern state should model his
conduct. The Senate is the expression of the general will of an
uncorrupted people. The supreme magistrate is the executor
of that will legally embodied. The true patriot's function is
service to the people, at whatever cost. An antique and formalized conception—the true republic—is set in direct contrast
to another: the tyrannical regime. Both are used to describe
Venice. Action is dependent on which conception prevails.

Isolating a fragment of the play in this manner risks
distorting the whole. *The Two Foscari* is far less of a political
play than *Marino Faliero*. The major emphasis is upon the
suffering of father, son and wife, and upon the extraordinary
patriotism of Jacopo who prefers torture in a Venetian jail to
exile elsewhere. His actions, like Faliero's, seem excessive, and
the question of 'political justice'—are the laws those of 'the
people' or 'a tyrant'?—only indirectly relates to the highly
personalized motive of revenge which drives Loredano, like
Shylock, to use the law to obliterate mercy.

With that caveat in mind one may, nonetheless, extend
the political theme into the private story by observing that the
law is not an abstract and ideal thing. It is made by people
(and by ruling classes). What happens to the respect due to
the rule of law and the constitution when those who make the
laws are corrupt? 'Political justice' may be justice politicized,
and personalized. When the Doge proclaims his 'strictest
reverence' for the laws he adds a proviso. Loredano has
'strained' them, and he adds: 'I do not speak of you but as a
single voice/ Of many ...'. At the beginning of the fourth
act Loredano puts the matter bluntly:

Barbarigo. But will the laws uphold us?
Loredano. What laws?—'The Ten' are laws; and if
    they were not,
I will be legislator in this business. (IV.i.37–39)

A wilful patrician can use the acquiescent 'Ten', or the Senate, to push through what he desires as legislator. If the state is the slave of a tyrant (or tyrants) who use its constitution, its courts and their power as 'legislators' to foster their own aims (as Loredano does), then 'justice' is merely the expression of the usurping self-interest of those able to manipulate power for their own ends. To use an analogy from the politics of Byron's time: 'the Ten', with Loredano pushing them on, are the historical equivalent to that power of the Crown which had increased, was increasing and ought to be diminished. Barbarigo attacks Loredano for using 'your Giunta' for his aims.

Loredano.   How!—*my* Giunta!
Barbarigo.   *Yours!*
    They speak your language, watch your nod,
        approve
    Your plans, and do your work. Are they not
        yours?
Loredano. You talk unwarily. 'Twere best they hear
    not
    This from you.
Barbarigo.   Oh! they'll hear as much one day
    From louder tongues than mine; they have
        gone beyond
    Even their exorbitance of power: and when
    This happens in the most contemned and
        abject
    States, stung humanity will rise to check it.
Loredano. You talk but idly.
Barbarigo.   That remains for proof.
        (V.i.141–50)

Moore wrote in the *Life* of Sheridan that 'Law is but too often ... the ready accomplice of Tyranny', and he sharpened the generalization to a criticism of the Pittite system which used legislation to encroach 'upon the property and liberty of the subject'.[27] No Marxist criticism of the relation between class and power could put the matter more clearly. It is tempting to act as a latter-day Hobhouse to point to the state trials of Hardy, the Hunts, Burdett, which must have been in Byron's mind, or even to look forward and observe how the submission of the martyrs of Tolpuddle to legal transportation mirrors the exile of Jacopo. But the text resists the local allegory. The debate is in terms of general principle only. Byron is concerned with the political philosophy which a historical record might teach, and, unlike *Childe Harold*, has no provocative commentator.

When the power of the state became 'exorbitant' then 'stung humanity will rise to check it' said Barbarigo. It is a Byronic 'prophecy'. It is the old theme of 'resistance' to 'tyranny' when the 'balance' of power is distorted. But one cannot isolate the passage this way to support a preconceived image of revolutionary Byron. Loredano is unimpressed: 'You talk but idly.' Loredano is quite correct. The historical fact about the Venetian state was that 'stung humanity' did nothing. Revolution was not inevitable. Faliero's curse was fulfilled. What followed was the 'euthanasia' of the constitution. Barbarigo's fear of speaking out—his lack of a 'loud tongue'—is symptomatic of reluctant acquiescence sinking to servility. (Compare, if one will, a free press, or the poet's voice.) But, on the other hand, what use was Faliero's resistance?

As for an appeal to the people ... Doge Foscari has the word 'citizen' often in his mouth, but *Il Popolo* do not have even a brief scene in this tragedy to express their admiration for a 'Friend of the People'. In any case, his name and fame rest on thirty-four years of war, not, for instance, on regulations concerning conditions of labour or the liberty of the press.

Venice—all the citizens collectively—is embodied only in Marina whose attack on 'murder by law' is magnificent but abstract. She accuses her country in the name of

> Men and Angels!
> The blood of myriads reeking up to Heaven,
> The groan of slaves in chains, and men in dungeons,
> Mothers, and wives, and sons, and sires, and
>   subjects,
> Held in the bondage of ten bald-heads ....
>   (III.i.240–44)

Marchand calls this 'the voice of rebellion that is never silenced by timidity or considerations of policy'.[28] But it is *not* rebellion. It is a protest delivered by an allegorical abstraction which has no result. Her demand for 'retribution' is as powerless as her earlier call for resistance. She represents no specific force within the orders of the state. It is only a voice, its helplessness emphasized by her sex.

But the man who acted, Faliero, likewise achieved nothing. Tormented by conscience he was executed as a criminal.

A recent lecture on 'Byron in Venice' spoke of Byron's 'iron revolutionary will'.[29] Wherever that may be found, it is not in the Venetian tragedies. They represent an impasse and inevitable decline. It was a classic dilemma. No redress for grievances can be obtained, Faliero tells Israel, neither for himself nor for the people. In this the teaching of history, and the historical record, supported Byron as the sober language of Rose's *Letter from the North of Italy* indicates in an appendix to the text: 'A state without the means of some change is without the means of its conservation,' wrote another classic historian. The words are those of Burke in the *Reflections on the Revolution in France*.

[...] The plays are monitory: take warning from history. In so far as they relate, in general, to the situation of 'Tory' Britain they do not show any 'progressive' way forward. The choice is between class revolution or the continuation, *sine die*, of 'corruption' in the form of a reactionary oligarchy opposed by a party which has lost all guts for reform. Whig constitutionalism is a dead letter; joining the radicals will bring in Hunt and Cobbett, worse than Robespierre or Marat. Faliero is in a position analogous to La Fayette or Mirabeau (or Lord Byron if revolution came). Foscari is as helpless as Byron in the Lords. There is nothing to be done. [...] Byron's political education, therefore, is not in revolution but in disenchantment. It is a process of learning the hard way. But it is learning about things as they are. [...]

NOTES

1. Feiling, *The Second Tory Party*.
2. *Ravenna Journal*, 13 January 1821. See also *The Revolt of Islam*, IX, xxvi.
3. Letters to Murray, 31 August and 29 September 1820. For *specific* relation between contemporary events and the plays see Ashton, 'The Censorship of Byron's *Marino Faliero*', pp. 27–44; Johnson, 'A Political Interpretation', pp. 417–25; Watkins, 'Violence, Class Consciousness, and Ideology', pp. 799–816.
4. Byron hoped for a Constitution on the American model; *Ravenna Journal*, 9 January 1821.
5. October 1820; to Hobhouse, 22 April 1820. See also to Hobhouse, 29 March 1820; the radicals should be 'dealt with' like Jack Cade or Wat Tyler.
6. To Murray, 21 February 1820; 'My Dictionary': Augustus; to Augusta Leigh, 15 October 1819. Burke is discussed by Madame de Staël in *Considerations*, II, 36.
7. To Hobhouse, 29 March 1820.
8. To Hobhouse, 22 April 1820 and 12 October 1821. Cf. Montesquieu in de Staël, to 'cut up the tree by its roots to obtain its fruit', op. cit., II, 383.
9. To Murray, 21 February 1820; to Hobhouse, 22 April 1820.
10. Russell, *Life of William Lord Russell*, p. xiii.
11. See Bamford, *Passages in the Life of a Radical*, II, 79, 96.
12. I adopt Carlyle's portrait from *The French Revolution*.

13. Marchand analyses the issue admirably in his *Byron: A Biography*, p. 841. Also relevant is Barrell's *English Literature in History*—a Marxist view of the role of the gentry.

14. My account is derived from Laqueur, 'The Queen Caroline Affair', pp. 417–66. See also Sales, *English Literature in History*.

15. To Murray, 17 August 1820; to Count Alborghetti, 23 November 1820.

16. To Hobhouse, 8 August 1820.

17. Brand, *Italy and the English Romantics*, p. 192, discusses numerous Italian patriotic tragedies, including Mary Russell Mitford's *Rienzi* (1828) and Bulwer Lytton's *Rienzi* (1835). Mitford also wrote *Foscari* (1826).

18. New, *Life of Brougham*, p. 3.

19. Byron, *The Complete Works* (London: Murray, 1832–33), XIII, 234.

20. New, *Life of Brougham*, p. 113.

21. *Faliero*, I.ii.64; III.i.32–33, 43; *Foscari*, I.i.240 f.; II.i.149 f.

22. Cited by Trench, *Portrait of a Patriot*, p. 311.

23. Boulton, *The Language of Politics*, pp. 226–32.

24. Marshal, *Italy in English Literature*, p. 354.

25. '[T]he populace are not interested—only the higher and middle orders', *Ravenna Journal*, 24 January 1821.

26. *Faliero*, I.ii.301 f., 461 f.

27. Moore, *Life of Sheridan*, I, 486, 467.

28. Marchand, *Byron's Poetry*, p. 102.

29. Programme of the 1985 Cheltenham Festival of Literature.

'Agonized Self-Conflict':
Marino Faliero

G. WILSON KNIGHT

The more spiritual and cosmic energies in *Manfred* and *Cain*—not incomparable with those of *Lear* and *Macbeth*—are in *Marino Faliero* and *Sardanapalus* closely housed in a realistic plot, lonely experience brought back to a human service: behind or within their at first sight quiet manner burn both cosmic vision and intense thought. These may respectively be compared with *Coriolanus* and *Antony and Cleopatra*; though Byron's order of composition *within* the series bounded by *Manfred* and *Sardanapalus* seems uncertain.

The royalist ideal central to the Shakespearian scheme we have watched losing prestige in Milton, Swift and Pope. Yet its essence persists for various basic reasons. Aristocratic scorn of the mob in a Shakespearian or Byronic hero reflects not so much snobbishness as the assertion of individual personality against a group-consciousness. Closely akin is the problem of soldierly honour. We have seen Byron both glorify and deplore military splendours. The thought of his day tends to push the revolutionary instinct of Pope's epistles against both church and throne farther: sometimes too far, making of revolution itself a positive. Byron now aims to preserve intact the royalistic spirit whilst rejecting its formal degradations. In pressing for a new *personal sanctity* he logically conceives a new *sovereignty*, dramatizing stories of (1) a revolutionary duke and (2) a pacifist king. His deep interest in the story of Marino Faliero, recorded in his long Preface and additional notes (where we can profitably watch a dramatist of

Shakespearian calibre revealing the historical interest behind his work), is understandable. For it strikingly symbolizes some of the most complex issues of post-Renaissance Europe: of which Byron, the revolutionary aristocrat, is himself a symbol. [...]

First, I offer a short description of Marino Faliero himself. His heroic service is emphasized, and also his original unwillingness to undertake supreme authority. But, having it, he has a deep sense of its dignity and honour. Though nearly eighty years old, his passions are still youthful, and his eye 'quick' and impatient (I.i.13). Hearing of Steno's sentence his proud and curbless temperament reveals itself in speeches of fiery and rising impetuosity. He would have the Saracens, Genoese or Huns victoriously overrunning Venice, his passion instinctively falling to treasonable thoughts. Then, alone, he meditates on the ducal cap, seeing it as a gilded 'toy' with the 'thorns' but not the 'majesty' of a crown: 'How my brain aches beneath thee! And my temples/ Throb feverish under thy dishonest weight' (I.ii.265–66). The Shakespearian depth is obvious; but complexities of a later day are now involved in both the associations of 'thorns' and the implications of a constitutional and limited monarchy. An essential falsity and insincerity is given by 'dishonest'. In a noble speech later, he expands on the mockery of his position as both man and ruler:

> Begirt with spies for guards, with robes for power,
> With pomp for freedom, gaolers for a council,
> Inquisitors for friends, and hell for life!
>
> (III.ii.358–60)

He longs both to 'free Venice' and 'avenge' his own 'wrongs'. This subtle continuity of personal and general emotions remains evident throughout the interview with Bertuccio (I.ii) which leads to his association with the conspiracy: if his people could share his 'sovereignty' and both together master the 'aristocratic Hydra', he would at last rule indeed. His agreement is most skilfully motivated; Bertuccio—formerly a

soldier—immediately channelling all his sense of comrade-
ship; and recollection of his son's death in battle being swiftly
turned to thoughts of his people's 'filial' love. Them, not the
senate, he served as a soldier. Left alone, he feels 'unworthy' of
his ancestors; yet in terms of that unworthiness must have
'revenge' on baseness and create true freedom. These paradoxes are emphasized.

We heard from Angiolina (II.i) that his passions go deep,
everything wearing in him 'an aspect of eternity'. He is thus a
true successor to other heroes. His faults are those naturally
allied with his military past: his fiery and patrician passions,
and a sense of honour so keen it approaches a 'vice'. The
analysis might suit Coriolanus in Shakespeare. 'Pride' is a fault
in both. She urges her husband in vain to give Steno's fault the
neglect its triviality merits, to dwell less on honour and more
on Heaven's charge of forgiveness. But when his passion does
cool its place is taken by a deadly and a hated duty. Especially
the betrayal of all honourable tradition appals him. His
integrity refuses to call it anything but 'treason' (III.i.50–57).
Success will win the gratitude of prosperity, but failure leave
only a record of baseness: a stern realism seeming to allow the
quality of an action to depend on its result. The nobles'
villainy itself forces the means. Yet again, asked whether all the
nobles should fall, he answers, 'Ask me not—tempt me not
with such a question—/ Decide yourselves ...' (III.ii.295–96).
His decision, tilted by remembrance of personal ingratitude,
is for general massacre, though afterwards recollections of
past social and military companionships crowd back to make
each 'stab'-to-be seem a 'suicide' (III.ii.472). But the strange
magnanimity of a prince who risks all in plotting for his
people is set in contrast to the conventionally honourable
'tyrant' impervious to remorse though he depopulate
'empires' rather than punish a few 'traitors'. And yet, just as
we are again convinced, mention of Steno elicits two lines
which recall with unerring insight the seething personal
resentment: 'Man, thou hast struck upon the chord which

jars/ All nature from my heart. Hence to our task!'
(III.ii.540–41). The balance of impure motive against revolutionary idealism is maintained.

As action draws near the Doge becomes calm:

> It was ever thus
> With me; the hour of agitation came
> In the first glimmerings of a purpose, when
> Passion had too much room to sway; but in
> The hour of action I have stood as calm
> As were the dead who lay around me.   (IV.ii.93–98)

Which is one of many deep human penetrations that need not
be limited to the person concerned. He determines to resign
after the plot's consummation and meditates again on the
wrongs and justice of his course. When his expectations are
reversed he bears sudden failure with stoic calm. At the trial
he recapitulates his unwillingness to take office and his resentment at the nobles' insult, but remains proud and aloof:

> I deny nothing, defend nothing, nothing
> I ask of you, but silence for myself,
> And sentence from the court.   (V.i.295–97)

Alone with Angiolina (V.ii) he tells how the priest he once
struck prophesied that in maturity a 'madness' would seize
him at an age when 'passions' should properly 'mellow' into
'virtues', Byron's respect for religion and uneasy relations
with priests both finding a home in this story too. He sees his
life as a 'maze' and his pride takes pleasure in yielding only to
an over-ruling 'power' greater than men's understanding. At
his final speech (V.iii.26–101), standing 'within eternity', he
bitterly denounces Venetian vices and prophesies a shameful
future; and he dies with a gesture more toweringly proud than
Coriolanus.

The human delineation is Shakespearian, especially in its
feeling for destiny interwoven with close ethical penetration
into the springs of action and the combining of personal traits

with general issues. The Doge could not exist in any other play; he and the action inform each other; the comments of others help, technically, to realize his personality. The texture of the whole is tight, yet we also get an insight into the man comparable to that we have, not of our friends, but of ourselves. He is complete and individual, an honourable past and some faint feeling for an undefined future lingering about the tragic conception.

Our quotations have already hinted at the verbal power. The language is reserved with no especial striving after any overlay of metaphor and image, every accent rising from the tense thought or smouldering passion concerned, every speech from the speaker's nature and situation's demands. The utterance is transparent, yet weighty, the weight now owing little or nothing to any poetic tradition. Yet Byron's Augustan apprenticeship has served to winnow away all trivialities, leaving him instinctively free for an unfettered, yet well-sorted, diction that carries quiet profundities with Shakespearian ease, as in

> ... as yet 'tis but a chaos
> Of darkly brooding thoughts: my fancy is
> In her first work, more nearly to the light
> Holding the sleeping images of things
> For the selection of the pausing judgment.
>
> (I.ii.282–86)

Continually comment strikes home into human psychology, into the human soul itself, as when the Doge remarks how, once bloodshed starts, 'the mere instinct of the first-born Cain' (IV.ii.56) will render brutal those to whom such acts were recently abhorrent. When a speech catches fire the passion curves up like a wave, fierce as a crested snake:

> Yet for all this, so full of certain passions,
> That if once stirr'd and baffled, as he has been
> Upon the tenderest points, there is no Fury

> In Grecian story like to that which wrings
> His vitals with her burning hands, till he
> Grows capable of all things for revenge.
>
> (II.ii.168–73)

The passion plays against the line-units, starting with a pointed intensity, relaxing to swift parenthetic realism ('as he has been ...'), then towering steadily to the moment of striking ('his vitals ... hands'), and next withdrawn, relapsing as an ocean breaker, at the close. It suggests and demands the pulsing vocal variation which is the very life-blood of stage utterance. Such variation works continually to define passionate depth against colloquial changes, and is here, as in Shakespeare, carried into manipulation of scene-movement too. The Doge's early dialogue (II.i) with Angiolina has a wavelike undulation, with, after extreme rhetorical fury, such a powerfully dramatic pause as 'What matters my forgiveness? an old man's/ Worn out, scorn'd, spurn'd, abused ...' (II.i.266–67). You almost hear the quiet voice and deeper note. Shortly the passion again rises (at 'this blight, this brand, this blasphemy'), though not so high as at first. He is what he says, an old man, tired. 'Come hither, child ...' (II.i.291) marks a new movement. Such changes are continually making psychic disclosures; and both suspense and discovery are age-old dramatic tricks, the one preparing for and the other reflecting that depth-seeing and revelation of new psychic dimensions, dark underground rivers or cloudy heights, that is the business of drama. Here both surprise and discovery are frequent. We wait anxiously for the court's first judgement. The Doge's interview with Bertuccio is a clever partnership in dual unmasking; his sudden appearance later among the conspirators a powerfully staged surprise; and the development of his mental conflict a gradual and ever more deep disclosure of tangles and emotions as you feel him tearing out his own existence at its roots. A key-incident is Bertram's discovery of the plot to Lioni. The whole action is by way of being one half-paralysed struggle to overthrow an invincible, though rotting, order; and one long suspense waiting for the pealing of the great bell in Act IV. At the last, the Doge works through a long and steadily rising invective to die in as sudden—even in that context—and shattering a stage climax as you will find in our literature. The mind is thus continually both awakened by surprise and distended by suspense to receive the deepest human, or other, revelations; and the play's weighted thoughts and emotions take on profound subjective importance. We are united to the action on a deeper plane than one of interest or entertainment.

Though the style is mainly direct and unmetaphoric and the whole most carefully constructed, yet the lucidity and care are both thoroughly organic. The reserved nature-imagery is subtle and important. As so often in Byron, human actions are felt shading into comparisons from animal life, and we have a normal assortment: scorpion, silk-worms, viper, tiger, raven, wolves, eagle, geese, adder, worm, dog, lion and a lamb 'bleating' before a butcher. The list speaks for itself, toning into the fierce and poisonous passions and thoughts that are involved. But more important are those directly relating human society to organic nature. My next quotations all occur in III.ii, the scene of the conspirators' meeting. The final massacre is to

> unpeople many palaces
> And hew the highest genealogic trees
> Down to the earth, strew'd with their bleeding fruit,
> And crush their blossoms into barrenness.
>
> (492–95)

The metaphor shows the aristocracy as having grown from the soil of its own past: the play sharing continually the typical Byronic sense of tradition, of a present deeply rooted in history. But the nobility are also felt as a single insidious, living body, to aim primarily at Steno being to 'lop the hand' rather than its 'head'. To show mercy to any individual is to give

> such pity
> As when the viper hath been cut to pieces,
> The separate fragments quivering in the sun,
> In the last energy of venomous life,
> Deserve and have.   (27–31)

The extraordinary virulence and impact derives from a strong feeling for biological energy, such being, paradoxically, most intensely realized when both (1) dangerous and (2) suffering destruction, as with the scorpion in *The Giaour*. Elaborate 'organic' metaphors cluster: we hear that all must die since it is the 'spirit' of the aristocracy that needs to be 'rooted' out, whereas one 'single shoot' of the 'old tree' would only 'fasten in the soil' and give rise to more 'gloomy verdure' and 'bitter fruit', the last phrases neatly characterizing the play's view of a forbidding, threatening, social combine. The whole passage (161–65) both recalls and reverses the logic of a similar speech and context from *Julius Caesar*; and might be used as evidence—if any were needed—to rebut any charge of plagiarism in these Shakespearian comparisons. Indeed, the play can quite safely hold its own with such a work as *Coriolanus* (which is similarly rich in 'organic' metaphors), at least with reference to political and social analysis in which, indeed, it strikes more cleanly to the heart of our contemporary situation than any Shakespearian plot. How modern rings the Doge's asseveration that the 'present institutes of Venice' nourish a 'fatal poison to the springs of life', to all 'human ties' and, finally, 'good order' itself (437–39). Though the proposed deed may be only hideously fertilizing in Bertram's horrified thought of 'blood which *spouts* through hoary scalps', another view may see the dead 'gather'd' in to 'harvest' and reaped with a 'sword' for 'sickle'. So all the nobles must die since

> all their acts are *one*—
> A single emanation from one body,
> Together knit for our oppression.   (285–87)

As in *Julius Caesar* the act is viewed as a divinely appointed 'sacrifice'. Moreover, the willed harmony-to-be is, very subtly indeed, conceived not precisely as a living organism but, being still a dream in the mind only, as a work of art, a temple. Opposed to the decadent and decaying living death of the present order imagined as a 'monster of a state' and 'spectre' to be exorcised with 'blood' is set the artistic vitality of a 'fair free commonwealth', a considered art-form with no 'rash equality' yet with 'equal rights', 'Proportion'd like the columns to the temple/ Giving and taking strength reciprocal', where no part may be removed without infringing the general 'symmetry' (165–75). The old order was not truly an organism, but a ghost only; and the new remains a planned symmetry with ever so faint a suggestion of the artificial. A deep reading of the whole play leaves any truly *willed* social development problematical.

The balance of sympathies is markedly just. You are continually caught by an unexpected reverse of what you thought the play's 'thesis', whereas the thinking is moving all the time on a deeper level. So, though the action depends on our recognition that the nobility are a poor lot, though they are imagined as 'a few bloated despots' and the Doge honestly thinks he is helping to free the 'groaning nations' from an ever-tightening grip, yet they are shown at the trial as perfectly just, though austere and cold. To them the Doge's treason is, quite naturally, a thing of unrecorded villainy (again emphasizing its relation, or lack of relation, to the past) comparable with 'earthquakes' and 'pestilence' (V.i.491). Their imputation of 'wild wrath and regal fierceness' strikes home. Moreover, they deliberately pride themselves on remembering what they consider the Doge himself has forgotten, his own 'dignity', and in the very order of his punishment acknowledge 'their prince', so that he dies in state (V.i.560–67). The terms are, however, not really kind since the cruelly apt reference to 'dignity' must be intolerable to so fiery-proud a temperament; and the Doge, himself sincere to danger-point, has for long been bitterly sickened by that hypocrisy of respect of which this formal mockery is but the last towering example. Indeed, we can strike something of a correct balance by regarding the Doge's final speech, which it will do us no harm to consider as levelled at ourselves. From the start the nobles' insult was subtly intangible and perhaps defensible in view of Steno's emphasized youth. Their virtues are all those of respectability, convention, and the outward shows of rectitude: correspondingly, their vices are anaemic and frigid. So the Doge, at the point of death, levels his last scalding and prophetic denunciation of future shame to Venice in the strikingly Lawrentian terms of

> Vice without splendour, sin without relief
> Even from the gloss of love to smooth it o'er,
> But in its stead, coarse lusts of habitude,
> Prurient yet passionless, cold studied lewdness
> Depraving nature's frailty to an art .... (V.iii.85–89)

Their 'smiles' shall lack 'mirth', their 'pastimes' bring no pleasure; and so on, up to the shattering climax. But, meanwhile, we have lived through precisely the mental territory of Pope's satires, just as Steno is a variation on Sporus.

The gloomy passions and shadowed thought throughout produce a dark impressionism. The word 'black' is peculiarly insistent. Steno's deed is a public 'blackening' of the Doge's wife; the nobles are men of 'black blood', their faults causing the 'black deeds' of the rebels whose action, if a failure, will be written 'black' in the calumnies of time, the dark day itself being henceforth one 'black' in the calendar, to be, perhaps, succeeded by days of brightness. Here is a typical phrase: 'When you lie down to rest/ Let it be black among your dreams ...', with a following suggestion of 'ill-omen'd cloud' obscuring the 'sun' (I.ii.244–47). The play works up to a 'funeral marriage' and 'black union' (V.ii.8). Throughout we have 'darkly brooding thoughts', and hear of senators 'In dark suspicious conflict with the Doge,/ Brooding with him in mutual hate and fear' (III.ii.378–79). 'Stifled treason' lurks in 'narrow places' and whispers 'muffled' curses to the night (IV.i.224–25). The nobles' vices are 'gloomy'. 'Freedom' is a sun and so is virtue, but the play emphasizes far more the presence of 'souls obscured'. The weather is gloomy, not violently tempestuous, since that would not suit its shadowed gravity, but rather sultry and ominous:

> *Doge.*   At what hour arises
>   The moon?
> *Bertuccio.* Late, but the atmosphere is thick and
>   dusky
> 'Tis a sirocco.   (I.ii.569–71)

Later Lioni remarks that 'the cloudy wind' blowing from the Levant has subsided to leave the moon unobscured. The play is, indeed, mostly in half-light. The Doge is at the 'twilight' of his life. Angiolina imagines Steno 'grovelling by stealth in the moon's glimmering light', and struck by conscience at 'every shadow' (II.i.41–43), to perpetrate his ugly deed. The Doge's fortunes are early seen 'Now darkling in their close toward the deep vale/ Where Death sits robed in his all-sweeping shadows' (II.i.501–03). He naturally dwells on death. Quite early he hints of an impending doom to make the 'cemeteries populous' and later feels the 'destroying angel' above Venice, finely imagined as a swooping bird. When he and his companions are in their 'graves' will future generations, he wonders, revere those 'tombs'? Death and moonlight pervade the atmosphere. The moon dominates, not for romantic glamour, but rather for its steely pallor suiting the hard ethical precisions, cold vices, and chaste virtues of the somewhat grave conception. The persons are all touched by the ghostly finger of it, and walk near death.

This more imaginative atmosphere is concentrated and focused into certain crystallizing scenes, somewhat as Enobarbus's description of Cleopatra distils the essential quality of the various tonings in *Antony and Cleopatra*. The

first discovers the Doge alone by the Church of San Giovanni
and San Paolo before which stands an equestrian statue. It is a
moonlit night. His sense of guilt imagines the midnight bell
pealing across the 'arch of night' to wake all sleepers from
hideous dreams of the fate overhanging them. Then in
weighted accents he addresses the church, home of his dead
ancestry, the building

>   whose dim statues shadow
> The floor which doth divide us from the dead,
> Where all the pregnant hearts of our bold blood,
> Moulder'd into a mite of ashes, hold
> In one shrunk heap what once made many heroes,
> When what is now a handful shook the earth—
> Fane of the tutelar saints who guard our house!
>
> (III.i.15–22)

He addresses the past which lives still in him. Two doges, his
'sires', rest there. He stands before them, sinks himself
beyond the transient moment to ask grace or condemnation
of the eternal. He would have the dead rise to people the dim
aisles, lending their 'high blood' and 'blazon roll of glories' as
witnesses to his integrity, even though in him their 'mighty
name' lies 'dishonour'd'. Such intuition of the living dead, of
the past within the present, you find nowhere outside Byron;
nor so noble a feeling for the ancestral honours of the race.
And both are one with the sacred building where those dead
rest. The Church is a symbol of eternity. So the Doge would
draw strength and justification from the dead, share with
them his scarcely endurable responsibility. 'Spirits! smile
down upon me,' he prays. His cause is theirs, their fame
mingles into his, and if he prospers he will make their city for
ever 'free and immortal'. The noble religious and ancestral
conception is so inevitable in its context that we may too
easily pass over its other interest in relation to that historic
eternity and respect for religion so important throughout
Byron's work. But here his deepest feelings are, as in

Shakespeare, unobtrusive, within, not crowning, the action. The Doge's soliloquy, that has already made of the Church an actor in our play, leads on to an even greater dramatic intensity after Bertuccio's entrance:

> *Bertuccio.* 'Tis not the moment to consider thus,
>   Else I could answer. Let us to the meeting,
>   Or we may be observed in lingering here.
> *Doge.* We are observed, and have been.
> *Bertuccio.*   We observed!
>   Let me discover—and this steel—
> *Doge.*   Put up;
>   Here are no human witnesses: look there—
>   What see you?
> *Bertuccio.*   Only a tall warrior's statue
>   Bestriding a proud steed, in the dim light
>   Of the dull moon.
> *Doge.*   That warrior was the sire
>   Of my sire's fathers, and that statue was
>   Decreed to him by the twice rescued city:
>   Think you that he looks down on us or no?
> *Bertuccio.* My lord, these are mere phantasies; there
>   are
>   No eyes in marble.
> *Doge.*   But there are in Death.
>   I tell thee, man, there is a spirit in
>   Such things that acts and sees, unseen, though
>   felt;
>   And, if there be a spell to stir the dead,
>   'Tis in such deeds as we are now upon.
>   Deem'st thou the souls of such a race as mine
>   Can rest, when he, their last descendant chief,
>   Stands plotting on the brink of their pure
>   graves
>   With stung plebeians?   (III.i.81–102)

I do not remember a more powerful instance of a stage-object used to share in, focus, and universalize the action. This is, precisely, the play's heart. Notice that a statue, as so often in poetry, symbolizes eternity.

Such an opening towards the infinite applies, as in *Sardanapalus* too, to *both* sides of the dramatic conflict. The cosmic symbolism of moonlight thus helps to bind the plot and realize a super-personal dimension. Our second example (IV.i) involves mainly spatial, as our first temporal, infinities. Lioni returns suddenly from a dance full of a foreboding that has chilled love-flirtations with deathly fears, turning the music to a 'knell'. Opening his window he watches the night's expansive 'stillness' under a 'broad moon'. An interesting repudiation of the erotic—the pleasure was explicitly one of 'love' in its way—follows, of age trying to appear young by artificial light and youth wasting its energies on misconceived attempts at pleasure. Feminine attractions and the whole 'dizzy' delusion of 'false and true enchantments', of 'art and nature' mixed, are both recalled and probed. Contrasted are the moon, stars, and waters, and buildings ghostly-sweet as vast 'altars' or ancient pyramids. Next he dreams of some true-love serenade in the moonlight, the phosphorescent plash of an oar, the twinkle of gondola lights. Both in its repudiations and serenity the speech is important; the moon, symbol of chastity, blends with a romantic integrity, but its steely truth is set right against those social superficialities the play, as a whole, strongly condemns (IV.i.1–110).

Later the Doge waits for the dawn that is to bring dark conspiracy to an open triumph: 'Will the morn never put to rest/ These stars which twinkle yet o'er all the heavens?' (IV.ii.71–72). He is impatient for daylight action after our play of half-light indecisions, anxiously sensing a 'morning freshness' and noticing that the sea looks 'greyer', while his keener-eyed nephew thinks he sees the dawn already 'dappling' the sky (IV.ii.110–12). The suspense is breathless: 'Thou day!/ That slowly walk'st the waters!—march—march on—' (IV.ii.138–39). But no dawn can come to Venice: for that we

must turn to *Sardanapalus.* The bell indeed strikes; but the
night of dishonesty and hatred is not lifted.

The great bell of St Mark's symbolizes an ultimate
authority. Its use by the Doge, who alone can sound it, as
the signal for massacre helps at first to justify his right as
sovereign to exert full power. He uses this 'last poor privilege'
left him to herald the last blow for justice. It is to strike 'at
dawn' (III.ii.245–53) and wake the city. The poetry is charged
continually with thought of the 'sullen huge oracular bell',
which 'knells' only for a 'princely death' or a 'state in peril',
pealing 'bodements'. This is to be its 'awfullest and last' office
(IV.ii.182–86). That office is, indeed, precisely, 'oracular'. The
bell with its traditional and royal associations becomes the
voice of those eternal dead to whom the Doge prayed; but
falls instead as a condemnation, throwing its balance against
the Doge. It overhangs the action, oppressive and awful, and
may be referred to that other irony of the Doge's guilty but
prophetic fancy of a great bell rousing the city from dreams of
conspiracy. The stage effect when at last it does strike should
be overpowering.

Angiolina alone expresses an ultimate righteousness. Her
original attitude to Steno's fault was one of pity or scorn,
almost unconcern. To her, shows and words mean nothing,
substantial values are everything. 'What is virtue', she asks, 'if
it needs a victim?' (II.i.57–58). She is undisturbed by slander.
To desire even 'justice' proves you prefer a name to a quality.
No 'base passions' rule her, no image of a younger lover than
the Doge ever entered her head. When told that others are less
pure-minded she replies: 'It may be so. I knew not of such
thoughts' (II.i.132). She is not even interested. She urges the
Doge to Christian forgiveness, and is, indeed, herself a
personification of uncompromising Christian idealism, point-
ing a solution beyond the mazed troubles and vices of the rest.
But when at the Doge's trial Steno asks Christian forgiveness
(V.i.400–07), her severe purity shows a doubtfully Christian
refusal of any emotional compromise. She recounts her

previous utter unconcern while remarking that some (like the Doge) cannot altogether remain unaffected by 'shadows', and are troubled by unreal conflicts; in whom resentment becomes a fault, especially at that sternest test of greatness, an insult to a 'proud name' and 'pinnacle' of honour. An 'insect' may well hurt beings of a higher order. She recounts examples from history of some communal disaster brought on by questions of personal honour; and even such a thing as Steno has now

> put in peril
> A senate which hath stood eight hundred years,
> Discrown'd a prince, cut off his crownless head,
> And forged new fetters for a groaning people.
>
> (V.i.445–48)

Her icy integrity easily involves all—Doge, Senate, and Steno —in a level, critical judgement, like the steely fluid of moonlight washing away both shadows and colours, levelling all under the one steady gaze. The white integrity of her attack recalls Pope's in the Horatian Epistles. Images of reptile and venom have elsewhere been applied to Steno, and, in view of the whole action, Angiolina's speech may well serve as a new clarification of Pope's satiric fury. The play's statement narrows down to condemnation of Lucio-like superficiality, sexual parasites such as Sporus, just as that in our thinking which makes them possible—and they are aspects both of their creators and of ourselves—might be named the root evil of our culture. Her words are cold and hard:

> Nothing of good can come from such a source,
> Nor would we aught with him, nor now, nor ever:
> We leave him to himself, that lowest depth
> Of human baseness. Pardon is for men,
> And not for reptiles—we have none for Steno,
> And no resentment: things like him must sting,
> And higher beings suffer; 'tis the charter

Of life. The man who dies by the adder's fang
May have the crawler crush'd, but feels no anger:
'Twas the worm's nature; and some men are worms
In soul more than the living things of tombs.
                                        (V.i.455–65)

The clever pauses and metrical disruptions, the mastery of
the colloquial, the reserved dignity and purity of winnowed
diction joined to scorn more scalding because less involved
in the object than even Pope's, witness Byron's powers in
maturity.

Angiolina's relentless, almost cruel, perfection will not, of
course, serve as a final Byronic solution, though his enduing a
feminine figure with an idealized distinction is normal
enough. The specifically sexual is here definitely under a
cloud. The Doge boasts of his utter mastery of such instincts
even in youth; Angiolina leaves even Shakespeare's Isabella
behind in chastity; and their marriage arrangements—
carefully described—do not appear to have been altogether
romantic. Here fiery pride is a lesser fault than sexual licence,
and Lioni's repudiation of the dance quite integral to the
general conception.

And yet the conspiracy fails through neglect not of firm
ethical principles so much as the personal feelings of the 'soft'
Bertram. His typically Byronic softness is vividly discussed
and sharply distinguished from cowardice (III.ii.49–78). That
is, destiny exposes the revolution's inorganic weakness
through Bertram's inability to crush *personal* gratitude. The
Doge himself has to fight against his own nature, crushing
memory of former aristocratic comradeships to be destroyed
in the approaching massacre. You can feel pressing through
the play's structure an implied pattern where the sexual and
soft personal emotions might *together* reach some solution.
For the chaste fervours of Angiolina are not all attractive and
blend with the play's moonlit, dawnless quality, while a fine
speech of the Doge's on virtue (II.i.379–98) has the icy ethical

touch of 'Comus'. Angiolina's utter scorn of Steno must be contrasted with her earlier unwillingness that his 'young blood' be shed. She does not compass the 'Christian' forgiveness Steno pathetically asks, in a speech finely exemplifying Byron's almost Shakespearian generosity of emotional balance. But the other pattern, which Byron exploits in *Sardanapalus*, is to be flooded by the sun, transfers sexual enjoyment to the more positive side of the conflict and presents not a revolutionary but a pacifist sovereign. Which is the more Christian? The Doge's deep meditations tremble on the brink of the solution:

> Oh world!
> Oh men! What are ye, and our best designs,
> That we must work by crime to punish crime?
> And slay as if Death had but this one gate,
> When a few years would make the sword
> superfluous? (IV.ii.166–70)

That is, from the view of eternity man's attempts at all justice are necessarily childish. Yet the very failure has its own eternal sanction:

> That moment would have changed the face of ages;
> *This* gives us to eternity. (IV.ii.275–76)

But again, had the plot succeeded, would not a better Venice have matured? Byron clearly, in his own prose comment, means us to realize that the Doge's prophecy of a shameful future has indeed been fulfilled. Does success or failure define the quality of a deed? Or does the quality determine the deed's ultimate success? But perhaps the plot was, ultimately, successful, in so far as its whole nature, including the judgement of St Mark's bell, that is, its condemnation, receives a full, though tragic, understanding. [...]

Byron's *Marino Faliero* and the Force of Individual Agency

A. B. ENGLAND

It is traditional, in discussions of *Marino Faliero*, to point out that when Byron wrote it he was becoming active with the Carbonari in Ravenna and that the play reflects some of his political interests of the time. In an essay that continues to be important, E. D. H. Johnson in 1942 stressed how intensely Byron was caught up in the 'revolutionary movement to establish the independence of Italy', and that he wrote the play 'in a mood of high hope for the emancipation of the Italians from the tyrannical government which was oppressing them'.[1] Johnson indicates that Byron not only felt a passionate interest in the idea of action intended to pursue a political autonomy the Italian states did not have under Austrian rule, but also believed in the possibility of such action being conceived and carried out. Certainly the tone of a letter he wrote to Murray on 22 July 1820, in which he says that he has just finished writing *Marino Faliero*, suggests that despite the disappointments he is in an optimistic mood about revolution:

> The tragedy is finished but when it will be copied is more than can be reckoned upon.—We are here upon the eve of evolutions and revolutions.— Naples is revolutionized—and the ferment is among the Romagnoles—by far the bravest and most orig-inal of the present Italians—though still half savage. —Buonaparte said the troops from Romagna were the best of his Italic corps and I believe it.—The

Neapolitans are not worth a curse—and will be
beaten if it comes to fighting—the rest of Italy—I
think—might stand.—The Cardinal is at his wit's
end—it is true—that he had not far to go.—Some
papal towns on the Neapolitan frontier have already
revolted.—Here there are as yet but the sparks of
the volcano—but the ground is hot—and the air
sultry.[2]

In contrast to this, much of the criticism of *Marino Faliero*
that has appeared in the last twenty years suggests that the
play is imbued with pessimistic feeling about the hero's
struggle to achieve an act that will both constitute a move
towards self-realization and cause his political and social
environment to reflect his advocacy of liberation from an
oppressive regime. It has appeared to some readers that the
several particular, individual, and idiosyncratic actions
performed by the play's characters are overshadowed by two
powerful features of the play's thematic and narrative structure: the first of these is the notion that the movements of the
individual characters are subject to an all-embracing deterministic scheme such as that referred to by the hero as 'fate',[3] and
the second is the fact that the plot ends with the hero's death
and his failure to achieve what his mind has been so purpose-
fully bent on throughout the play. Thus, although Jerome
McGann points at the end of his account to the values of
'consciousness' and 'vital passion' animating Faliero's final
speech, he argues in the body of that account that 'neither the
conspirators nor the oppressors are masters of their own
wills', and that the Doge 'goes to his demise with a clear and
terrible understanding of his own helplessness'.[4] Similarly,
Philip J. Skerry says that the human individuals in the play are
controlled by 'forces that are at once more powerful than man
and unintelligible to him' and that the combination of these
forces may be referred to as 'Fate' (p. 105).[5] On the matter of
the narrative outline, Peter J. Manning has suggested that it

indicates 'how limited the opportunities' for effective heroic 'action' have become in the world that Byron now knows, that an 'air of frustration hangs over the action', and that the plot carries its central figure towards a state of 'complete stultification'.[6] And Malcolm Kelsall links *Marino Faliero* and *The Two Foscari* as 'two plays ... indicative of a total impasse producing ... decline and eventual extinction': Faliero is unlike the Foscari in that he does act decisively, but he achieves 'nothing', and his line of 'resistance' offers no 'way forward'.[7] These reading experiences, obviously, suggest that Byron's play has little power to be encouraging in its treatment of the hero's attempt to achieve individuating and significant action. Yet it seems to me that this pattern of response is at odds with some features of the play's spirit and texture, and that Byron might well have been dismayed by it. An exception to the dominant critical mood is an essay by Thomas L. Ashton, who finds considerable force in the revolutionaries' words about a continuing influence after death and concludes that Byron's 'poetry of politics' has a genuine power to invigorate: the poetry of the play 'binds us to the creative fulfillment of Byron's prophetic politics, in our immediate conception of other equally "hopeless" conflicts'.[8] My own account of the play will be in some ways consistent in tone with Ashton's. But I shall concentrate less on the theme of 'politics' than on the treatment of the hero's attempt to achieve self-definition and some approach to autonomy through the manner in which he acts. For Marino Faliero is, for much of the play, seeking to achieve on a personal and psychological level something analogous to what Byron as a member of the Carbonari believed he was helping Italy to achieve politically.

When Byron refers to the historical event on which his play is based he defines himself as having been powerfully struck by its singularity. 'The conspiracy of the Doge Marino Faliero is one of the most remarkable events in the annals of the most singular government, city, and people of modern history,' he says at the beginning of the Preface,[9] drawing the reader's attention to several levels of uniqueness that throw the event into stark relief. He also says that the event is extraordinarily 'dramatic in itself', and in correspondence with Murray during 1817 he was more specific about this: 'I mean to write a tragedy on the subject which appears to me very dramatic; an old man—jealous—and conspiring against the state of which he was the actual reigning Chief—the last circumstance makes it the most remarkable—and only fact of the kind in all history of all nations' (*BLJ*, V, 174). Faliero's act represents an extraordinary clash between individual intent and the expectations generated by his social position, and later in 1817 Byron reiterates his sense that the event is marked by an arresting disjunction of act and context when he describes the story as a case of 'the head conspiring against the body' (*BLJ*, V, 203). In *The Autonomy of the Self from Richardson to Huysmans*, Frederick Garber suggests that the figure acting out of the 'hunger for autonomy' will seek to construct an 'edifice of self' that is not only 'distinctive' but 'distinct',[10] and Byron's comments on the story show that a major reason for his being drawn to it was a sense that the Doge's act was dramatically effective in thus making himself distinct. In leading and co-ordinating a conspiracy against the state of which he was the head, Faliero achieves a radical form of action in the sense that it is defined by David A. Crocker during his discussion of Aristotle's and Hannah Arendt's concepts of *praxis*: he says that 'to act is to initiate an unexpected novelty that confirms the agent's uniqueness and discloses it to others'.[11] And Byron's play dramatizes the hero's struggle to achieve the difficult act of choice through which he will become conscious and deliberate in the initiation of such a 'novelty'.

The action of the play begins with the protagonist's highly individual response to a cluster of words. Michael Steno has defaced the Doge's throne by carving on it words that question his wife's reputation. They have evoked in Faliero such a tremendous energy of opposition, demanding its fulfilment in action, that when the sentence upon Steno is read out and it utterly fails to match the force of his anger, he experiences a kind of vertigo and has to be physically supported (I.ii.70–74). His response is certainly a testament to the power of a particular cause (in this case verbal) to produce an effect. But the effect does not seem to his nephew, Bertuccio, commensurate with the cause: the 'fury doth exceed the provocation' (I.ii.136). In this way he defines Faliero's response as individual to the point of being idiosyncratic, and we are made to feel the particularity, the specialness, of the cause and effect sequence that Byron has chosen to dramatize.

Faliero believes that the present imbalance in his psyche will be counteracted only by some form of action carrying a force at least equivalent to that which his response has given to Steno's. His first desire is that Venice should be subjected to some physical threat, so that he might engage in the kind of co-ordinated physical violence upon which much of his reputation has been built (I.ii.88–94). Although the thought evokes nostalgia for that 'full youth' when body 'served' soul as a 'steed' under the control of his 'lord', Faliero understands the limitations of age, and in a manner that implies faith in the capacity of his intelligence to initiate and co-ordinate change, he says that he must 'look round for other hands/ To serve this hoary head' (I.ii.275–80). By this point he has identified the essential opposition to his psychic peace as the 'hundred-handed senate' that has failed to punish Steno adequately (I.ii.269), and what he has begun to contemplate is an action that will be powerfully far-reaching in effect and will thus imprint his personality on the world in a manner so forceful as to obliterate Steno's mark: there is no wonder that he refers to it as a 'task/ Herculean' (I.ii.281–82). As his imagination becomes active, Faliero describes the energetic and creative subjectivity of his approach to circumstance. As yet, he says, his mind is 'but a chaos/ Of darkly-brooding thoughts':

> my fancy is
> In her first work, more nearly to the light

Holding the sleeping images of things
For the selection of the pausing judgment.—
The troops are few in—   (I.ii.282–87)

The movement from 'fancy' to 'troops' is vividly symptomatic
here, expressing a relationship between mind and act similar
to that described by Coleridge in his account of men of
'*commanding* genius' who 'must impress their preconceptions
on the world without, in order to present them back to their
own view with the satisfying degree of clearness, distinctness
and individuality'.[12] Despite his view that the ruling group of
Venice has been unresponsive to his mood, Faliero expresses
faith throughout this speech that he can still produce an effect
on his environment: 'In my life I have achieved/ Tasks not less
difficult' (I.ii.271–72), he says, and the particular placing of
words around the line-break gives powerful emphasis to what
he sees as his continuing capacity for distinctive praxis.

When Israel Bertuccio appears to complain about his treatment by an aristocrat, Faliero at once strategically defines him
as a representative of the discontented 'people' (I.ii.298) and
begins to think about using the tensions in the social structure
for his own individual purposes and fulfilment; in a single,
dramatic act he might 'free Venice, and avenge [his] wrongs'
(I.ii.316). Israel Bertuccio, of course, has his own use for
Faliero. And the scene in which they converse is dominated by
language that defines the force of human agency, the power of
individual psyches to generate specific acts. Both men are
strongly aware that their own histories have been marked by
such agency. When Faliero describes himself as having
'traversed land and sea in constant duty/ Through almost sixty
years' and says that this long and active life has been devoted
to the cause of 'Venice,/ My fathers' and my birthplace'
(I.ii.433–35), he causes himself to seem for a moment like
Wordsworth's Michael, a figure also marked by radical intent
and agency, but whose story, it seems to me, is in the end
considerably bleaker than Faliero's. Faliero's energies have

been devoted to a social and political, rather than a natural, context, and his use of the active verb makes clear his sense of how much purchase he has been able to achieve in that context: he has 'commanded' and 'conquer'd', he has 'made and marr'd peace oft in embassies' (I.ii.430–31). He has been able, in Eliot's terms, to 'murder and create' in drastic and visible fashion. Bertuccio, for his part, is the 'chief of the arsenal, employed/ At present in repairing certain galleys/ But roughly used by the Genoese last year' (I.ii.350–52). Not only is he now supervising the rehabilitation of Venice's navy, but for much of his life he has been in 'command' of a galley, responsible for directing the movement of a human group through an unruly and dangerous medium. Not surprisingly, the conversation between these two men is full of thrusting, active, forward-looking processes of thought. Each has recently suffered a blow to his sense of his power to affect his environment, and thus, as Bertuccio puts it, to his 'self-esteem' (I.ii.374). In Bertuccio's case, it has been a physical blow to the face and it has produced blood, 'the first shed by a Venetian hand' (I.ii.336). When Faliero incites him to action by saying, '... something you would do—/ Is it not so?' (I.ii.342–43), he initiates the play on 'thing' that, as we shall see, appears frequently: according to Faliero's analysis, the Senate has reduced the people to 'nothing' (I.ii.270), and he incites Bertuccio to an act that would give him and the people a new substantiality in the community (not, of course, the inert and block-like thing-ness that he attributes to his own position when he suggests that the Senate has *reduced* him to a 'thing'). Each man is ready to use the other for his own 'project' (I.ii.568), which is, of course, nothing short of a revolution that will destroy the existing social structure. There is a sense throughout the scene that they both use language as a means to the end of social and political action: Bertuccio most specifically draws attention to this when he says, 'Then, in a word, it rests but on your word/ To punish and avenge' (I.ii.405–06), when he says that in order to achieve his great purpose he 'will speak/ At every hazard' (I.ii.476–77), and also when he says that his words of open complaint against the aristocrat, Barbaro, can camouflage his revolutionary agenda. The link between the two men is further formalized when the Doge discovers that they have been 'comrades' in battle (I.ii.363). However, because of Faliero's social position, his deliberate choice of revolution is a more radically self-individuating act than is Israel's, and at the end of Act I he is clearly uneasy about his intention. When he imagines his ancestors reaching out to hold him back, he says 'Would they could!' and recognizes a need to suppress feelings that his awareness of ancestry generates: 'Alas! I must not think of them' (I.ii.587). The sensation of insecurity here and the use of 'must' are ominous signs of how his thinking will develop at a later stage.

In the crucial conversation with Angiolina in the second act Faliero struggles to counteract this unease. Turned by her presence from the political field towards the private and marital, he begins to speak in ways that claim some control over his own and her emotional experience—'But let that pass.—We will be jocund' (II.i.160)—and indeed, when he says to her, 'Speak, and 'tis done' (II.i.167), he implies that in this realm he can find access to a reassuring sensation of omnipotence. But Angiolina's responses soon challenge such an implication. The only request she makes is for an ameliora-tion of his disturbed mental state, thus drawing his mind back to the problem of achieving self-command. She then refuses to change the subject at his request (II.i.212), and argues that since Steno has not harmed the emotional reality of their marriage Faliero should not so desperately desire public vindi-cation. Since his need remains, the argument leads to a stale-mate. And his next bid for psychic control of the marital precinct is an attempt to ensure that Angiolina will regard him with kindness and respect after his death. His stance and his words again evoke Wordsworth's Michael establishing the covenant with his son at the site of the projected sheepfold.

Like Michael, Faliero tries to control the future by invoking the past, as he offers Angiolina (to whom he is now referring as 'child') an account of how he brought about the marriage and what he attempted to achieve in it. The marriage is presented as having been a refuge or shelter, an extension of her father's parental protection of her, designed to provide 'safety' within a perilous social territory (II.i.299–301), and bearing a distinct resemblance to the type of 'autonomous refuge' described by Garber, which in certain circumstances 'the mind can build beautifully and with perfect success if it learns to eject and cut off'.[13] As the major agent in the construction of this marriage, Faliero says that in his youth he 'sway'd' passions that might damage its purity (II.i.313), and that the shelter he so conscientiously made safe has been presided over by 'patriarchal love' (II.i.363). When Angiolina contemplates all of his deliberate activity in the construction of experience, she says, 'You have done well' (II.i.377). But what Faliero feels he has been forced to witness, and this distinguishes him from Michael at the stage of addressing Luke at the sheepfold, is the destruction of what has been so laboriously built. A conversational sequence intended to be reassuring thus leads suddenly into crisis, and when Faliero talks of how his old age has been 'blighted' (II.i.456) by Steno he appears to be drifting into despair. On the other hand, this acknowledgment of a kind of psychic defeat is accompanied by an impulse to re-establish the force of his political presence in the face of the Forty's indifference: 'I will be what I should be or be nothing' (II.i.454). And Angiolina unconsciously encourages him when she refers to his performance on the battlefield at Zara, where he 'saved/ The state' (II.i.469–70) and thus achieved a mode of consummate action. Expressing a somewhat nostalgic and unfocused feeling about the transforming power of the single, supreme act, she says that 'Another day like that would be the best/ Reproof to them, and sole revenge for you' (II.i.472–73). Since it seems that at this stage of Faliero's life such an action would be unlikely, her

words are potentially alarming in that they appear to emphasize the superiority of an irrecoverable past to a difficult
present. But the reader knows that Faliero's capacity to originate action is not exhausted, and that he is being pragmatically
duplicitous rather than despairing when he says that there can
be no hope of repetition because 'one such day occurs within
an age' (II.i.473). In a certain sense, as he knows, there will be
no repetition because the action he intends will be radically
unlike those of a past from which he is in the process of extri-
cating himself. But it will at least be continuous with that past
in its dramatic force. When he says, 'There's much for me to
do—and the hour hastens' (II.i.481), it becomes clear that he
has emerged from the emotional ebb and flow of the
encounter with Angiolina with his faith in the power of individual action intact. And at the end of the scene he stresses
again the idea that through action he will seek to materialize in
the state, to counteract the oppressive sensation of non-exis-
tence. Here, when he refers to the idea of being 'nothing', he
is thinking of what he will be after death; but what he wants to
become in life is a 'thing' that she will remember and that will
cast a 'shadow' in the domain of her 'fancy' (II.i.509–12).

At the beginning of the third act, however, Faliero's anxiety
about his chosen role has developed to the point where it
causes him to construct an overarching deterministic scheme
within which his particular act will be included. He argues that
because of the moral decline of the aristocracy Venice has
become a 'proud city' (III.i.7) needing to be punished. When
he says that the city '*must* be cleansed of the black blood
which makes [her]/ A lazar-house of tyranny' (III.i.8–9, my
italics), he invokes a notion of historical necessity which
presupposes that corruption is virtually axiomatic. On the
basis of this, Faliero envisages a great purification being
brought about by a pattern in communal history of which this
moment is a part: 'the hour' has come, he says, 'whose voice,/
Pealing into the arch of night, might strike/ These palaces
with ominous tottering' (III.i.1–3), as if the palaces are to be

struck by the process of time, rather than by particular men. A crucial feature of the moment is that it will be, in its exposure of aristocratic corruption, vigorously apocalyptic. And Faliero even suggests that the collective unconscious of the tribe is aware of its approach: the coming hour will be capable of 'waking the sleepers from some hideous dream/ Of indistinct but awful augury/ Of that which will befall them' (III.i.5–7). If he can place his act within such a context he can almost remove the burden of individual responsibility: 'the task/ Is forced upon me, I have sought it not' (III.i.9–10). He does acknowledge the force of immediate causes such as Steno's idiosyncratic act and his own intense resentment, but these are now subordinated to a pattern originating with a primary cause more powerful than either Steno or himself. Faliero uses the language of logical design to invest the primary cause with a sense of purpose: 'therefore was I punish'd', in order that he would eradicate the 'patrician pestilence' (III.i.11–12). When he says that this pestilence has 'spread on and on' (III.i.12) he imagines a process by which it has become all-pervasive in Venetian life. This process has culminated in his own pain brought about by the pestilence's manifestation in Steno's words: corruption has spread until 'at length it smote me in my slumbers,/ And I am tainted, and must wash away/ The plague-spots in the healing wave' (III.i.13–15). Apocalyptic fervour asserts itself again here, as he argues that he was hurt in order that he would perpetrate a version of the flood: again this defines him as the immediate cause of the communal purification, but also as a figure playing a historically deter-mined role. Such thinking has by this point gained a powerful hold on Faliero's mind, as we see again later in Act III, when as he contemplates those who will be killed in the revo-lution he says that they 'will then be gather'd in unto the harvest,/ And we will reap them with the sword for sickle' (III.ii.263–64), suggesting that the violence will be a sign of a historical process come to natural fruition. When he thinks in this way, he is able to regain a sense of connection or continuity between his present action and the past. For he argues to himself that the 'mighty name' of all his ancestors has been dishonoured in the particular case of his mistreatment by the Senate, and that the spirits of those ancestors will therefore embrace his performance with approval (III.i.33–40).[14]

This mode of conceptualizing his intended act is clearly useful and enabling for Faliero: if he can feel that he is in the secure embrace of historical destiny, it will be less starkly apparent that he is engaged in a radical and adventurous act of individual choice. The impulse to 'merge with history'[15] and with his ancestral past rather than to mark himself as severely distinct from it is vividly expressed when, in asking for the approval of his ancestors, he refers to their 'fame' and 'name' being 'all mingled up in mine,/ And in the future fortunes of our race' (III.i.43–44). Such thinking is a natural human reflex to the prospect of an acutely challenging act. But several features of the text dramatize very different approaches to experience from this and have the potentiality to undermine it. For example, there are all those signs of the individual agent's power to originate action that were given such full life and reality in Act I, especially in Faliero's conversation with Israel Bertuccio. Also, although both of these figures do at other points express the belief that their acts are sanctioned by the past, there is a sharp difference between the two concepts of historical process that enable them to do this. Bertuccio and the revolutionaries can take it for granted that their actions arise out of a great traditional divide. But Faliero has to construct the notion that a small group within a privileged minority will feel that their name has been so severely demeaned as to justify the bringing down of the whole governmental structure. This notion is obviously not a very solid base on which to found historical support. Furthermore, if we are to feel that Faliero's assertion of manifest historical destiny is convincing, we need to be shown that the ruling group is as patently vicious as Faliero says it is. And at the start of the next act Byron introduces what seems to be a strategically placed soliloquy by the aristocrat, Lioni, that does nothing to support Faliero's analysis and a good deal to undermine it. Peter Manning is correct, I think, when he says that 'Byron provides little evidence in *Marino Faliero* from which it can be decided whether the revolution Faliero embarks upon is justified.'[16] The analyses of Venetian society offered by the revolutionaries cannot be seen as necessarily reliable. And even when her husband is about to be executed at the command of the Forty, the most severe reference to the issue by Angiolina is that the effects produced by Steno's lie will include 'new fetters for a groaning people' (V.i.447), a comment certainly not meant to suggest that she considers the revolution to be justified: her virulence is directed at the individual Steno, whom she distinguishes from the rest of the ruling group and describes as a 'thing', an 'adder', and a 'reptile' (V.i.457–61). The question is a complicated one, of course, and I am deeply sympathetic to Daniel P. Watkins' argument that the 'ruling class value system does not serve the Venetian citizenry at large' (p. 802); it should also be noted that, as Anne Barton has pointed out, Angiolina tends to be a 'conservative' witness.[17] But Byron makes no move in the text sufficient to challenge the notion that Faliero's claim to manifest historical destiny emerges from a subjective approach to his world and that it involves some degree of both mystification and denial. It seems important that when he keeps his appointment with the conspirators and first articulates his notion of historical destiny, he arrives early. Faliero places great emphasis on the notion that a crucial 'hour' has come, but also says, 'I am before the hour' (III.i.1).[18] And this seems to underline the critical disjunction between his analysis and the dramatized reality. For the play does not show that the time for revolution patently has come, and it appears to define Faliero's action as the result of particular circumstances and an idiosyncratic choice. The hero is clearly in a different relationship to time from, say, Shelley's Prometheus, whose notion of historical inevitability is corroborated by many accounts of how drastically human life has deteriorated.

Despite all these subversive implications Faliero's analysis has exerted a powerful influence on the play's readers. We have already seen some endorsements of his idea that what he does is required by the imperatives of a great deterministic scheme. Similarly, both John P. Farrell and Jerome McGann refer to the rulers of Venice in such a way as to associate them with that general and manifest corruption upon which Faliero repeatedly insists: Farrell calls them 'sordid plutocrats', McGann machine-like and inhuman 'things'. McGann also refers to Faliero's image of the 'blighting venom' inherent in Steno's act and says that this venom is 'organic' in the state of Venice, stressing Faliero's view that Steno's act is both a stimulant to and a symptom of 'general poison'.[19] Again, such a notion is powerfully enabling to Faliero in his quest to define himself as historically ordained to restore Venice's health. But Steno's action is seen quite differently by Angiolina, who does not have a vested interest in transforming it into an emblem of widespread disease; she defines it as isolated and eccentric, a 'rash' performance endowing Steno with a momentary prominence she sees as 'absurd' (II.i.19, 241). It may be said, of course, that Angiolina has her own reasons for defining the action as in this way peculiar to Steno, but what that may remind us of is simply that each view of the action is subjective and partial, including Faliero's.

During the rest of Act III Byron implies again and again that if the 'great change' is to occur it will depend upon the sharpness of Faliero's individual will, cutting against the grain of his past in order to achieve a highly idiosyncratic (and historical consequential) act of choice. It has always been clear that the external forces moving Faliero towards the act of revolution are intrinsically less impressive than those that would move him against it, and Faliero's insistence that his act of choice is difficult hardly surprises us. One feature of his quest is that he seeks to counteract the sensation of having been reduced to a 'puppet' by the checks and balances of the Forty (III.ii.194) and by their response to Steno's insult. The most obvious way of doing that would be to achieve as radical a degree of deliberate consciousness as he can in the process of perpetrating an act that boldly imprints his presence on his environment. He believes that he has within his self the 'individual means and mind' that are necessary for such an achievement (III.ii.203). And when he says that he will 'stake' his 'heart' and 'soul' on his performance, he implies that his psyche will prove its strength both in the making of the choice and in the pursuit of the public act to which that choice leads. Malcolm Kelsall says that Faliero is vague in his articulation of what the great change will bring when he talks about the 'general symmetry' of the new 'commonwealth' and that his language is inappropriate to the 'pragmatic situation' because it resists specific reference to immediate circumstances (in this volume, pp. 50–51). Reading Kelsall's analysis, one can sense a potential analogy between what Faliero's language does here and the process of generalizing mystification that he engaged in when he sought to provide himself with the assurance of historical destiny. But in this sequence it is not long before his language moves from a generalizing metaphor (in this case architectural) to an insistence on particular actions: 'I tell you you must strike, and suddenly,' he says (III.ii.237), 'when you hear/ The great bell of Saint Mark's, which may not be/ Struck without special order of the Doge' (III.ii.245–47). This last bit of authority is the 'last poor privilege they leave their prince' (III.ii.348), and he finds piquant appeal in using it for such a purpose. He is obviously constructing a scenario that will be arresting in shape, and through which he will forcefully establish his presence in Venetian history. And Israel Bertuccio confirms this idea when he draws attention once again to the uniqueness of Faliero's intended act: 'until this hour,/ What prince has plotted for his people's freedom?' (III.ii.437–38).

Soon after this reminder Faliero undergoes his most

extreme crisis of will, evoked by his memory of a time when those to be killed were so closely bonded with him that he can say, 'Each stab to them will seem my suicide' (III.ii.473). The crisis is analysed by Israel in fairly familiar and necessarily unsympathetic terms: Faliero is lapsing into a shameful form of 'childhood' in failing to subdue the involuntary emotion; he displays 'shallow weakness' and must 're-man' himself (III.ii.474–500).[20] These brutal terms underline just how strenuously deliberative Faliero's act of choice has become, and how powerful is the barrier against which he must struggle in order to be able to say, '*This will* I' (III.ii.496). When Israel says, continuing to reprimand Faliero for vacillation, 'You acted, and you act on your free will' (III.ii.502), his comment carries weight because what Byron appears to have dramatized is indeed a full-fledged act of conscious will, achieved despite the trembling brought on by involuntary emotion, and in which the protagonist's self has struggled towards the state of being 'undetermined and unconditioned' which Peter L. Thorslev, Jr. defines as a criterion of freedom.[21] Faliero himself, however, in another comment which seems to deny or obscure the responsibility that would accompany the quest for autonomy, disagrees: 'And yet I act no more on my free will,/ Nor my own feelings—both compel me back' (III.ii.517–18). He realizes the obvious fact that he cannot satisfy all the conflicting impulses of his psyche. And he chooses at this point to see his anger and his revolutionary impulse as further instances of involuntary passions that subdue him: echoing Milton's portrait of Satan, he says, 'there is *hell* within me and around,/ And like the demon who believes and trembles/ Must I abhor and do' (III.ii.519–21). Although on the one hand this stresses the 'potency of his subjectivity', it also defines Faliero's belief that he is the 'victim of his fierce inner life'.[22]

Thus, as he contemplates the enormity and the uniqueness of his intended act, Faliero again feels the need to define himself as moved by forces over which he has no control.

However, in his present argument against his own free agency he makes no reference to the earlier notion that he has been chosen by some force embedded in the patterns of history. That notion included the possibility that his initial anger was instilled by historical circumstances so as to provide the volitional energy that would enable him to make the difficult act of choice: thus he could see himself, even in strenuously making that choice, as a functionary within a larger system. However, at this point he defines his lack of freedom solely by reference to his own psyche. What makes him unfree is precisely that idiosyncratic emotional response that marked him out from others at the start of the play and that continues to exert, according to his own analysis, a powerful pressure on his behaviour. Thus, whatever we may feel about the philosophical clarity of his analysis of free will, it seems at this stage that the issue has to do with the structure of his own psyche, which is being considered as a force independent of larger, non-human structures. His language implies that if the question about his autonomy is to be settled, it is to be settled by reference to his own self and its characteristics, rather than to any overarching system within which it might be contained. Also, if the intended political action is to occur, it will be brought about by what is achieved within his own distinctive and still turbulent psyche. Since the end of his conversation with Angiolina in Act II most of his psychological and verbal energy has been devoted to preparing himself for this single act. And when, at the end of Act III, he says to Israel, 'I am resolved—come on' (III.ii.529), he claims to have reached the point where he is ready to perform it.

Lioni's soliloquy at the start of the next act embodies a mode of discourse utterly different from that which has so far dominated the play. A major desire expressed in its early stages is for sleep, which Lioni sees as a lapsing away into 'tranquil' unconsciousness that is an inner reflection of the evening's 'stillness' and thus the opposite of that vigilant pursuit of conscious self-direction which has recently absorbed Faliero (IV.i.21–27). As Lioni ponders the contrast between the peaceful external scene and the frantic activity of the festival he has left, he develops the traditional and quite typically Byronic argument that so much of the activity pursued eagerly by both 'Age' and 'Youth' is futile (IV.i.35–50). This is not, of course, an argument that has been given much life in the play so far, since the major characters have needed to believe in the potential value of action in order to dwell so tenaciously and with such passionate intensity on the means of achieving it. After this, Lioni's speech dwells with increasing detail on the scene he contemplates from the window of his palazzo, and it becomes clear that he is now seeking through language to describe the quality of a perceptual experience, rather than to reach after a mode of action or a state of mind that will enable him to act. One activity that *is* embedded in the details of the description is that of the moonlight 'serenely smoothing o'er' the variegated surfaces of the walls and buildings of the city (IV.i.74–78). But rather than bringing about actual change in the structure of the external world, this activity modifies the perceptual experience of contemplating that structure. The moonlight also creates a visual unity out of diverse elements: we know how illusory this image is in its relationship to the actuality of the city's inhabitants, but it is deeply satisfying to Lioni's imagination. We are reminded of the play's perpetual emphasis on the idea of transformative public action when Lioni says that the great palaces on the waterfront 'seem each a trophy of some mighty deed/ Rear'd up from out the waters' (IV.i.80–81). But what his mind focuses on here is a series of still, peaceful objects transformed by the imagination into symbols of action that has receded into the past and of which the observer is barely conscious. When Lioni says, 'All is gentle: nought/ Stirs rudely; but, congenial with the night,/ Whatever walks is gliding like a spirit' (IV.i.85–87), he offers to the mind an image that is comprehensively distinct from the divided and confrontational world of the play, a world full of solid objects threatening to collide. When, after this movement of the mind towards stillness and unconsciousness, Lioni is stimulated by Bertram's nervous behaviour to intervene decisively in the revolutionary plot, he merely adopts the course of action that circumstance and his responsibilities as a member of the Forty appear to demand. To say that Lioni in this sequence 'doffs his human identity for his role as mechanical senator'[23] suggests that a descent from imaginative sensibility to harsh automatism has occurred. But the probing and pragmatic acumen that he shows in the conversation with Bertram is not clearly more 'mechanical' than his earlier mode of discourse. It is simply a movement back to an interventionary and active mode from which he has experienced a brief interlude.

It is this mode, of course, that again dominates the play in its last stages, where the Doge does finally perform the great action that he has contemplated for so long and with so much energy of intent. That is, having chosen to lead the revolution and to set it in motion, he does cause the tolling of St Mark's bell, which is the initiating signal that he himself has designed. Both before and after the performance of this act, there are signs that he is able to confront the stark reality of his own agency more directly than at some stages in the past. Late in Act IV, for example, he progresses beyond the argument that he cannot approach autonomy or freedom of choice because of his subjection to involuntary anger: when he says that he is 'settled and bound up' (IV.ii.73) he means that he has now achieved command over the 'hell within' and has become truly deliberate. When he refers to the great purification that he imagines his act can cause, he does not define it as the result of historical destiny but of difficult personal choice: 'The very effort which it cost me to/ Resolve to cleanse this commonwealth with fire,/ Now leaves my mind more steady' (IV.ii.74–76). Both the protraction of the infinitive by the initial line-break here and its close connection with the first-person pronoun work to stress individuality of action. As a consequence of this struggle for self-command, Faliero is now able to compare his movement through time and circumstance with that of 'the pilot of an admiral galley' (IV.ii.80). He acknowledges his position as originator of the revolutionary sequence when he defines himself as the 'master-mover' of events (IV.ii.196). And when, after the failure of the revolution and the sentencing of Faliero, Angiolina defines herself as having been the 'unconscious cause' of the catastrophic sequence, he insists, 'Not so: there was that in my spirit ever/ Which shaped out for itself some great reverse' (V.ii.11–12). In the same conversation he stresses the force exerted even in defeat by his individual act of choice: 'in one hour/ I have uprooted all my former life' (V.ii.107–08). According to this, not only has he separated himself from his past, but he has also abruptly deprived that past of its life.

All this is not to suggest, of course, that the mental processes by which he confronts real characteristics of his act of choice are thoroughly admirable (though they are more honest than some of his earlier obfuscations). Indeed, there are still many problems and ambiguities in these processes. For example, when he aligns his present decision with his earlier modes of action on the battlefield and argues that the act of choice has been infinitely more difficult, his language takes on a (potentially enabling) brutality which goes a long way to supporting those analyses which suggest that deliberative acts of will in Byron tend to be dehumanizing:[24] he has had to 'steel' himself in this instance in order to be able to 'spill/ The rank polluted current from the veins/ Of a few bloated despots' (IV.ii.85–87). Also, Faliero falls into the error of believing that sheer deliberation has the power to confer value: he argues that he has become able to 'make revenge a virtue by reflection,/ And not an impulse of mere anger' (IV.ii.103–04). Moments like these again suggest that the extraordinary act of choice is achieved at great psychological cost. Furthermore, there are signs that Faliero cannot consistently confront the notion of individual human agency in a direct manner. For instance, after he has defined his own

'spirit' as having 'shaped out' its reverse 'for itself', he
surrounds this notion with a battery of omens, prophecies,
and signs of predestination that do a good deal to blur his
individual responsibility (V.ii.13–41). It is in this same conversation with Angiolina that he introduces a generalizing
comment that has exerted considerable influence on some
published accounts of the play:

> And yet I find a comfort in
> The thought that these things are the work of Fate;
> For I would rather yield to gods than men,
> Or cling to any creed of destiny,
> Rather than deem these mortals, most of whom
> I know to be as worthless as the dust,
> And weak as worthless, more than instruments
> Of an o'er-ruling power; they in themselves
> Were all incapable—   (V.ii.65–73)

With its reference to 'gods' the speech introduces a kind of
determinism rather different from that historical inevitability
which earlier attracted Faliero's mind: here the forces
depriving him of free agency take on a more distinct materi-
ality and personal life. What is very clear about the speech is
that it is an expression of desire for a reassuring way of
perceiving experience. The notion it advances seems untrue to
the experience that has been dramatized, and particularly to
that cut and thrust of individual action that has dominated the
play's most recent events. Faliero has been brought down
precisely by those 'mortals' he says he despises, and most
recently we have seen the revolution aborted because of the
particular human impulses of Bertram and the pragmatic
acumen of Lioni in responding to them. I would suggest,
therefore, that the kind of thematic status given to this speech
by McGann and Skerry may be misleading. McGann connects
the speech with the notion of a superhuman 'power' to which
the individuals in the play are subject. This power is not quite
identical to those that Faliero invokes: it is more destructive

than the historical inevitability that he imagined to be using him to restore Venice's health, and it does not take such distinctly personal form as his 'gods'. It is rather some inevitability in the pattern of Venetian and perhaps all human life, it is described by metaphors such as an 'infernal machine' and an indestructible 'beast', and it causes the behaviour of human beings to degenerate to brutalism. It is thus not a force that Faliero would quite be able to define for himself. But even though it appears to derive its life from the behaviour of particular human beings, this force is consistent with Faliero's 'Fate' in that it deprives human beings of the power of choice and is describable as something other than human. The process of delineating this metaphysical power, it seems to me, generates a degree of mystification comparable to Faliero's own: when McGann says that 'everyone becomes an unwilling instrument of "this monster ... this spectre"', he quotes words through which Faliero refers very directly to the human group with which he is contending, and when he says that 'the plebeians are the ignorant "accomplices" of its designs', he quotes from a speech in which Benintende is making a legalistic statement about who has worked with whom in organizing the revolution.[25] One consequence of viewing the action in terms consistent with Faliero's speech about fate is that McGann and, later, Skerry can see the world of the play as analogous to that of Greek tragedy. Skerry says of Faliero's speech that fate now appears in the play as an 'actual force: the will of the god', and that it introduces a Greek concept of experience which 'suggests the unknown forces that guide man's destiny'. And McGann argues that the Doge's 'helplessness' is a sign that 'the fates of Agamemnon and Oedipus are as certain as those of Byron's dramatic heroes'.[26] But although Faliero and Oedipus have a good deal in common—each is a highly energetic man who thinks he is seeking to cleanse the state over which he presides—Oedipus is surely a good deal more beset by forces outside the arena that individual human beings can command.

Once it becomes clear that the attempt at revolution has failed, Faliero's mind continues to be restlessly active, now in the pursuit of a conceptual mode that will subvert the implications of public defeat. He argues that the individual 'spirits' of those who perpetrated the revolution can still exert influence, now through the irresistible force of example, as they advance into the territory of the future in order to achieve a new form of action: they 'shall yet go forth/ And do what our frail clay, thus clogg'd, has fail'd in' (IV.ii.310–11). Faliero knows that, in order to take on this exemplary force, he does not have to achieve any further act other than to die. Benintende draws attention to the astonishing mark that he has already made on the history of Venice simply by performing an act of choice. He has made himself 'the greatest traitor upon record/ In any annals' (V.i.130–37), and he has forced the government to enact a new law to cope with the unprecedented (V.i.193). Faliero also knows that when the place where his portrait should be is left 'vacant' and covered with a 'death-black veil', attention will again be drawn to his action in a classic example of absence conferring presence (V.i.494–504). He is able to understand this as his mind continues indefatigably (and convincingly) to see even his failure as confirming his ability to intervene in history. When he says, 'I stand within eternity, and see/ Into eternity' (V.ii.88–89), he is trying to explain to Angiolina that he can maintain such a poised mental stance because he feels sure that he will be instrumental in the future decline of Venice. In all this activity his mind shows considerable resilience and resource, as he now transcends his earlier and rather limited notion that the value of his action depended on its 'success'.[27]

Faliero also thinks about and in the end achieves a further, alternative mode of public action. That is, rather than having 'done with Time' (V.ii.6) and making his stand within 'eternity' as soon as he is defeated, he chooses during the last moments to engage again with the immediate realm of temporal event. And the medium through which he seeks to

act is language. When he contemplates the notion that he
might speak at some length before death, he says, 'true *words*
are *things*,/ And dying men's are things which long outlive,/
And often times avenge them' (V.ii.288–90).[28] In one way,
Faliero's phrasing brings us back to that play on variants of
'thing' that seemed so important to his desire to materialize as
a force with weight and mass in the Venetian community.
Just a little earlier he has used the word's reductive potential
in addressing the Signor of the Night as a mere 'thing'
(IV.ii.252): his own word turns against him, however, because
the Signor has arrested Faliero and has thus intervened materi-
ally to help abort the revolution. Immediately after the signs
of defeat Faliero says, 'There now is nothing left me save to
die' (IV.ii.261), and close to the time of his death, 'I have
nothing left' (V.ii.104). On the other hand he also senses stirring within him 'something of the blood of brighter days'
(V.i.272). And when he says that words can be things, he is
obviously seeking to suggest that they can carry a force like
that of material objects. The status of language, of words, has
been in question at several points in the play.[29] Angiolina has
said that virtue is meaningless if it has to depend merely 'upon
men's words' (II.i.57–58), but she has also acknowledged
the possibility that Pietro may have 'words of weight'
(II.i.154) to communicate to Faliero when she hesitates to
break into their conversation. Calendaro, one of the revolutionaries, is impatient with the relative insignificance of
speech when he says, 'may this be/ The last night of mere
words: I'd fain be doing!' (III.ii.387–88), but he has also
acknowledged that the 'unmanly creeping things' which
constitute the government are somehow able to 'command
our swords, and rule us with a word/ As with a spell'
(II.ii.117–19). Faliero himself has said that there is in truth 'no
such thing' as the duke of Venice since the office has become
just 'a word—nay, worse—a worthless by-word' (I.ii.100), but
his response to what Steno wrote on the throne has suggested
that words are capable of very great power. And at the end it is

as if he is seeking to generate in his own words a power not just equivalent to that which Steno has exerted but radically exceeding it. Before he utters the great curse on Venice, the ducal cap is removed from his head. He responds to this by saying that the Doge has now become 'nothing' and that the speaker is simply once again Marino Faliero (V.iii.1–2). In the speech that follows he attempts to suggest that he himself is markedly other than 'nothing', that his words can take on massive substantiality. He knows that only the ruling group can hear him, since the outer gates of the ducal palace are closed: 'the people are without,/ Beyond the compass of the human voice' (V.iii.24–25). Although some influence can presumably be exerted on these few auditors, and perhaps that is why Faliero says that he is still speaking to 'Time' as well as to 'Eternity' (V.iii.26), his preoccupation now is with achieving a form of action through speech consciously addressed in the present moment to the universe that he thinks of as eternal. Rather than speaking directly to 'man', he says that he is communicating with the 'elements' (V.iii.28). And the manner in which he addresses waves, winds, earth, stones, skies and sun bears some relationship to what Byron wrote in his Journal less than two years after composing *Marino Faliero*:

> Why should not the Mind act with and upon the Universe?—as portions of it act upon and with the congregated dust—called Mankind?—See—how one man acts upon himself and others—or upon multitudes?—The same Agency in a higher and purer degree may act upon the Stars etc., ad infinitum. (*BLJ*, IX, 46)

The tone is also distinctly Shelleyan. When Faliero refers to his association with 'eternity,/ Of which I grow a portion' (V.iii.26–27) his words are suggestive of Shelley's depiction in the following year of how the spirit of Adonais becomes a 'portion of the Eternal' (l.340), and when he says to the 'elements' that he wants them to 'let my voice be as a spirit/ Upon you!' (V.iii.29–30), he speaks in the manner of the poet in the 'Ode to the West Wind' who wants the wind's 'spirit' to become his own so that he can move humanity as it moves the waves. As Faliero makes this last attempt at self-defining and self-assertive action, the reader may well feel unsure of how Byron is seeking to place it within the context of the play. Faliero has been utterly baffled in his attempt at revolutionary action, the Venetian populace cannot hear his speech, and his words are not written down. On the other hand, it does seem clear that Byron is not seeking to reduce the attempt to an absurd gesture.[30] For example, he underpins the prophecy with a series of footnotes that draw attention to the accuracy of even the most outlandish of his forecasts. And he provides the speech with a considerable feeling of authority in its grammatical structure. It is dominated by a single sentence of almost forty lines, stretching from just before its mid-point to its conclusion. The verb forms in the sentence keep changing from future to present tense, as if bringing the future into contemporary life, and finally, at the climax, to the past tense, as Faliero contemplates an achieved degradation of Venice to the 'worst of peopled deserts' (V.iii.95). The many clauses defining Venice's future are subordinated to the long delayed reference to Faliero's death, which is what he hopes the inhabitants of Venice will remember at the end of the city's long decline. In this way his execution is transformed into a sign marking the corruption that will cause the long fall. It is as if Faliero is making a final, energetic bid to mark his autonomy and his force through the power of grammatical construction. Whatever status the reader might feel inclined to grant this speech, it seems clearly to represent a further and vigorous attempt by Faliero's mind to find ways of transcending the immediate actualities of political defeat and death and to counteract the sensation of nullity that these and so many other events have induced.

Thus, although the plot may dramatize defeat for the

protagonist, it does not clearly endow defeat with thematic priority. [...]

[...] [A]lthough the given narrative about Faliero appears to be historically defined as an example of conspicuous failure, Byron's exploration of the hero's psyche dwells on a (somewhat intermittent) process of growth, or at least on a struggle that enables Faliero in the end to cope with the reality of patent historical failure. In describing what his investigation into the history of this figure has led him to, Byron writes: '... it may be inferred, that Marino Faliero possessed many of the qualities, but not the success of a hero; ... Petrarch says, "that there had been no greater event in his times" (*our times* literally) "nostri tempi," in Italy. ... Had the man succeeded, he would have changed the face of Venice, and perhaps of Italy' (*CPW*, IV, 538–39). Insisting on certain human characteristics that survive the historical narrative of defeat and that he discovers through his own individual act of literary creation, Byron pays tribute here to the energy and *élan* inherent in Faliero's act of choice, and to the enormous potential residing in the human individual for achieving transformative influence on circumstance.

NOTES

1. Johnson, 'A Political Interpretation', pp. 418, 420.
2. *Byron's Letters and Journals*, ed. Leslie A. Marchand (London: John Murray, 1977), VII, pp. 137–38: hereafter cited as *BLJ*.
3. V.ii.66. Quotations and act, scene, and line references are from *Lord Byron: The Complete Poetical Works*, ed. Jerome J. McGann (Oxford: Clarendon Press, 1986), subsequently referred to as *CPW*: *Marino Faliero*, edited by Barry Weller, is in Vol. IV; *Don Juan* is in Vol. V.
4. McGann, *Fiery Dust*, pp. 214, 209, 208.
5. Skerry, 'Concentric Structures', pp. 99, 105. For a third example of this critical tendency, see Robinson, *Shelley and Byron*: Byron implies that

'fate determined the actions of the Doge' (p. 157) and that therefore 'the Doge was not morally responsible for his actions' (p. 158).

6. Manning, *Byron and His Fictions*, p. 120.
7. Kelsall, *Byron's Politics*, pp. 91, 115.
8. Ashton, 'Byron's "Poetry of Politics"', p. 13.
9. *CPW*, IV, p. 300.
10. Garber, *The Autonomy of the Self*, pp. 17–18.
11. Crocker, *Praxis and Democratic Socialism*, p. 51.
12. *The Collected Works of Samuel Taylor Coleridge*, I, p. 32.
13. Garber, *The Autonomy of the Self*, pp. 19, 40.
14. Manning refers to Faliero's 'need to feel aligned with his heritage' and to the 'casuistry' by which he transforms a 'willful choice' into an assigned duty: *Byron and His Fictions*, p. 113. Although my discussion of the beginning of Act III has a good deal in common with Manning's, his general emphasis on approaching the play is quite different from mine.
15. The phrase occurs in an interview with Don De Lillo, discussing *Libra*, his novel based on the assassination of John F. Kennedy. He says, 'To merge with history is to escape the self': *Rolling Stone* (17 November 1988), p. 117.
16. Manning, *Byron and His Fictions*, p. 110.
17. Watkins, 'Violence, Class Consciousness, and Ideology', pp. 799–816; Barton, '"A Light to Lesson Ages"', p. 148.
18. Jerome Christensen also stresses Faliero's 'prematurity' here, but for an entirely different purpose, in '*Marino Faliero* and the Fault of Byron's Satire', p. 323.
19. Farrell, *Revolution as Tragedy*, p. 152; McGann, *Fiery Dust*, pp. 209–11.
20. Gleckner makes interesting comments on this sequence in *Byron and the Ruins of Paradise*, pp. 315–16.
21. Thorslev, *Romantic Contraries*, p. 10.
22. Garber, *The Autonomy of the Self*, p. 36.
23. McGann, *Fiery Dust*, pp. 213.
24. This is Gleckner's position in *Byron and the Ruins of Paradise*. Faliero's militaristic language here also offers support to Daniel P. Watkins' notion that many of Byron's characters are socially conditioned in damaging ways. Watkins has expressed this notion in a number of essays, but perhaps most fully in *Social Relations*.
25. McGann, *Fiery Dust*, pp. 207, 209, 210, 211, concentrating on *Marino Faliero*, III.ii.165–66 and V.i.27.
26. Skerry, 'Concentric Structures', pp. 105–06; McGann, *Fiery Dust*, pp. 208, 206.
27. For a clear statement of this notion, see Manning, *Byron and His Fictions*, p. 113.

28. For a full treatment of Byron's thinking about the relationship between words and things, see Marshall, '"*Words* are *things*"', pp. 801–22. As she points out, variants of the statement I have quoted appear in *Don Juan* and 'The Prophecy of Dante'.

29. For some of the following discussion of the status of language in the play I am indebted to Jennifer Gustar, a student in my graduate seminar on Byron in the fall of 1987.

30. McGann takes the speech very seriously, and his full statement about the 'values' it 'upholds' is as follows: 'The first, and most important, is consciousness itself, which if it does not save life at least redeems man from its immediate evils and enables him to affirm its larger designs. Secondly, when he denounces the hollow men of Venice we are given our last sight of his outraged humanity, and the expression of that vital passion which has been at once his human doom and human redemption' (*Fiery Dust*, p. 214).

Marino Faliero and the Fault of Byron's Satire

JEROME CHRISTENSEN

Ordinarily, when one thinks of Byron's satire it is *Don Juan* and not *Marino Faliero* that comes to mind. The horizon of my interest, to which this essay aspires, is *Don Juan*. It will do so without proposing a reading of any particular canto or passage and with scant attention to the anatomical peculiarities of that protean beast. Instead I intend to be more specific about both fault and satire than about *Juan* itself. I shall try to demonstrate that *Marino Faliero*, a play written during the composition of *Juan* and situated within its generous precincts, is the best approach to Byron's most powerful poem because *Faliero* represents, with all its faults, a poetics of Byron's satire. [...]

Marino Faliero, Doge of Venice, a work wherein romantic ambition labours in a theatre of baroque inconsequence, was the first play to be written under the general dispensation of *Juan*. The action begins in abeyance as Faliero awaits the verdict of the Forty (the patrician ruling élite) on Michael Steno for scrawling on the ducal throne a charge of infidelity against the Doge's wife Angiolina. When to the offence of Steno is added the insult of a lenient punishment by his peers, the Doge, inflamed with resentment, lends his ear to the seditious plot of the discontented plebeians, becomes convinced they have a common cause, and assumes leadership of the incipient rebellion. The Doge persuades his followers to strike quickly, and they agree to converge at St Mark's on the sunrise signal of the bell. The plot, however, is betrayed, the uprising

117

quelled, and Faliero and his lieutenants apprehended. Faliero is tried and executed within the palace, where there is no possibility that his words or demeanour could incite the volatile populace; after his death his engraved name in the gallery of the doges is covered by a black veil, eternal mark of his treason.

Marino Faliero both represents and enacts Byron's ambivalence about his own social status and about the possibility for effective political action in contemporary England. Faliero's greyheaded uselessness within a society that, secure from foreign threat, is intent on routinizing charisma reflects both the post-Napoleonic dejection of a man who had once aspired to noble deeds and who now is convinced that in Wellington the English have gained the hero they deserve, and the post-*Childe Harold* cynicism of a poet who appreciates that the charismatic quality of his previously published poetry was only the trumpery of the marketplace. Faliero's biography also telescopes Byron's own idealization of his family history. In *Hours of Idleness* Byron had exposed himself to Henry Brougham's ridicule by his jejune celebration of his nobility; Brougham mockingly exposed not only the poet's graceless boastfulness but more tellingly Byron's insecurity about his aristocratic status, which emerged in the poet's Ossianic exertions to concoct and retail a past that proved his nobility was not only ancient but *earned* in glamorous highland skirmishes.[1] The aged bitterness of the Doge is not simply another trope of Byronic world-weariness, but, as a scene in his ancestral mausoleum makes clear, a vehicle to render the return of the fathers in the son: they are at once addressed and impersonated that they might see and suffer the disgrace administered by time and men. Moreover, the plot of *Faliero* shows Byron working out in dramatic form some of the political preoccupations that circulate throughout this correspondence. Having become financially solvent enough to worry about *keeping* rather than *finding* money, Byron shifted his financial anxiety from moneylenders to investments. His letters are studded with queries about the current state of 'the funds', imperious instructions about the management of his interest in them, and dire predictions of financial collapse.[2] Indeed, forecasting catastrophe became something of a hobby for Byron; it allowed him to indulge the fantasy that he might return to England during the ensuing chaos as the man on the horse who would command the rebellious masses and shape a new social and economic order—a fantasy in which it is typically difficult to disentangle the purely personal motive from the more generally political one. Again, however, that tangle imitates the doubleness of the motives of Faliero: he is offended in his person but takes that offence as an insult to the sovereignty of an office which is the only guarantor of the legitimacy of the state; he allies himself with republicans but only as the supervisory mind might condescend to act through the soiled instrument of the body. [...]

The vacillations in Byron's exchanges with John Murray about the possible staging of *Marino Faliero* enact the ambivalence he represents. Scholars disagree about Byron's intentions. Some argue that despite his vehement protests he really wanted *Marino Faliero* to be staged and denied that aim in full confidence (justified by events) that Murray would go ahead and arrange for its production anyway, thereby enabling Byron to deny his interest in the performance should it fail or, in case of triumph, to receive the plaudits like a champion who conquers offhandedly.[3] I do not intend to enter that dispute. What is important here is to note that in the failure of the funds to fail, and in the absence of any other pretext for Byron's physical return to England (the indefatigably drab Southey could not be provoked into a duel), the theatre represented the next best thing, a symbolic return made as good as real by its occurrence in a space where symbols have a virtual life. It is crucial to realize, however, that the next best thing would, in this case, also have been the worst. Such a triumph would be poisoned at its heart, since it would merely replay the ironic relation between sovereignty and theatricality that

Byron had already exposed in the Bonaparte stanzas of *Childe Harold* III.[4] What triumph Byron could have achieved would have had its transitory reality only in the effervescent admiration of a tyrannous audience and would in any case not have been fully *Byron's* triumph, since Byron was experienced enough in the practices of Murray and the management of Drury Lane to be certain that in the passage to the stage the text would fall into various hands which would prune his drama to customize its force. 'Byron' could only appear in London as a lame monarch, one whose sovereignty was conditioned by its self-evident theatricality, one who was hedged about by a peremptory administrative machinery, and one whose acts would only be dim imitations of the sort of executive actions occurring in a real world elsewhere. Byron's irresolute management of *Marino Faliero* dramatizes the ironic thesis common to that play and to the later *Sardanapalus*: sovereignty can only exert its authority through a self-imaging, but that staging submits that authority to potential humiliation. Sovereignty cannot survive what Byron called its 'cursed attempt at representation'.[5]

Nothing I have said about the relations between representation and enactment challenge the conventional reading of *Marino Faliero* as a historical tragedy about a grand risk and a glorious failure. And it is surely the case that it was as a piece of tragic sensationalism à la mode that *Faliero* appealed to Murray and his colleagues. Actually, however, the play is not about failure but about success or, to be precise, about the social machinery for transforming failure into success. Faliero's ascendancy to the dogeship was the direct result of his heroic salvation of the state from its foreign enemies. Far from demonstrating that such heroism is irrelevant in an age of impersonal bureaucratic efficiency, the play dramatizes the ritual advantages the hero-king provides for the modern state: Faliero's action in the play neatly repeats the service by which he was originally exalted. Crucial to this interpretation is Faliero's acknowledgement prior to his meeting with the plebeian conspirators, 'I am before the hour' (III.i.1). This indication of prematurity is reinforced by the conspirators' expressions of surprise at Faliero's indignant impatience with any counsel of delay. Whatever Faliero's intentions, the effect of his leadership is to precipitate rebellion prematurely, to practise a kind of political homeopathy, infecting the state with a discord of such weakness that it could be localized and contained, thus allowing the germs of civil conflict to exhaust their malignancy before they could fester into a mortal illness. In this schematically Girardian reading, the execution of the Doge is a scapegoating which does not deny his sovereignty but decisively consummates it. He has rescued the state from civil war, and his service is sealed by his identification as the monstrous double who is beheaded and forever marked as unique by the covering of his engraved name in the gallery of the doges.[6] That black veil puts an endstop to all the emulous strife that unsettles the established order. It naturalizes order by attributing strife not to, say, an irreconcilable class conflict, but to the anarchic passion of a prodigy of nature. The king who betrays the state saves it—such is the plaguey paradox kept under quarantine by the black veil, so that the deep truth may remain nameless.

If we can agree that the secret stratagem of Faliero's revolt is to induce homeopathically what he calls this 'game of mutual homicides' in order that his sacrificial death can bring the game to a close, we may have resolved most of the effects of the play, but we are still left without any grasp of the causes. We could, of course, pursue a Girardian reading further and argue that the effect is fundamentally the *same* as the cause: that all the actions of Faliero are governed by the final cause of the preservation of hierarchical stability, that his drama is a ritual enactment of ostensible rivalry and civil war performed in order to provide the scapegoat whose succinct execution defuses a divisiveness (represented by the doublings that propagate throughout the play) that might otherwise explode into anarchy and promiscuous bloodshed. In other words, the full scale Girardian reading would require us to interpret *Marino Faliero* as theatrical all the way down: a play about the essentially dissimulative character of a politics solely designed to satisfy symbolically the demands of a brute nature that can only be imagined as a chaos of blood and poison.

Such attention to the final cause, whether we find it reassuringly orderly or tyrannously pre-emptive, has the tendency to efface the potency of Steno's lampoon. That tendency conforms to an implicit convention observed by all parties. Patriarch, patrician and plebe all deny that the scrawl has any consequences. No cause in itself, Steno's lampoon is merely the pretext for an action proceeding from a source of more gravity. Faliero, who urges his nephew to 'think upon the cause' (I.ii.272),[7] subsequently offers a diagnosis that turns on Mandeville: 'Our private wrongs have sprung from public vices' (III.ii.154). He specifies the crisis twice, each time identifying it with his election as Doge: 'Their own desire, not my ambition made/ Them choose me for their prince, and then .../ Farewell all social memory. ... [N]o friends, no kindness,/ No privacy of life—all were cut off' (III.ii.325–27, 348–49). To be made the Doge is to feel the full imposition of the public in the joke of sovereignty; to assume the ducal authority is to submit to the constraint of an absent power which the sovereign can never possess but must always represent. As representation the sovereign is incapacitated, not deprived of power exactly, for to become doge is to learn that one cannot lose what no one has, but stripped of the watery, bourgeois surrogate for power, privacy. Consequently, the provocation of Steno's gibe, according to Faliero, lay in its final spoliation of the one fragile refuge of privacy that remained to him, his domestic life with Angiolina.

Given the synonymity of the public and the theatrical, Faliero's account squares with my own, except in its insistence on an opposition between the private and the public and on some dramatic moment in which the former is violated by the latter. But such a theory cannot be credited. Certainly Steno's lampoon does not violate any privacy; for in the dialogue between Faliero and Angiolina in which they recall their betrothal, arranged by Angiolina's dying father, it is evident that nothing that could be called privacy ever subsisted between them, no subjective space in which a theoretical liberty could be exercised. Faliero reminds her, '[Y]ou had/ Freedom from me to choose, and urged in answer/ Your father's choice.' Angiolina agrees: 'My lord, I look'd but to my father's wishes ...' (II.i.322–24, 342). A choice so given is no choice at all; and the freedom of a virtuous woman is not liberty, since virtue is a fixed source of light:

> Vice cannot fix, and virtue cannot change.
> The once fall'n woman must for ever fall;
> For vice must have variety, while virtue
> Stands like the sun. and all which rolls around
> Drinks life, and light, and glory from her aspect.
>
> (II.i.394–98)

The *helos* of that sun, who fixes the woman within a solar system of virtue, is the father, whose wishes have the authority of a cosmological given. Thus in its form Faliero's marriage 'proposal' to Angiolina, made at the behest of her father, recapitulates the bind in which *he* was placed by his election as Doge: in proposing marriage he cuts himself and his wife off from all 'social memory'. Any proposal made by authority addresses a subject whose choice can only be nominal, since to reject the proposal would be to remove oneself from the line of the father which confers the very possibility of choice. There is no power to choose what is not authorized: but it follows that authority is delegated every power except that of conferring the power freely to choose. Every well-formed statement in Venice is a variant of Angiolina's 'My Lord, I look'd but to my father's wishes', even, or rather especially, Faliero's pathetically curtailed self-assertion, 'I will be what I should be, or be nothing ...' (II.i.453). The ironical equivocation of that 'should' displays the blind vanity of the will that indulges the fancy of a destiny different from that which is designed by the father, who has said and is continually saying the same thing. Embedded in the inexorable conjunction of 'will' and 'should' is the endless reiteration of the compliance of all subjects with the wish of a father who wishes to identify himself with a father ideal making the same wish—a circuitous submission to an ideal authority which is faulted by its structural incapacity to will anything but what it should, a circuit which, in its dynamic iterability, is the expression of an absent cause.

The play not only gives us no grounds to think that Angiolina is unfaithful, Byron takes pains to dispel the possibility that anyone in Venice could suspect the virtuous wife of the Doge of adultery. Steno's slander, then, is, by all accounts, impotent: it exposes nothing nor does it propagate rumour. Indeed, Faliero's irate response, a 'fury [that] doth exceed the provocation,/ Or any provocation' (I.ii.136–37), does not take the form of a repudiation of the incredible charge of wifely infidelity but of a denial of his own passion for his wife:

> 'T was not a foolish dotard's vile caprice,
> Nor the false edge of aged appetite,
> Which made me covetous of girlish beauty,
> And a young bride: for in my fieriest youth
> I sway'd such passions; nor was this my age
> Infected with that leprosy of lust
> Which taints the hoariest years of vicious men,
> Making them ransack to the very last
> The dregs of pleasure for their vanish'd joys;
> Or buy in selfish marriage some young victim,
> Too helpless to refuse a state that's honest,
> Too feeling not to know herself a wretch.
>
> (II.i.310–21)

The lust that Faliero denies is the obverse of the innocent 'patriarchal love' he affirms (II.i.363). Steno's scrawl does not discover, let alone cause, any infidelity; it marks the exclusion from the Venetian patriarchy of any physical passion that could be anything other than infidelity or incest by bringing to visibility the incestuous format imposed on all private relations between husband and wife, 'father' and 'daughter'. The determination in the last instance is not the father, but a discourse that puts any man, any husband, any sovereign in the position of a father who can have no desire except that which is already scripted as incestuous. Steno's mark is a provocation not because it speaks of facts but because it signifies at all levels a proscription of desire.

All relations in Venice, even the most intimate, are statements in a discourse which allows for no digression or, what is the same thing, no unintentional, non-hierarchical, wordless sensuality. [...] It is only an apparent paradox to assert, however, that from the 'point of view' of power everything that occurs in Venice, all actions and words of all parties, the whole discourse of society, is nothing but digression. Digression, like theatrical representation, is empty, purposeless speech. [...] The text of *Marino Faliero*, however, extends the digressively theatrical to include *all* social and political speech and behaviour, which is not framed by any supervisory purpose, and which is distinguished from theatrical representation proper only in that it is both mystified in its production and afflicted with nostalgia, uttered by actors who believe in their parts. [...]

We can agree with Faliero then that Steno's ribaldry is not the cause of the civil disturbance in Venice. Yet Faliero wants to go further, to claim that the scrawl is nothing at all. He calls it the 'mere ebullition of vice' (III.ii.403)—a figure that oddly anticipates the trope that T. S. Eliot would later use to characterize Byron's poetry: 'We have come to expect poetry to be something very concentrated, something distilled; but if Byron had distilled his verse, there would have been nothing whatever left.'[8] [...] Although vice itself, the vile substrate from which poisonous ebullitions like Steno's effervesce, Venice is queerly figured as compounded of the same fantastic element as Steno's scrawl; it is a something that can be reduced into nothing. This view of Venice has been called 'organic',[9] but it is surely a root and branch organicism, indistinguishable from the sort of nihilism that shadows a swollen, frustrated, so-called 'Byronic' narcissism. Faliero's 'political' programme is indistinguishable from the project of the ego to which I have already referred: 'I will be what I should be, or be nothing', a zero-sum egoism which allows for no action that is not the doomed extension of a wish, or the wishful extension of a doom. Faliero is thus like Eliot, who flaunts a magical power to extinguish, which he, however, graciously restrains. And like, curiously enough, a more efficient practitioner of the art of extinction, Robert Elliston, manager of Drury Lane, who in his application for a licence for *Faliero*, which he had assiduously cut to eliminate all traces of contemporary political comment, stressed that 'we have so curtailed [the play] that I believe not a single objectionable line can be said to exist'.[10] Elliston regarded the political gestures of *Faliero* as a 'mere ebullition of vice', a digression from an innocuous Byronic entertainment that might be distilled, that, he claimed, he *had* distilled into nothing.

Hence when, at the end of the play, members of the populace, frustrated in their desire to get within hearing distance of the exchanges of Faliero's execution, 'curse ... the distance' and vent the forlorn wish, 'would we/ Could but gather one sole sentence' (IV.iv.11–14)—as if that sentence would distil and resolve the confusing events that have been acted out in the streets of Venice—they are in the same situation as the Drury Lane spectators who watched the mutilated result of Elliston's censorship (which did not include this final scene). All objectionable sentences have been lopped off and hauled away; nothing salient remains. *This is no loss.* There could be nothing truly objectionable in a sentence spoken by Faliero or any actor who might impersonate him. Indeed, the play demonstrates the homology between gathering, distillation and extinction: there is no substantive difference between the fetishism of distillation, whether it be the Eliotic notion of a crystalline touchstone or the popular wish to gather a single explanatory sentence, and the murderous ambition to extinguish all, to censor the objectionable out of existence: essence and nothingness turn on the same idealist pivot. The twin beliefs in a distillation that will return either to an essence or to nothing partake of the same alchemical faith, the same mystery-mongering politics. The very attempt to look for a sentence is to look to one's father's wishes.

What remains is the black veil, neither essence nor nothing. It is the mark beyond the sentence of Faliero and its execution—something added to the sacrificial machinery of the state in order economically to seal once and for all the flawlessly sufficient hegemony of the state machine. Intended as an *index expurgatorius* which would put a stop to all further talk, the black veil was itself censored by Elliston; indeed, it is the sign in the play of that censorship, which the veil anticipates and entails as the type ordains and is (all but) cancelled by its antitype. Venetian censorship is expunged by a new censorship, which may disable the play as theatre but realizes it as a text that has a forcefulness which is not under the control of the monopolistic discourse of patriarch, patrician, and patriot. The veil marks and its censorship remarks the necessity of a certain craftsmanship of repression. [...]

I would claim that *Marino Faliero* is a poetics of satire in abbreviated form. Byron's satire, like all satire, finds fault; what distinguishes Byron's satire is that what it finds is what it *is*. The only possible power that can accrue to satire in a disciplinary society managed by a discourse that remains invisible, a power that no one can speak, is to mark the digressiveness of all authoritative utterance by an abbreviation without authority that contingently produces its own reproduction as the track of its own aboriginal digression. If the fault of Byron's poetry is its digression, a digression that invokes no authority, nor prospects any teleology, that fault is its indubitable strength. Byron's digression is the stenographic signifier that cannot be gathered into one sole sentence, that cannot be disciplined. This, I say, is a political act, if not, in the absence of any shibboleth, a political programme. If, then, Byron participates in what Richard Sennett calls 'the fall of public man', he does not reify a zone of 'privatized freedom' as a transcendent refuge of the self from the arena of public expression and display; rather he dramatizes the yearning for such a refuge and the futility of that yearning, shows that the notion of a secret place of self-expression and unencumbered personal relations, of any sort of transcendence, is an illusion that is constituted by and functional within a pervasive disciplinary discourse.[11] Byron opposes every explanation of the private that is in any way systematic but observes the impossibility of proposing any alternative that would not be subject to 'this cursed attempt at representation'. [...]

In my view it is less important that Byron was 'born for opposition', than that he was made for apposition: to *add, juxtapose, apply*. His is the only poetry that we can place in apposition to the writings of a Pope: he is the true, if necessarily contingent and unpropertied heir of that poet who could spawn only bastards. Taking on Pope's power without his authority, the scapegrace stenographer puts his master, all masters, to shame. A stenograph that is a digression, a digression that is a stenograph—that is how *Marino Faliero* characterizes *Don Juan*; that is the mark of Byron, the fault of his satire.

NOTES

1. Brougham, *Edinburgh Review*, January 1808, in Rutherford, *Byron: The Critical Heritage*, pp. 27–32.

2. See, for example, *BLJ*, VIII, 135, 137 and 181.

3. The classic statement of Byron's ambivalence is David Erdman's essay, 'Byron's Stage Fright', pp. 219–43.

4. These passages are discussed in my essay 'Byron's Career', pp. 72–74.

5. *BLJ*, VIII, 66.

6. Girard, *Violence and the Sacred, passim*. See also Jerome McGann's fine reading of *Marino Faliero* in *Fiery Dust*, which is attentive to the doublings and ironic reversals in the play. McGann concludes, however, that despite the general wreckage, the values of consciousness and expressing 'vital passion' are upheld—a 'human redemption' that is, in my view, an idealization of Byron's more radical critique (*Fiery Dust*, pp. 205–15, esp. 214–15).

7. Cf. Byron's defence of his characterization to John Murray: 'The Doge *repeats*; *true*—but it is from engrossing passion—and because he sees *different* persons—and is always obliged to recur to the *cause* uppermost in his mind' (*BLJ*, VII, 195).

8. Eliot, 'Byron', pp. 193–94.

9. McGann, *Fiery Dust*, p. 209.

10. Ashton, 'The Censorship of Byron's *Marino Faliero*', p. 28. The contemporary political events that *Marino* most touched upon were the divorce proceedings initiated against Queen Caroline by her royal husband and the discovery and quashing of the Cato Street conspiracy. Closer to home, Byron surely had the recent (December 1819) arrest and imprisonment of his long-time friend John Cam Hobhouse for 'scandalous libel in contempt of the privileges and constitutional authority of Parliament' in mind as a pattern for Steno's political prank. For the details of Elliston's handiwork, see pp. 34–38.

11. Sennett, *The Fall of Public Man*, p. 217.

EDITORS' BIBLIOGRAPHICAL NOTE

Of Byron's three historical dramas (as they are usually called), *Marino Faliero* and *Sardanapalus* have received by far the most critical attention and consistent praise. Indeed one of the most recent books on Byron is entirely devoted to this trilogy: Lansdown's *Byron's Historical Dramas*; and almost

100 pages of Corbett's *Byron and Tragedy* are similarly focused. At the opposite end of the spectrum of critical appraisal essentially launched by Chew's *The Dramas of Lord Byron* is Blackstone's curious *Byron: A Survey* in which both *Marino Faliero* and *The Two Foscari* are labelled 'obsessional drama', 'neurotic' in contrast to *Manfred* and *Sardanapalus*, their heroes 'ineffective', the 'mise-en-scène cramping', the drama 'impoverished'. Two other books (the first actually a published lecture) devoted entirely to Byron's plays deserve mention here along with Chew's: Dobrée's *Byron's Dramas* and Ehrstine's *The Metaphysics of Byron*.

I. Specifically on *Marino Faliero* are the following, arranged alphabetically by author:

Ashton, 'The Censorship of Byron's *Marino Faliero*', pp. 27–44.
Ashton, 'Byron's Poetry of Politics', pp. 1–13.
Cooke, 'The Restoration Ethos', pp. 569–78 (also on *Sardanapalus*).
Farrell, 'The Betrayal of Prometheus: *Marino Faliero*', in his *Revolution as Tragedy*, pp. 150–62.
Franklin, 'Angiolina [in *Marino Faliero*]', in her *Byron's Heroines*, pp. 182–91.
Hassler, '*Marino Faliero*', pp. 55–64.
Johnson, 'A Political Interpretation', pp. 417–25.
Kernberger, 'The Semiotics of Space', pp. 69–73.
King, 'The Influence of Shakespeare', pp. 48–55. Cf. Richard Lansdown's Appendix: 'Shakespearian Allusions in *Marino Faliero*', *Byron's Historical Dramas*, pp. 237–44.
Manning, *Byron and His Fictions*, pp. 109–22.
McGann, *Fiery Dust*, pp. 206–15.
Skerry, 'Concentric Structures', pp. 81–107.
Spence, 'The Moral Ambiguity of *Marino Faliero*', pp. 6–17.

II. On *Marino Faliero* along with *The Two Foscari* and *Sardanapalus* the following are most useful:

Barton, '"A Light to Lesson Ages"', pp. 138–62.
DeSilva, 'Byron's Politics', pp. 113–36.
Elledge, *Byron and the Dynamics of Metaphor*, pp. 97–151 (includes *Cain* in lieu of *The Two Foscari*).
Gatton, '"Put into Scenery"', pp. 139–49; and '"Pretensions to Accuracy"', pp. 57–67.
Marchand, *Byron's Poetry*, Chapter 8.
Martin, *Byron*, Chapter 6.
Ruddick, 'Lord Byron's Historical Tragedies', pp. 83–94.

Steiner, *The Death of Tragedy*, pp. 201–09.

Watkins, 'Violence, Class Consciousness, and Ideology', pp. 799–816.

III. Briefer comments on *Marino Faliero* in omnibus studies of Byron's works:

Cardwell, 'Byron: Text and Counter-Text', pp. 7–23.

Cox, *In the Shadows of Romance*, has a section entitled 'Byron and Tragedy: Mysteries and Histories'.

Foot, *The Politics of Paradise*.

Joseph, *Byron the Poet*, Chapter 4.

Watson, 'Mental Theatre', pp. 24–44.

'Studiously Greek': *The Two Foscari*

JEROME J. McGANN

Marino Faliero and *The Two Foscari* [often] have been [...] disapproved for not dramatizing the causes of the struggle: both [have been said to] open with the opposing forces already arrayed. But Byron maintained that his procedure was 'studiously Greek',[1] and if the Venetian plays are to be faulted for opening in this way then so are the works of Aeschylus and Sophocles. The fates of Agamemnon and Oedipus are as certain as those of Byron's dramatic heroes.

This matter of structure is intimately related to the peculiar themes which Byron deals with in his Venetian plays. The *Agamemnon* does not involve a viable struggle against fate but is concerned with the gradual revelation of the meaning of a particular fatality in terms of a developing and concatenated system of images, symbols, and dramatic confrontations. Though important and functional, characterization is itself subordinate to the religious or symbolic spectacle whose first intention is to unfold meaning, to explore the significance of the central themes. This perspective seems to me remarkably similar to Byron's. His Venetian plays have 'action', of course, but not in a Shakespearian sense. As in Aeschylus and Sophocles, action in Byron is not so much 'struggle' as it is 'spectacle'—dramatically symbolic revelation. [...] Further, the revelations are made by developing the relations between, and thereby the significance of, certain predominant images and symbols. As in Aeschylus, Byron's characters are often the pawns of the poetry in which they are involved. Like Agamemnon or Clytemnestra, they perform acts of their free will, but the continuum in which these acts are caught up is not subject to human manipulation. Something inexorable strides abroad, a fatality, and this power is captured for our perception in the poetic relations in the plays. [...]

The Two Foscari [however] will seem a poor imitation of *Marino Faliero* if we see it only as a warmed-over version of Byron's earlier Venetian play. Samuel Chew has rightly noted that many of the same themes are carried forward:[2] we note particularly those of civic pollution, the vision of governors as slaves to a mysterious and non-human force, and the unre-solvable conflict between patriotism and personality. But the play does not have the metaphoric thickness of *Marino Faliero*. In the latter, Byron leans heavily upon closely woven image patterns to secure an effect of a developing revelation of meaning. *The Two Foscari* is less single-minded a work, is not exclusively or perhaps even primarily an anatomy of ideas. Rather, it attempts something *Marino Faliero* left untouched except in the case of the Doge: it attempts to dramatize the effect that life in Venice has upon a number of different, and very specific, people. *Marino Faliero* has only one 'person-ality'—the Doge—and two or three fairly interesting 'charac-ters' (Bertram, Israel Bertuccio, Angiolina). *The Two Foscari*, on the other hand, has three distinctive personalities—the Doge, Marina, and Loredano—and at least one extremely engaging character—Barbarigo.

Before we consider this aspect of the play, however, we ought to make some examination of its ideas and imagistic motifs. *Marino Faliero* has at least four potent dramatic symbols: the ducal cap, which represents the illusion of human power; the equestrian statue of the Doge's ancestor (III.i), which is a portent of doom and a sign of its trans-temporal dominion; the mask and cloak of the aristocracy which they wear in public as the badges of their secrecy and inhumanity alike; and the bloody sword waved over the people at the end, another sign of death and doom (and one that distinctly recalls Aeschylus). Each of these symbolic props is the locus of one or more image sequences in the play. *The Two Foscari* contains three dramatic symbols of this sort: Loredano's account book, the goblet of Venetian crystal which he gives to the Doge at the end, and the dungeon of the younger Foscari.

Loredano's accounting tablets are made the framing symbol of the play, and they epitomize both the spectacle of Venetian justice and the moral code of all who serve it. Such justice and such a code scrupulously put out of court all human concerns. When Marina bursts in upon her husband's trial in the first act the court immediately adjourns, for she suddenly focuses the tribunal's attention on the inhuman artifice of the law which they serve.

> 'T was a dreadful sight
> When his distracted wife broke through into
> The hall of our tribunal, and beheld
> What we could scarcely look upon, long used
> To such sights. (I.i.364–68)

The pattern repeats itself throughout the play: the automatic forms of tradition and law are meant to cast out human consciousness, and they tend to retreat (for a time) when such consciousness is forced aggressively upon them. Loredano is the only one among the senators who does not follow this rule. He is not shamed by his consciousness of the law's brutality, and—unlike his fellow council members—he does not try to suppress his understanding of realities beneath a hypocritical assertion of patriotic duties.

The principal image related to Loredano's tablets is that of the balance, which is used literally and figuratively throughout the play. At the beginning Barbarigo is disturbed by their increasing cruelty as judges. He is Loredano's chief partner in the plan to limit the power of the Foscari, but his conscience has begun to bother him. Not so Loredano, however, who is determined to pursue his 'hereditary hate' until his books are 'balanced' (I.i.18 and 54). Barbarigo is a just man, but his soul

has been long delivered up to his official duties. Loredano, on
the other hand, cares little for the state as such. He uses the
state for purely personal ends, in this case to revenge himself
on the man whom he believes to have murdered his father and
uncle. But just as double-entry accounting is Loredano's
direct inheritance, he also receives a patrimony of attitudes
and convictions that make him act the way he does. This is
what makes the idea of a balanced account so effective as
poetry: it is a hereditary idea, like his hate and his whole
mental procedure. Byron suggests that his belief about the
Doge's guilt is unfounded in fact, but he also indicates why
Loredano can scarcely help believing what he does. Loredano
understands the inhuman character of Venice's institutional
processes—this is precisely why he can manipulate them so
well to his purposes—so that its history of crimes wrought in
secrecy, and covered with a legal form, becomes for him the
sign of the Doge's guilt and the norm by which he must be
judged.

> *Loredano.* When the Doge declared that he
>   Should never deem himself sovereign till
>   The death of Peter Loredano, both
>   The brothers sickened shortly: he *is* sovereign.
> *Barbarigo.* A wretched one.
> *Loredano.*   What should they be who make
>   Orphans?
> *Barbarigo.*   But *did* the Doge make you so?
> *Loredano.*   Yes.
> *Barbarigo.* What solid proofs?
> *Loredano.*   When princes set themselves
>   To work in secret, proofs and process are
>   Alike made difficult. ...   (I.i.35–43)

Loredano knows that the very inhumanity of the legal
forms in Venice makes them wonderful instruments of
torture, and he acts accordingly. The Doge has been, like
Loredano, a power in the state and a manipulator of its laws so

that he perceives clearly what Loredano is doing and makes no outcry against him. Near the end of the play the Doge says that he is beyond both good and evil, and when Barbarigo offers a brief word of good will the Doge rebukes him: 'I spoke not to *you*, but to Loredano./ *He* understands me' (IV.i.238–39). Marina is passionate in her denunciation of Loredano's and Venice's brutal artifices, but the Doge tells her: 'Woman, this clamorous grief of thine, I tell thee,/ Is no more in the balance weighed with that/ Which—but I pity thee, my poor Marina!' (II.i.132–34). A gulf separates the standards of public and private life; understanding this, the Doge dutifully renders to Caesar the things that are Caesar's and tries as best he can to preserve the capacity for making purely human responses as well. Loredano preys upon his human feelings by exploiting this split in the Doge's character: he directs the torture of his son in a process over which the Doge is the presiding officer. The scheme is doubly effective just because the Doge strives so hard to maintain an impersonal demeanour and to fulfil the duties of his office to the letter. By serving the state the Doge is forced to destroy and feed upon his own children. Marina reiterates this theme a number of times in the play, in reference to the Doge and Venice at large. Barbarigo is the first to introduce it when, at the opening, he describes the Doge's strict adherence to his civic obligations in a gruesome metaphor: 'he,/ With more than Roman fortitude, is ever/ First at the board in this unhappy process' (I.i.24–26). But Barbarigo seems only half conscious of the brutal character of the tribunal, for he tells Jacopo Foscari that the law is merciful which permits a father to serve in the council of accusers (I.i.84–87). The balance image recurs as an ironic sign that Venice and most of her important citizens are imbalanced, and that they are incapable alike of remedying their condition or even clearly understanding its nature: 'To balance such a foe, if such there be,/ Thy father sits among thy judges' (I.i.81–82).

The crystal goblet is one of the focusing symbols for the

idea that Venice is destructively corrupt both in spite of and because of the forms of justice and honour which she outwardly maintains.

> *Doge.* 'T is said that our Venetian crystal has
>   Such pure antipathy to poisons as
>   To burst, if aught of venom touches it.
>   You bore this goblet, and it is not broken.
> *Loredano.* Well, sir!
> *Doge.*   Then it is false, or you are true.
>   For my own part, I credit neither; 't is
>   An idle legend.   (V.i.294–300)

The Doge's last remark is a brilliantly economical revelation of his complete understanding not only of the malice of Loredano, but of the sham purity of 'Venetian crystal'. Like the Doge Faliero, he goes willingly to his death, for he sees that Venice is no more able to protect herself against the destructive passions of a Loredano than Loredano is able, given his traditions and environment, to redeem himself.[3] Venice, with her secrecy and machine-government, has made Loredano what he is, and thus she is as much the fitting instrument of his purposes as her 'pure' crystal is of his death potion.

As in *Marino Faliero*, the state is here conceived as a productive agent, a parent who passes on to its children its own unnatural life. Jacopo cannot take his children into exile with him for, as Loredano says, 'they are the state's' (III.i.387). Marina answers scornfully that 'if/ They live, they'll make you soldiers, senators,/ Slaves, exiles—what *you* will.' The state is a self-perpetuating instrument of death, and Marina more than anyone else clarifies this for us. Just after Jacopo dies of his prolonged torture the Doge says to Marina, 'Your children live.' Her answer summarizes the truth that to serve Venice is to be her victim, as are all the people in the play to one degree or another. It is also one of the crucial speeches in the play's dramatic action, for these are the words which finally release the Doge's austerely controlled emotions and put him beyond both his office and his enemies (which are, in a sense, the same thing):

> My children! true—they live, and I must live
> To bring them up to serve the state, and die
> As died their father. Oh, what best of blessings
> Were barrenness in Venice!   (IV.i.208–11)

Immediately the Doge falls to embrace his dead son, and in doing so he finally chooses between his person as father and his rôle as governor. Up to this point he has struggled unsuccessfully to fulfil the claims of both. Now he is resolved. When the deputation from the assembly comes to request his abdication he refuses, not because he is attached to his office but because he will not violate himself in the interests of the state any longer—he will not break '*my* oath' (V.i.47; Byron's italics). Twice before he had asked to be relieved of his post in order to live the private life of a citizen. He was refused because the state needed him. Now the state deems his abdication necessary, but he refuses to serve its wishes.

The character of Jacopo Foscari is little short of disastrous, but his dungeon ruminations are an important event in the play. The dungeon itself is an effective dramatic symbol of the city as a whole. The prison is a place of continuous sorrow, despair, and death; as such, it is the true record of Venice's history, which is more 'like an epitaph' than anything else (III.i.20). It is also a place of darkness and deep silence, so that the chronicle of woe graven on the rough cell walls seems unlikely to be read by anyone but 'wretches' like Jacopo. But Jacopo insists that 'The tyranny of silence is not lasting.' 'Use and time' have taught him 'Familiarity with what was darkness' (III.i.79 and 60–61), and like his father he comes through suffering to understand (to quote out of context) that 'on the shores of darkness there is light'. The play's dark truths cannot be kept from men because, as the Doge says just before the prison scene, 'we are slaves,/ The greatest as the meanest' (II.i.57–58). The history of Venice is everywhere one of human grief and frustration, so that when Jacopo says 'such a chronicle as this/ Which ... only can be read, as writ, by wretches' (III.i.27–28), we are to understand that it is a truth for all those who would dare acquaint themselves with it.

Thus the prison cell suggests that the glorious and vital appearance which Venice outwardly maintains is really an illusion:

> these walls have been my study,
> More faithful pictures of Venetian story,
> With all their blank, or dismal stains, than is
> The Hall not far from hence, which bears on high
> Hundreds of doges, and their deeds and dates.
> (III.i.117–21)

The true story of Venice is learned in the dungeon chronicles where we see that men are alive and admirable only insofar as they try to become familiar with the darkness in themselves and struggle to oppose its progress. The Venice of apparent glory is both a lie and a misery, but the Venice of her dungeon is, if a misery, at least the truth. The Doge Foscari, like Marino Faliero, gives a trenchant speech on the innate sin and frailty of man. 'Mortals,' he says to Marina,

> who can read them
> Save he who made? or, if they can, the few
> And gifted spirits, who have studied long
> That loathsome volume—man, and pored upon
> Those black and bloody leaves, his heart and brain,
> But learn a magic which recoils upon
> The adept who pursues it. All the sins
> We find in others, nature made our own....
> All is low,
> And false, and hollow—clay from first to last,
> The prince's urn no less than potter's vessel.
> Our fame is in men's breath, our lives upon

Less than their breath; our durance upon days,
Our days on seasons; our whole being on
Something which is not *us*!—So, we are slaves,
The greatest as the meanest—nothing rests
Upon our will; the will itself no less
Depends upon a straw than on a storm;
And when we think we lead, we are most led....

(II.i.332 ff.)

Such an awareness does not in itself redeem man's fate, but it does represent a *sine qua non* for the visions of the earthly paradise expressed in *Sardanapalus*, *Beppo*, and especially *Don Juan*.[4] The active mind prevents 'man's worst—his second fall' and thus preserves man human in a world which is—morally speaking—both contingent and cyclically regenerative.[5] This idea of the second fall is Byron's version of the sin against the Holy Spirit. It is the denial of the obligation to selfconsciousness, the refusal to see, and represent, the light in the darkness. Besides being preservative, such knowledge ennobles, for it is not easily won. The deepest misery is also the deepest darkness, or that in which the Ten are involved as well as all those who enslave their minds to the 'mysterious' illusions of the state.

But unlike *Marino Faliero*, *The Two Foscari* does not primarily involve an apocalypse of its fundamental themes. A much more 'dramatic' work, the later play presents a related sequence of character studies, and its plot hinges upon the moral education of the Doge and Marina. The most obvious example of all this is the Doge, who vacillates for most of three acts between his human and his civic personalities. When he first appears in the play the strain of his office is beginning to wear upon him. He is preoccupied with his son, and fumbles even his most perfunctory civic duty (II.i). His exchanges in Acts II and III, particularly with Marina, illustrate with what difficulty he keeps his feelings under control while he witnesses, and meditates, the torture of his son. He keeps telling Marina to be calm, but his own emotional unrest is as manifest in its taut restraint as is Marina's in her passionate outbursts. He rebukes the compassion offered by the senator too forthrightly (II.i.25 ff.), and protests too strongly to Marina when she suggests he is to be pitied (II.i.145 ff.). In fact, when Loredano directs the torture of Jacopo he is aiming more at the father than at the son, as the Doge well knows. Thus Jacopo's vain attempt to maintain his composure under the Question reflects his father's attitude, and suggests that their agonies are as comparable as their determinations to resist. When Jacopo finally dies the Doge says, 'He's free' (IV.i.193), and the event signals the beginning of the Doge's freedom. Moved by Marina's bitter denunciation of Venice's child-murdering, he finally gives expression to his cruelly stretched emotions. At this point he too undergoes a death, and when he rises up from embracing the body of his son to answer the summons of the Ten, he, like Jacopo, is free. 'How fare you?' Marina asks Jacopo just before he dies, and his last word—'Well'—foreshadows the Doge's release. 'Sirs, I am ready,' he says to Loredano and Barbarigo, for 'nothing further/ Can touch me more than him thou look'st on there' (IV.i.228 and 234–25). Before this moment the 'stoic of the state' (as Marina scornfully calls him) manifests a control like that of Charles XII in 'Mazeppa', but afterward he shows the self-possession of a Mazeppa.

Loredano is a fine example of Byron's ability to invest a completely villainous character with life, and secure for him strong dramatic sympathy. Byron apotheosized the characters of Satan, Richard III, Iago and a host of other literary miscreants, not because he thought them good or evil, but because they were themselves in a grand way, because they had a passionate integrity. Loredano is of their number. Barbarigo has all the right sentiments but is Loredano's lackey nonetheless for, as Loredano sees clearly, he is never 'fix'd in purpose' (IV.i.49). Barbarigo represents whatever conscience the Venetian nobles still possess, but he also mirrors their moral irresolution. They live in a kind of hell and have, as Homer would say, 'strengthless heads'. Thus Loredano rules them like slaves. The Doge respects his conscious malice, Marina hates him for it, but both have only contempt for Barbarigo and the other councillors. Throughout the play Loredano directs a legal process for personal vengeance; unlike Barbarigo and the other nobles, he never rationalizes his cruelty with an appeal to patriotism (his patriotic arguments are always completely cynical), nor does he justify a sense of shame with a show of compassion. In fact, he has no need of shame for he does not serve the illusion of the state, but only himself. This is nicely brought out in the fifth act when the Chief of the Ten asks the Doge if he will abdicate according to the council's wishes. 'Your answer, Duke!' the Chief demands, and Loredano immediately demands in turn: 'Your answer, Francis Foscari!' (V.i.177). Loredano has scrupulously maintained the proper civic forms, including forms of address, throughout the play, but now he addresses him as a private citizen to dramatize his moment of triumph. Thus, when Barbarigo says to him,

> You are ingenious, Loredano, in
> Your modes of vengeance, nay, poetical,
> A very Ovid in the art of *hating*....   (V.i.134–36)

he summarizes the dramatic success of Loredano's passionate evil—to his own shame as well, for Loredano's perverted vitality is morally superior to Barbarigo's good, but ineffectual, intentions.

A superficial reading of the play might lead one to conclude that Barbarigo finally discards his sycophancy when he comes to understand the depth of Loredano's hatred. Through the first four acts he is completely Loredano's tool, but from the opening of the play he shows signs of a troubled conscience. These feelings grow with the play's development, but his will to act is not affected until the end of Act IV. Loredano then proposes to strip the Doge of his office, and Barbarigo 'protests'. 'Are you then thus fix'd?' he asks Loredano, and

when Loredano asks in turn, 'Why, what should change me?'
he answers: 'That which changes me' (IV.i.321–22). When the
council meets to decide the matter Barbarigo does indeed
fight against Loredano's proposal, and in the following scene
he again actively opposes Loredano's wishes (V.i.151 ff.), but
again in vain.

Barbarigo does at last free himself of the dominion of
Loredano, but only because he is terrified by the enormous
reality of the man's evil, by its 'poetical' character. He seeks
a safer place, one where his nakedness will not show so clearly,
and he finds it in the Ten. At the end he becomes what
the aspiring sycophant Memmo so longs to be: 'an unit/ Of
an united and imperial "Ten"' (I.i.194–95). This fact is well
dramatized in the great concluding scene of the play. Just
before his death the Doge tells the nobles that he will leave the
palace in the manner that he came. They are quite upset by
this, since his gesture will scandalize their actions before the
people. Unlike the Chief of the Ten, Loredano appears
unmoved, but he saves the council from public embarrassment
by poisoning the Doge. He does not intend to save them but
merely to settle his personal account, to balance his books.
When the Doge dies the Chief of the Ten and Barbarigo speak:

> *Chief of the Ten.* If it be so, at least his obsequies
>   Shall be such as befits his name and nation,
>   His rank and his devotion to the duties
>   Of the realm, while his age permitted him
>   To do himself and them full justice. Brethren,
>   Say, shall it not be so?
> *Barbarigo.*   He has not had
>   The misery to die a subject where
>   He reigned: then let his funeral rites be
>   princely.
> *Chief of the Ten.* We are agreed, then?   (V.i.310–18)

To the question, as Byron's stage direction puts it, '*All, except*

Lor., *answer,* Yes.' For all his evil Loredano remains, as always, completely superior to such moral rationalizations.

Marina is quick to expose the poverty of spirit in men who, like Barbarigo and the Chief of the Ten, need to cover their shame with such magnificent gestures.

> Signors, your pardon, this is mockery.
> Juggle no more with that poor remnant, which,
> A moment since ...
> You banished from his palace and tore down
> From his high place with such relentless coldness;
> And now, when he can neither know these honours,
> Nor would accept them if he could, you, signors,
> Purpose with idle and superfluous pomp
> To make a pageant over what you trampled.
> A princely funeral will be your reproach,
> And not his honour.   (V.i.320–32)

'Splendour in hypocrisy' Marina calls this elaborate funeral and the phrase is equally applicable to the men who conceive and agree to such hollow pageants.

In this last scene Marina achieves that complete nobility of person which she did not have before. She rails at Loredano and the Doge throughout the play, but her passion is—as the Doge says—excessive and useless. Marina knows something is radically wrong in Venice, but her grief for Jacopo, her pained bewilderment at the Doge, and her indignation at Loredano all obscure her understanding of herself and of the events around her. More, they obscure the obligation *to* understand which Byron places on all his characters.[6] Marina does not want to understand, however; she wants to save Jacopo (and, later, the Doge). This is why the Doge's speech on innate human frailty and fate in Act II is so important for her. It is an instruction in the futility of putting any dependence upon our hopes or designs, in the necessity of being *conscious* of this futility. At that time Marina replies to the Doge that 'I do not think of such things,/ So I be left with [Jacopo]' (II.i.375–76). When he dies Marina throws the Doge's wisdom back in his face in a fit of despair. 'Where is now/ The stoic of the state?' (IV.i.213–14) she cries at him. He accepts the rebuke as just, for not until Jacopo's death does he experience himself complete human emptiness. When he makes his stoic speech to Marina, for example, he is still confident that some hopes are sure, that Marina and Jacopo will, if exiled, at least have each other: 'Thus much they cannot well deny.' But events finally do take away all his surety on life and the truth of his own wisdom is proved upon himself. He stands the final test, but Marina continues to torment herself with her sense of injustice: 'Oh, for vengeance! ... Well, well; I have sons, who shall be men' (V.i.99 and 101–02).

When the Doge dies, however, Marina seems so struck by the enormity of this history, or perhaps by its radical absurdity, that she yields up her demand to force her will upon such an existence. The defect lies not in the malice of Loredano but in the ignorance of those who are his dupes, and of those who made Loredano what he is. Her consciousness of the need for consciousness makes her turn to Barbarigo and the other nobles to urge their awareness of what a self-reproach will be a splendid funeral for the Doge. They do not listen, of course, but neither does she berate them. She exposes the horror of their lives as clearly as she can, and for the rest: 'Well, sirs, your will be done! as one day,/ I trust, Heaven's will be done too!' (V.i.361–62). Heretofore Marina's passion has been no more than the expression of her sense of ineffectualness. She was 'distracted', but now her understanding becomes a concentrate and her personality self-possessed. The education in self-knowledge which Barbarigo misses at the end Marina gains. After she has made their hypocrisy plain to the councillors she is warned by the Chief of the Ten:

> Know ye, Lady,
> To whom ye speak, and perils of such speech?

Her reply:

I know the former better than yourselves;
The latter, like yourselves; and can face both.
Wish you more funerals?

and Barbarigo's:

> *Heed not her rash words;*
> Her circumstances must excuse her bearing.
>   (V.i.362–67; my italics)

are the exact measure of what she has won and what he has lost.

Readers of Byron have argued for a long time about his attempt to 'reform' the theatre. He called his plays a dramatic 'experiment' and he said that his models were the classics, the Greeks. He said the plays were not political, that the unities were his 'great object of research', and that 'they might as well act the Prometheus of Aeschylus' as try to put *Marino Faliero* on the stage.[7] But Byron never explained why the unities appealed to his aesthetic sense, or why he turned to the Greeks, or what specifically he expected a mental theatre to achieve. In fact, the whole question of Byron's intentions in this matter remains obscure, and—worse luck—suggestively obscure. We know what he did not like—melodrama and excessive sentiment; we know at least the direction that his likes took—towards the Greeks, Alfieri, and certain things in a few modern dramatists; but we do not know what his purposes were other than to get people to *think* while at the theatre.

Some people have simply thrown over the subject as another example of Byron's deliberate obscurantism. His respect for the 'older' dramatists is deemed merely another example of his sentimentality about the classics and the past, and his admiration for Alfieri's *Mirra* is regarded as no more than a psychological response to the incest theme (Byron said he wept at a performance of the play). Some of this may be true, but how much we will never know, any more than we will ever be able to resolve once for all Byron's thoughts on the entire affair. It is nonetheless clear, from all his harping on the matter and all the work he put into the plays, that he was quite serious about his efforts and had something (at any rate) in mind.

To understand Byron's purposes we might usefully draw a distinction between his theatrical and poetic ends. His work with the Drury Lane Theatre committee seems to have stimulated his desire to reform the stage, to produce a theatre that was free of the melodrama so prevalent in his own day (and often exemplified in his own work *Manfred*). Bring back the unities, bring back a less spasmodic dramatic spectacle; let passion be dramatized not by ever more extravagant displays but by the very restraint in its display. These are theatrical ends. Poetically, Byron sought—particularly in his Venetian plays—to write about the same kinds of themes that we find in his tales: the nature of a sick or doomed society, the dilemma of a man caught in such a milieu. The two purposes merge very nicely, however, for his Venetian plays are not concerned with the issue of events but with their meaning. The plays do not aim to arouse suspense about the outcome of a plot development, as melodrama so frequently does; on the contrary, they are intended to make the audience thoughtful and self-conscious, to force an understanding of the nature and causes of the fatality which the plays dramatize. *Marino Faliero* and *The Two Foscari* certainly have a parable-like quality to them, and it is not at all unlikely that Byron's term 'mental theatre' was meant to have a significance somewhat beyond its specialized meaning of simple 'closet drama'.[8]

NOTES

1. *The Works of Lord Byron: Letters and Journals*, ed. Rowland E. Prothero (London: John Murray, 1898–1901), V, 347, hereafter referred to as *LJ*.

2. Chew, *The Dramas of Lord Byron*, p. 99.

3. See Marina's speech on the corrupt atmosphere in Venice: III.i.366–82.

4. This point of view in Byron's poetry, especially the later work, has often been incidentally noted by scholars. Hirsch has done well to reiterate and focus the idea in a brief, generalized form. See his 'Byron and the Terrestrial Paradise', pp. 467–86. His essay confines itself almost exclusively to *Don Juan*.

5. The theme is typically Byronic. See *Childe Harold's Pilgrimage IV*, stanzas 93–98, 179–84, etc.

6. Again, a constant theme in Byron. Compare *Childe Harold's Pilgrimage IV*, stanza 127.

7. *LJ*, V, 67, 84, 229, 313.

8. The general Byronic theme of the need for self-consciousness tends to suggest this. Moreover, the term 'mental theatre' seems to be another of Byron's verbal equivocations intended to mean both 'drama of self-consciousness' and 'closet drama'. David V. Erdman ('Byron's Stage Fright', pp. 219–43) has shown quite conclusively that Byron did indeed have hopes that his plays might be successfully performed, and that his many disclaimers were intended to absolve him from blame if his plays should have failed on the stage.

'Suppressed Passion': *The Two Foscari*

PETER J. MANNING

The line by Sheridan that Byron selected for the epigraph to *The Two Foscari* encapsulates its themes: 'The *father* softens, but the *governor's* resolved.' At the centre of the drama is the trial of Jacopo Foscari for alleged treason against Venice, over which his father the Doge is required to preside. The situation contains the already familiar elements: a father who figures as the oppressor of his son, and, as in *Marino Faliero* and *Sardanapalus*, a conflict between obligation to the state and private freedom. The outward circumstances of the play might thus be loosely termed political, but it is striking that Byron imparts little of the information needed to assess the charges and countercharges of the plot. Jacopo is pursued until he dies by Loredano, who thereafter relentlessly forces the resignation of the Doge, knowing it will kill him, because he believes the elder Foscari poisoned both his father and uncle. However, neither Jacopo's guilt nor Loredano's accusation is ever fully clarified, and to a point the inscrutability pays dividends. In the first speeches Byron refers to the torture inflicted upon Jacopo as 'the Question', and the recurrent phrase is a sign of the interrogative role the reader must adopt. Because the secondary characters do not wholly comprehend the events before them the drama evolves as much in their uncertain responses as in the clash of the principals, and their attempt to puzzle out the action is the prototype for the reader's. Yet in the end the drama is weakened by the doubts that Byron permits to surround the basic facts of the story, and his want of concern with them alerts the reader that his interests lie elsewhere than in the feud between Loredano and the Foscari.

'I have been so beyond the common lot/ Chastened and visited', Jacopo says sadly in Act IV, 'I needs must think/ That I was wicked' (IV.i.166–68). All Byron's heroes are haunted by this sense of a guilt anterior to any action which drives them towards self-punishment, and here the note of bewildered innocence is not unwarranted: Jacopo is a victim of the hate aroused by his father, and it is thus appropriate that the Doge appear as his persecutor. The Doge seems dimly to realize that Jacopo is his scapegoat; he tells Jacopo's wife Marina that 'they who aim/ At Foscari, aim no less at his father' (II.i.86–87). By his action he in effect consents to the substitution, and when Marina reproaches him for complicity and he replies by arrogating the words of Christ on the cross the bitter variation of Christian symbolism becomes explicit: 'I forgive this, for/ You know not what you say' (II.i.125–26). 'You have seen your son's blood flow, and your flesh shook not,' she exclaims in horror (II.i.129), but the Doge feels only that Jacopo is a 'disgrace' to their house and it is left to her to insist that the Venetians should 'implore/ His grace' for their cruelty (II.i.171–72). Byron counterpoints the suggestion that the dedication of the Doge to Venice is a secular analogue of the Gospel declaration that God so loved the world that he gave his only begotten son to redeem it with a characteristic allusion to *patria potestas* hinting at an adversary position devoid of charity: Barbarigo describes the Doge 'With more than Roman fortitude ... ever/ First at the board in this unhappy process/ Against his last and only son' (I.ii.24–26). An Old Testament parallel conveys the Doge's attitude more accurately than the New; it is clear that he has cast himself as the martyr of the piece in the image of Abraham commanded to slay Isaac:

I have observed with veneration, like
A priest's for the High Altar, even unto
The sacrifice of my own blood and quiet,
Safety, and all save honour, the decrees,
The health, the pride, and welfare of the State.

(II.i.255–59)

I do not know precisely how much weight Byron meant us
to give to echoes like these, but their frequency (like his life-
long fascination with, and opposition to, the intricacies of
Christian dogma) testifies to the appeal made to his imagination by episodes of a son slaughtered by a father.

The dimensions of the family conflict in *The Two Foscari*
extend to every area of the plot. Jacopo is in prison because he
is unable to exist apart from Venice; already in exile for a
previous offence, he opened a treasonous correspondence in
order to be discovered and recalled. He knows that he will not
survive his return but he is compelled to it by the irresistible
impulse that his welcome to death reveals: 'my native earth/
Will take me as a mother to her arms' (I.i.142–43). Jacopo
exclaims that the brief glimpse of the city he is allowed while
out of his cell makes him feel 'like a boy again' (I.i.93), for to
him it represents the innocent peace of childhood. His happy
memories of swimming in the ocean and racing gondolas
along its surface further illustrate the nature of his desire
to regress to a fostering maternal environment. 'I was a boy
then,' he concludes wistfully, and the reply of the guard seals
the impossibility of ever recapturing that lost bliss: 'Be a man
now: there never was more need/ Of manhood's strength'
(I.i.122–23).

The Doge calls his son's compulsion 'womanish', and it
is indeed produced by identification with the mother, but
he too transfers to the city the emotional force usually
inspired by women. In this context, as in *Marino Faliero*, the
feminine gender customarily employed in referring to Venice
acquires special significance. The common usage resonates

disconcertingly when at his first appearance the Doge recounts his service to Venice while the city destroys his son:

> I found her Queen of Ocean, and I leave her
> Lady of Lombardy; it is a comfort
> That I have added to her diadem
> The gems of Brescia and Ravenna; Crema
> And Bergamo no less are hers; her realm
> By land has grown by thus much in my reign,
> While her sea-sway has not shrunk.   (II.i.17–23)

The language confirms that Venice stands at the apex of an oedipal triangle in which the brand of traitor enforces Jacopo's position as the defeated son and the Doge's eminence magnifies his status as the triumphant father and husband. His rationale for rejecting Marina's plea that he intervene in Jacopo's behalf exposes his complete identification with paternal authority:

> *Doge.* I found the law; I did not make it. Were I
>   A subject, still I might find parts and portions
>   Fit for amendment; but as Prince, I never
>   Would change, for the sake of my house, the
>   charter
>   Left by our fathers.
> *Marina.*   Did they make it for
>   The ruin of their children?
> *Doge.*   Under such laws, Venice
>   Has risen to what she is—a state to rival
>   In deeds, and days, and sway, and, let me add,
>   In glory (for we have had Roman spirits
>   Amongst us), all that history has bequeathed
>   Of Rome and Carthage in their best times,
>   when
>   The people swayed by Senates.
> *Marina.*   Rather say,
>   Groaned under the stern Oligarchs.

Doge.   Perhaps so:
   But yet subdued the World: in such a state
   An individual, be he richest of
   Such rank as is permitted, or the meanest,
   Without a name, is alike nothing, when
   The policy, irrevocably tending
   To one great end, must be maintained in
     vigour.
Marina. This means that you are more a Doge than
    father.   (II.i.395–413)

The deadly juggernaut the Doge makes of the state is a reflection of the ruthless self-control he practises upon himself, for
he loves his son but will not be seen to unbend. 'I cannot
weep,' he tells Marina, 'I would I could' (II.i.78), and the
hypersensitivity that perceives sympathy as condescension
explodes when she attempts to commiserate: 'Pitied! None/
Shall ever use that base word, with which men/ Cloak their
soul's hoarded triumph, as a fit one/ To mingle with my name'
(II.i.146–49). The first consequence of such repression is as
always the sense of a hostile, determinist universe; 'So, we are
slaves,/ The greatest as the meanest—nothing rests/ Upon
our will,' the Doge laments of his self-created hell (II.i.357–
59). Jacopo's death is the counterpart (and in some measure
the result of) his own stifled tenderness. 'And this is
Patriotism?' Marina asks unbelievingly; 'To me it seems the
worst barbarity' (II.i.427–28). She likewise denounces her
husband's attachment to Venice as 'Passion, and not
Patriotism' (III.i.143), and through her it is realized that the
fanatic loyalty to Venice that links the otherwise unlike father
and son is the mark of a crisis of which the harshness of the
one and the softness of the other are the twin faces.

   Marina is a second, sexual focus of the disguised situation
expressed in *The Two Foscari*, and she occupies a position
congruent to that of Venice in the complex of feelings represented by the two men. On the surface she and the city are

polar opposites: whereas Venice is the exalted lady of the Doge and the devouring mother of Jacopo, Marina is the loyal wife of the latter and the courageous antagonist of the former. This symmetry, however, discloses a deeper similarity. Jacopo's weakened condition makes him so dependent on Marina for support, forensic and physical, that she becomes to him the nursing protectress that she is to their children, a portrait of the ideal aspects of the fantasized mother figure even as Venice is of the negative. Yet since the structure of the drama places as much emphasis on the intimacy between Marina and the Doge as on the marriage relationship, Jacopo seems to the reader to be in competition with his father for her attention. The advantage he enjoys in our minds by actually being her husband is offset when his early death leaves Marina and the Doge alone together. In the end the Doge too is reduced to dependence on Marina by his grief-stricken collapse and removal from office, and in the configuration of the elderly widower watched over by his son's wife the motif of the redemptive daughter observed throughout Byron as a primary manifestation of his central ambivalence towards women recurs. Indeed, Marina's strength has sinister implications. Marina is proud not to have 'left barren the great house of Foscari', but the reader knows too well the connotations of such sternness not to be taken aback when she declares that she refused to cry out in the pain of childbirth 'for my hope was to bring forth/ Heroes, and would not welcome them with tears' (I.i.240–47). The corollary of her maternal fierceness is the terrifying capacity for passion that from Gulnare through Myrrha and Semiramis Byron distrustfully ascribes to his female protagonists. If Marina is the exponent of charity pleading against the savage world of men her instincts also make her a destructive force within that world: 'I have some sons, sir,/ Will one day thank you better,' she warns Loredano (III.i.269–70). The anticipation of revenge entails upon future generations the misery that afflicts the Doge and Jacopo, and

hints that Marina is a mother who, like Venice, may consume
the life of her children.

Byron's characterization of Loredano is the perfect complement to the internal dynamics of the Foscari family. The
cynical contempt for legitimacy he displays in answering
Barbarigo's objections to the planned deposition of the Doge
calls into doubt the elder Foscari's sacramental vision of the
immutable institutions of Venice:

> *Barbarigo.* What if he will not?
> *Loredano.*   We'll elect another,
>   And make him null.
> *Barbarigo.*   But will the laws uphold us?
> *Loredano.* What laws?—'The Ten' are laws; and if
>   they were not,
>   I will be legislator in this business. (IV.i.36–39)

The Doge's exaltation of the state is cast in a still more
ambiguous light when even after this flagrant admission
Loredano rebuts Barbarigo's argument that the Doge has
already suffered enough in the death of his son by turning
against him exactly the principle the Doge invoked in refusing
to aid Jacopo, sanctimoniously proclaiming that 'The feelings
of private passion may not interrupt/ The public benefit'
(IV.i.265–67). The immediate effect of this hypocrisy is
undoubtedly to confirm Loredano's wickedness, but with it
Byron also reminds the reader that the forms of the state can
be manipulated to mask personal ends; the play is less
concerned with apportioning individual guilt than with adum-
brating the common motivation of the enemies. Like the
Doge, Loredano is obsessed with the need to fulfil the imagined expectations of paternal authority; he is driven to retribution by the 'hereditary hate' he carries engraved on his tablets,
an apt emblem of his psychological fixity. He is a scourge to
the Foscari only because he must prove that he is a good son
to his own forebears, and his thirst for vengeance will be the
inheritance of Marina's children in the next cycle, when the

rôles of persecutor and victim will appear reversed. The inter-
generational continuity of the strife is further evidence for
apprehending the warfare between the families as a displaced
image of the tensions within the family; it should be observed
that in overthrowing the Doge Loredano acts out the resentments against the father that Byron excludes from the portrait
of the weakly submissive Jacopo, who is so thoroughly an
overshadowed son that he never becomes a man. Just as
Jacopo's fate is an instance of the child's worst fears for
himself, Loredano's triumph and curious escape from punishment are perhaps to be explained as an image of his wishes.

As the play proceeds it becomes increasingly obvious that
the notion of an autonomous state with a will of its own is a
convenient fiction men elaborate to conceal their culpable
aspirations and impulses. A conversation between Memmo
and an unnamed senator invited to lend by their neutral presence an air of disinterestedness to the cabal against the Doge
displays the temptation of power clothed in the specious
respectability of 'duty':

> *Memmo.*   As we hope, Signor,
> And all may honestly, (that is, all those
> Of noble blood may,) one day hope to be
> Decemvir, it is surely for the Senate's
> Chosen delegates a school of wisdom, to
> Be thus admitted, though as novices,
> To view the mysteries.
> *Senator.*   Let us view them: they,
> No doubt, are worth it.
> *Memmo.*   Being worth our lives
> If we divulge them, doubtless they are worth
> Something, at least to you or me.
> *Senator.*   I sought not
> A place within the sanctuary; but being
> Chosen, however reluctantly so chosen,
> I shall fulfil my office.

Memmo.   Let us not
    Be latest in obeying 'The Ten's' summons.
Senator. All are not met, but I am of your thought
    So far—let's in.
Memmo.   The earliest are most welcome
    In earnest councils—we will not be least so.
                                              (IV.i.82–98)

Byron deftly imitates the interior duplicity by which the
moral sense is laid asleep and equivocation changes into
enthusiasm. His demonstration of the pervasive allure of the
state as a pliable sanction for individual aggressiveness makes a
comment the passage of time renders still more significant
than it was in the 1820s. Because of their stunted inner lives
the heroes of most of Byron's tales must derive their sense of
themselves from the outside; they exist only so long as they
are in motion, conducting war and wreaking revenge. Faliero
extends this syndrome, and it is because his image of himself
requires continuous public confirmation that he cannot accept
the distinction Angiolina draws between honour and reputation. The Doge bewails the diminished opportunity to base a
public identity on valorous exploits, but as his translation of
Steno's insult into an affront to Venice reveals, he compen-
satorily aggrandizes himself by identifying with the state, an
expedient Byron had presciently intuited the conditions of
modern life would favour. It may thus be understood how the
rebel Faliero foreruns his apparent opposite, Foscari, who
defines—and enhances—himself by his exaggerated devotion
to Venice. The gambit fails both men, however: Faliero is frustrated by the state's anonymity and finally bows to the weight
of established authority, and Foscari's prestige, as Memmo
remarks in the first scene of *The Two Foscari*, is that of 'a
gilded cipher' (I.i.196). He is defeated by the artful Loredano,
whose chicanery shows that in the mass state the grand Titans
are superseded by the cunning exploiters of form and ritual.
    The supposed omnipotence men idolize in the state in

order to satisfy their own needs levies with growing severity the penalty of psychological evasion as *The Two Foscari* advances. Jacopo is sentenced to fresh exile, and Marina tries in vain to reconcile him to the decree the country he loves passes against him. 'Obey her,' she urges, "tis she that puts thee forth,' but he replies despondently, 'Ay, there it is; 'tis like a mother's curse upon my soul ...' (III.i.185–87). Marina is permitted to accompany him, but the sentence includes the proviso that their sons must remain behind:

> *Jacopo.* And must I leave them—*all*?
> *Loredano.* You must.
> *Jacopo.* Not one?
> *Loredano.* They are the State's.
> *Marina.* I thought they had been mine.
> (III.i.386–88)

The restriction is horridly apposite, for it recapitulates Jacopo's self-destructive exaltation of Venice; in the fate of his children the negative aspects of the mother figure represented by the city win out over Marina, their complement and double. Divorced thus from his maternal native land, forced to abandon his father and sons, weakened from the torture that is the embodiment of these spiritual sufferings, Jacopo dies. The Doge throws himself prostrate on the body in sincere grief, but Marina's sharp remark enables the reader to see beyond the pathos of the situation and comprehend the Doge's responsibility for the anguish he suffers:

> Aye, weep on!
> I thought you had no tears—you hoarded them
> Until they are useless; but weep on! he never
> Shall weep more—never, never more.   (IV.i.214–17)

The half-buried echo of Lear's words over the body of the daughter his folly has destroyed points up the Doge's collaboration in the circumstances of which outwardly he is only the victim; the source of his misery is the sternness he cherishes in himself and its reflection, the state.

The last act fully discloses the pernicious hollowness of the ideal to which the Doge has given himself. The Ten force him to abdicate, and the common usage he employs as he resigns the ducal ring and bonnet returns the reader to the fundamental level of the drama: 'The Adriatic's free to wed another' (V.i.192). An otherwise gratuitous conversation with Memmo renders the oedipal content still more explicit:

> *Doge.* Methinks I see amongst you
>   A face I know not.—Senator! your name,
>   You, by your garb, Chief of the Forty!
> *Memmo.*   Signor,
>   I am the son of Marco Memmo.
> *Doge.*   Ah!
>   Your father was my friend.—But *sons* and
>   *fathers*!   (V.i.195–99)

His tormentors hypocritically insist that the Doge leave the palace with an honorary escort, but in a final terrible irony he dies when he hears the bell announcing his successor. Having repressed the areas of the self that lay outside his office, the Doge no longer has any existence apart from it. The Ten decree magnificent obsequies, and though Marina rightly protests that the elaborate courtesy mocks them, the irony cuts in the other direction as well: it is in the name of such insubstantial grandeur that the Doge sacrificed his family and, at last, himself.

'What I seek to show in *The Foscaris*,' Byron told Murray, 'is the *suppressed* passion ...' (*LJ*, V, 372). The multiple repressions of the drama offer the most complete illustration of the conflict that dominates Byron's imagination: through them may be seen from all angles the resentful, helpless son and the rigid posture he adopts in defence, together with the awesome mother whom he alternately desires and fears.

'My Hope Was to Bring Forth Heroes': *The Two Foscari* and the Fostering of Masculine *Virtù* by [a] Stoical Heroine

CAROLINE FRANKLIN

Thought of the state of women under the ancient Greeks—convenient enough. Present state a remnant of the barbarism of the chivalry [chivalric?] and feudal ages—artificial and unnatural. They ought to mind home and be well fed and clothed— but not mixed in society. Well educated too, in religion, but to read neither poetry or politics—nothing but books of piety and cookery. Music—drawing— dancing—also a little gardening and ploughing now and then. I have seen them mending the roads in Epirus with good success. Why not, as well as hay-making and milking?

(Byron's Journal of 6 January 1821)

While the burlesque world of *Don Juan* is one of monarchical tyranny and female domination, that of the political plays set in Venice is its obverse: an androcentric republic. In both the mock epic and the political plays the poet's concern is with the question of re-establishing republican masculinity. According to Enlightenment political thinkers such as Montesquieu and Rousseau, the classical republics had been successful in ensuring the disinterested patriotic service of the (male) citizen, because private interests were rigorously separated from the public arena. This had been achieved by rigid sexual rôle differentiation, and the low status of women, as Byron sardonically observed in his Journal. Writing from the perspective of the failure of the French Revolution, but in the years which saw revolutionary conspiracies in both England and Italy, he now questioned the neoclassical ideology of a gendered nation-state which underpinned his own republicanism.

Marino Faliero and *The Two Foscari* were among a group of political plays which appeared at this period, set in classical or medieval Italy. [...] In both *Marino Faliero* and *The Two Foscari*, Byron's heroes exemplify that notion of self-controlled manliness which emanated from an eighteenth-century interpretation of the classical tradition of stoicism. This ideology was a feature of the period's neoclassicism particularly adopted by male Jacobins, who often self-consciously compared themselves to heroes like Brutus and Cato of Utica.[1] Like the actual French revolutionaries, Faliero compares his allies to Brutus and Cassius (V.vi.178), and the plot to the Catiline conspiracy (I.ii.596–97). The masculine ideal was self-command and even sacrifice of personal senti-ment, in order to take authoritative political action. This reflected the contemporary cult of the individual. The virtue —or more properly *virtù*—of a great man guaranteed that public life was free from the corruption of the feminine (the personal and subjective).

In both the Venetian plays, therefore, the sexual temptation of women must be repressed—Faliero's marriage is platonic. Moreover, as female chastity is the measure of masculine authority, then the female equivalent of *virtù* is a narrowly sexual definition of virtue. Marino Faliero's actions are designed to demonstrate the interrelatedness of masculine *virtù* and feminine virtue in the gendered republic. In *The Two Foscari*, the theme is extended: here the patriarch must repress the 'feminine' familial values of sentiment and nurture for the good of the state. But this seemingly ideal Rousseauistic relationship between the sexes is interrogated in both plays.

For neither Faliero nor Foscari is a vigorous or effective statesman, creating or maintaining an ideal republic. Both are helpless octogenarian puppets of a corrupt oligarchy. The republican ideal fostered by the liberal aristocrat's idealization of the classical *polis* has ossified in both Venice and, by implication, Britain. Moreover, it is questionable whether rigorous separation of the private emotions from the public sphere, by sexual rôle differentiation, can foster a revival of true republican masculine heroism. Does this ideology of two separate gendered spheres merely facilitate the perpetuation of patriarchal power, creating an oligarchic gerontocracy impervious to humanitarian concerns?

In *The Two Foscari* [as in *Marino Faliero*] Byron continues to give the heroine a lofty character. Again she speaks for the individual's subjectivity of conscience, arguing in turn with the men who preference civic duty. But Marina is integrated with the action of the second Venetian play in a way that Angiolina was not. Instead of keeping gracefully aloof from male public affairs she intrudes and interrupts. She opposes Loredano, who manipulates Venice's laws for his own purposes; she confronts the Doge, whose mission to guard those laws outweighs humanitarian considerations. She disputes with her husband Jacopo, whose loyalty to the place is stronger than love of life itself. Marina's volubility was harshly criticized by contemporary critics, whether Whig or Tory, as offending against femininity. Jeffrey commented on the venom of her tongue and her vehemence in the *Edinburgh Review*; T. N. Talfourd in the *London Magazine* described her as 'vociferous'; the reviewer of the *Monthly Review* called her 'something of a scold', as did Bishop Heber in the *Quarterly Review*. Perhaps it is significant that the *Lady's Magazine*, on behalf of its female readership, was almost alone in singling out for praise 'The noble spirit ... and the conjugal affection and fidelity of Marina'.[2]

Instead of keeping silent until asked to speak, Marina

argues and contradicts. Because of her intrusion into state business, and the constant repudiation of her values by the male leaders of society, she thrusts into view the discrepancy between the theoretical reverencing of women by the chivalrous aristocracy and the reality of contempt for female powerlessness.

The heroine's brave quest to save her husband illustrated the powerlessness of woman, deemed necessarily a private individual, in combating the mechanisms of state power. Like Mary Wollstonecraft, Byron is challenging Rousseau's assertion that the objectivity of republican government can only be maintained by the rigorous separation of reason and sentiment through a policy of rigid differentiation of sexual rôles. Wollstonecraft, in *A Vindication*, concentrates on her assertion that women are by nature as rational as men. Byron's Marina, Angiolina and Myrrha also illustrate this premise. But as a Romantic poet, rather than a proponent of Enlightenment rationalism, Byron strives to demonstrate the indivisibility of reason and passion in both men and women. *The Two Foscari* is an important examination of the artificiality of Rousseau's characterization of republicanism as necessitating stoic suppression of subjectivity by limiting it to the 'feminine' sphere.

Again Byron uses the vulnerable figures of the venerable patriarch of the republic and his virtuous daughter (in law) to illustrate his fear of the inability of liberal ideals to be transmitted to future ages:

> And the deep agony of his pale wife,
> And the repress'd convulsion of the high
> And princely brow of his old father, ...
> ... these moved you not?
>
> (I.i.355–60)

Once more the obscuring of motives and the silencing of words makes the climax of the tragedy not death itself (as this Doge is also over eighty), but lack of communication of the meaning of political events to the people. The subjugation and murder of Foscari after his refusal to submit any further to the oligarchy is obscured by a screen of secrecy and the hypocrisy of a state funeral. Though she is the most vocal and eloquent character in the play, Marina is also the most obviously disregarded. (Her lack of importance is evidenced by the fact that she is allowed to survive.) Marina embodies the tragedy of individual subjectivity: the inability of the powerless either to effect reform even of the grossest tyranny, or to make their words heard in the world at large. A closer examination of the play will show that Marina's words are the privileged discourse of the play, reflecting the frustration of the Romantic poet at the marginalization of his own expression of individual subjectivity, which is considered as effeminately irrelevant to the male world of public affairs.

When Marina enters, her husband has been taken into the secret torture chamber of the state for the third time. In answer to a senator's chivalrous greeting in bidding her command him her wishes, she retorts bitterly—repudiating the hypocritical pretence of female power enshrined in such courtesy: '*I command!*—Alas! my life/ Has been one long entreaty, and a vain one' (I.i.200–01).

When he understands that her wishes involve state business (her husband's interrogation), however, he refuses to answer her. When she retorts that the only permitted form of questioning and answering in Venice is performed with the connivance of the rack, he cuts short her words with a reproof that she is out of her correct domain, both literally and figuratively, and thus has no right to speak: 'High-born dame! bethink thee/ Where thou art' (I.i.204–05).

Marina replies that she is in her 'husband's father's palace', her home and thus her rightful feminine domain. But Memmo corrects her: '*The Duke's* palace'. His emphasis stresses that public roles have precedence over private. To illustrate the extent to which all subjective feeling has been suppressed or relegated to the separated and powerless 'feminine' sphere of

mere private life the groans are now heard which signify the
Doge's supervision of the torture of his own son, who is
accused of treason. We could compare the tableau enacted in
this play with that of Jacques-Louis David's neoclassical
painting *The Lictors bringing Brutus the Bodies of his Sons*
(1789), [where] the masculine republican stoic ability to
divorce public from private is celebrated in the polar opposition of the sexes after Brutus' condemnation of his own sons
to death for conspiring against the republic. The division of
the composition into heroic male citizens on the left and
mourning women on the right is emphasized by the classical
column separating stoicism and sentimentalism. Yet, as
Ronald Paulson comments, 'The power of the picture lies in
its being on a secondary level a psychomachia, an image of
divided loyalties ... deriving from the mixed emotions of the
father himself.'[3]

In Byron's play, as the epigraph indicates, the patriarch is
not permitted paternal feelings. Marina, as a woman, is sanctioned to express the emotions which have to be suppressed
by the ethos of masculine republican stoicism. But she will not
retire to weep in the appropriate manner, and hopes her
husband will deny the Council of Ten the satisfaction of
hearing him cry out under torture, so that a senator questions
the extent of her (permitted) feminine 'feeling'. But, refusing
to have her responses stereotyped, Marina retorts that she is
measuring the extent of Jacopo's heroism by the standards of
her own stoic bravery in childbirth:

> We must all bear our tortures. I have not
> Left barren the great house of Foscari,
> Though they sweep both the Doge and son from
>   life;
> I have endured as much in giving life
> To those who will succeed them, as they can
> In leaving it....   (I.i.239–44)

She again repudiates the passivity of the feminine rôle when the senator, under the guise of gallantry, tries to usher her away from this place, the inner sanctum of government, as it is presumed that the news that Jacopo has been rendered unconscious will overpower her feminine sensibilities. Brusquely she shrugs him away: 'Off! *I* will tend him' (I.i.253).

Though the rôle she claims is the traditionally female one of nurse and comforter, Marina eschews feminine delicacy and modest demeanour, arguing with the senators and rudely barging her way into the 'great arcanum' where not even the senators themselves are allowed:

> They shall not balk my entrance ...
> Who shall oppose me? ...
> ... Yet I'll pass.
> ... there is
> That in my heart would make its way through hosts
> With levell'd spears; and think you a few jailors
> Shall put me from my path? Give me, then, way....
> (I.i.257–70)

Patronizingly the senators let her pass, confident of her impotence: she will not be admitted, and if she were she would be ignored (I.i.276–79).

In fact the council breaks up in disarray when Marina bursts in. She does not have to speak. Just the presence of a woman is an uncomfortable reminder of their repressed subjective feelings, to the officers of the law:

> ... 'Twas a dreadful sight
> When his distracted wife broke through into
> The hall of our tribunal, and beheld
> What we could scarcely look upon, long used
> To such sights. (I.i.364–68)

Loredano is incredulous that the appearance of a mere woman could have such an effect:

And so the Council must break up, and Justice
Pause in her full career, because a woman
Breaks in on our deliberations?   (I.i.314–16)

His business is only with the male members of her family:
father-in-law, husband and sons. Jacopo must confess because
his reputation must be besmirched. His capacity for transmit-
ting his power or beliefs to a future generation must be
eradicated; his children must be disinherited or destroyed.
Marina is an irrelevance because she has no such power. As she
herself acknowledges, her only form of transcendence is
through physical generation: '... my hope was to bring forth/
Heroes ...' (I.i.246–47).

Act II opens with an image of the state's bureaucracy: the
Doge is signing papers. The peace treaty rewrites the republic
as an empire. The history of Venice will be passed on in such
official records. But there is a discrepancy, dramatized in the
play, between the spontaneous words of its citizens and its
public written documents. Their composure temporarily shat-
tered by the sight of Marina's grief, the Ten had granted her
permission to visit her husband in prison. But she finds their
spoken words, generated by feeling, are powerless to grant her
admittance to the Bridge of Sighs unless confirmed in writing
(II.i.51–62). Catch 22 is that they only reconvene when they
resume Jacopo's torture, which he is not expected to survive.

The Doge's acquiescence in this processing of words by
eliminating the 'feminine' subjective, and by excluding her
personal relationship with Jacopo ('the holiest tie beneath the
Heavens', II.i.68) from consideration, leads to an outburst of
Marina's anger against her father-in-law. She repudiates his
patriarchal role: 'Call *me* not "child!"/ You soon will have no
children—you deserve none' (II.i.70–71). When her husband
dies, she will again refuse the appellation 'daughter' from
him, contemptuously rejecting his comfort: 'Hold thy peace,
old man!/ I am no daughter now—thou hast no son'
(IV.i.195–96). Now, when he tells her that the Ten still refuse

her request to accompany Jacopo in his exile, she—a fertile young mother—execrates them as a gerontocracy:

> ... The old human fiends,
> With one foot in the grave, with dim eyes, strange
> To tears save drops of dotage, with long white
> And scanty hairs, and shaking hands, and heads
> As palsied as their hearts are hard, they counsel,
> Cabal, and put men's lives out, as if life
> Were no more than the feelings long extinguish'd
> In their accursed bosoms.   (II.i.108–15)

This hatred and resentment at the rule of old men, which finds expression in seventeenth-century drama like *Venice Preserv'd*, and even more forcibly in the *Sturm und Drang* plays of Schiller and Goethe, expresses impatience with the constraining strait-jacket of authority. As the first Christian republic, Venice could be perceived in two ways: either as a model of constitutional government reverenced throughout the world, perfectly balancing the claims of the aristocracy and the people; or as a former ideal, now corrupted into an oligarchy, and in the process of becoming an imperial power. For Venice, read Britain. Byron's selection of Faliero and Foscari—the only notable representatives of dissent in the history of the republic—indicate the poet's preoccupation with the decline of the ideal. As venerable patriarchs, they symbolize the precious heritage of republicanism; yet the image of an old man superintending the mangling of his son to the point of death is also one of stultified tradition blighting the future (even more than the January and May marriage dramatized in *Marino Faliero*). Unlike the vigorous and statesmanlike Brutus of David's painting, who has saved the republic by his heroic action, the frail and feeble octogenarian, Foscari, has merely been the unwitting tool of Loredano's dynastic rivalry.

It is the republican matron, representing the future fertility

of the state, who articulates the protest against the rule of old
men. As a woman, Marina speaks on behalf of natural feeling:

> ... could it be else that
> Men, who have been of women born and suckled—
> Who have loved, or talk'd at least of Love—have
> given
> Their hands in sacred vows—have danced their
> babes
> Upon their knees, perhaps have mourn'd above
> them—
> In pain, in peril, or in death—who are,
> Or were at least in seeming, human, could
> Do as they have done by yours, and you yourself—
> *You*, who abet them?   (II.i.117–25)

Note the separation of 'men' from the 'human' in her syntax.
The pledges of marriage, the events of the life-process are
designated effeminate and excluded from importance in the
making of history. But by repudiating them, men become less
'human', and women are marginalized. Marina demands in
frustration: 'What are a woman's words?' (II.i.130).

The substitution of the claims of the state for personal
commitment is achieved by the displacing of women from
public life, and the corresponding imaging of *Venice* as a
woman. Venice is personified as a haughty courtly queen
shrouded in feminine mystique: '... she knows not herself,/ In
all her mystery' (II.i.85–86). The dogeship is a marriage
service; Foscari wears the wedding ring, a sign of his overriding commitment until he is forced to relinquish it in Act V:

> ... every hour has been the country's.
> I am ready to lay down my life for her,
> As I have laid down dearer things than life....
>   (V.i.52–54)

The sons of Venice likewise express their patriotic feeling in
terms of mother love. Jacopo feels like Cain cursed by Eve

when exiled: "'tis like a mother's curse/ Upon my soul—the mark is set upon me' (III.i.186–87). Like his father he prizes Venice above life and his real family.

When disputing the superior claims of her rival, Venice, on her menfolk, Marina refuses to be reprimanded for her unpatriotic thoughts (II.i.276–77). She accuses *Venice* of being dishonoured (II.i.163–64) and a traitress (II.i.386–87). Whereas the Doge would give willingly all his sons for the state's service, Marina cries out for individual feeling: 'Accursed be the city where the laws/ Would stifle nature's!' (II.i.418–19). *The Two Foscari* is an important examination of patriarchy as a fundamental principle of government. The distortion of natural relationships it produces in the Foscari family mirrors the stranglehold with which the male oligarchy subjugates all other members of the body politic of Venice.

When Loredano brings the news that the Ten, after another session of torture unproductive of a confession, have decreed Jacopo's banishment, Marina enquires if permission has been granted for her to accompany him, but Loredano is non-committal. The Doge attempts to stem her bitter attack on the villain by advocating the feminine posture of silence and passivity. This leads Marina to make Loredano define her own status: 'well, then, you're a prince,/ A princely noble; and what then am I?' (II.i.292–93). The answer, framed both by Loredano and Marina herself is: 'The offspring of a noble house ... And wedded/ To one as noble' (II.i.294–95). Her class is defined only in terms of her relationships with men. As a noblewoman, she has outward status but no immanent power. She is therefore in a perfect position to criticize the tyranny of the oligarchy disinterestedly but from the inside. Since the torture chamber has done its worst with her husband, the Ten have no hold on her. Loredano tells her to silence her free thoughts in the presence of representatives of Venetian law. The Doge concurs. She should be deferential to the city's male rulers. Marina contemptuously repudiates such silence and respect:

                                                    Keep
Those maxims for your mass of scared mechanics,
Your merchants, your Dalmatian and Greek slaves,
Your tributaries, your dumb citizens....
                                        (II.i.299–302)

Proudly citing her nobility of birth, she refuses to produce the
submissive behaviour expected of women. She challenges the
oligarchy to punish her insubordination by force, as they did
her husband. But, as Loredano drily informs her, her words
will never leave the chamber. They are as fruitless as those
scrawled on Jacopo's prison wall.

   This bitter irony is underlined by Jacopo's plaintive request
when she visits him in prison that she save him from oblivion
by telling his story: 'All then shall speak of me:/ The tyranny
of silence is not lasting' (III.i.78–79). He has been refused his
request for history books while in prison, but finds an alternative record of the past in the graffiti on the cell wall. The
building itself is indicative of the process of suppression of
dissent: above it is the splendid Doge's palace, with its official
tradition of republican freedom commemorated in chronicles
and portraits of the city's rulers; below sea level are the
dungeons where subversive writing on the wall speaks of past
tyranny, read only by those themselves deemed traitors, and
then only by dint of the sense of feeling in the total darkness.
In *Marino Faliero*, the graffito was an unintentional self-reve-
lation of corruption by the aristocracy themselves. In *The Two
Foscari*, the play ends with Loredano's writing on his tablets
his account of the story, while the words on the prison wall
remain in obscurity.

   Like Wollstonecraft, Byron, in the Venetian plays, portrays
the ideal rôle of woman as a republican matron. In the letter to
Talleyrand which prefaces *A Vindication* Wollstonecraft's
rhetoric strives to demonstrate that woman's domestic rôle
has a civic purpose: 'If children are to be educated to understand the true principle of patriotism, their mother must be a

patriot.' The feminist version of nineteenth-century domestic ideology still saw motherhood as woman's primary vocation, but sought equality for her private sphere by construing it as the nursery to the state. The portrayal of Marina interrogates this idea. Her marriage is based on friendship between equals, as Wollstonecraft advocated. Jacopo greets Marina as his 'true wife' and 'only friend', while she tells him to 'divide' his sorrow with her (III.i.215). However, Marina finds that family love is not in harmony with her patriotism. As a woman, Byron portrays her as closer to nature than society, and thus an oppositional voice to state authority.

The rôle of the young woman in rejecting patriarchal control of her fertility is thus a central Byronic concern. Because her rôle in Venetian society is not immanent, but contingent on her relationships, a woman's loyalty is seen by Byron as purely personal in nature. Marina sees herself as accountable to no one but her husband, and in his defence she can therefore articulate an individualism untrammelled by 'masculine' law. Personal liberty is her first priority: she suggests that they could find happiness abroad. Patriotism is to her a childish clinging to mere 'climes and regions': allegiance to Venice is abrogated now that the republic has become 'an ocean Rome' of imperialism (III.i.146–54). She wants to forge a new life with Jacopo (III.i.198–202). Personal loyalty and liberty are not preferences to Marina but 'duties paramount', to which all other scruples and feelings must be secondary. Jacopo may be compared to Abel, Japhet and Hugo—Christlike oppressed sons who forgive their stern fathers—who trust that good will eventually ensue from their suffering, who fundamentally believe in the justice of patriarchal authority in spite of the injustice visited on them. When Marina curses Venice, Jacopo points proudly to his silence—his absence of protest.

But Marina, as a woman not permitted to participate in the public sphere, speaks on behalf of all silenced subjects of Venice of

> The blood of myriads reeking up to heaven,
> The groans of slaves in chains, and men in
>   dungeons,
> Mothers, and wives, and sons, and sires, and
>   subjects,
> Held in the bondage of ten bald-heads....
>
> (III.i.241–44)

While her husband acts with dignified restraint, Marina attacks Loredano as the personification of state tyranny (III.i.252–55, 263–66, 268–69). When Jacopo tries to silence her, Loredano, like the senators, gives her a chivalrous answer: 'Let the fair dame preserve/ Her sex's privilege' (III.i.268–69). Loredano now informs Marina he has given permission for her to accompany Foscari only because he is 'One who wars not with women' (III.i.280). She attempts to repudiate both this patronizing chivalry and his underlying contempt for women by asserting that an individual's quality of nature, like that of a thoroughbred horse, overrides mere categorization by birth (III.i.289–303). In other words she asserts herself his moral superior, even though a woman. She harangues his degeneration from the ideals of the nobility (in his cowardly and corrupt manipulation of the law for personal vengeance) and triumphs in his discomfiture when the hit strikes home.

Though Marina has proved that she is qualitatively equal to her oppressor by her breed and blood, and morally superior in her unstained honour as wife and mother, she is shown just how hollow is her victory when Loredano insists that her children must remain in Venice as they belong to the state. Previously she had threatened him with her sons' revenge in the future (III.i.269). Now she is informed: 'They are the state's' (III.i.387). She now realizes that her maternal rights over them relate only to the menial tasks of breeding and rearing:

> That is
> In all things painful. If they're sick, they will

Be left to me to tend them; should they die,
To me to bury and to mourn; but if
They live, they'll make you soldiers, senators,
Slaves, exiles—what *you* will; or if they are
Females with portions, brides and *bribes* for nobles!
(III.i.389–94)

Her own metaphor of horse-breeding has rebounded upon her.[4] She discovers that all her nobility and chastity are not in fact valued as *individual* superiority at all, for female virtue is highly prized only to ensure the purity of blood of the male line. Her body is as much at the state's disposal as Jacopo's. A woman's only value in society is in the provision of male heirs to power. A female's inherent worth is so little that daughters are given away as gifts by their fathers, pawns in the power struggle, and even then they must be accompanied with 'portions' or bribes of money to give them value.

When Jacopo dies before they can board the boat that is to take them to exile, and Marina now wishes to join him in death, the Doge reminds her of her duty to live for the sake of the children. She now repudiates what she had previously boasted of—the sanctity of motherhood:

My children! true—they live, and I must live
To bring them up to serve the state, and die
As died their father. Oh! what best of blessings
Were barrenness in Venice! Would my mother
Had been so!   (IV.i.208–12)

Marina's despair is based on her realization of the extent to which the state controls all processes of life. Her simple belief in her aristocratic superiority of 'blood' comes into conflict with the dynastic system of ensuring the perpetuation of power by using and overseeing her biological function as a mother. Her grief at the state's regulation of motherhood is echoed by the Doge's tears—as he, for the first time, mourns Venice's destruction of his benevolent rôle as loving father (both of his bodily son and of the city in his charge). Before, he had been ashamed of weeping, pretending his eyes were misty from age (II.i.5–7) and sternly commanding his son to desist from effeminate weakness: 'Boy! no tears' (III.i.415).

He now acknowledges his own subjectivity to 'feminine' feeling, and paradoxically this gives him the strength to oppose the state's manipulation of his integrity any further. Now he has the dignity to refuse to abdicate when this is demanded. Previously the request to resign the dogeship had been refused, and he was even constrained to sign an oath that he would not repeat the request. When he is deprived of power, Learlike, he is reunited in sorrow with Marina. He declares to the oligarchy that his allegiance shall henceforth not be restricted to his own class but to a consensus of government: in Rousseau's words, 'the *general* will' (V.i.56). The discrepancy between the term 'general will' in Chapters I and II of *The Social Contract* (which may be ideally taken to represent all subjects of the state) and the specific exclusion from citizenship of the lower classes and women (in the later section on the republic of Sparta) constitutes a dilemma which the play leaves unresolved. Wollstonecraft reacted by claiming citizenship for women by denigrating the concept of 'feminine' subjectivity and adopting the 'masculine' criteria of reason for both public and private spheres. But Byron's play cries out against both the silencing of woman and the suppression of masculine emotion in the juxtaposition of Marina and the Doge.

When he is deprived of office, Foscari, as a mere private citizen, like Marina, is urged to leave the precincts of power (V.i.212–20), and his passionate words (on the subjugation of the Venetian people) are rebuked, as hers had been (V.i.261). But, as Loredano recognizes, the pathos of the sight of the city's patriarch forced to quit his palace on the arm of his widowed daughter-in-law, would communicate an unforgettable image to the citizens, which would speak even louder than his silenced words. The republic should, like Venetian crystal, reveal the presence of corrosive poison within it by its instant antipathy. But neither stands the test, and the Doge is murdered, his murderer undiscovered, and Foscari's words of dissent obliterated by the 'princely' funeral rites which betoken unbroken allegiance to the status quo.

Like Angiolina Faliero, Marina Foscari is central at the close of the play, her outspoken condemnation of the Council of Ten guiding the audience's response. She sardonically claims as a woman's duty (like the care of the aged) her right to the burial of her dead father-in-law, as well as her husband. Her only legal property—her dowry—will give her the means:

> Though his [the Doge's] possessions have been all
>   consumed
> In the state's service, I still have my dowry,
> Which shall be consecrated to his rites....
>
> (V.i.344–46)

Her request for a private funeral is, of course, refused. Death, like life, is the state's business. Again she is reproved for her impudent excoriation of the male rulers and threatened with punishment, but, in view of the circumstances, reassured that her words will not be written down. The irony of this pronouncement of the futility of Marina's speech is accompanied by Loredano's simultaneous gesture of crossing out words (his grudge against the Foscari family) in his account book. The impotence of the passionate expression in words of individual subjective judgement is the final image of the play. The fact that this is the subject of a poem by Byron makes it a double irony.

NOTES

1. Outram, *The Body and the French Revolution*, Chapter 5.
2. Reiman, *The Romantics Reviewed*, part B, II, 924; IV, 1614; V, 2072; III, 1127.
3. Paulson, *Representations of Revolution*, p. 33.
4. Wollstonecraft's *Vindication* closes by comparing a woman to a horse, in her treatment by man.

EDITORS' BIBLIOGRAPHICAL NOTE

For critical essays on *The Two Foscari* that include comment on *Marino Faliero* and *Sardanapalus* as well, and for general studies that include briefer comments on *The Two Foscari*, see the Editors' Bibliographical Note appended above to the essays on *Marino Faliero* (pp. 129–31). Other than those, there are relatively few treatments of the *Foscari* except for the most recent *Byron's Historical Dramas* by Richard Lansdown, Chapter 6, and *Byron and Tragedy* by Martyn Corbett, pp. 115–43. So far as we know, only W. G. Bebbington has written, and slimly at that, on the play: 'The Two Foscari', pp. 201–06, and it may be even more notable that George Steiner and G. Wilson Knight all but ignore it, the former dismissively adjudging the play as 'a convincing example of what Aristotle meant when he advised dramatists to avoid those occurrences in history which were more implausible than fiction' (*The Death of Tragedy*, p. 206), the latter apologetically noting only that he should have liked 'to have noticed the psychological tension of *The Two Foscari*' (*The Burning Oracle*, p. 286), and 27 years later in *Byron and Shakespeare* settling for a small handful of scattered quotations with no comment at all on the play.

What remains are Chew's old-fashioned, though still useful in certain ways, *Byron's Dramas*, Ehrstine's *The Metaphysics of Byron*, and brief comment by Blackstone in *Byron: A Survey*; even briefer by Knight in *The Golden Labyrinth*.

'Simple' and 'Bright': *Sardanapalus*

G. WILSON KNIGHT

The Byronic conflicts achieve an all but final resolution in *Sardanapalus*. The hero is a king sternly criticized for lax rule with a corresponding abandon to sensuous delights. His brother-in-law Salemenes is given authority to crush a rebellion which nevertheless through the king's clemency ultimately succeeds. A powerful love-force is present in the person of Myrrha, a Greek slave for whom the king has left his own wife. Sardanapalus, after showing extreme though futile bravery, dies finally with Myrrha on a lighted pyre. As in *Antony and Cleopatra* a certain relaxation of sexual ethic deliberately aligns a fiery eroticism with certain positive values against efficiency and war.

Sardanapalus is, however, not rashly idealized. He enters to 'soft music', 'effeminately dressed, head crowned with flowers, and his robe negligently flowing'. Salemenes hates the 'lascivious tinklings' of his attendant music and the 'reeking odours of the perfumed trains' (I.i.29–30, 38). He accuses the king of 'sensual sloth' and lack of 'virtue', despising his 'feasts', 'concubines' and 'lavish'd treasures' (I.ii.70, 234–35). Elsewhere the king is called an 'effeminate thing', 'silkworm' and '*she* Sardanapalus' (II.i.95, 87, 404). He himself admits having 'wasted down' his 'royalty' (IV.i.275–76). Salemenes' faithfulness has in contrast a manly strength:

> I will not see
> The blood of Nimrod and Semiramis
> Sink in the earth, and thirteen hundred years
> Of empire ending like a shepherd's tale.   (I.i.5–8)

References to ancestry are even more continual here than in *Marino Faliero*. The rebels would extinguish 'the line of Nimrod'. Nimrod and Semiramis are frequently quoted to shame the king. They symbolize respectively the chase and war, which Salemenes equates with health and glory while disgusted that his king takes part in neither. 'A line of thirteen ages' comes to an end with Sardanapalus' fall (III.i.234).

But the hero makes out a good case. When confronted by the ancestral example of Semiramis in leading her people as far as the Ganges and returning unvanquished though with only twenty guards, he has a powerful answer:

> *Sardanapalus.*　　　　　　And how many
> 　　Left she behind in India to the vultures?
> *Salemenes.* Our annals say not.
> *Sardanapalus.*　　　　　　Then I will say for them—
> 　　That she had better woven within her palace
> 　　Some twenty garments, than with twenty
> 　　　　guards
> 　　Have fled to Bactria, leaving to the ravens
> 　　And wolves, and men—the fiercer of the three,
> 　　Her myriads of fond subjects. Is *this* glory?
> 　　Then let me live in ignominy ever. (I.ii.131–39)

To him she was only 'a sort of semi-glorious human monster'. He realizes he might quite easily have himself shed blood 'by oceans' till his name became a 'synonym of death', at once 'a terror and a trophy'. He has not 'decimated' his people with savage laws, or 'sweated' them to build pyramids, but instead pursued civic ambitions, founding cities:

> 　　what could that blood-loving beldame
> 　My martial grandam, chaste Semiramis,
> 　Do more, except destroy them?
> 　　　　　　　　(I.ii.181, 187, 404–05, 230–31)

His motto 'Eat, drink, and love; the rest's not worth a fillip' (I.ii.252), though it may at first shock us, sinks deeper as you meditate it; and set against his ironic picture of a trophy raised over fifty thousand dead certainly makes one pause. His aim is that all—not only the privileged— should be happy. He has aimed to lessen 'the weight of human misery' (I.ii.263–64) not increase it, He loathes 'all war and warriors' and prefers the pleasure that 'sparkles' at a feast to all 'Nimrod's huntings' or 'my wild grandam's chase in search of kingdoms' (III.i.4–6). His logic is often witty:

> *Myrrha.* Look to the annals of thine empire's
>   founders.
> *Sardanapalus.* They are so blotted o'er with blood, I
>   cannot.
>   But what would'st have? The empire *has been*
>   founded.
>   I cannot go on multiplying empires.
>
> (I.ii.547–50)

Yet he is simultaneously aware of his limitations. Salemenes is 'stern' as he 'heedless', and 'slaves' deserve to feel a 'master' (I.ii.387–89): so he gives his brother-in-law authority to crush the suspected insurrection. We are shown a king quite lacking in that particular hardness so often conditioning virtue and efficiency. He can regard his strong supporters as better men than himself. But also a conscious royalty renders him proudly independent of the 'vile herd', whether in 'noisy praise' or 'noisome clamour', and a superb confidence rings in his threat to prove himself more fierce than 'stern Nimrod' conjured from his 'ashes', should his people insist on brutality of rule and refuse their potential humanity (I.ii.341–43, 373).

He is a man of unpractical enlightenment beyond the superstitions of his day. When the Greek Myrrha shows surprise at his actually enjoying, like Cassius, a thunderstorm that strikes others with awe, and says how she herself respects all such portents as 'auguries of Jove', he replies:

> Jove!—ay, your Baal—
> Ours also has a property in thunder,
> And ever and anon some falling bolt
> Proves his divinity—and yet sometimes
> Strikes his own altars.   (II.i.548–53)

Notice the clever touches in 'your Baal' and 'property'.
Sardanapalus shamelessly blasphemes 'the worship of the land'
and shocks the priest Beleses. For to him the stars are most
wonderful when unsullied by religious connotations:

> Oh! for that—I love them;
> I love to watch them in the deep blue vault,
> And to compare them with my Myrrha's eyes;
> I love to see their rays redoubled in
> The tremulous silver of Euphrates' wave,
> As the light breeze of midnight crisps the broad
> And rolling water, sighing through the sedges
> Which fringe his banks: but whether they may be
> Gods, as some say, or the abodes of gods,
> As others hold, or simply lamps of night,
> Worlds, or the lights of worlds, I know nor care not.
> There's something sweet in my uncertainty
> I would not change for your Chaldean lore....
> (II.i.252–64)

Such an immediate contact with a living universe is set against
the horror of being 'sermonised' and 'dinn'd' with memories
of 'dead men', 'Baal' and 'Chaldea's starry mysteries'. We
are clearly made to feel the faults of priestcraft, traditional
superstitions and ancestral domination. Salemenes accuses
Beleses of 'smooth words and juggling homilies', and even
Arbaces sees in him a 'subtle spirit' of more 'peril' than a
'phalanx'. Priests have 'codes', 'mysteries' and 'corollaries' of
right and wrong far too tortuous for a 'plain heart' to understand (II.i.232, 379–82). The satire may be very up to date and
amusing, as when Sardanapalus says the gods never themselves

speak to him except through the priests, and then usually for some 'addition to the temple'. Yet, with all this, there occurs one powerful and typically Byronic example of respect to religious office, when Sardanapalus, meeting Beleses in battle, refuses at first to dip his hands in 'holy blood' (III.i.273–74). There is deliberate emphasis on the priest's magic insight: his prophecy proves true, suggesting, as in *Marino Faliero*, an almost superstitious feeling of the Church's invisible power, however the enlightened hero may enlist our immediate sympathies. Our response to him is usually direct. When the overflowing Euphrates breaks its bulwark and strikes awe into Pania, Sardanapalus answers curtly: 'I can forgive the omen, not the ravage' (V.i.198). He repudiates conventions and superstitions in the cause of a health, sanity, and realism that his opposers cannot understand.

He is, even to himself, something of a paradox, at once effeminate and exceptionally brave. Salemenes, he says, should have been king: 'and I—I know not what, and care not', in which we can detect a resemblance to earlier, and darker, heroes. To his wife he is humble:

> My gentle, wrong'd Zarina!
> I am the very slave of circumstance
> And impulse—borne away with every breath!
> Misplaced upon the throne—misplaced in life.
> I know not what I could have been, but feel
> I am not what I should be. (IV.i.329–34)

His very truth to central impulses makes him a continual paradox. He is not exactly effeminate; and indeed analyses the dangers of the feminine temperament, how it may become 'timidly vindictive' to a 'pitch of perseverance' beyond masculine passion (II.i.586–90); and talks of a mother lion 'femininely' raging 'Because all passions in excess are female' (III.i.378–81). Yet Myrrha speaks some exquisite lines on the basic nature of the specifically feminine behind all man's activities; the earliest and the latest troubles of his existence being nursed by maternal or some other feminine gentleness (I.ii.509–15). The hero, poet-like, is somewhat bisexual, aiming to fuse man's reason with woman's emotional depth, while repudiating the evil concomitants. Sardanapalus is a 'man-queen', though the phrase is used by Salemenes as a condemnation of pure effeminacy. There is, perhaps, evidence of some womanly streak in the incident of the looking-glass (III.i.163 ff.): but next the action drives him to a pitch of efficiency far surpassing, yet perhaps including, all soft and generous qualities. It teaches a simple thing: the value of water, as opposed to wine, a significant contrast suggesting an advance beyond the sensuous. 'All the gold of earth' could not repay 'the pleasure' of this water (III.i.360–61). The plan demands that he should show himself to lack no atom of that manliness characterizing his inferiors in vision. But, though astounding every one by both his swift efficiency and valour when tested, his scorn of military glory persists:

> *Salemenes.* This great hour has proved
>   The brightest and most glorious of your life.
> *Sardanapalus.* And the most tiresome. (III.i.342–44)

His arms are 'toys', the sword-hilt hurts his hand, his throne is uncomfortable. He must mock at all the baubles of respectability. He is, indeed, 'inscrutable'. He is Byron's 'superman'.

Like the Duke's in *Measure for Measure*, his clemency, however unwise, is conscious and purposeful:

> To love and to be merciful, to pardon
> The follies of my species, and (that's human)
> To be indulgent to my own.   (I.ii.276–78)

This, not glory, is the only 'godlike' thing about him. The execution of rebels would leave him no sleep. His virtues are felt to be one with his sins which 'have all been of the softer order' (IV.i.397–98). He is of 'softer clay' than his rock-like brother-in-law, is our 'soft sovereign'; the word is recurrent.

His first entrance was heralded by 'soft music'. It is an *Antony and Cleopatra* favourite, and Antony was the 'soft triumvir' in *The Corsair*. Sardanapalus deliberately aims to avoid piling burdens on a mortality already overweighted, and to set instead an example of 'mild reciprocal alleviation' (I.ii.353) of life's agonies; to make his 'inoffensive rule' an 'era of sweet peace 'midst bloody annals' (IV.i.511–12). That is 'the sole true glory' and the only victory he has ever coveted. 'Bloodshed' is a 'mockery' of a 'remedy' against evil (II.i.466–67) and conquest no renown. Idealized romance in 'Grief cannot come where perfect love exists' blends into the wider implications of 'I seek but to be loved, not worshipp'd'; and that into a gentle, pastor-like concern and a desire to convert the realm 'to one wide shelter for the wretched' (II.i.599, III.i.36, 41–42). Whatever the exact prophetic statement intended, the firm erotic basis is undeniable. Such thoughts as 'My very love to thee is hate to them' and 'I cannot love thee when I love mankind' from *The Corsair* have matured to a wider unity. Love's 'devotion', though it makes him faithless to his wife, comes on him like a 'duty'. The very softness and weakness of which we hear so much is a duty, as in a wider context it is felt to be a strength. 'I have loved and lived', he says, and 'my life is love' (I.ii.400, 406), all empires being nothing to that one blazing central fire he would express; hence his strong desires for a simpler, rustic life, apart from the 'falsehood' of his 'station'. He asks Myrrha to define that 'unknown influence' and 'sweet oracle' of love that makes wordless communion between him and her:

> *Myrrha.* In my native land a God,
>   And in my heart a feeling like a God's,
>   Exalted; yet I own 'tis only mortal.
>   (I.ii.424–30)

Like Sean O'Casey today Byron closely entwines his most positive statement with a fearless eroticism:

> I would not give the smile of one fair girl
> For all the popular breath that e'er divided
> A name from nothing.   (I.ii.338–40)

Yet a deeper, or at least a more tranquil, a more Words-worthian, experience is elsewhere shadowed, though still in association with 'errors' of a gentle sort:

> If I have err'd this time, 'tis on the side
> Where error sits most lightly on that sense,
> I know not what to call it; but it reckons
> With me ofttimes for pain, and sometimes pleasure;
> A spirit which seems placed about my heart
> To count its throbs, not quicken them, and ask
> Questions which mortal never dared to ask me....
>   (II.i.524–30)

This is a state of listening passivity. Sardanapalus is conceived as, in essence, a saint. 'If then they hate me, 'tis because I hate not' (I.ii.412) he says. There is a profound insight elsewhere (IV.i) in a discussion of ingratitude: how kindness too often raises precisely its reverse; while those on whom one has no claim 'are faithful'. But, unwise or not, Sardanapalus is the 'king of peace'. His courage is that of warrior, king and martyr in one. He forgives 'royally', yet fights 'like a king'. It is, too, an innate royalty:

> Methought he look'd like Nimrod as he spoke,
> Even as the proud imperial statue stands
> Looking the monarch of the kings around it,
> And sways, while they but ornament, the temple.
>   (II.i.352–55)

'Sway' is earlier contrasted with 'subdue'. A closely Biblical and Shakespearian use of royalty enlists all the splendours of an outworn value to establish poetically a new. So Sardana-palus refuses a strong plain helmet for one lighter and more regal, against all advice given on grounds of practical utility and danger of recognition by the rebels, with the shatteringly royal phrase: 'I go forth to be recognised' (III.i.143). He would quell rebellion with spiritual, not merely martial, authority. His bounty to his followers after disaster is golden as Antony's. The sublime pride and utter scorn of compromise often catches some essence from the New Testament drama. He is, as Christ, utterly alone in his instinctive royalty:

> *Sardanapalus.*   This is strange;
>   The gentle and the austere are both against me
>   And urge me to revenge.
> *Myrrha.*   'Tis a Greek virtue.
> *Sardanapalus.* But not a kingly one.   (II.i.578–81)

At the herald's infuriating message after the final defeat he first, in a flash of anger, determines to execute swift punishment; but, being implored in the name of a herald's 'peaceful' and 'sacred' office, replies, with a New Testament echo blending into a delicate irony:

> He's right—Let him go free—My life's last act
> Shall not be one of wrath. Here, fellow, take
> This golden goblet, let it hold your wine
> And think of *me*; or melt it into ingots,
> And think of nothing but their weight and value.
>   (V.i.335–39)

When early in the action his friends kneel to him as a god, the conception is pagan; but when at the last his soldiers throng round 'kissing his hand and the hem of his robe', we have been trained to a deeper insight.

Byron maintains, however, a happy balance of sympathies to counteract any danger of an excessive idealism. Against the hero Salemenes stands out with a manly and conventional kind of strength demanding respect, his allegiance remaining unaffected by a sister's cruel treatment. As in Dryden's *All for Love* the hero's sexual fault is emphasized by the actual entry of his wife and frequent mention of his children, though it is

also suggested that no warm-blooded king can be bound by
a state marriage. The uncomplaining and faithful Zarina is
beautifully drawn, and at his interview with her in Act IV
Sardanapalus seems to recognize both a value and a virtue
beyond him, while foreseeing the remorse which attends on 'a
single deviation from the track of human duties'. The old
Byronic guilt is not quite exorcised; and the conception of
Sardanapalus, though of greatest importance, is never left *in
vacuo* as an absolute. For that we must consider the whole
play, conclusion and all. Myrrha, the Ionian slave and
Sardanapalus' mistress, is similarly important. Her devotion
puts Greece and all its emotional and cultural connotations,
literary and political, at the hero's feet: such Greek references
being frequent and contributing an added richness to the scin-
tillating impressionism. She serves as a critical standard, as it
were, meditating on the meaning of her love for so strange a
man, and variously relating his weaknesses and nobility to her
native traditions. Both Zarina and Myrrha are beautifully
drawn, ranking high among Byron's succession of fine
women.

There is a very pleasing interplay of glittering impressionism to which the many proper names, whether Greek or
Assyrian, contribute; with, moreover, a happy blend of nature
with a romantic humanism in the many rose-references, as
when the hero is 'crown'd with roses', refuses to crown
himself 'with a single rose the less' whatever dangers are afoot,
prefers a cottage with Myrrha and 'crowns of flowers' to his
kingdom's 'dull tiara', or equates his own fall to that of a
'pluck'd rose'. The bee gathering 'honey' from 'wholesome
flowers' only is beautifully contrasted with mankind's ability
to transmute evil to good. We have an adder and flowers and
there are references to natural disturbance such as tempests,
and some larger symbols to be noted shortly; but Sardanapalus loves tempests as a pleasing variation. His new strength
is compared to a 'twilight tempest' thundering from out a hot
summer's day (III.i). The suffusing tone is summery, as in the

'gay pavilion' thought of as the king's 'summer dotage', and 'the big rain pattering on the roof'. Moreover, the moon breaks through in 'brightness' after storm, and the king's 'silk tiara' and 'flowing hair' are seen making 'a mark too royal' in its 'broad light'. Beleses points to the 'earliest' and 'brightest' of the stars 'which so quivers/ As it would quit its place in the blue ether' (II.i.63–64). There are Sardanapalus' lovely star-lines already quoted. The heavens are alive here, bending down and speaking alike to saintly king and plotting priest. The priest reads their hieroglyphic meanings, but Sardanapalus feels rather an exact coincidence of the cosmic on the human. His flowery banquet

> Shall blaze with beauty and with light, until
> It seems unto the stars which are above us
> Itself an opposite star....   (I.ii.555–58)

But the most indicative and compact of all minor impressions here is that of a 'crimson' blush on Myrrha's cheek 'Like to the dying day on Caucasus/ Where sunset tints the snow with rosy shadows' (I.ii.42–44), or that of her arms 'more dazzling with their own born whiteness' than the sword-steel she brandishes (III.i.394–96). Such fusion is compact and twined in further with many brilliances of human civilization, with 'glittering spears', a sword that shall 'out-dazzle comets', the flash of steel generally in heroic combat, Sardanapalus' mirror 'of polish'd brass from India', his diademed helmet and continual gold—the 'golden realm of Ind', 'all the gold of earth', a 'golden reign of peace', Nimrod's chalice as a 'golden goblet thick with gems', the 'golden goblet' and other gold treasure at the close. Especially beautiful is Sardanapalus' thought of himself as a poor miner and Zarina as a 'vein of virgin ore' which he may discover but not himself possess though it 'sparkles' at his feet (IV.i.344–49). And all blends with and clusters about the king's throne, the music and feasting and wine so deeply praised, and the fiery conclusion. These many transverse glintings of a rosy nature, sparkling heavens and flashing civilization, like shot silk or the iridescence of a bird's plumage, both combine with the scintillations of the hero's wit, and at once irradiate, enliven, and interpret the whole massed statement.

The use of impressionism, and still more the dramatic value of stage symbolism, is Shakespearian, as is the music, garlands and banquet, and the interruption of the latter by storm and thunder; the comments thereon; and the rising Euphrates. The play comes indeed so close in feeling (and phrase-reminiscence) to Shakespeare that it runs inevitable risks, but the cohesion is thoroughly organic. It has depth as well as a beautiful surface clarity. It is not one of those many would-be poetic dramas where you cannot 'find a heart within the beast'. I point next to the negative and positive pulses of that heart: which relate respectively to (1) the ancestral taboos against which the hero is fighting; and (2) that cosmic and fiery energy of which his life is conceived as an immediate and spontaneous expression.

The negative extreme is given in Sardanapalus' nightmare in Act IV. We start with Myrrha's lovely lines spoken over his sleep after the battle (i.1–42). One might compare the exquisite sleep-speech in *Lara*, a fine example of Byron's Shakespearian ability to maintain a purely objective and human reserve to realize an ultimate mystery. The 'God of Quiet' is felt as brother to Death, as in Shakespeare. She watches the 'play of pain' on his features, and exquisitely the poetry uses natural imagery in service to human description: the 'sudden gust' that 'crisps' the 'reluctant' mountain lake, the blast ruffling autumn leaves. Now Sardanapalus' dream concerns (1) Nimrod the Hunter, and (2) Semiramis the fighter. These two, founders of his Assyrian empire, represent all traditional values, and suggest the dark ingrained fear of ancestral authority whose weight so often masquerades as conscience. They oppose respectively Byron's sympathy with the sanctities of animal and human life and may be equated with the 'ancestral voices prophesying war' of 'Kubla Khan'.

Sardanapalus is shown in the play as not having used his 'bow'
and 'javelin' for years, not 'even in the chase'. Now, yet half in
his dream, he cries:

> Hence—hence—
> Old hunter of the earliest brutes! and ye,
> Who hunted fellow-creatures as if brutes!
> Once bloody mortals—and now bloodier idols,
> If your priests lie not!   (IV.i.27–31)

Both are 'bloody'. But he awakes to find their opposite:
Myrrha, symbol of *pure sexual* passion. It is a move from death
to life: 'I've been i' the grave—where worms are lords.' He has
seen 'a legion of the dead' (ll. 48, 64). Something of *Cain* is
neatly entwined with Sardanapalus' experience. He describes
Nimrod as possessing a certain cold dignity with a 'haughty,
dark, and deadly face', his quiver holding 'shaft-heads feath-
er'd from an eagle's wing' (ll. 84–85, 90). The scene is a guest-
hall and he invites his ancestor to fill the cup between them;
next fills it and offers it himself; but the vast figure with
changeless expression refuses the symbol of convivial joy,
preserving a deadly immobility. He turns and faces Semiramis.
She is a more gruesome figure: bloody, withered, 'sneering'
with the passion of 'vengeance' and 'leering' with that of 'lust'
(ll. 102 ff.). Sexual suggestion is entwined with cruelty: which
is clearly symbolized by her goblet 'bubbling o'er with blood',
the connotation being similar to that transmitted by Flecker's
Hassan. There is another goblet whose contents are left undefined. Other figures are there, but none of them either eat
or drink. They are opposites of the festive and sensuous. He
feels himself turning to stone, yet alive and breathing, like
them. There is a 'horrid sympathy' between these dead and
the living—indeed, the nightmare figures are made of the
negative elements of the old Byronic hero as Sardanapalus
mainly of his 'softness', and a state is outlined next of living
death, apart from both heaven and earth. At length the lips of
both smile. At this extremity a 'desperate courage' infuses his

limbs (ll. 140 ff.) and, fearing them no longer, he laughs 'full in their phantom faces'. He grasps the hunter's hand, which melts away. There is a reconciliation: the man at least looked a 'hero'. But the woman is less easily conquered. She attacks him with 'noisome kisses', spills both goblets till their 'poisons' flow round him, while he shrinks as if he were the son who slew her for 'incest'. Loathsome objects cluster round. He is dead, yet feels; buried, yet raised; consumed by worms yet purged by flames; withered in air yet—the rest is vague save that he searches for Myrrha and awakes to find her beside him. The reaching of a positive beyond death by relegating death's realisms to a dream state is a clever mechanism implied also by the structure of *Hassan*. The progress through death is found in Keats' 'Hyperion', a very similar statement; and the hideous woman and the figures round her point to Keats' 'Belle Dame'. The dream is loaded with suggestions of incest and cruelty and may be related variously to an over-emphasis of power-instincts to the exclusion of sexual health; to the domination of ancestral authority; and to sadism. Semiramis is a 'homicide and husband-killer'. Nimrod comes off better, but every time he is called 'hunter' there is blood-insinuation. The death-impressions are icily sculptural, suggesting a forbidding eternity: 'If sleep shows such things, what may not death disclose?' (ll. 52–53). The answer can only be in terms of a corresponding awakening or some vast apprehension of cosmic life hinted by Myrrha's reply: 'The dust we tread upon was once alive/ And wretched' (ll. 65–66). This, then, is the negative heart: its dramatic place is apt— Sardanapalus has been fighting, shedding blood. The leers and sneers and welcomings have an obvious reference to this, just as the Weird Women get Macbeth after a bloody battle. Myrrha sees it as 'mere creations of late events': it is that—and more. Afterwards, the king reports again how his ancestors have been trying to 'drag me down to them' (IV.i.176).

For the positive pulses of the heart, to Byron the sun is all

but God, as in the opening of Canto III of *The Corsair*. His
early tales are, of course, set by choice in sun-warmed regions.
Manfred has an interesting invocation, close to the sun-
worship in *Cymbeline*, and central to an understanding of
Byron's mind and work:

> Glorious orb! the idol
> Of early nature, and the vigorous race
> Of undiseased mankind, the giant sons
> Of the embrace of angels, with a sex
> More beautiful than they, which did draw down
> The erring spirits who can ne'er return.
> Most glorious orb! that wert a worship, ere
> The mystery of thy making was reveal'd!
> Thou earliest minister of the Almighty,
> Which gladden'd, on their mountain tops, the hearts
> Of the Chaldean shepherds, till they pour'd
> Themselves in orisons! Thou material God!
> And representative of the Unknown—
> Who chose thee for his shadow!   (III.ii.174–87)

Notice that the sun's sacred life is related to some past golden
age. It is next the 'chief star' and 'sire of the seasons', alone
making earth 'endurable'. Also the 'inborn spirits' of man still
have a 'tint' of it: the relation is all-important, the sun having
powerful psychological associations. On that thought Byron-
Manfred plays, asserting that sun-qualities of 'life and warmth'
have been of a 'fatal nature' to him. Arimanes, grand divinity
of nature, is throned above a 'globe of fire'. Now *Sardanapalus*
powerfully develops the symbol. As with the moon in *Marino
Faliero*, the sun here covers both sides of the human conflict,
though with subtle differences in conception.

It is first entwined with worship of Baal, the orthodoxy of
the realm. The priest Beleses watches its setting and searches
for its 'edicts', would read the 'everlasting page' of this 'true
sun', this

> burning oracle of all that live,
> As fountain of all life, and symbol of
> Him who bestows it....   (II.i.1–17)

His understanding is superstitious in comparison with Sardanapalus', but he has his own dignity. Why, he asks, must the sun's 'lore' be limited to 'calamity'? Why not herald a day more worthy its own 'all-glorious burst from ocean'? Why not a 'beam of hope' to replace omens of 'wrath'? He talks of fear and sacrifices. His religion is negative: but in terms of it the sun is felt as a dominating force. Its red setting appropriately gilds this scheming revolutionary. We watch it, as it were, deserting its worshipper: 'While I speak, he sinks—is gone.' The speech concludes with an equation of sunset and death (ll. 17–36). Later Beleses is shocked at the king's disrespect for Chaldea's 'starry mysteries'. Yet Sardanapalus has, as we have seen, his own way of worship, and his particular approach—at once erotic, aesthetic and agnostic—is developed further in our second sun-incident in Act V.i.1–58. Two great sun-symbolisms thus frame the central storm and nightmare movements of Acts III and IV. Moreover, this, as tragedy gathers round, is not a sunset, but a sunrise, relating to the spiritual victory of Sardanapalus and his love. Myrrha and Balea are at a window. Storm has broken night's loveliness. The contrast in nature is beautiful, but what, she asks, of that other stormy chaos on earth of evil passions? What dawn-fire of resolution can rise on that? As with Shakespeare and Pope (in his *Essay on Man*) the human-tempest analogy is exact. The dawn is splendid:

> And can the sun so rise,
> So bright, so rolling back the clouds into
> Vapours more lovely than the unclouded sky,
> With golden pinnacles and snowy mountains ...
>   (V.i.9–12)

till it makes heaven a glorious replica of earthly forms. This sun-splendour is related precisely to the 'soul' of man. It 'dwells upon', 'soothes' and 'blends into' the 'soul'. Sunrise and sunset are the 'haunted epoch' of 'sorrow and love' (the respective arrangement seems a slip). Both are needed for spiritual insight: they are 'twin genii' that 'chasten' and 'purify', more sweet than 'boisterous joys', and build palaces for choice souls to possess peacefully apart from, while enduring, the agonies of existence. 'Pain' and 'pleasure' are 'two names for one feeling' surpassing speech, like some 'Kubla Khan' dome above antinomies, a unity 'which our internal, restless agony' would 'vary in the sound' (V.i.1–38). Myrrha describes the super-consciousness all poetry aims to create. She speaks with the dawn streaming in on her, flooding her with gold. She, knowing like Antony she may not see its rising again, regrets having not felt more of the 'reverence' and 'rapture' due to that power which keeps earth warmly living though mortals die. She almost becomes a 'convert' to Baal. Once, says Balea, the sun reigned on earth, the usual golden-age reminder. But Myrrha prefers him in heaven, where he sways more powerfully than any 'earthly monarch', each ray more potent than empires: which precisely relates to Sardana-palus' preference of love to kingdoms of the earth. The sun is, indeed, here expressly the transcendent reality. Balea calls it, surely a god. Myrrha answers that her own, Greek, belief is the same: yet she thinks it rather the abode of gods than itself one of the 'immortal sovereigns', repeating Sardanapalus' concep-tion of the stars. The meaning of all this goes far beyond my transcription. The rising, flooding, sunlight increases with developing stage dialogue. It is dramatically active. Moreover, the usual association of royalty, sun and love becomes a personified association, since Myrrha is the play's love-force. So the moving dialogue adds wonder to wonder till the blaze shuts out the world, dissolving it in light which Myrrha can no longer face. The sun all but equals the divine, though with a slight reservation felt also in *Manfred* where Arimanes, with his globe of fire, is not all-powerful over the protagonist. The human, in Byron, must preserve its integrity to this extent: hence the sense of the stars earlier and the sun here being the 'abode' of more human gods rather than themselves divine.

The sun thus dominates imaginatively, in twin rhythms of evening and morning associated with the two sides of the conflict, but more directly with Myrrha, the love-centre, to whom the king earlier compares the stars. A golden haze encircles, aureoles, the central action of battles, storm and nightmare, the sun blazing from each side. And when there is more battling and tragic failure, the movement dissolves into a sovereign nobility as the lovers die on their chosen sacrificial pyre, loaded with frankincense and myrrh, the throne its 'core'. This is the dawn implied by Myrrha's earlier question; it is a 'leap through flame into the future' (V.i.415). Sardanapalus wants the *future* to 'turn back and smile' on his reign, recalling Marino Faliero. So, too, he addresses his ancestors, bearing home to them the insignia of his lost empire through the 'absorbing element' of fire. His faults have been great, but he writes his name on the memory of centuries:

> Time shall quench full many
> A people's records and a hero's acts;
> Sweep empire after empire, like this first
> Of empires, into nothing; but even then
> Shall spare this deed of mine....   (V.i.442–46)

The blazing palace shall be more firmly established than Egypt's pyramids. A torch from Baal's shrine 'lights' the lovers 'to the stars', in an embrace of 'commingling fire' (V.i.450, 471). The orthodoxy of the realm contributes to the originally conceived sacrifice.

Sardanapalus is a less complex and at a first reading probably a less profoundly moving work than *Marino Faliero*; but the simplicity is integral to its peculiarly monistic statement, and the final violent equating of dawn-fire with human tragedy is necessarily not easy to probe though obvious enough to the view. It marks the resolution of former conflicts and corresponds to *Antony and Cleopatra* in the Shakespearian sequence—though its cool classic purity of diction and beautiful lucidity of symbolism differ slightly from Shakespeare's more masked effects. What is implicit in Shakespeare is continually here, as often in *Marino Faliero* also, explicit. The ritual-conclusion is, for example, definitely a 'sacrifice', Myrrha pouring a libation to the gods and Sardanapalus drinking a formal farewell to his pleasures. There is, too, something statuesque about the whole and a new plastic quality in certain references to sculpture, in longer visual-descriptive passages of persons, as in that of Myrrha fighting, with 'her nostril dilated from its symmetry', and in stage-pictures that differentiate it from Byron's more usual inward and energic effects and mark a transition to certain elements of *Don Juan*.

Sardanapalus ranges a non-moral eroticism with a Christian idealism, and the transference is quite pivotal. Though forcing as well both a tragic conclusion and a subtle humour, its positive alignments might be said to dramatize eternity in action and hence it has a certain stillness, a plastic quality. [...]

'A Problem Few Dare Imitate': *Sardanapalus* and 'Effeminate Character'

SUSAN J. WOLFSON

I

Sardanapalus, Byron's staging of an 'effeminate character' in the idiom of ancient Assyria, was published late in 1821; the following year, Hazlitt produced an essay 'On Effeminacy of Character'.[1] The congruence of his delineation with the hero of Byron's tragedy, at least in the early scenes, would have struck anyone who had read the play or the generous excerpts supplied in the reviews of 1822. Here are Hazlitt's opening sentences:

> Effeminacy of character arises from a prevalence of the sensibility over the will: or it consists in a want of fortitude to bear pain or to undergo fatigue, however urgent the occasion. We meet with instances of people who cannot lift up a little finger to save themselves from ruin, nor give up the smallest indulgence for the sake of any other person. They cannot put themselves out of their way on any account.... They live in the present moment, are the creatures of the present impulse.... [B]eyond that, the universe is nothing to them. The slightest toy countervails the empire of the world. (VIII, 248)

Byron clearly understood the degree to which *Sardanapalus* would provoke interest in the 1820s not only as a historical subject, but also within contemporary discourses on gender and the fate of empire. Hazlitt's characterization of the effeminate reiterates the complaints Byron had given the frustrated allies of Sardanapalus' empire: 'Will you rouse the indolent procrastinator to an irksome but necessary effort, by shewing him how much he has to do? He will only draw back the more for all your intreaties and representations' (p. 250).

These compelling alliances are crossed in Hazlitt's essay by two more complicated perspectives, however: Hazlitt at once broadens the field of analysis to concede a general tendency to effeminacy in the male character and, despite the remarkable congruence of his subject with Byron's play, attempts to absolve the fascinating, and questionable, figure of Byron from such imputation. [...] Yet as soon as he mentions the more overtly ambiguous Byron, he allows the excuse of aristocratic affectation and emphasizes the manliness of the literary performances: 'Lord Byron is a pampered and aristocratic writer, but he is not effeminate, or we should not have his works with only the printer's name to them!' (p. 254).[2] Despite such insistence, however, the issue remains open. The tone that governs this logic is ironic, and the evidence equivocal: the absence of the author's name may indicate manly risks sufficient to provoke legal action, but the dodging of public accountability also reports a certain failure of manly nerve.[3]

Byron's representation of 'effeminate character' in *Sardanapalus* predicts these problems of interpretation: not only does Byron associate it with a politics of evasion, he also embodies it in a hero cast as pampered, aristocratic and effeminate all at once. Moreover, he perplexes the judgements of fault that Hazlitt tries to settle: the play sets the spectacle of effeminacy amid a swirl of often conflicting forces, aligning it variously with hedonism, eroticism, class privilege, sloth, self-mystification, ideological critique, political idealism, and humanitarianism. [...] [T]he complex of attributes that Byron was trying to synthesize was transparently 'Byronic'— both in the sense of the character publicly identified with him by the early 1820s, and its way of drawing on private questions of character, prompted in early 1821 by his life as Cavalier Servente and frustrated supporter of Italian liberation.[4] *Sardanapalus* is not just personal allegory turned to spectacle, however. [...] By placing an 'effeminate character' in a historically specified social configuration, Byron's play requires attention to how judgements about gender are produced within networks of political and cultural concerns.[5]

Gender is the template of the play's investigation of how 'social freedom' (IV.i.81) is to be managed, power secured, and the integrity of a culture maintained and perpetuated. As the terms 'feminine', 'effeminate', 'manly', and 'unmanly' are applied to the king, they also limn codes of conduct and sensibility that bind Assyrian—or any—culture.[6] Concentrating this vocabulary on Sardanapalus and his awakening into political and military action, Byron shades it with an array of complementary figures. On one side are the patriarchs, whose example applies the harshest judgement to the present king's 'mode of life or rule' (I.ii.246)—chiefly Nimrod, 'the hunter-founder of [the] race' (IV.i.179), and his most direct political descendant, Salemenes, royal advisor and voice of empire. On another side are the palace women: the harem, especially Sardanapalus' 'favourite', his Greek slave Myrrha; and more remotely, but still with a claim on his gentleness, his queen, Zarina. Sardanapalus' oscillation between these gendered sets tempts some to view him as 'a tragic hero with masculine and feminine tendencies in irreconcilable conflict'.[7] Yet an important effect of Byron's play is to make essentialist formulations of 'masculine' and 'feminine' themselves sites of conflict. If the company of women draws Sardanapalus away from concerns of empire, their sphere is not simply opposed to 'masculine' empire, but overlaps and merges with it. Zarina, mother of princes, bears issues of dynasty; and Myrrha, no

less than Salemenes, despairs of the civic and political consequences of Sardanapalus' negligent luxury: although her
motive is love rather than nationalism, she, too, urges care for
'thy past fathers' race,/ And for thy sons' inheritance'
(I.ii.589–90)—so much so, that one reviewer called her a
'female Salemenes', a voice of 'just apprehensions and manly
counsels'; and, at moments of crisis, she displays capacities
usually identified as masculine.[8] The deepest confusion of
gender is stirred by Sardanapalus' legendary ancestor,
Semiramis, the warrior 'Man-Queen' (I.i.43). A reciprocal of
the present 'she-king', it is she who epitomizes everything he
finds most repellent in the imperatives of empire.

These confusions intensify at the centre of the play into a
bewildering, and revelatory, set of transformations. Byron
makes the battle, historically a proving-ground of masculinity,
into an arena of crisis and violence in which usual signs of
gender dissolve. Here Sardanapalus' effeminacy is not so
much revoked as propelled into a new register, a spectacular
androgyny: with 'silk tiara and his flowing hair', he 'fights as
he revels' (III.i.205, 213), scarcely to be distinguished from
Myrrha, who appears waving a sword over 'her floating hair
and flashing eyes' (III.i.384), not only mirroring him, but also
evoking the warrior Semiramis. Byron amplifies these weird
mirrorings with a psychic correlative, Sardanapalus' nightmare
of 'a horrid kind/ Of sympathy' with his dynastic progenitors,
'the hunter' Nimrod and 'the crone' Semiramis (IV.i.124–25,
132)—the former oddly passive, the latter a ghastly embodiment of imperialism and sexual aggression. At the end of the
play, Byron will suppress these confusions and reinvest orthodoxy just before a theatrical climax masquerading as an act
transcending history. But the interval of disruption persists as
a challenge not altogether contained by this plot.

That Byron can stage these confusions only as events of
psychic and political crisis reflects his difficulty in imagining
any social form capable of sustaining a new term against polar-
ized distinctions of gender. Sardanapalus' effeminacy is always

represented as concealing rather than cancelling a latent masculine character. Byron's source, Diodorus Siculus, by contrast, presents a freakish hybrid, a man not only effeminate but also given to fetishistic transvestism and bisexuality:

> [H]e lived the life of a woman ... spending his days in the company of his concubines and spinning purple garments and working the softest of wool, he had assumed the feminine garb and so covered his face and indeed his entire body with whitening cosmetics and the other unguents used by courtesans, that he rendered it more delicate than that of any luxury-loving woman. He also took care to make even his voice to be like a woman's, and ... to pursue the delights of love with men as well as with women. (I, 427)[9]

Although Byron urged his publisher to have this 'story translated—as an explanation—and a *note* to the drama' (*BLJ*, VIII, 128–29), the proposal is of dubious value.[10] For what Diodorus reveals—indeed, casts into relief—is the emphatically heterosexual character of Byron's 'effeminate'. This revision is crucial: a heterosexual masculinity at once implies a power in reserve and releases effeminacy as a sign of something other than sexual decadence or incapacity.

This revision is animated for Byron both by personal concerns and social judgement, and always inflected by class privilege. On a public level, Byron's Sardanapalus summons the whole issue of masculinity in Regency dandyism and his own association with it; on a private level, the compound of flagrant effeminacy and heterosexual virility projects an oblique, and ultimately heroic, figure for the issue of gender of deepest concern to Byron, his bisexuality.[11] [...] Dandyism manages gender-testing with a self-conscious theatricality, paraded with the aristocratic licence Hazlitt grants Byron's social behaviour. [...] 'As a social, even political phenomenon, with repercussions in the world of ideas,' Ellen Moers writes,

> dandyism was the invention of the Regency, when
> aristocracy and monarchy were more widely
> despised (hence more nastily exclusive) than ever
> before in English history. What the utilitarian
> middle class most hated in the nobility was what the
> court most worshipped in the dandy.[12]

The differentiation of class that Moers sees as stimulating the dandy's performance is also what licenses his attitude towards gender: namely, the privilege of flirting with the appearance of effeminacy.

Yet, as Hazlitt's essay implies, dandyism could strain such licence when it threaded into the social fabric at large, corrupting the national character. Not coincidentally, this corruption was frequently diagnosed as contamination by continental style, and to more than a few critics, Byron was an index of the symptoms. [...] Concern was expressed not just by middle-class commentators but by the older order of aristocrats: both sides saw in dandyism a default of virile manhood, and the fate of the empire hung in the balance. This is the 'dandy' side of Sardanapalus, theatricalized with the tone of indifference Moers describes: 'a Hero so evidently at the centre of the stage that he need do nothing to prove his heroism'. [...]Byron's record of the life he was leading in Ravenna as he was shaping both *Beppo* and *Sardanapalus* not only reveals his sensitivity to this association of the dandy with political default and effeminacy; it also provides a kind of motivating text for why beneath the surface of Sardanapalus' pleasure-seeking he signals 'latent energies' (I.i.11) pointed towards a plot of masculine emergence. The soldiers' amazement in the middle act that 'Baal himself/ Ne'er fought more fiercely to win empire, than/ His silken son to save it; he defies/ All augury of foes or friends' (III.i.312–15) shimmers as a fantasy script of Byron's own longing, as jaded dandy and politically defunct expatriate lord, for self-renewal through political crisis. Unlike Sardanapalus' Nineveh, Byron's

Ravenna was already under foreign domination; its politics were astir with revolt and subversion, and Byron was participating with money, advice and collaboration.[13] In this respect, he was more like a rebel satrap than Sardanapalus. At the same time, however, his aversion to violence and his aimless routine of entertainments and amorous intrigue with Teresa Guiccioli defined him as a kind of Sardanapalus—and not without the sense, confessed in his journals and voiced by the play's secondary characters, that he must be roused for ends more worthy. Uneasy in the role of Cavalier Servente (by which he felt effeminized, more like the slave Myrrha than her master), restless, alternately bored and amused by local revels, he felt himself all too prone to the 'Italian manners' that Roberts warned against.[14] Intermittently, he was reading history about the lives of heroes and longing for release from a 'lifetime, more or less *ennuyé*'; the only cure for his 'depressed spirit', he sensed, was 'Violent passions' (*BLJ*, VIII, 15).

This seemed possible to him in Italy in early 1821, when, as Leslie Marchand reports, 'revolutionary excitement had risen to the fever pitch ... with the Austrians poised for the invasion of Naples'.[15] By mid-January, Byron is involved in local politics and 'sketch[ing] the ... tragedy of Sardanapalus, which' he says, 'I have for some time meditated. Took the names from Diodorus Siculus, (I know the history of Sardanapalus, and have known it since I was twelve years old), and read over a passage in the ninth vol. octavo of Mitford's Greece, where he rather vindicates the memory of this last of the Assyrians' (*BLJ*, VIII, 26). [...] [T]he vindication of Sardanapalus appeals to Byron, but its potential script for self-renewal is contradicted by what he records in his journal for 14–16 January (*BLJ*, VIII, 27–28). It is a story of sustained lethargy amid trivial entertainments and ultimately futile political intrigue. All January he is absorbed in these random activities, their aimless motions aggravated by a birthday: 'I shall have completed thirty and three years of age!!!' Byron moans on the 20th; 'I go to my bed with a heaviness of heart at having lived so long, and to so little purpose' (VIII, 31). Yet he seems helpless to change his course: 'Read—Rode—fired pistols, and returned. Dined—read. Went out at eight—made the usual visit', he notes on the 23rd; 'Heard of nothing but war,—"the cry is still, They come"'—a rueful allusion to Macbeth's taunts at the invading army before his defeat (V.v.1–2). 'The Car[bonar]i seem to have no plan', he complains; 'nothing fixed among themselves, how, when or what to do. In that case, they will make nothing of the project, so often postponed, and never put in action' (*BLJ*, VIII, 32). They merely multiply and magnify his own aimlessness, as if everyone had become a Sardanapalus:

> Half the city are getting their affairs in marching trim. A pretty Carnival! ... met some masques in the Corso—'Vive la bagatelle!'—the Germans are on the Po, the Barbarians at the gate, and their masters in council at Leybach ... and lo! they dance and sing, and make merry, 'for to-morrow they may die.' ... The principal persons in the events which may occur in a few days are gone out on a *shooting party* ... a real snivelling, popping, small-shot, water-hen waste of powder, ammunition, and shot, for their own special amusement. (*BLJ*, VIII, 33)

By February, Byron [...] had thoroughly compounded the imaginative energies invested in the drama with those of the projected revolt: 'To-day I have had no communication with my Carbonari cronies; ... It is a grand object—the very *poetry* of politics. Only think—a free Italy!!! Why, there has been nothing like it since the days of Augustus' (*BLJ*, VIII, 47). But events in modern Italy pretty much came to a halt on 7 March, when the Austrians defeated the Neapolitan army at Rieti. Although Byron insists to his publisher (writing on the anniversary of Bastille Day) that *Sardanapalus* should 'not be mistaken for a *political* play—which was so far from my intention that I thought of nothing but Asiatic history' (VIII,

152; Byron's emphasis), his surrounding accounts disclose scenes of action which persistently implicate the play's 'poetry of politics' in larger stages of social reflection and political play.[16]

II

Byron's first image of Sardanapalus, a reading by Salemenes, is of a character in default. Like Philo on Marc Antony, the Assyrian speaks as a chorus, lamenting the prospect of 'the blood of Nimrod and Semiramis/ Sink[ing] in the earth, and thirteen hundred years/ Of Empire ending' (I.i.6–8)—a motion he would reverse. He will soon urge the king 'beyond/ That easy—far too easy—idle nature.... O that I could rouse thee!' (I.ii.61–63). He rehearses the agenda, emphasizing the key word, 'rouse':

> He must be roused. In his effeminate heart
> There is a careless courage which corruption
> Has not all quench'd, and latent energies,
> Repress'd by circumstance but not destroy'd—
> Steep'd, but not drown'd, in deep voluptuousness.
>
> (I.i.9–13)

It is an important aspect of this reading that Sardanapalus the 'man' (I.i.14) is not so much usurped as masked by effeminate corruptions. The paradigm is that of the prodigal: 'Not all lost, even yet he may redeem/ His sloth and shame, by only being that/ Which he should be', namely, one who would 'sway his nations' and 'head an army' rather 'than rule a harem' (I.i.18–23).

Yet the substitutions Salemenes names also disclose a political emergency. Effeminacy is not just an embarrassment to royal decorum; it is a danger to the security of empire: 'All the nations ... thy father left/ In heritage, are loud in wrath against thee,' he warns (I.ii.98–100). A 'king of all we know of earth' may not simply heed 'lulling instruments, the softening voices/ Of women, and of beings less than women'; for while he 'lolls crown'd with roses', his 'diadem/ Lies negligently by to be caught up/ By the first manly hand which dares to snatch it' (I.i.29–36). Byron's framing of this critique as a crisis of gender—unmanning influences betraying a father's heritage to other manly hands—exposes the power politics of oppositions and polarities. Within such a structure, a king's effeminacy cannot be a capable principle of reform: its confusions provoke revolt because they corrupt the conservative foundation of masculine culture and the discourses that bind it—'what all good men tell each other,/ Speaking of him and his', as Salemenes puts it (I.i.45–46). Even as rebels, men feel compromised, diminished by the prospect of 'woman's warfare' (II.i.82). As one complains,

> To have pluck'd
> A bold and bloody despot from his throne,
> And grappled with him, clashing steel with steel,
> That were heroic or to win or fall;
> But to upraise my sword against this silk-worm....
>
> (II.i.83–87)

Another says that it makes him 'blush'—as if effeminized—that their antagonist is a mere 'king of distaffs' (II.i.344).

This widely voiced title, with which Salemenes confronts the king, epitomizes the scandal of substitutions. When Byron has Sardanapalus answer the charge of having turned 'the sword ... into a distaff' by arguing that 'the Greeks ... related/ The same of their chief hero, Hercules,/ Because he loved a Lydian queen' (I.ii.324–30), he exposes his partiality. Hercules was not enamoured of, but enslaved by, this queen, who effeminized him by dress and enforced tasks of spinning and weaving while she took over his lion-skin and club. The Greek Myrrha confirms this degradation when she celebrates Sardanapalus' heroism on the battlefield by comparing his erstwhile 'effeminate arts' to Hercules 'shamed in Lydian

Omphale's/ She-garb ... wielding her vile distaff' (III.i.218–20). This image, moreover, casts Hercules as a masculine hero shamed by bondage, rather than liberated into effeminacy. A more potent scandal for Assyrian culture is Sardanapalus' gross abuse of the symbols of Nimrod's patriarchy. It is in the 'hall of Nimrod' that he stages his 'evening revel' (I.ii.635), and it is 'Nimrod's chalice' that he use to toast Bacchus (I.ii.160)—deified, he reminds his critics, not as the conqueror of India but as patron of 'the immortal grape' (I.ii.166, 174), a bequest that Sardanapalus deems superior to 'Nimrod's huntings,/ Or my wild Grandam's chase in search of kingdoms/ She could not keep when conquer'd' (III.i.5–7).

This Grandam, however, poses a problem to the substitutions and inversions with which Sardanapalus would fashion his politics of effeminacy: this man-queen's androgyny does not complement and legitimize his effeminacy; rather, as her frequent pairing with Nimrod indicates, it joins her to the imperial patriarchy. Her honour to 'Nimrod's line' (I.ii.86) poses a double embarrassment to Sardanapalus: 'Semiramis—a woman only,' Salemenes chides, 'led/ These our Assyrians to the solar shores/ Of Ganges' and returned 'like a *man*— a hero; baffled, but/ Not vanquish'd' (I.ii.126–30). When Salemenes first heralds the entry of 'the grandson of Semiramis, the man-queen' (I.i.43), a nasty syntactic ambiguity regenders both king and queen—or applies its androgynous compound to both, with a difference for Sardanapalus: the queen is masculinized exactly in proportion as the grandson is feminized. Byron's first stage direction stresses the latter for the readers whom he considered his primary audience: '*Enter* SARDANAPALUS *effeminately dressed, his Head crowned with Flowers, and his Robe negligently flowing, attended by a Train of Women and young Slaves*' (I.ii). With national identity 'won' and sustained by 'blood, and toil, and time, and peril' (II.i.118), an effeminate king can only engender political disorder. The terms are everywhere linked: 'As femininely garb'd, and scarce less female' than his company of 'glittering girls,/ At once his chorus and his council', the king is 'subject to his slaves' (I.i.39–42, 47).

Yet as this charge is broadcast, Byron complicates it with other values. If the play's first image of effeminacy is controlled by voicings of distress over the fate of empire, Byron shows this culture also using the same set of terms to scorn any merciful and pacifist nature. This extension enables us, as Gordon Spence argues, 'to regard Sardanapalus both as guilty in his indolence and contempt for his subjects and as admirable in his pacifism and humanity'—or perhaps not even guilty: for Leslie Marchand, this is no 'indolent wallower in voluptuousness, but a contemplative character whose inaction was owing partly to his humanitarian hatred of war and violence and partly to his contempt for the ends of worldly ambition and the lust for power.'[17] To Byron's Sardanapalus, these ends are hollow: Myrrha's speaking the 'names,/ Lord—king—sire—monarch' produces 'a chill' in his 'heart, a cold sense of the falsehood/ Of this my station' (I.ii.443–49) that he links to a contempt for 'ungrateful' people who 'murmur'

> Because I have not shed their blood, nor led them
> To dry into the desert's dust by myriads,
> Or whiten with their bones the banks of Ganges;
> Nor decimated them with savage laws,
> Not sweated them to build up Pyramids,
> Or Babylonian walls.   (I.ii.227–32)

In the Assyria of Sardanapalus, such social policy gets judged only as effeminacy. Thus when the arrested conspirator Arbaces confesses his admiration for Sardanapalus' mercy, remarking that 'Semiramis herself would not have done it' (II.i.373), his ally calls him a 'Sardanapalus!/ I know no name more ignominious' (II.i.368–69), and then mocks him for a 'spirit shrunk/ Into shallow softness ... the *pardon'd* slave of *she* Sardanapalus' (II.i.397–98, 404). The italics, redundant to metrical stress, punctuate the gendered contempt.

The discourse of softness, for better and for worse, inflects these values. First heard in Sardanapalus' praise of luxuriously 'soft hours' (I.ii.8), it is then judged with shame by Myrrha; she feels 'fallen/ In [her] own thoughts, by loving this soft stranger' (I.ii.653). Yet it is also associated with gentleness: Zarina says of her husband that 'he was soft of voice and aspect,/ Indifferent not austere' to her (IV.i.241–42). This attitude is continuous with public policy. Resisting the 'too severe ... Hard' temper of Salemenes, Sardanapalus thinks of himself as 'softer clay, impregnated with flowers' (II.i.522), his metaphor also a regendering. When he idealizes himself as one who 'loves his fellows/ Enough to spare even those who would not spare him' (II.i.316–17), he evokes women's values: 'what they ask in aught that touches on/ The heart, is dearer to their feelings or/ Their fancy, than the whole external world' (IV.i.221–23).

It is this culture, Byron suggests, that determines Sardanapalus' 'effeminate character'. A sensibility fundamentally averse to its dynastic script of oppression, violence and military imperialism can refuse this male-identified rôle only by cultivating effeminacy, idealizing this resistance as a progressive humanitarianism. Sardanapalus' swerve from his dynastic precursors is also Byron's swerve from precursor texts: his Sardanapalus indulges hedonism not in default but, as Daniel Watkins argues, in 'protest against the ideology of the society he is born to rule'.[18] To conceive a ruler in such terms is a bold enough gesture in the reactionary political atmosphere of post-Napoleonic Europe, when emphatic shows of force were deemed essential. So seductively does Sardanapalus articulate his principles of pacificism and mercy, that for many critics problematic corollaries are obscured.[19] [...] Neglected in such analyses are facts Byron's play keeps in view: namely, the relation of Sardanapalus' pacifism to a social structure sustained by slavery, hereditary privilege, powerless women, and royal prerogative—one in which a king may deal with people as property and treat wife and children as political factors: 'I married her as monarchs wed—for state,/ And loved her as most husbands love their wives', he protests, thinking this bond superior to what links a 'peasant to his mate' (I.ii.213–16). The system of slavery is submitted to the least critical pressure, in no small part because its chief embodiment is Myrrha, who also figures into a sentimental representation of gender: feminine devotion to a masculine master. Under the force of this romance, Byron tends to avoid representing slavery in the play as an ideological problem. It becomes, instead, an idiom of self-pity. When Sardanapalus pleads excuse to 'gentle, wronged Zarina' by asking her to see him as 'the very slave of circumstance/ And impulse .../ Misplaced upon the throne—misplaced in life' (IV.i.330–32), the social and political facts of slavery are not only not addressed but sentimentalized. Despite Byron's own position against slavery, it is a measure of his desire to keep Sardanapalus sympathetic that he lets this trope remain uncriticized: the fault of Sardanapalus is evasion, not slave-owning.[20] The conversion of slavery from historical referent to sentimental trope is a process repeated with another historical referent in this scene, one to which McGann's recent work has attended, Byron's representation of his scandalous separation from Lady Byron in terms of a husband's remorse and a wife's forgiveness. But the result is deeply unstable, for the other scandalously derelict husband in the English press was George IV: English readers in Byron's day would be reminded of both, with conflicting effects on their sympathies with Byron's hero.

Indeed, *Sardanapalus* seems almost gratuitously to exploit popular antipathy to George IV, by provoking attention to a mistreated queen and to lavish palace revels funded at public expense.[21] Such a context, though in code, haunts the character of Sardanapalus with a degree of self-interest: his 'disposition/ To love and to be merciful, to pardon/ The follies of my species, and (that's human)/ To be indulgent to my own' (I.ii.275–78) is also a disposition, Byron suggests, to rationalize and romanticize a self-serving luxury. Even a reviewer such as Bishop Heber, who finds the character 'admirably drawn', has to note such 'selfishness' and its social default: 'He affects to undervalue the sanguinary renown of his ancestors as an excuse for inattention to the most necessary duties of his rank; and flatters himself, while he is indulging his own sloth, that he is making his people happy.'[22] Byron makes this affectation particularly legible by writing Sardanapalus' self-defence in terms that conveniently project rigid alternatives: a king either revels or is a tyrant. 'Byron's most impressive achievement', Peter Manning argues, is to expose 'the problematical motives beneath unimpeachable sentiments.'

One of the most deeply problematic motives of Sardanapalus' luxuriating effeminacy is, paradoxically, its value as self-restraint:

> if they rouse me, better
> They had conjured up stern Nimrod from his ashes,
> 'The Mighty Hunter!' I will turn these realms
> To one wide desert chase of brutes, who *were*,
> But *would* no more, by their own choice, be human.
> *What* they have found me, they belie; *that which*
> They yet may find me—shall defy their wish
> To think it worse.   (I.ii.372–79; Byron's emphases)

With warnings such as this, Byron marks Sardanapalus' effeminacy both as a protest against cultural values and, as Manning perceptively writes, 'the sign of an effort to escape the heritage of violence he fears in himself'[23]—a resistance to 'something bloody and cruel in his nature by refusing to give it any opportunity to break forth', in Allen Whitmore's elaboration.[24] It is suggestive in this respect that the ghost of Nimrod not only represents a despised cultural heritage, but conjures a bloodline that feeds a latent identity: 'He look'd like Nimrod', an astonished adversary remarks of an angry Sardanapalus (II.i.352).

To show Sardanapalus bearing this legacy even as he resists its dictates is also to imply his deep allegiance to its gendered polarities. Byron's analysis is shrewdest in his understanding of how even a sensibility inclined to cultural critique may reproduce the culture's syntax. The lurking of Nimrod behind Sardanapalus' effeminate masquerade is one sign; his orthodox view of the feminine is another. When Salemenes shames him with Semiramis, a woman who acts like 'a man', Sardanapalus reacts in terms that are utterly conservative about gender, however scathing his critique of imperial 'glory':

> she had better woven within her palace
> Some twenty garments, than with twenty guards
> Have fled to Bactria, leaving to the ravens,
> And wolves, and men—the fiercer of the three,
> Her myriads of fond subjects. Is *this* glory?
> Then let me live in ignominy ever.   (I.ii.134–39)

Weaving and spinning are Hercules' humiliation. This conservative view is also, tellingly, Byron's own: women 'ought to mind home ... not [be] mixed in society', he remarks of their 'artificial and unnatural' situation in contemporary Europe, deeming the contrasting 'state of women under the ancient Greeks' (which he was gleaning from Mitford) not only 'convenient' but ideal (*BLJ*, VIII, 15). [...]

Byron casts Sardanapalus' entry into military action in other terms, ones that seek to retain effeminate pleasures in the midst of masculine imperatives. Thus, the epiphany Myrrha announces—'He ... springs up ...// And rushes from the banquet to the battle/ As though it were a bed of love' (III.i.221–24)—involves banquet and battle in the same energy. A mirror scene marks this involution. In a complex self-regard that Byron thought 'natural in an effeminate character' (*BLJ*, VIII, 128), Sardanapalus calls for a mirror to preview himself in military garb: 'This cuirass fits me well, the baldric better,/ And the helm not at all. Methinks I seem [*Flings away the helmet after trying it again*]/ Passing well in these toys; and now to prove them' (III.i.163–65).[25] His preening suggests, in its very campiness, that he will become a 'man' less by repressing effeminacy than by giving it a larger arena of action. The provenance of the mirror is a predictor: it is a spoil from Semiramis' Indian campaign. Byron does not reject the idea that Sardanapalus' behaviour is 'natural' as well as socially cultivated, but he attempts to revise what its expression can encompass—an accomplishment that some see as a sort of brief for Byronism.[26]

A more troubling complication of the military stage is a revelation of feminine power as no less violent than the masculine terms Sardanapalus would escape. Byron has him first sense this affinity in the wake of an earlier, successfully quelled conspiracy. Recoiling from Myrrha's exhortation for swift revenge, he explains his policy in terms of sexual difference: revenge, he says, is 'too feminine, and springs/ From fear' (II.i.584–85):

> your sex, once roused to wrath,
> Are timidly vindictive to a pitch
> Of perseverance, which I would not copy.
> I thought you were exempt from this, as from
> The childish helplessness of Asian women.
>
> (II.i.586–90)

This gendering links him to general cultural attitudes: one conspirator scorns the apprehensions of another as 'weakness—worse/ Than a scared beldam's dreaming' (II.i.349–50). As the crisis intensifies, however, distinctions of gender unsettle. The verb Sardanapalus joins to Myrrha's wrath, 'roused', is the same that his allies use to name the emergence desired of him ('He must be roused'). If cultivating an effeminate character promised an escape from violence, the revelation of feminine wrath thwarts that prospect.

This contradiction was always implicit in Semiramis, but because her motive was empire, not love, her energy could be demonized. Myrrha is a more problematic revelation. The night of battle did not send her 'herding with the other females,/ Like frighten'd antelopes' but, as we learn from

Sardanapalus himself, included her in the newly 'made warriors' (III.i.377–78, 385). This equivalence poses a fascinating and disturbing disruption to his understanding of the feminine. When he reports that Myrrha appeared on the field 'like the dam/ Of the young lion, femininely raging' (III.i.378–79), his simile is doubly impressive: not only does it suggest a capacity 'natural' in a *feminine* character (to turn Byron's phrase), but 'dam' also evokes the bloodline to Semiramis, the 'blood-loving beldame,/ My martial grandam' (I.ii.238–39). Myrrha confronts Sardanapalus with wrath that is not a perversion of the 'feminine' but a new definition: 'Femininely meaneth furiously,/ Because all passions in excess are female', he is moved to surmise (III.i.380–81). His tone is wonder, contrasting his sarcastic judgements of Semiramis, but the note of 'excess' betrays how unsettling this spectacle of feminine fury is to him, even when motivated by love: it challenges all the terms of difference by which he had preserved self-regard and justified his effeminized principles of pacifism.

Byron deepens this crisis with Sardanapalus' nightmare during his rest from battle, one not staged but told to Myrrha as if to make her bear its import. It is a colloquy with his ancestors in which the grandam emerges as a grotesque of Myrrha. Sardanapalus' dream of Semiramis does more than unveil the ancestral past, Caroline Franklin proposes; it is also an anxious vision of 'how Myrrha could change' in the catalyst of violent events.[27] That the central syllables of S*emira*mis chime *Myrrha* predicts on the subrational level of phonics the nightmare's figurative logic: Semiramis usurps the lover's 'place in the banquet', substituting for her 'sweet face' (IV.i.102–03)

> a grey-hair'd, wither'd, bloody-eyed,
> And bloody-handed, ghastly, ghostly thing,
> Female in garb, and crown'd upon the brow,
> Furrow'd with years, yet sneering with the passion
> Of vengeance ....   (IV.i.104–08)

Semiramis embodies a bloody dynasty: she appears with Nimrod and a host of other 'crowned wretches,/ Of various aspects, but of one expression' (IV.i.114–15); 'All the predecessors of our line/ Rose up, methought, to drag me down to them', shudders Sardanapalus (IV.i.175–76). But more disturbing than her inclusion in the line of violence is her perversion of Sardanapalus' orthodoxy of gender. The real horror of this 'thing' is its near effacement of its feminine gender; the garb is the only sign. It is the female wretch who provokes the starkest alienation from bloodline and empire alike: a 'ghastly beldame!/ Dripping with dusky gore, and trampling on/ The carcasses of Inde' (IV.i.31–32). This psychically evolved spectre of the feminine—one which Byron exaggerated over and against competing accounts of Semiramis—is the event that most forcefully confronts Sardanapalus with the error of cultivating effeminacy as ideological resistance: not only does this royal redefinition of self fail to reform masculine culture but, Byron suggests, it involves a fundamental misapprehension of what is possible in a female garb.[28]

It is this second revelation that Byron has Sardanapalus sensationalize. Among the company, Semiramis alone leers with the passion of 'lust' (IV.i.107) as well as empire. So effectively does she embody these twin aggressions that men may be redundant; we are soon reminded that she is a 'homicide and husband-killer' (IV.i.180). Sexuality in her becomes a force of death:

> The female [...] flew upon me,
> And burnt my lips with her noisome kisses
> [...] she still
> Embraced me, while I shrunk from her, as if,
> In lieu of her remote descendant, I
> Had been the son who slew her for her incest.
> (IV.i.149–50, 155–58)

This nightmare of female sexual aggression assaults Sardanapalus' understanding of men as masters and women as their slaves. He shrinks in horror as these roles are reversed and perverted. Sexuality and violence, two energies he thought to keep opposed, are here wound together, even as they were when he entered battle 'as though it were a bed of love' (III.i.224). Neither the feminine nor the erotic secures an escape from violence, and Sardanapalus finds himself a victim of both. The psychic consequences are inevitable: 'Then— then—a chaos of all loathsome things/ Throng'd thick and shapeless: I was dead' (IV.i.156–60).

The end of the play is forecast: a release from biological and cultural heritage alike in a determined act of self-cancellation. In the nightmare of history that Byron writes for Sardana-palus, the masculine ancestors offer no refuge, though there is a momentary desire for acceptance by the 'noble aspect' of Nimrod and the race of fathers. They retain an attractiveness that exposes a need to secure a kind of masculine allegiance against the terror of female aggression: 'The hunter smiled upon me', Sardanapalus recalls (IV.i.133–34). Yet his more habitual repulsion rebounds as a fantasy of rejection: as he grasps Nimrod's hand, 'it melted', and Nimrod vanishes into 'nothing but/ The memory of a hero' (IV.i.144–46). This disappearance, repeated by his father's reticence ('he,/ I know not why, kept from me' [IV.i.177–78]), leaves the dreamer trapped between an impossible longing for masculine valida-tion and a horror at his feminine ancestry. So intimately involved is Sardanapalus' ideology of gender with his alien-ation from empire that the latter is made, ultimately, to concentrate on the spectre of the unnatural woman. Cast into the phantasmic and the demonic, Semiramis is exiled by this nightmare, spoken of no more in the play.

This purging allows Byron to attempt, in the remaining scenes, one final reordering of sexual and political priorities. It is not surprising to read in his Preface that he 'prefer[s] the more regular formation of a structure, however feeble, to an entire abandonment of all rules whatsoever' (*CPW*, VI, 16). He means dramatic structure—the 'unities' as a universal 'law of literature'—but the play makes evident the implication of social structure and distinction of gender as well. Francis Jeffrey clearly sensed this when he dismissed Byron's summoning of 'law' as 'mere caprice and contradiction': 'He, if ever man was, is *a law unto himself*—"a chartered libertine"; [a pointed phrase from the Archbishop of Canterbury's mildly sarcastic wonder at Prince Hal's transformation into King Henry V: 'when he speaks,/ The air, a chartered libertine, is still' (I.i.48–49)]—and now, ... tired of this unbridled license, he wants to do penance within the *Unities!* This certainly looks very like affectation.'[29] The correction of the libertine by classical decorum, as Jeffrey implies, has to do with more than dramaturgy. As in the case of King Henry, Byron's formalist rigour bears on Byron's self-regard and, not coincidentally, this reform emerges as the covert social allegory of the play itself.

In a cultural syntax of gendered polarities, the terms of conservative restoration are already in place, even as the empire crumbles. When Sardanapalus' eagerness to enter the final fray prompts Salemenes to remark that he sounds 'like a young soldier', he replies, 'I am no soldier, but a man'—expressing his 'loath[ing]' of 'soldiership', not with effeminacy this time but with a superior order of masculine pride (IV.i.565–67). This higher masculinity pulses throughout the play's final stages, as Byron has Sardanapalus repeatedly face down threats of unmanning. When he fears that sending his sons away 'may/ Unman [his] heart' (IV.i.210–11), the verb is reproof; when accused of indulging a 'feminine farewell' with his wife (IV.i.363), he hears the caution: 'I grow womanish again, and must not;/ I must learn sternness now. My sins have all/ Been of the softer order—*hide* thy tears ...//... they unman me/ Here when I had remann'd myself' (IV.i.396–98, 402–03); when taking leave of his remaining soldiers, he exhorts them, 'Let's not unman each other' (V.i.401). This restraint coincides with a new concern for dynasty. Diodorus reports that Sardanapalus had daughters and sons; Byron hones this into a male line, which Sardanapalus belatedly honours with regret that he has left to his 'crownless Princes' the paltry heritage of a 'father's sins', even as Zarina assures him that they will know only 'what may honour/ Their father's memory' (IV.i.276–83). His tone is affectionate and rueful, compared with Salemenes' consolation that the rebels will 'have miss'd their chief aim—the extinction of/ The line of Nimrod' ('Though the present King/ Fall, his sons live—for victory and vengeance' [IV.i.376–79]), but the fidelity is the same. Just before setting the conflagration that will keep '[his] fathers' house' (V.i.208) from delivery to the rebels, Sardanapalus bids 'Adieu [to] Assyria! ... my fathers' land' (V.i.492–93).

Sardanapalus becomes tragic to the degree that it represents the defeat, within the structures of civic life, of any effort to reform the gendered politics of patriarchy. Yet it is part of Byron's intelligence about this tragic paradigm that he lets it expose what it cannot organize and subsume—specifically, an excess of problematic individual motives. Even as Sardanapalus utters allegiance to the fathers, Byron reveals the habitual self-concern. When he imagines that in consequence of losing the kingdom, his sons will hear 'all Earth ... cry out, "thank your father!"/ And they will swell the echo with a curse' (IV.i.289–90), Byron makes his egotism indistinguishable from his care for dynastic defeat. This is also the flow of Sardanapalus' reiterated pacifism: 'To me war is no glory—conquest no/ Renown .../ ... I thought to have made mine inoffensive rule/ An era of sweet peace midst bloody annals .../ ... Sardanapalus' golden reign./ I thought to have made my realm a paradise,/ And every moon an epoch of new pleasures' (IV.i.506–19). The self-idealizing that is everywhere interwoven with this political idealism—and the self-concern evident in its easy shift from 'sweet peace' to 'paradise' to 'new pleasures'—betray motivation by an unredeemed, and ultimately unexamined, egotism. There is always critical pressure on the pathos.

The one uncritical sentimentality that Byron allows himself

is Myrrha, whom he refeminizes into heroically devoted subordination. 'Appropriately enough,' suggests Paul Elledge (who sees Sardanapalus moving 'closer toward the reconciliation of his masculine with his feminine impulses'), 'Myrrha's role as "masculine" counterpart diminishes in importance and the Greek slave assumes her proper place as a subservient, deeply affectionate companion to the king.'[30] Whether or not we share this sense of propriety, we can see how the play elicits it. Rejecting freedom, Myrrha asserts that it is 'the woman's [part to die] with her lover' (V.i.373), and Sardanapalus concurs in this essentialism: asking if she feels 'an inward shrinking' from the flames, he assures her that he 'will not love [her] less; nay perhaps more,/ For yielding to [her] nature' (V.i.414–17). Masking ideological grid as emotional necessity, Byron has Myrrha pledge herself to the suttee, doing 'for love, that which/ An Indian widow braves for custom' (V.i.466–67). If this stoic firmness produces an outcome equivalent to that gained by the 'childish helplessness of Asian women' (II.i.584–89), Byron's suppression of this question by a drama of individual desire and aesthetic spectacle is potent enough that some readers deem self-immolation a 'worthy ... apotheosis', a '*Liebestod*' (the terms are McGann's and are frequently echoed).[31] Byron's poetics of mystification are enhanced by the symbolic associations of the 'frankincense and myrrh' (details not in Diodorus) that he has Sardanapalus order for their pyre (V.i.280). These elements set the stage for an elevation beyond the mortal; they are the properties of apotheosis.

Nothing is more revealing of the way Byron's sentimental elaborations may introduce wayward complications, however, than the multivalence of this seemingly straightforward enhancement. For if 'myrrh' evokes a ritual of Christian sanctification, it also bears a second, more troubling association from a pre-Christian text: it is the shrub into which Myrrha, in Ovid's *Metamorphoses*, is transformed as a release from the agony of a birth engendered by incest with her father. In

Sardanapalus, Myrrha's name, in alliance with 'myrrh', cannot but summon this reference—one reinforced by Alfieri's sensational tragedy (1789), which Byron knew well.[32] Although his own play evades the full import of this complicated association, Myrrha's name means that it cannot be escaped entirely —especially since Ovid's story of Myrrha's incest poses a potential reciprocal to the nightmare Byron invents for Sardanapalus, of sympathy with the son who is the object of his mother's 'incest' (V.i.58).

The effect is to display yet one more phase of how Byron develops meaning by a visible revision of precursor texts. This process virtually shapes Sardanapalus' moral character in the final scenes. In a decisive recasting of Diodorus' Sardanapalus, Byron does not merely make his Sardanapalus a man; he also makes him a gentleman, one whose behaviour contrasts with the series of brutal enforcements in Diodorus' account. After sending 'much of his treasure' away with his children (I, 439), Diodorus reports, the king closed himself, his remaining 'gold and silver as well as every article of the royal wardrobe, and ... his concubines and eunuchs in the room which had been built in the middle of the pyre, [and] consigned both them and himself and his palace to the flames' (I, 441). Byron's Sardanapalus is the epitome of chivalry: he arranges the escape of his wife and sons; he cares for the safety of his harem (III.i.121, 148–49); he frees his slaves and 'all the inmates of the palace, of/ Whatever sex' (V.i.257–59); and he distributes his treasure to his soldiers, even as his favourite concubine volunteers, in love, to join him in death.

It is a short step from such idealizing to a final effort at aesthetic transcendence. Earlier English accounts, unlike Byron's play, read the scandal of gender in the king's suicide. [...] Byron, by contrast, drives towards a conclusion that effaces the social system which made gender matter. As the conflagration absorbs plot into spectacle, immediate history, with its entanglements of gender and empire, is cancelled. In the play's early scenes, Byron had Sardanapalus confront self-cancellation in different but related terms: forgoing the responsibilities of office, he has become 'a nothing' in public eyes (I.ii.103). Byron has him recall and reclaim this nullity just before he mounts the pyre; addressing a country no longer under his sway, Sardanapalus indulges one last piece of theatre, for an audience that is now only a figure: 'Adieu, Assyria! ... I satiated thee with peace and joys; and this/ Is my reward! and now I owe thee nothing' (V.i.492–95).[33] The idiom serves to project the immolation beyond the spectacle of the moment and onto the stage of universal mythology:

> the light of this
> Most royal of funereal pyres shall be
> Not a mere pillar form'd of cloud and flame,
> A beacon in the horizon for a day,
> And then a mount of ashes, but a light
> To lesson ages, rebel nations, and
> Voluptuous princes.   (V.i.436–41)

Ending the play in this fiery glow has the effect, on the level of spectacle, of endorsing Sardanapalus' script, transforming his artifice into a symbol of universal value and effacing particular problems in a clarified transcendence. Yet even as Byron bedazzles us with these higher significances, he also unsettles them with the suggestion that the pyre is merely the latest and the last sign of a consuming self-interest that habitually masks itself as higher consummation. This minor vibration remains part of the play's total expression.

What also remains is the problem of gender. In the first reviews the question was either stabilized or conspicuously evaded. Myrrha is routinely lauded as a model of feminine devotion, and the more complicated challenge of Sardana-palus' effeminacy is either effaced or recast in the paradigm of 'effeminacy transformed'. The *Examiner* declared that the king 'preserves frankness and generosity to the last'. And, long before Marchand, Jeffrey was insisting that Byron's hero 'is not an effeminate, worn-out debauchee ... but a sanguine votary of pleasure, a princely epicure.... He enjoys life ... and triumphs in death.' [...] Although Heber notes the 'selfishness' and 'self-indulgence' mixed into Byron's characterization, his willingness to subordinate these to the script of heroism written by the character himself is a telling response.[34] In happy complicity, English theatrical productions emphasized the spectacle, especially the immolation. [...] Along the way, the complex and intractable issue of the king's effeminate character is downplayed. Both William Macready and Charles Kean cut the preening mirror scene from their productions, in 1834 and 1853 respectively, and only George Henry Lewes seems to have minded. He was especially irritated by Kean's interpretation. [...] Lewes longingly fantasizes, with elaboration, the scene he misses, and he is aware of the implication, speculating that 'as [Kean] also omits to give *any* indication of the effeminacy, he, perhaps, instinctively felt that detail would raise a titter!'[35]

The suppression of Sardanapalus' potentially unheroic implication with the feminine was not absolute, however. In a production in New York in 1854, an actress named Mrs Shaw-Hamblin essayed the title role.[36] As her experiment helps us see, Byron's examination of gender holds a mirror to the culture in which it is performed: we read his understanding of gender only by becoming self-conscious about our own. If Byron allows Sardanapalus to stage his story as 'a problem few dare imitate, and none/ Despise' (V.i.447–48), the staging of *Sardanapalus* is less lofty and more perplexed. The final conflagration imitates a heroics that would transcend all ideologies, including the ideology of transcendence itself; but the problem of effeminate character continues to reproduce its daring and conflicting strains of definition.

NOTES

1. Byron's reference to Sardanapalus as an 'effeminate character' appears in *Byron's Letters and Journals*, ed. Leslie A. Marchand, 12 vols (Cambridge, MA: Harvard University Press, 1973–82), VIII, 128. Subsequent citations appear parenthetically in the text as *BLJ* with volume and page number; Hazlitt, *Table Talk*, reprinted in *The Complete Works*, VIII, 248–55. Subsequent citations are by page number.

2. David Bromwich gives perceptive attention to how Hazlitt's sympathy with Byron's liberal politics and his admiration of his genius interact with certain elements of class antagonism—as well as irritation at Byron's self-will, egotism and aristocratic contempt for the herd (*Hazlitt*, pp. 326–34).

3. Compare, for instance, Byron's gendering in acknowledging his authorship of *The Corsair* in this passage from Thomas Medwin: 'Contrary to the advice of my friends, I affixed my name. The thing was known to be mine, and I could not have escaped any enemies in not owning it; besides, it was more manly not to deny it' (*Medwin's 'Conversations'*, p. 144).

4. 'Such a character, luxurious, energetic, misanthropical', observed the *Quarterly Review*, 'is precisely the character which Lord Byron most delights to draw' (Heber, 'Lord Byron's *Dramas*', p. 494); Rutherford identifies the reviewer (*Byron: The Critical Heritage*, p. 236). In a recent paper, Marilyn Butler argues that Byron's patent echoes of several Shakespearian texts (notably, *Antony and Cleopatra*, *Hamlet*, *Richard II*) and their tragic heroes assist this identification of Byron with his hero. Once English readers recognized *Sardanapalus* as a 're-reading or misreading of Shakespeare', then 'it is a short, Coleridgean step to take the socially inaccessible private Byron to be speaking through the hero' ('John Bull's Other Kingdom', pp. 285–86).

5. Quotations from *Sardanapalus* are from *Lord Byron: The Complete Poetical Works*, ed. Jerome J. McGann, 7 vols (Oxford: Clarendon Press, 1980–91). Volume VI, which includes *Sardanapalus*, is co-edited with Barry Weller. Parenthetical citations indicate act, scene and line number. References to this edition of Byron's poetry are given as *CPW* with volume and page number; McGann's cogent remarks about the implication of *Childe Harold's Pilgrimage* in political and social contexts also articulate the larger poetics of *Sardanapalus*: 'The central ideological focus of the entire myth involves the question of personal and political freedom in the oppressive and contradictory circumstances which Byron observed in the world of his experience. More than anything else this book says that the most personal and intimate aspects of an individual's life are closely involved

with, and affected by, the social and political context in which the individual is placed' (McGann, 'The Book of Byron', p. 261).

6. Jerome McGann's shrewd perspective on the Eastern tales of the previous decade (note 5) may be extended to *Sardanapalus*: the play is the latest in this 'series of symbolic historical and political meditations on current European ideology and politics' (McGann, 'The Book of Byron', p. 262).

7. Spence, 'Moral and Sexual Ambivalence', p. 69.

8. Heber, 'Lord Byron's Dramas', p. 495.

9. Quotations, here and subsequently, follow *Diodorus Siculus*, trans. C. H. Oldfather. Parenthetical citations in my text indicate the volume and page number of Oldfather's edition.

10. 'For the historical account,' Byron writes to Murray, 'I refer you to Diodorus Sicilus' (*BLJ*, VIII, 128–29). In the first editions, Murray did not comply with Byron's request. Diodorus' basic perspective—especially the details of 'effeminacy' and cruelty—would have been available in Lemprière's popular, much published *Classical Dictionary*; my text is *A Classical Dictionary*, 'Fifth American Edition, Corrected and Improved by Charles Anthon', as well as Lydgate's *Fall of Princes*.

11. As he awaited publication of *Sardanapalus*, Byron recalled 'the Dandies' and their 'hundred fooleries': 'I liked the Dandies,' he writes in his journal: 'I had a tinge of Dandyism in my minority—& probably retained enough of it—to conciliate the great ones—at four & twenty.— —I had gamed—& drank— & taken my degree in most dissipations' (*BLJ*, IX, 22).

12. Moers, *The Dandy*, p. 47.

13. For a well-informed account of the flux of events and Byron's shifting engagement, see Marchand, *Byron: A Portrait*, pp. 336–43.

14. Elsewhere, I discuss Byron's uneasy sense of being feminized by his role as Cavalier Servente and its effects on his representation of Juan's simultaneous transvestism and enslavement in another Eastern culture, that of the Turkish Sultana Gulbeyaz (Wolfson, '"Their She Condition"', pp. 585–617, see especially pp. 604–05). Byron was composing this episode at the time he was working on *Sardanapalus*.

15. Marchand, *Byron: A Portrait*, p. 338.

16. The substitution of literary exercise for politics continued to divert Byron during these months. By the end of April, when it was clear that Italian liberation had failed, he could at once insist to Thomas Moore that 'no time nor circumstances shall alter my tone nor my feelings of indignation against tyranny triumphant', and yet still recommend, 'And now let us be literary:—a sad falling off, but it is always a consolation' (*BLJ*, VIII, 104–05).

17. Spence, 'Moral and Sexual Ambivalence', p. 60; Marchand, *Byron:*

A Portrait, p. 343.

18. Watkins, 'Violence, Class Consciousness, and Ideology', p. 806.

19. E.g. Joseph, *Byron the Poet*, p. 116; Marchand, *Byron's Poetry*, p. 103; Corbett, *Byron and Tragedy*, pp. 114–15, 98; Knight, 'The Two Eternities: An Essay on Byron', *The Burning Oracle*, p. 225; Farrell, *Revolution as Tragedy*, p. 164; McGann, *Fiery Dust*, pp. 233, 239 and 236, respectively. In 'Hero With a Thousand Faces', McGann sharply analyses several more problematic aspects of Byron's characterization of Sardanapalus (pp. 295–314).

20. Byron himself indulges a similar displacement into the figurative, abetted by the idiom of feudal romance, when he offers his play to Goethe as 'the homage of a literary vassal to his liege lord' (*CPW*, V, 8). In *Sardanapalus*, terms of slavery, sounded 42 times, most often name a social fact, usually in relation to Myrrha; but Sardanapalus, the principal slave-owner, applies 'slave' to traitors and enemies, to a restless and complaining populace, and finally to himself to excuse his failings. Byron's poetry refers frequently to slavery in classical, feudal and Eastern cultures. [...] Back home, the English press continued to expose the brutalities of the slave trade: one horrifying account appears in the same volume of the *Edinburgh Review* in which *Sardanapalus* is reviewed (pp. 34–52).

21. Thomas More, quoted in J. B. Priestley, *The Prince of Pleasure*, p. 41.

22. Heber, 'Lord Byron's Dramas', pp. 494–95.

23. Manning, *Byron and His Fictions*, p. 128.

24. Whitmore, *The Major Characters*, p. 73.

25. On the punning possibilities of 'Myrrha' as the true 'mirror' of Sardanapalus, see Christensen, *Lord Byron's Strength*, pp. 280–81.

26. This bisexual ideal is read in both personal and political conduct, often with an essentialism that matches or even exceeds that of the play's most orthodox discourses. G. Wilson Knight finds Sardanapalus 'poet-like' in a bisexuality that 'aim[s] to fuse man's reason with woman's emotional depth' ('The Two Eternities', *The Burning Oracle*, p. 247). Elledge (*Byron and the Dynamics of Metaphor*) reads the 'images of "bisexuality"' similarly.

27. Franklin, *Byron's Heroines*, p. 215.

28. Voltaire's *Sémiramis* (in *The Works of Voltaire*, XVII, 147–225) is almost an entirely sympathetic, tragic figure: she is as haunted as any Byronic hero by past sins, and her guilt is a 'dreadful malady' that weakens her grip on the 'reins of empire' (p. 149); we see her beset by base manipulators and longing for death. The incestuous desire that Byron emphasizes in the dream is recast by Voltaire as innocent (Sémiramis does not know her son and thinks he is the agent of restoration promised in the prophesies), and she welcomes his unwitting murder of her as 'the fate I merited' (p. 224).

29. Jeffrey, 'Lord Byron's Tragedies', pp. 422–23. I quote from Gary Taylor's edition of *Henry V* (London: Oxford University Press, 1984).

30. Elledge, *Byron and the Dynamics of Metaphor*, p. 121.

31. McGann, *Fiery Dust*, p. 230.

32. See Book X (II, 84–99). Myrrha, tormented by incestuous passion for her father, insinuates herself into his bed. When, after several encounters, he unmasks her, she flees to a foreign land and begs the gods for relief as she labours in the birth of their child; they change her into a myrrh tree. In Vittorio Alfieri's drama, *Mirra* (1789), she commits suicide at the mere confession of her desire. [...] Byron was violently affected by a performance in the summer of 1819: 'I am not very well today,' he writes to Murray; 'Last night I went to the representation of Alfieri's Mirra—the last two acts of which threw me into convulsions—I do not mean by that word—a lady's hysterics—but the agony of reluctant tears—and the choking shudder which I do not often undergo for fiction' (*BLJ*, VI, 206); several days later, he reports that he has 'never been quite well since the night of the representation of Alfieri's Mirra—a fortnight ago' (p. 217). Byron's subsequent formation of Myrrha in *Sardanapalus* as a transgressor of national rather than familial codes and as a willing suicide for love seems motivated in part by an effort to reconceive the horrors of Alfieri's 'representation' and its possible evocation of his own incestuous affair with Augusta.

33. The echoes of 'nothing' extend to Byron's complaint in his Preface that his 'private feelings' about keeping his plays off the stage seem destined 'to stand for nothing' (*CPW*, V, 9). For both playwright and hero, the authority of private selfhood exists in tension with social stages of action. But paradoxically, the idiom of the stage proves convenient for declarations of individual agency: against the 'nothing' that cannot protect *Sardanapalus* from the theatrical establishment, the 'nothing' Byron writes for Sardanapalus indulges a highly theatrical self-authorizing. Byron's shifting attitudes about the value of the stage are illuminated by Erdman in 'Byron's Stage Fright' in this volume, pp. 5–32.

34. Heber, 'Lord Byron's Dramas', pp. 493–94.

35. George Henry Lewes, 'Charles Kean and *Sardanapalus*', *The Leader* [25 July 1853]; reprinted in Archer and Lowe, *Dramatic Essays*, p. 252.

36. Howell, *Byron Tonight*, p. 80.

EDITORS' BIBLIOGRAPHICAL NOTE

The amount of critical work devoted to *Sardanapalus* rivals that on *Manfred* and *Cain*, not only in quantity but in quality as well. Byron thought it his finest play and recently that judgement has implicitly been reattested by the fall 1992 issue of *Studies in Romanticism* devoted entirely to it. Since that issue in effect forms a mini-book of the most recent criticism of *Sardanapalus* we have been reluctant to borrow from it for our purposes here, but its worthiness as a valuable companion to the essays included in this volume should be obvious from the range of its contents and the distinction of its corps of critics. The issue includes the following:

Butler, 'John Bull's Other Kingdom', based on the proposition that Byron shared with the other Romantics a drive to play 'a part in modelling the English sense of national identity', indeed to construct 'models of the nation in literature'.

McGann, 'Hero With a Thousand Faces', on the 'symmetries between constructs [and characters] in the play and correspondences [to characters in Byron's life and] in the world', the play's characters facing always 'in two directions, "referentially" toward certain socio-historical frameworks, and "reflexively" toward the poetic environments within which they are aesthetically active'.

Kelsall, 'The Slave-Woman in the Harem', which focuses on Myrrha (and Greece's) enslavement as 'sexual politics' in its 'widest signification', an argument set in the context of the work of Godwin, Wollstonecraft and the Shelleys—as well as owing a debt, one that Kelsall acknowledges, to Caroline Franklin's *Byron's Heroines*, which includes in Chapter 7 ('The Fostering of Masculine *Virtù* by the Stoical Heroines of the Political Plays') an excellent section on Myrrha.

Christensen, 'Byron's *Sardanapalus*', whose section titles provide some sense of the richness and scope of his analysis: 'From Despotic Politics to Economic Despotism', 'The Eighteenth-Century Background' (its 'British discourse of despotism'), 'The Political Economy of Sex', and 'Committing Anachronism' (that is, a Lukacian conception of characters expressing feelings and thoughts about historical relationships in a clearer way than the real people of the time could have done).

Corbett, 'Lugging Byron Out of the Library', on the 1990 Yale production of the play, which, he argues, reveals it to be 'a masterpiece of literary drama' as well as 'a masterpiece for the stage'; and Biggs, 'Notes on Performing *Sardanapalus*', by the director of the Yale production, who, as Marilyn Butler notes in her essay, brought out 'this astonishing play's varied possibilities: the highly theatrical remote world it evokes, the modernity and intellectuality of the issues it addresses'.

The *Studies in Romanticism* issue also contains an invaluable 'Select Bibliography for *Sardanapalus*' (pp. 387–90) compiled by Yu Jin Ko that need not, therefore, be repeated here; we content ourselves with only those few critical essays, sections of books and briefer commentary not included there:

Bell, *The Central Self*, pp. 43–52.

Brewer, 'Byron's *Sardanapalus*', pp. 77–91.

Cardwell, 'Byron: Text and Counter Text', pp. 7–23.

Clancy, 'Death and Love in Byron's *Sardanapalus*', pp. 55–71.

Manning, *Byron and His Fictions*, pp. 123–36.

Steiner, *The Death of Tragedy*, pp. 206–08, remarkable mainly for its judgement that 'nowhere else is Byron more completely a master of his means. He comes near to writing the only dramatic blank verse in the English language from which the presence of Shakespeare has been entirely exorcised.'

Byron's *Cain* and the Antimythological Myth

DAVID EGGENSCHWEILER

> The poet,
> Admired for his earnest habit of calling
> The sun the sun, his mind Puzzle, is made uneasy
> By these solid statues which so obviously doubt
> His antimythological myth....
> (W. H. Auden, 'In Praise of Limestone')

Despite the quintessential Byronism of *Manfred*, which makes it a standard anthology piece, *Cain* is Byron's most exciting and complex drama. The causes of this excitement, however, continue to change. Initial readers were justifiably shocked by the blasphemies: the occasional parodies of Genesis and the apparently reversed sympathies with the characters. But this response could not outlast the fears and tastes of the age; the various Higher Criticisms and a string of dark heroes longer than Banquo's succession made these excitements into historical curiosities. Then, modern criticism turned the play psychological and quite rightly found Cain to be an existential hero caught up in irresolvable conflicts between spirit and matter, knowledge and love—an angry young man, rebelling against a world he had not made. Yet, now, having lived and read a good way into the postmodern age, we may find that fragmented consciousnesses and vitalities of despair seem a bit quaint, that they make the play seem too comfortable. So, if we find the play more exciting than our interpretations of it, we try to find out why in order to clarify and intensify our response.

Rereading *Cain* with a confident sense of the philosophical and psychological issues that recent criticism has defined, we should still be discomforted by Byron's handling of his biblical source. If we are no longer shocked that Byron occasionally mocks the literalness of Christian faith, we may still be disturbed and interested to find him doing perplexing things with one of our main cultural myths, the story of the Creation, the Fall, and the slaying of Abel. We could feel more comfortable if we could classify his treatment of the myth—a satiric inversion or an intellectual modernization or even a framework for satiric and philosophical digression—but to do this we would have to amputate too many asymmetrical parts of this baggy dramatic monster. We would have a tidier but a less interesting play, and, besides, we would be left with an appendix of deformed parts that should feel as embarrassed together as the naughty passages exiled to the appendices of Juan's schoolbooks.

A useful way to avoid most of these simplifications is to consider *Cain* to be a play *about* the biblical myth, such that the variations in structure, style, invention and imitation, theme, characterization and point of view are all means of controlling our complex relationship to the traditional myth. This approach might seem too intellectual for the dramatic effects of the play; but, on the contrary, it should clarify those effects by showing some of the means by which Byron manipulates his reader's (or rare viewer's) responses. In fact, this reading owes less to literary criticism than to later plays—such as Shaw's *Man and Superman*, Anouilh's *Antigone* and MacLeish's *J. B.*—in which traditional myths are also explored and evaluated. Of course, Byron does not examine his myth as explicitly and obviously as later playwrights, perhaps because he was more conservative in his attitudes towards dramatic illusion. He was quite willing to play fast and loose with such illusion in his narrative poems, subverting the reader's suspension of disbelief willy-nilly in *Beppo* and *Don Juan*; but he had a stronger regard for dramatic properties, even to the point of defending the musty unities against their abuse in the contemporary plays he read for Drury Lane. So, no characters turn actors to discuss with the audience the parts they are playing; no choric commentators step through the illusory arch to lecture us about the play; in such matters of point of view Byron's play is less modern than *The Knight of the Burning Pestle*. Nonetheless, through his more conservative and often more powerful means, Byron also creates a richly complex examination of the myth he uses.

As the play begins we are given a comfortably familiar Byronic conflict (and by 1821 it should have been familiar to any literate Englishman): a gloomy rebel, upholding truth, justice and freedom, opposes an arbitrary tyrant and those who would submit in fear and self-abasement. Given some easy inversions of values, the biblical myth would do quite well to supply us with our outlaw-hero and the powerful forces he must challenge; and, to prepare us for the heroic conflict, the elevated style of the opening hymn promises that 'some samples of the finest Orientalism' will follow. But, if we are not intent on reducing the characters to the sides they represent in the politics of paradise, we should soon become pleasantly uncomfortable, not because the characters betray their political positions but because they do not consistently present them in the grand manner we had expected. Byron's sense of potential comic types (which he had already demonstrated well in the first canto of *Don Juan*) begins to qualify his mythic cast of characters. In attitudes and occasionally in style they suggest the possible outlines of a middle-class comedy or melodrama. Eve, the first woman, has become the first mother, trying to keep her children out of trouble, to see that they are hard-working, respectable family men. One of a long line of fictional mothers who wring their hands at thankless, back-talking sons, she tries to keep Cain under control through her maternal maxims. Addressing him as 'My boy', she tells him, 'Content thee with what is' (I.i.45).[1] She regrets that she and Adam were not content in their youth, but she hopes that she can spare her son those errors of innocence (how conveniently she can forget the strength of her youthful hungers). She follows with still more telling lines: 'Cain, my son/ Behold thy father cheerful and resigned,/ And do as he doth' (I.i.50–52). The touches of archaic diction only intensify the inappropriateness of this middle-class advice, which might remind us that Eve was the first Jewish mother.

Adam is as Eve describes him here, a pleasant paterfamilias, our first dad. The comment that causes Eve to recommend him as a model is his call to work:

> Our orisons completed, let us hence,
> Each to his task of toil—not heavy, though
> Needful. The earth is young and yields us kindly
> Her fruits with little labour.   (I.i.47–50)

The faintly Miltonic style does not quite overcome the blandness of Adam's comment: confronted by his son's blasphemies and his wife's fears, Adam retreats into work and duty with the uplifting assurance that things are not so bad after all. Given this kind of opposition, it is no wonder that Cain cannot fully sustain heroic proportions in his blasphemy; it is hard to remain dignified or intellectual when arguing such touchy issues with one's parents. Cain's first attack is a cheap shot at his father: when Adam points out that the rest of the family has prayed fervently, Cain replies, 'And loudly. I/ Have heard you' (I.i.24–25). Of course, Cain makes some valid points about the goodness of knowledge and the dubious justice of original sin; but throughout Acts I and II he often falls back into the petulance with which he first spoke. Even his repeated complaints that he did not ask to be born and that he should not have to suffer in a world his parents made are the frightful clichés of grumbling adolescents. In such matters we sympathize to a large extent with the frustrated Cain (as we do with Joyce's Stephen, O'Neill's Jamie Tyrone and Roth's Portnoy as they feel the frustrations of being sons),

but the touch of domestic dilemma takes some of the heroic
edge off Cain's protest.

Abel and Adah speak little in the opening of the play, but
their later appearances fit them perfectly into domestic types.
Abel is the favourite younger son, his mother's blue-eyed boy,
who never doubts that he is loved by all. He is obedient,
gentle, loving, and not overly bright. Adah is Cain's loving
and lovable wife. Although she cannot understand Cain's
frustrations and ambitions, she tries to soothe him and help
him find joy in their son and their extended family. She is also
faithful and plucky: she will stick by her husband no matter
what. Zillah, whose part is very small, is the fourth child of
Adam and Eve (the family relationships are necessarily complicated), but she always seems like Abel's wife, the sister-in-law.

Obviously I have exaggerated in describing these characters
as flat comic types. In characterization and language they
usually come much closer to their biblical prototypes. Nevertheless, the comic family pattern is there, and the characters
occasionally live down to it. Because of that pattern the play
sometimes drops from its mythic heights, and we should feel
the sense of discrepancy that we do in many modern colloquial adaptations of myths: how odd to hear Eve and Cain
quarrelling like other mothers and sons! Byron uses this
technique much more in 'The Vision of Judgment', where he
presents Satan as an old nobleman down at the heels and St
Peter as a gruff old gatekeeper. But there he is playing for
broad comedy; he is mocking the heavenly heroics of Southey
and Milton. In this play he is using the technique sparingly as
one means of distancing us from the myth, of giving us
another literary perspective on the myth without trying to
subvert it entirely.

As soon as Cain is alone he begins a soliloquy that takes us
further from the biblical source:

> And this is
> Life. Toil! And wherefore should I toil? Because

My father could not keep his place in Eden?
What had *I* done in this? I was unborn;
I sought not to be born; nor love the state
To which that birth has brought me. Why did he
Yield to the serpent and the woman? Or
Yielding, why suffer? What was there in this?
The tree was planted, and why not for him?
If not, why place him near it, where it grew,
The fairest in the centre? They have but
One answer to all questions, ''Twas *his* will
And he is good.' How know I that? Because
He is all pow'rful, must all-good, too, follow?

(I.i.64–77)

The style here is as important as the attitude it presents. The rhetorical questions, each generating its answer in yet another question, are a parody of Socratic method. The series of brief sentences, unconnected grammatically and leading to aphoristic statements, is a parody of Baconian prose. It is not important whether or not Byron was intentionally parodying specific authors; he gave Cain a style that, since the Renaissance, had been associated with sceptics and free-thinkers. He took Cain out of the Bible and placed him in another tradition. We should recognize, though, that Cain is not entirely a disinterested sceptic: his questions are mostly rhetorical and his mind already made up. He is presenting his grievance, which is partly a just one, in the semblance of inquiry; he is using a rationalistic technique of discourse in order to attack the Old Testament faith from which he originated. This is made clearer when Lucifer enters and speaks of God in a similar style:

If he has made,
As he saith—which I know not nor believe—
But if he made us, he cannot unmake.
We are immortal! Nay, he'd have us so,
That he may torture. Let him! He is great,

> But in his greatness is no happier than
> We in our conflict. Goodness would not make
> Evil, and what else hath he made?   (I.i.140–47)

Cain's rationalistic manner has turned into Lucifer's wonderfully fanciful and self-indulgent sophistry. With the advantage
of a later perspective we might hear the voice of one of
Lucifer's descendants, Browning's Caliban, who will argue
with almost the same ideas and style to justify himself against
Setebos. Lucifer and Cain are more intellectually acceptable
than Caliban (as Byron was more sceptical than Browning),
but they also argue a 'natural theology' that has forced its way
into Genesis.

Lucifer takes us again outside the myth as he uses his supernatural foreknowledge to become a scholarly commentator on
Scripture. He objects strongly that he is not to be identified
with the serpent that tempted Eve, and he implicitly cites
Scripture as his authority: 'It is not written so on high'
(I.i.219). Byron makes this citation explicit in his Preface
when he points out that Genesis does not identify the serpent
as a demon, but it is one thing for Byron to cite the Bible in
defence of his version and quite another thing for Lucifer to
do so. It is a sophisticated bit of irony to have a character from
a myth referring us to the original text in order to refute the
traditions about him that developed in later 'fable' (which
must include *Paradise Lost* as well as theological traditions).
The effect is similar to Shaw's Devil in *Man and Superman*
taking offence at Dante's and Milton's descriptions of Hell: it
makes the character both more realistic (he is a plain-spoken,
factual fellow) and more fictional (he calls attention to his
fictional nature by debating it). In both ways it undercuts the
myth by making it self-conscious, by making it recognize
itself as myth. Lucifer does this again when he tells Adah
that the kind of love she has for her brother will one day be
considered a sin (I.i.363–90). Knowing Byron's personal and
literary preoccupations, as his contemporary readers did, we

get the point at once: by having Lucifer and Adah cite scriptural precedent for incest, Byron is again baiting his moralistic critics. He is sidetracking the tale into his own scandal and tipping us the wink as Lucifer slips out of the myth and into Byron's personal life.

Finally, the most direct means of distancing us from the Bible in Act I is Cain's frequent refusal to consider the Fall in its full symbolic meanings. At times he is doggedly literal and thinks of the Fall in strategic terms, trying to figure out how his parents could have outwitted God and obtained the benefits of both the tree of knowledge and the tree of life. At other times he is philosophically idealistic, searching for reality in the abstractions Lucifer praises and considering the story of the Fall to be a set of wearying metaphors for those abstractions. So, he can pun sarcastically on the main symbols of the story: in answering his own question of whether or not God must be all-good because all-powerful, he says, 'I judge but by the fruits—and they are bitter—/ Which I must feed on for a fault not mine' (I.i.78–79). The effect here is much different than when Adam and Eve play upon these images: 'The fruit of our forbidden tree begins/ To fall' (I.i.30–31). Their puns are complex conceits, true for them in both the literal and the figurative senses with universal truths existing in realistic images; they speak from within the myth. But Cain's puns are satiric and antithetical; they play the figurative senses against the literal ones. He subverts the images of the myth. At his most sarcastic and rationalistic he says of Adam and Eve, 'What do they know? That they are miserable?/ What need of snakes and fruit to teach us that?' (I.i.461–62). Byron is being dramatically audacious. By changing the snake and the fruit into the generic plural, Cain is thumbing his nose at the whole business. He is refusing to take the Fall seriously because, as he said earlier to Lucifer, it does not correspond with his own experiences:

Thou speaks't to me of things which have long
   swum
In visions through my thought. I never could
Reconcile what I saw with what I heard.
My father and my mother talk to me
Of serpents and of fruits and trees. I see
The gates of what they call their Paradise
Guarded by fi'ry-sworded cherubim,
Which shut them out, and me.   (I.i.167–74)

Here he describes his two 'real' worlds as worlds of sight: there is the physical world of solid obstruction that he can see with common sense and common senses, and there is the visionary world of his mind. Because it is both common-sensical and abstract, Lucifer's discourse on God fits both of these visual worlds; but the tale of serpents, fruits, and trees (again the plurals) fits neither, for it is a mythic tale and cannot be explained by literal or intellectual vision. Cain resembles Auden's poet with his 'earnest habit of calling/ The sun the sun, his mind Puzzle,' and he, too, constructs his 'antimythological myth' out of the literal and the mental. Of course, Cain does not realize that his antimythological truths are the fictions of his own countermyth of heroic individualism, rationality, and rebellion; if he did, he might be more prepared for the collapse when it is his turn to become a tragic actor in the biblical myth.

Similarly, we are so much controlled by Byron's antimythological techniques—his ironic devices of characterization, style, point of view, and wit—that we almost forget that Cain must eventually be initiated into the symbolic tale. Almost, but not quite, for Lucifer reminds us with suitable double meanings: when explaining to Cain the two rulers of the universe, he says, 'not worshipping/ Him makes thee mine the same'; when Cain asks, 'And what is that?' he replies, 'Thou'lt know here and hereafter' (I.i.319–21). Philosophically, Lucifer is referring to what he will later describe as the 'two

Principles', and Jerome McGann has convincingly cited this passage to demonstrate that Lucifer, like God, is an orthodox dualist of spirit and matter.[2] But we should not let the philosophical sense completely obscure the quiet taunt of foreboding. Lucifer is also reminding us that Cain will become his through violence, that Cain will eventually learn what this means and will thereby be changed forever. Behind the face of the philosophical angel we see for a moment the traditional devil.

In Act II Byron makes his representation of the biblical myth even more ironic, almost absorbing it in an elaborate countermyth about the structure of the universe. Because his techniques are much more obvious, we may be brief. As Lucifer takes Cain on a universal grand tour to complete his sceptical education, we are taken not only from the literal setting and plot of Genesis but from its cosmology as well. As Cain soars into outer space and Paradise seems to become smaller and smaller, he sees other worlds and other times, including the more glorious earth before it was resolved into the chaos from which Jehovah created the present earth. As commentators have noted, Byron has immersed the traditional account of Creation in the sceptical solvent of nineteenth-century science and pseudo-science.[3] He has not directly denied the story of Genesis; he has instead surrounded it with vast stretches of time and space and with other kinds of creatures whose possible existence he has inferred from modern archaeology and astronomy. The effect on Cain and on readers is to make the act of Creation seem second-rate, to make man seem an insignificant being in the universe, and to make the Fall seem a tempest in a very small teapot. Also, since we have the advantage of Byron's Preface and some knowledge of nineteenth-century religious and scientific controversies, we realize what Cain cannot: Lucifer has read Cuvier's *Essay on the Theory of the Earth*, or at least he is taking sides on some clearly modern issues. The effects here are similar to those in

Act I when Lucifer argues the morality of incest or the relation between himself and the serpent. Byron is being very witty; he is having one of the principal characters in the Christian myth give us the inside story about contested details of that myth. And, although Lucifer cannot speak *ex cathedra*, we must amusedly admit that he is in a better position to know about such things than are nineteenth-century theologians. For the dramatic effects of the act we need not decide how seriously Byron himself took his theorizing or his sources (although knowing that would help us to know better how to evaluate Lucifer); more importantly we must appreciate the ironic techniques that distance us from the biblical myth and from a serious mythic form. Byron's cleverness does this quite as effectively as do his philosophical themes.

But, as in Act I, Byron subtly hints that this distancing is temporary. Cain asks to be shown Lucifer's or God's dwelling, and Lucifer replies, 'I could show thee/ Both, but the time will come thou shalt see one/ Of them for evermore' (II.ii.398–400). Again Byron reminds us of the impending murder and its consequences, and, as he has taken us further from the myth, so his hint of our return to it has become more ominous. There is a muted horror in that 'for evermore', a horror that Cain cannot yet recognize but the reader can.

In Act III Cain returns to earth and first suffers a conflict between his love for his wife and child and his despair caused by hurt pride, by a sense of undeserved suffering, and by the knowledge received from Lucifer. Cain's opening dialogue with Adah gives us a summary of his attitudes to this point, and it emphasizes the main theme of Act III, the opposition between kinship and defiant individualism. It is a quietly transitional scene: while it maintains the issues and attitudes of the first two acts, it returns us to 'the Land without Paradise' and prepares for the climax and reversal that follow. With the entrance of Abel and the making of the sacrifices, the biblical action of Cain's story begins. Until now, all has been prologue, a series of reflections on the past and its consequences. Scorning obeisance to Jehovah and the ritual of blood sacrifice, Cain speaks as he has spoken throughout; but, as he strikes Abel, he acts, he enters the myth and truly becomes Cain. Byron uses a wonderful touch of dramatic irony in having Cain say, immediately after the blow, 'Where's Abel? Where/ Cain? Can it be that I am he?' (III.i.322–23). Although in his strange new circumstances the character feels that he is no longer Cain, for us he has become the true Cain, the first murderer, the killer of his brother. Until now, he has been a composite character masquerading as Cain in an imaginary setting interpolated between chapters three and four of Genesis. He has been what many commentators have called him: a deist, a nineteenth-century liberal, a political revolutionary, a sceptic, a cousin of Childe Harold and Manfred and Lara. This masquerading has caused the greatest ironic detachment from the myth, since Cain has been an anachronism, commenting on the myth in which he finds himself and in which he knows he does not belong. This technique enables Byron to attack the moral, religious and political values that he associates with the worship of a Nobodaddy God. Byron could have continued in this manner; he could have treated chapter four of Genesis as ironically as he had treated the first three chapters on the Creation and the Fall, and he would have had a more uniform, more satiric play that was better suited to old-fashioned stereotypes of the Byronic. But he would also have had a more facile, less moving, less intelligent play.

Until he killed Abel, Cain considered himself the victim of circumstances. He complained often that he did not ask to be born, that he did not pick the fruit, that he and his children suffer for the acts of others. Since, as far as he could see, he merely happened to be Cain, the unfortunate son of Adam and Eve, he could stand apart from his parents' story, from their God and their sins and their guilt. But now the story has become his story, the sin his sin, the guilt his guilt. As this happens, the play becomes more dramatically intense and more mythic. Before, Cain considered the tale in intellectual terms: he analysed the politics of Paradise, the strategic blunders of the Fall, the injustice of original sin, even the metaphysical structure of the universe. He usually thought about things in either practical, literal terms (Adam and Eve should have stolen the fruit from the tree of life) or in representative, allegorical ones (God, whom he has never seen or heard, stands for tyranny). Because such ways of thinking are rational, the best philosophical interpretations of the play have usually concentrated on them and on the first two acts. With the murder, however, Cain begins to perceive both more personally and more symbolically. As he truly enters the myth, he begins to experience and understand it as myth, not merely as fact or didactic fable. He thereby loses a good bit of cleverness, but he gains much more in imaginative insight. The most pointed instance of this change is his deeper understanding of exile. Several times Cain had referred to the loss of Eden as the loss of his and his children's 'just inheritance'; he spoke as though it were a family estate that a heavenly shyster had diverted from the rightful heirs. But as he reacts in horror to his dead brother, he speaks differently: 'This is a vision, else I am become/ The native of another and worse world' (III.i.342–43). These lines anticipate the later curse, adapted from Scripture, that he must become a fugitive, banished from the face of the earth; and these lines interpret that curse in its most profoundly personal and mythic sense: that 'worse world' is primarily a spiritual and psychological state that Cain enters through violence. His exile occurs in the murder; the later, literal banishment is a symbolic enactment of that spiritual exile. This had also been true of the Fall and the subsequent banishment from Eden, as even Adam and Eve had been aware when they hid their nakedness in the Garden. But Cain could not understand such symbolic geography until he, too, had become an actor in the myth and entered a new state through violence, until he could say, 'I am awake at last—a dreary dream/ Had maddened me' (III.i.378–79).

This new world has its own language as well as its own appearance, for we should not expect Cain to speak as he had before the murder, just as we should not have expected Adam in Act I to speak as he had when he walked about Eden naming the creatures. Styles change with the territory and are important ways of controlling the readers' relationship to the myth. As Cain bends over the dead body, he speaks in short phrases that in their logical progression superficially resemble his arguments of Act I:

> His eyes are open. Then he is not dead.
> Death is like sleep, and sleep shuts down our lids.
> His lips are too apart; why then he breathes.
> And yet I feel it not. His heart! his heart!
> Let me see, doth it beat? Methinks—No—no.
>
> (III.i.337–41)

Yet the effects of these lines are very different from those of earlier speeches, partly because the motivation is different (Cain is desperately trying to convince himself rather than sarcastically playing with his certainties) but also because we hear echoes of Lear, bending over the body of Cordelia. When Byron is trying for big scenes (as throughout *Manfred*), he often pirates or alludes to Shakespeare. So, Cain echoes Lear, Eve in her distraught curses echoes Lady Macbeth, and even Zillah, as she kisses her dead husband, borrows phrases from Juliet's last speech. Such allusion, or unconscious imitation, reflects the changed style as the play has developed from an ironic to a tragic mode, from a commentary on the myth to a performance of it.

As the Angel of the Lord enters to pass judgment on Cain, Shakespeare yields to Scripture, and Byron writes a close metrical adaptation of Genesis. The angel, decorously standing in for God, asks, 'Where is thy brother Abel?' and Cain replies, as he must, 'Am I then/ My brother's keeper?'

(III.i.468–69). We have waited for this line, knowing that it would come, knowing that it was waiting for Cain to speak it; otherwise he would not be Cain but an imposter. And the line is thrilling, partly because it has been so tritely quoted that it is strangely renewed by its original context, partly because we are moved as we realize that Cain has found his way, after his unusual mental and physical wandering, to this familiar landmark in his myth. This feeling of fulfilment and closure is far more important than any theological issues of fatality that Byron may have been dabbling with in the play. Our sense of inevitability comes not from Cain's universe but from Byron's source, from our persistent realization throughout the play that no matter how far Cain departs from the actions and emotions of Genesis, he will end up here, as surely as Anouilh's Antigone will end up in the tomb or MacLeish's J. B. will end up abhorring himself and repenting. There are certain things that Antigone or J. B. or Cain must do; otherwise, their plays would be completely ironic, and the ironies would have nothing substantial to work against; the sources would be merely points of unrestrained departure.

Yet, Byron does not completely dissolve his play into the biblical myth. His control of context and character is better than that would permit. Cain's scornful reply to the angel is not morally or emotionally worthy of the character who shortly before realized that he had brought death into the world and made himself brotherless. Although Cain experiences his own sense of guilt and accepts responsibility for the suffering he has caused his family, he still recoils from Jehovah's judgement. His reply is a scornful but forced gesture of defiance, an attempt to hide his guilt from an opponent. After the angel sentences him to be a fugitive, Adah fears that 'whoso findeth him/ Shall slay him', and Cain replies again in proud defiance: 'Wouldst they could! But who are they/ Shall slay me? Where are these on the lone earth/ As yet unpeopled?' (III.i.481–84). Byron is being very good here. He is not only restoring for a moment Cain's sarcastic wit; he is also allowing Cain to step out of the myth once more, to comment like a clever sceptic on a logical absurdity in Genesis. But the effect is much different from what it would have been in Act I, because we now are too much out of sympathy with Cain's posing; in this context, the wit seems too strained and adolescent. And it sets him up for the angel's breathtaking reply: 'Thou hast slain thy brother,/ And who shall warrant thee against thy son?' (III.i.484–85). This comment shatters Cain's brittle detachment and restores us suddenly to the central meaning of the myth, a meaning that makes Cain's quibbles seem like a tinkling cymbal. In killing Abel he has destroyed the bonds of human kinship, the most important bonds that remained after the Fall. As Adah pleads that her son be not the slayer of his father, it is now the angel's turn to be flippant: 'Then he would be but what his father is' (III.i.489). The sarcasm of this grim joke does not lessen its horror or its importance. As the archetypal killer, Cain has set a precedent for all mankind.

Were Cain not so defensive at this point, he would not need the angel to explain the larger significance of his act. Earlier in soliloquy, without the need to defy or pose, he intuited that significance precisely: 'What shall I say to him? My brother? No,/ He will not answer to that name, for brethren/ Smite not each other' (III.i.353–55). He realized that his blow had destroyed brotherhood. Just as the action of the play has moved circuitously but inevitably toward the murder, and the ironic speeches have moved inevitably towards the lines from Genesis, so the moral themes have moved towards this realization. Cain's resentment of his parents, his suppressed jealousy of Abel, his feeling that his wife could not sympathize with his mind, his preferring to consort with spirits, his journey away from earth and mankind, Lucifer's advice that Cain should withdraw into his own inner world, and in general Cain's distancing himself from the biblical myth of the exiled family of man—all have led towards Cain's destruction of kinship and his realization of how much is thereby lost. Throughout

Acts I and II, Adah insisted on the importance of their human ties, even to the point of claiming that she and Cain could create another Paradise as long as they had each other, their son, parents, brother, and sister. But Cain could not feel how vital these ties were until he had destroyed them. Surely this theme of broken kinship accounts for Byron's interpolated scene in which Eve stridently curses her son and Adam disowns him. That scene is not gratuitous histrionics or further satire on our psychologically unenlightened first parents. It is an acting out of the broken human community, a sign that the angelic banishment of Cain is not only a divine decree, but that it is a statement of what has already happened among men and within Cain's mind and spirit. If we have been led by this point of the play to respond to the central moral gestures, we should have come to understand this symbolic meaning of the myth.

In concentrating on the moral themes of Act III, however, we should not assume that Byron has negated the political and religious satire of the first two acts. The third act does not justify the ways of God to man; it does not make tyranny or vengeance palatable; and it does not excuse ecclesiastical misuses of Scripture. These protests still stand, although protest itself has been shown to be an incomplete way of living. And Cain does not become an orthodox worshipper, although he learns more about himself and what he needs. So, he continues to assert his own self and his rights against the angel who tries to make him grovel, but he also expresses his sorrow and responsibility for what he has done to his brother: 'That which I am, I am. I did not seek/ For life nor did I make myself. But could I/With my own death redeem him from the dust—' (III.i.509–11). We should not see him as either a convert to Adam's church or a failed revolutionary, mainly because those issues are not important in the conclusion of the play. Cain remains firm enough in character that we need not assume he has changed his mind about the injustices and cowardly acts he scorned earlier, but he is much more gentle and humble as he talks about what he has done to Abel. There is only one phrase that might suggest a changed attitude towards God: Cain says to his dead brother, 'I think thou wilt forgive him, whom his God/ Can ne'er forgive, nor his own soul' (III.i.532–33). The use of 'his God' might imply a more personal relationship with God, but we must not overly generalize the point: he accepts the vindictive God here because he feels that in this instance the vindictiveness is just. Furthermore, that God is surpassed in forgiveness by Abel, who in his last speeches is clearly associated with Christ and who points towards an ethic of forgiveness that should replace the Adamic religion of retribution. This is not to say that Abel should be taken as an ideal; he is far too tepid and obtuse for that. But he does have qualities that Cain needs, as Cain admits in some of the last lines of the play:

> And he who lieth there was childless. I
> Have dried the fountain of a gentle race,
> Which might have graced his recent marriage couch
> And might have tempered this stern blood of mine,
> Uniting with our children Abel's offspring.
>
> (III.i.556–60)

This calls not for conversion but for merger: of gentleness and sternness, justice and forgiveness, and—in Lucifer's terms— knowledge and love. This conclusion is an appropriate summary for the whole play, because the reader must also reach such a balance as he tries to comprehend the complete form. He must balance the predominant scepticism, wit and ironic form of the first two acts with the traditional morality, directness, and tragic form of the third. And he must appreciate the clever, detached playing upon and against the myth yet still be able to enter into the myth when the time comes, for only in that way can he apprehend the biblical myth in the complex ways that Byron requires, as he wittily and intellectually reveals its absurdities, evils and dangers, then passionately absorbs us in its basic symbolic truth.

Although Byron does not work with myth in such a controlled and precise way in his other poems, he does similar enough things that we can feel reassured in this approach. George Ridenour, Robert Gleckner and Michael Cooke have shown us extensively that Byron treats the myth of the Fall as both an object of ridicule and as a serious symbol of man's state.[4] In the Haidée cantos of *Don Juan* Byron moves in and out of a pastoral myth at will, sometimes treating it as an ideal and sometimes playing with it as though it were a fictional stage full of puppets. And the moral and psychological complexities we have found in *Cain* are even more pervasive in Byron's works. In theme and general technique *Cain* is at home in Byron's canon. But in its specific uses of traditional myth it is an extraordinary dramatic experiment and a forerunner of much modern drama.

NOTES

1. The text cited throughout is Truman Guy Steffan's variorum edition of *Cain* (Austin: University of Texas Press, 1968). I have adopted without comment Steffan's changes in punctuation, capitalization and use of italics.

2. McGann, *Fiery Dust*, pp. 256–58.

3. In *The Romantic Ventriloquists*, pp. 284–86, Edward Bostetter pointed out that the nineteenth-century scientific speculations of Act II destroy the reader's suspension of disbelief. He considered this act, however, to be largely at odds with the rest of the play, to disrupt a straightforward treatment of Genesis in Act I and to prevent a successful return to the treatment in Act III.

4. Ridenour, *The Style of 'Don Juan'*, Chapters 2 and 3; Gleckner, *Byron and the Ruins of Paradise*, Chapter 11; Cooke, *The Blind Man Traces the Circle*, Chapter 5.

Byron's Lapse into Orthodoxy: an Unorthodox Reading of *Cain*

WOLF Z. HIRST

Although Byron repeatedly protested the orthodoxy of *Cain* (1821), the vast majority of critics regard his play as unorthodox, iconoclastic, or downright sacrilegious. I propose to demonstrate that this work is not a blasphemous vindication of man's rebellion against a malignant deity, but rather a biblical drama reflecting divine inscrutability. This paper does not deal with sectarian doctrines: by using the word 'orthodoxy' in my title and pleading that *Cain* is basically neither iconoclastic nor sacrilegious I do not wish to imply that Byron's play is free of all heresy, but I do claim that it is not anti-religious, that it accepts rather than reverses the Scriptural position, and that the hero's attacks upon God are dramatically invalidated. [...]

I

It has often been falsely assumed, in Byron's times and in ours, that since Cain's sacrilegious utterances reflect the author's views they may be taken as stating the work's doctrine, but an analysis of the ironic pattern in the play will establish that although Byron projects himself into his hero, *Cain* retains sufficient dramatic objectivity to bring it closer to a conventional justification of God's ways to men than to the iconoclastic attacks voiced by its protagonist. The latter's evolution from uncompromising pride to relative resignation follows the classical development of the tragic hero from hubris through peripeteia to *anagnorisis*: like Oedipus, Cain, ironically, achieves the opposite of what he intends, for he too acts in ignorance 'maddened' by 'a dreary dream' (III.i.378–79). Spiritually blinded by his pride, he causes the death of a close relative, and then gains moral insight and self-recognition as he faces a God Who remains as inscrutable as ever. In the course of this process he becomes at least vaguely aware of the irony of his actions.

Few literary episodes are more pregnant with irony than the act of fratricide in Byron's drama. The irony of Cain's surrender to fury, to irrationality, after vainly pleading with his brother for reason, is enhanced by the circumstance that Cain's murderous frame of mind was caused by Lucifer, the advocate of reason. Cain felt cursed unjustly and taunted his parents with their expulsion from Eden for eating of the tree of knowledge, with rashly causing mortality; yet Cain himself effects a new curse, Cain's own quest of knowledge made him ally himself with Lucifer, and Cain recklessly brings death into the world. Though denouncing animal offerings for God he sacrifices a human victim to his own rebellious nature (an irony reinforced by 'the imagistic framework of the drama'[1]), after harping on the theme of innocent suffering he makes the innocent Abel and Zillah suffer, and having vainly longed for more satisfactory communion with his fellow men he now asks in despair: 'Who makes me brotherless?' (III.i.335). Restless and never at peace with himself, he has acted as if branded by an imaginary mark of Cain, at last earning the real mark which is set upon his brow.

This accumulated irony undercuts Cain's blasphemies; his sacrilege is not the play's. Inasmuch as the hero is the author's self-portraiture, the ironic attitude makes clear how inadequate Byron felt his impious sentiments to be. But we must treat Cain, the basically noble but flawed hero, as tragic protagonist. Although the play may fall short of tragedy in some respects, it fits Richard B. Sewall's definition of the

tragic vision, which 'sees man as questioner, naked, unaccom-
modated, alone, facing mysterious, demonic forces in his own
nature and outside, and the irreducible facts of suffering and
death', and which 'impels the man of action to fight against his
destiny, kick against the pricks, and state his case before God
and his fellows'.[2] The ironic treatment of Cain's hubris, again
true to the classical pattern, tends to vindicate the powers
against which the hero arose and to reaffirm the cosmic order.
Cain has been falsely credited with a 'Satanism' which is
condemned by its very logic.[3]

Byron's own analysis in his letter of 3 September 1821 to
John Murray casts Lucifer as tempter preparing the catastrophe:

> Cain is a proud man: if Lucifer promised him king-
> doms etc., it would *elate* him; the object of the
> Demon is to *depress* him still further in his own esti-
> mation than he was before, by showing him infinite
> things and his own abasement, till he falls into the
> frame of mind that leads to the Catastrophe, from
> mere *internal* irritation, *not* premeditation, or envy
> of *Abel* (which would have made him contemptible),
> but from the rage and fury against the inadequacy of
> his state to his conceptions, and which discharges
> itself rather against Life, and the author of Life, than
> the mere living. (*LJ*, V, 470)

Cain's dejection is caused by a discrepancy between the
consciousness of his own insignificance (II.ii.420–21) and the
infinite world encompassed by his imagination (II.i.98–109),
between his real 'state' and his ideal 'conceptions'. By guiding
him through space and Hades, Lucifer stimulates both Cain's
yearning for knowledge and his sense of limitation, thus
aggravating his 'internal irritation', and if such a 'frame of
mind' leads to disaster, Lucifer is the scheming tempter of
orthodox tradition. But critics ignore, misinterpret or reject
Byron's own interpretation and see the demon as representing

the rational good opposing human frailty within Cain. Leslie A. Marchand, for example, takes the extreme view that 'the roles of god and devil are reversed, for Lucifer is a champion of the "good principle"'.[4] Granted, Lucifer counsels reason and Cain's irrational anger brings about the catastrophe, but the conflict between reason and unreason is formulated as a choice 'betwixt love and knowledge' (I.429), and despite Adah's plea Cain chooses knowledge. Equally poignant is Cain's later repartee to Lucifer that he pities the latter 'who lov'st nothing' (II.ii.338). The externalization of Cain's inner conflict shuttles him between the advocates of love (Adah and Abel) and reason (Lucifer). Both love and reason are forgotten in the act of murder, so that Cain not only lapses from pure reason into defective humanity, but also becomes traitor to warmth, compassion and fraternal love. The irony of the rationalist's most irrational act is compounded by Cain's interposition between Abel and his sacrifice in the name of a love for all living things which he tragically fails to exhibit towards his brother at the very moment. Unremitting love and unconditional forgiveness—Adah's and Abel's humanity—can be emulated by mankind and would have prevented the catastrophe. But the suppression of all human sentiment for the sake of an abstract rationality—Lucifer's postulate—is ultimately untenable for man. Cain, by virtue of his human limitations, will never escape into Lucifer's realm. Lucifer's rôle thus falls into an archetypal pattern: reason untempered by love is evil, as are, for example, Iago's diabolical intellect and the narrow logic-chopping of Goethe's Mephistopheles. Byron's unfeeling demon glories in splendid isolation, whereas for the sensitive Adah 'solitude seems sin' (I.i.474). Cain's ironic reversal from self-imposed loneliness to enforced exile teaches him that man forsakes the dictates of sympathy and companionship at his own peril. No amount of stoicism, rationalistic argument, or Faustian aspiration will compensate for denial of feeling. Redemption can be brought about only by wedding the understanding to love (as

Shelley's Prometheus is reunited with Asia), and if reason clashes with love, man is to choose the affections of the heart over the meddling intellect.

This critique of unmitigated rationalism invalidates the traditional view of the play's bias towards sacrilege. True, the spokesmen for God's position (Adam, Adah and Abel) are so much Cain's intellectual inferiors as to provide no match for him, let alone for the subtle Lucifer, as has repeatedly been pointed out. [...] But since Byron wrote drama and not a theological disputation, we must modify the charge that Lucifer, and Cain when voicing the opinions of Lucifer (the 'more ironic and sophisticated Cain'[5]), have all the best arguments: although Adah's and Abel's simple speeches sound less persuasive than Lucifer's and Cain's high rhetoric, their attitude is vindicated by the play's ending. It might be argued that a divine tyrant ironically exploits the noble Cain to further His own malicious purpose, since the ignoble (because submissive) Adah and Abel do not lend themselves to such exploitation. I view the ironic contrast differently: the passive Adah and Abel accept imperfect justice and achieve good, whereas Cain thirsts for reform and compounds injustice. As M. G. Cooke remarks, Cain's problem is that he 'seeks to equate the logical ability to perceive imperfection with the practical ability to renounce and remove it'.[6] *Cain*, like *Oedipus Rex*, demonstrates how man's limited reason is an inadequate guide in a world ruled by mysterious power. This theme is already far from blasphemous, and yet it might be restated in even more orthodox terms. Since the act of fratricide ironically demonstrates how the hero achieves the opposite of what he intends, the play not only vitiates Cain's acceptance of Lucifer, which involves rejection of love (I.i.429), but it also seems to suggest that the hero would have escaped his fate had he embraced the principle opposing Lucifer—God—and that this principle requires love. Symbolically, the victory of human love over knowledge might be seen as the triumph of divine love, Cain's choice of reason over love as renunciation of God, and Abel's Christ-like forgiveness combined with Adah's passionate constancy as the persistent watchfulness of providence despite man's repudiation. The latter interpretation develops Christian concepts only hinted at in the text. Nevertheless, the very possibility of even suggesting a formulation of the action in these terms reinforces my contention that the play ultimately establishes the inscrutability of divine providence.

II

Just as the author's self-dramatization and Lucifer's rational-istic arguments do not make the play blasphemous, so Byron's romanticizing of the biblical figure, 'part of a new trend to transform Cain from villain to hero',[7] does not constitute a glorification of his defiance of God. Scripture condemns the crimes perpetrated by hero-villains like the Corsair, Manfred and Cain but not their Romantic features: obsession with a curse, regret for lost innocence, oppressive awareness of ephemerality and the futility of aspirations, life-weariness, disillusion—though these are conducive to rebellion. In one instance (Job) rebellion itself is almost condoned. In fact Scripture is not only the source of Byron's subject (and of his language) but of a number of Romantic traits of his hero.

A prominent biblical feature of the Byronic hero is of course the curse of the 'fugitive and vagabond', the Cain curse. But the mark of Cain, always a symbol of homelessness, was experienced most acutely by several Romantic heroes, for example the Ancient Mariner, the different versions of Ahasuerus, Chateaubriand's René, or Byron's own Harold, Giaour, Selim, and Manfred. In *Cain* homelessness becomes restlessness, which, in turn, as in other Romantic hero figures, is associated with a pursuit of eternal repose, a longing for death. Byron's Cain is the Romantic wanderer, the spirit searching for mental quiet, which is most poignantly expressed in the play's last line with Adah's parting wish of 'Peace be with him', and Cain's desperate reply: 'But with *me*!' Yet, paradoxically, Byron's protagonist exhibits restlessness, the symptom of the mark of Cain, long *before* his monstrous crime produces the mark itself. When the hero reminds us: 'Never/ Knew I what calm was in the soul' (III.i.204–05), we realize that one of the causes of the murder—feverish unrest —is a trait that logically should only result from it. Further-more, the poet induces in us an unconscious association between father and son by means of the protagonist's imagi-nary portrait of Adam's expulsion from Paradise 'with death/ Written upon his forehead' (II.i.74–75), a connection which strengthens the impression that a particular curse pervades Cain's world quite independent of the act (the sin of fratri-cide) that led to it. What Adam, however, has bequeathed to his son is not restlessness, but hard labour (III.i.109–10), so that before Cain draws upon himself the curse of fratricide he is already twice accursed: he bears an invisible mark of Cain and he has inherited the consequences of his parents' disobe-dience.

The biblical Fall motif, impersonal and remote when related to other Romantic heroes, becomes personal and immediate for Cain, who suffers for the sins of his own parents; and whereas others may yearn for a vague Eden or golden age of the distant past, Cain gazes back in despair at tangible Paradise. There is hence little sentimentality about his cry for the irrevocable yesterday, as in his lament over the fate of his 'disinherited boy' (which is also his own fate). Although Adah must admonish her brother not to whisper 'Such melancholy yearnings o'er the past' (III.i.32, 36), Cain's gloom is less mawkish than the ill-defined longing of most Romantic heroes. Similarly, Cain's plaint over the impermanence of human existence is not sentimental and has the full force of its meaning, since he cannot take comfort (like Job and his imita-tors) that it has been so for countless generations. Byron borrows an image from the previous chapter of Genesis (3:19) to express Cain's sense of ephemerality: 'being dust and grov'ling in the dust/ Till I return to dust' (III.i.114–15). This Romantic hero does not merely protest mortality but dramatically reproaches his parents for his condition.

Cain's protest exhibits the same psychological dilemma as Job's: in both the death wish co-exists with the lament over death's inevitability. When Job bemoans the ephemerality of life (10:20 or 14:1–2) he thinks of man's fate in general; when he exclaims 'Would I had never been born' (3:3) he refers to his private misfortune. But Cain, more paradoxically, speaks of himself in both instances: 'Must I not die?' (I.i.29) and 'Would I ne'er had been/ Aught else but dust!' (I.i.291–92). Cain yearns for death because, like Manfred and Faust, he is overcome by a sense of the futility of life that but leads to death (I.i.109–10), so that although he does not seek it he 'would behold at once what [he]/ Must one day see perforce' (II.i.195–96), and on achieving this preliminary object he pleads further:

> Since
> I must one day return here from the earth,
> I rather would remain. I am sick of all
> That dust has shown me; let me dwell in shadows.
> (II.ii.106–09)

In the second half of this quotation Cain expresses his death wish as *taedium vitae*, another typically Romantic sentiment to be found in the Bible, especially in Ecclesiastes. In Cain the cause of this life-weariness is entirely intellectual: unlike the Preacher he has not drunk life to the lees. He shares, however, the Preacher's insight into his own limitations, not only the sense of human ephemerality but also the consciousness of mental inadequacy, 'for we *know* nothing' (II.ii.61). As the example of Ecclesiastes shows, these two causes of frustration—the sense of transience and the recognition of the impassable bounds of knowledge—are in turn produced by heightened understanding. Ultimately increased consciousness goes back to the Fall, but in *Cain* only the cursed hero remains affected by it. It is this sharpened awareness—the analytical intellect of a Lucifer or Mephistopheles—that instils in Romantics the feeling of weariness with life, the frustration that makes Cain exclaim: 'I feel the weight/ Of daily toil and constant thought' (I.i.174–75). The 'daily toil' Cain recognizes as the punishment of Adam, but he does not associate the 'constant thought' and 'The mind which overwhelms' him (I.i.189) with that knowledge that Adam and Eve acquired by eating of the forbidden fruit. Until after the peripeteia Cain fails to recognize the curse inherent in the attainment of knowledge and perceives only its positive aspect:

> The snake spoke truth. It *was* the tree of
>   knowledge;
> It *was* the tree of life. Knowledge is good,
> And life is good, and how can both be evil?
>
> (I.i.36–38)

In both Genesis and *Cain* the gift of knowledge is ambivalent. In the Bible the tasting of fruit from the tree of knowledge is forbidden, but the text does not state that the apple itself is wicked, or that the 'knowledge of good and evil' is iniquitous. Adam and Eve sin through disobedience and are punished, yet, by this fall, man gains 'knowledge of good and evil'; he achieves that moral awareness which is put to the test throughout the Bible and most immediately in God's warning to Cain (Genesis 4:7). In Byron's drama Cain does not quarrel with Lucifer's variation upon the *felix culpa* theme, his parting remark that despite the apple's 'fatal' consequences it bore a 'good gift ... reason' (II.ii.459–60). As for other Romantic heroes, for Cain the positive aspect of reason lies in the unlimited possibilities of human aspiration. But Cain forgets it is the rational mind that curses man with consciousness of his own imperfections. Reason teaches that 'the human sum/ Of knowledge' is 'to know mortal nature's nothingness'

(II.ii.421–22). Reason reminds man of his lost paradise, shows him the injustice of the world, and makes him aware of life's transiency and his inferiority to his desires and conceptions (II.i.82–83). It is the tension between man's knowledge of his ephemerality, his shallowness, pettiness and blindness—in short his limitation—and his Faustian longings for infinitude, for perfection, absolute knowledge and eternal life that constitute Cain's *Weltschmerz*.

[...] Yet, the most striking feature of the Byronic hero, as distinct from the Wordsworthian solitary for example, is his recusant and ungovernable nature, whether as gloomy social outcast, descendant of the Gothic villain in *The Corsair* and *Lara*, or as the defiant Promethean and metaphysical rebel in *Manfred* and *Cain*. The charge of iconoclasm revolves around Byron's treatment of Cain's rebellion. It can be argued that if we sympathize with Cain merely for his suffering the play may be orthodox, but if we are made to identify ourselves with Cain's rebellion the work is sacrilegious. Here again a comparison with Job will be enlightening. There is an undeniable element of rebellion in Job's persistent questionings of divine justice and in his refractory self-justifications when seen against the meekness of the Three Comforters. What we admire in Job, however, is not revolt *per se* so much as the acute sense of right from which this revolt derives. Just as we respect Job's insistence on his innocence, so we esteem Cain's quest for absolute justice (I.i.77, II.ii.238, 289–305). As long as rebellion is sustained by such sentiments neither work condemns it.

Unlike Job, however, Cain's sense of right (together with reason and love) forsakes him momentarily when he is blinded by murderous frenzy. Cain is punished with exile not for his sacrilegious speeches but for his criminal act: 'Cain, what hast thou done?' (III.i.469). Yet Byron connects the crime with rebellion. Cain's rebellion (like that of Doctor Faustus) attracts Lucifer and encourages him to exploit Cain's mood for murder. To quote Byron's letter again: 'the object of the

Demon is to *depress* him [Cain] still further in his estimation', and the slaying of Abel is an act 'which discharges itself rather against Life, and the author of Life, than the mere living'. This is rebellion gone astray. In retrospect the indictment for murder warns against the blinding danger of rebellion. The book of Job, on the other hand, censures the blindness of the rebel's opponents (the Three Comforters) more than the rebel's own. Byron's play damns rebellion more than does the book of Job because Job rebels and gets away with it.

I now seem to have made Byron's drama more orthodox than Scripture. This alarming conclusion will be rectified if we bear in mind that the infinitely more blasphemous Cain deserves more than a comparatively mild rebuke. [...] Another difference between Job and Cain is that while Job ends in complete humility, Cain's recantation is halfhearted. Cain's submission is interrupted by two outbursts of his former recalcitrance: 'Am I then/ My brother's keeper?' (III.i.468–69) and 'That which I am, I am. I did not seek/ For life nor did I make myself' (III.i.509–10). In the first Byron transforms the biblical Cain's cowardice into defiance. But this outburst does not undermine Cain's newly gained submissiveness, for Cain has simply forgotten himself under the impact of his crime. Nor can the second speech be read as proof of Cain's unchanged obstinacy, because it expresses new disillusionment with himself as much as old rebellion against God and is immediately followed by a Christ-like sentiment: 'But could I/ With my own death redeem him from the dust—' (III.i.510–11). The two temporary lapses into former revolt indicate an attitude more ambivalent than Cain's earlier uncompromising blasphemy, but they are no less consistent with a reformed temper than the momentary flicker of old pride at the end of *Oedipus Rex* and *Othello*. Cain too has undergone tragic discovery and self-recognition. The discovery is Death and the insight his new sense of responsibility (III.i.371–74). He is 'awake at last' (III.i.378), and as he bids his dead brother farewell a new tone of humility creeps into his voice:

> if thou see'st what I am,
> I think thou wilt forgive him, whom his God
> Can ne'er forgive, nor his own soul. Farewell.
> I must not, dare not touch what I have made thee.
>
>   (III.i.531–34)

After the fratricide Cain's submissiveness markedly predominates over rebelliousness, so much so that it is he who warns his usually humble sister–wife: 'No more of threats' (III.i.525). Suffering has taught him wisdom. [...]

III

Let us now take a closer look at the portrait of the malignant deity painted by Lucifer and Cain. The latter's most clearly formulated assault upon divine justice occurs in the first soliloquy:

> The tree was planted, and why not for him?
> If not, why place him near it, where it grew,
> The fairest in the centre? They have but
> One answer to all questions, ''Twas *his* will
> And he is good.' How know I that? Because
> He is all pow'rful, must all-good, too, follow?
> I judge but by the fruits—and they are bitter—
> Which I must feed on for a fault not mine.
>
>   (I.i.72–79)

Cain's allegation is threefold: first, God is blamed for supplying the temptation, not man for succumbing to it. Second, the punishment is undeserved by Cain since the transgression was his parents': the innocent are made to suffer. And third, the nature of the penalty (the 'bitter fruits') is incompatible with divine benevolence.

The last of these accusations questions God's mercy rather than his justice. Of the various 'bitter fruits'—expulsion from Eden, toil, painful childbirth, mortality—Cain is most preoccupied with the sentence of death, which indeed was the penalty predicted for eating of the tree of knowledge. Whereas Cain seems to regard the paradox of God's granting eternal life to Adam in Paradise only to withdraw it again in punishment for disobedience as a malicious design to make man lament his loss, he fails to realize that, alluring as the fruit of the tree of life—immortality—appears, there is no reason to assume that it would have been less bitter than the equally alluring apple of knowledge. God's timely intervention may have spared him and his descendants unknown misery. On the other hand neither in the biblical nor in Byron's version is it clear whether seizure of the forbidden fruit of knowledge caused mortality or merely an awareness of it. Part of the ironic treatment of the protagonist lies in his failure to consider the second possibility. Cain complains that before Adam 'plucked/ The knowledge, he was ignorant of death' (I.i.296–97) without recognizing that his words may be literally true: perhaps Adam did not pluck death but the knowledge of death. Cain's attack upon the 'bitter fruits' of the Fall rests upon misunderstanding, since the fruit of knowledge with its burden of ever-increasing awareness is what he himself pursues. To an aspirer such punishment is merciful—indeed, it is as much reward as punishment.

Cain's charges concerning the suffering of innocence and the nature of temptation are more difficult to dismiss. Byron neatly solves the moral problem involved in Cain's inheritance of his parents' sin by making him repeat it, by transferring the motif of the Fall from parents to son (just as the mark of Cain motif is expanded from son to father). This motif is further developed in the series of falls from the beautiful pre-Adamite creation (II.ii.124), through Eden and then the present 'young' world of Cain and Abel (I.i.49, II.ii.216, III.i.20), into the still greater misery of subsequent generations (II.ii.223–27). The reference to future incest (I.i.363–67) is not only an illustration of Byron's obsession with the theme but also a dramatically justified prediction of a world still further fallen. This decline is paralleled in the Bible: Adam and Eve, Cain, Noah's generation and the repeated sins of the Israelites ultimately punished by exile. The fall of Cain in Byron corresponds precisely to the fall of our first parents in the Old Testament. For Lucifer is a tempter. Although the demon, being of spiritual nature, would have scorned to assume the shape of a creeping thing of earth—and Byron corroborates in the Preface that Lucifer is not the serpent—he lies when he insinuates that spirits never tempt men (I.i.217–42). Lucifer and the serpent perform the same function: they tempt with knowledge, only half fulfil their promise and cause tremendous sorrow. With the forbidden fruit Adam and Eve procured knowledge, knowledge of death, and yet their eternally dissatisfied son seeks to know more of this enigma. Under Lucifer's influence Cain initiates mankind into further knowledge of death by supplying the concrete example: 'Death is in the world!' (III.i.370), and yet it remains a mystery. Preoccupied with his parents' fall, Cain is ironically unaware that Lucifer tempts him as the serpent tempted Eve, an analogy instinctively made by Adah (I.i.392–93, 400–05). Furthermore, the demon produces what Byron's letter calls 'the frame of mind that leads to the catastrophe'. Adah testifies to the spirit's evil effect on the temper of her husband (III.i.45–51), whose old frustrations are now intensified by the cosmic journey and intelligence of future misery, and Cain's own account reflects how Lucifer has succeeded in aggravating his victim's self-abasement by stimulating his imagination (III.i.65–69). Lucifer fosters Cain's jealousy (II.ii.338–54), which alone—unlike that trait in his biblical counterpart—would never have made a murderer of Byron's rational Cain, but this submerged trait is nevertheless released in the blind fury of rebellion. By leaving Adah and accompanying his tempter Cain takes the first step in his repudiation

of love and brotherhood. In his surrender to Lucifer's temptation of knowledge, he is, like his parents, undeterred by the
threat of death: he would gaze upon 'the great double
myst'ries' even if he were to perish in the event, thus evoking
Lucifer's apt retort: 'There/ The son of her who snatched the
apple spake' (II.ii.403–09). Though Cain did not pluck the
forbidden fruit himself, he betrays his complicity by
condoning Eve's disobedience ('if it be such a sin to seek for
knowledge'), so that even Adah must convict him: 'Alas! thou
sinnest now' (III.i.92–93).

Adah's pious innocence, like Abel's, obviously serves as a
foil to the sacrilege that leads to murder. Yet it is easily overlooked that since Adah does not blaspheme she is not cursed.
The curse is portrayed in the play as dread of death, but Adah
does not brood over human transience, is happy 'despite of
death' (I.i.468), and does not feel 'The want of this so much
regretted Eden' (III.i.40). Although all four children of Adam
and Eve eventually suffer, only Cain, who repeats his parents'
rebellion, feels pained and doomed throughout, which implies
that the sins of the fathers are not indiscriminately visited
upon the children. With the catastrophe Cain might have
pleaded the murder and its consequences as bearing out his
contention that God punishes an innocent son for his father's
sin (or an innocent family for the crime of one of its
members), but although he does not openly withdraw his
earlier allegation of divine injustice, his present silence is a
kind of retraction. Similarly, without explicitly rescinding his
indictment of God for exposing Adam and Eve to forbidden
fruit, he fails, significantly, to repeat his accusation in more
personal terms: why didst thou lead *me* into temptation? Cain
begins to recognize his own responsibility: by ignoring the
lesson of his parents' fall he succumbed to a like temptation,
first Lucifer's and then that of his own irrational impulse, his
murderous frenzy; by slaying Abel he has indicted himself for
causing the very injustice against which he inveighed—innocent suffering. Obsessed with his guilt he senses that he

cannot press his earlier charges and thus they lose their effect. Whereas in a court of law, as in life in general, no argument is vitiated by its advocate, yet in drama the ironic situation of a blinded protagonist tends to undermine his case, especially if he abdicates it himself as the result of newly gained insight. Although they have not been disproved in so many words, the course of events has dramatically nullified the insinuations in Cain's first soliloquy that God trapped man and meted out merciless and unjust punishment.

Cain's explicit assumption of responsibility (III.i.371–75) also undermines the two refractory eruptions discussed above, the fatalistic but irrefutable comment 'nor did I make myself' (III.i.510) and the defiant 'Am I then/ My brother's keeper?' (III.i.468–69). Cain's free choice of knowledge over love has already proved that the play is not a fate tragedy and forced the question of predestination into the background: whether Cain was preordained to sin becomes as irrelevant as whether Abel's (or Job's) innocence is due to grace. In Genesis 4:7 God's warning to the future fratricide (omitted by Byron to make the murder unpremeditated) establishes Cain's freedom of choice. The poet follows the Genesis story in emphasizing his hero's free will and leaving it unreconciled with divine providence, so that the indictment of Cain is not an indictment of the Lord who created Cain; and God, Abel's real 'keeper', does not become a murderer for failing to prevent murder.

This does not mean that Byron reveals why God allowed fratricide to occur, or, as Walter Scott would have liked, 'the reasons which render the existence of moral evil consistent with the general benevolence of the Deity' (*LJ*, VI, 3). Abel's devout assertion that 'Nothing can err, except to some good end' (III.i.234) does not explain innocent suffering, his own, or Zillah's, or a wounded lamb's (II.ii.289–305), or the human condition in general, the woe caused Cain by 'the inadequacy of his state to his conceptions'. But the poet's failure to solve the intractable dilemma of theodicy does not make his play sacrilegious. The false impression of sacrilege is created because accusations, logically formulated by Lucifer and Cain, receive no convincing verbal refutation from their pious opponents, and it is overlooked that such refutation would in fact constitute the solution of insoluble questions. [...] Lucifer's and Cain's sacrilegious indictment is dismissed not through logical debate in the dialogue but by means of an artistic pattern of conflict, irony, reversal, and recognition. [...] Byron does not aim at establishing any doctrine. I admit that Byron gives the problem of theodicy a prominence lacking in the biblical version and has Cain and Lucifer pose it in unusually vitriolic terms. This emphasis, however, renders the dramatic rejection of sacrilege more conclusive and enhances the poetic effect by creating a more powerful contrast and poignant *anagnorisis*. The forcefulness of Byron's question must not be interpreted as a blasphemous answer.

Byron faithfully transfers an unsolved theological dilemma from Scripture to drama. By substituting an angel for the Lord he avoids increasing the crudity of biblical anthropomorphism which the introduction of God on the stage would have entailed (see *LJ*, VI, 16). But Byron's drama conveys a sense of the inscrutable God of Genesis. Since the question of innocent suffering must remain unanswered, it would have been easier to convict a deity appearing before the audience than one unseen and unheard. Better no answer than one unsatisfying. Cain's crime, however, does receive its answer: the remonstrance 'The voice of thy slain brother's blood cries out/ Ev'n from the ground' (III.i.470–71) reinforces the murderer's sense of guilt by objectifying the voice of his conscience. Only who is to express this remonstrance? If Lucifer represented the play's ideal, a Prometheus championing mankind against a malignant deity, it is he who should have upbraided Cain for the act of fratricide, for abandoning the dictates of reason. On the other hand Cain would not be able to accept the angel's reproach if it were the taunt of a fatuous messenger (like Aeschylus' Hermes) sent by a mali-

cious tyrant. To make one more comparison with the book of
Job, which also depicts the legitimate quest for a solution to
the dilemma of unmerited pain: the answer Job receives out of
the whirlwind asserts divine providence and leaves it a
mystery. This disappointment is lessened in *Cain* for two
reasons: Byron does not arouse our expectations by introducing the Lord to offer a reply, and God or his messenger
owes no explanation to a murderer. The question of divine
justice is solved in the book of Job no more than in *Cain*. If
Cain's punishment—eternal exile and mental self-torture—
exceeds his crime, the restoration of Job's family and wealth is
inadequate compensation for innocent suffering. Since Job's
guilt is dubious at most and Cain's undeniable, the balance of
crime and punishment is not fairer in Job than in *Cain*.

Nor is it fairer in Genesis. Whereas the sentence of the
biblical Cain is more deserved because his fratricide is
premeditated, Byron's hero, in glaring contrast with the pious
humility of his brother, explicitly causes the divine rejection
of his offering through his blasphemy (III.i.246–47) and
Manfred-like refusal to kneel (III.i.269–70). If Cain's rebellious stance may be condoned elsewhere, during the sacrifice
it is dismally out of place. Furthermore, the enlightenment
and at least partial reformation of Byron's hero and Abel's
Christ-like forgiveness suggest a divine purpose which
remains more obscure in the Bible.

Finally, if we were to insist that *Cain* comprises an explicit
theological statement, we would have to conclude that it is
more orthodox than Milton's conscious attempt to 'justify the
ways of God to men'. By transferring the motif of the Fall
from Adam to a murderer, to a man who should have been
forewarned by his parents' fate, Byron facilitates the task of
vindicating God. But of course *Cain* makes no categorical
assertion at all, blasphemous or otherwise, though tone and
structure convey an overall point of view, which we may now
redefine: the futility and danger of reason's rebellion, even in

the name of justice, against the human condition and against the mystery of the cosmic order.

IV

[...] Cain is biblical in spirit despite Byron's radical transformation of his source character. This metamorphosis is obvious, but the opposite process, the Bible's part in modifying the 'Byronic hero' concept, has not yet been fully appreciated. For this hero has evolved. Although Cain exhibits most of the 'Byronic' traits of the poet's earlier creations, the author's extravagant and one-sided posturing has given way to a more conventional, balanced and critical attitude. We have seen that Cain's lament over lost Eden and immortality is not as sentimental as in other Romantics but dramatically justified. Moreover, although Cain feels no less cursed and isolated from mankind than his precursors, pariahdom and alienation are no longer the insignia of unequivocal superiority as they were in Childe Harold and Manfred, for example. These heroes almost succeeded in an impossible attempt to suppress all feeling, 'to steel/ The heart against itself' and battle to the end 'cursing the heart by which [their] very humanity survives'. In the peripeteia of *Cain*, however, the act of murder and the ensuing impact are entirely emotional. Like Harold and Manfred, Cain longed to be a spirit free from 'clay', but this hubristic aspiration is rejected by the tone of the biblical drama and abandoned by the remorseful hero himself. The glorified Byronic revolt against accepted values, primarily social in *Childe Harold's Pilgrimage* and the Oriental Tales but assuming cosmic proportions in 'Prometheus', *Manfred* and *Cain*, is ironically reversed in the last and yields, if not to unmitigated humility and resignation, yet to repentance and new acknowledgment of the limits of human understanding. Cain is a more tragic figure than his predecessors. [...] Rebellion is no longer vindicated.

[...] Byron's subsequent work proves that the biblical mood reflected in *Cain* does not represent his settled *Weltanschauung*, but then he never seems to have acquired a definite system of thought or belief: he was a Romantic seeker, a metaphysical 'Pilgrim of Eternity'. Not only as authentic biblical drama but as manifest assertion of the tragic vision, *Cain* conveys a standpoint too absolute for Byron's philosophy of uncertainty. His relativism found its outlet in the shifting poses of *Don Juan*, where, as David Leigh has pointed out, the poet 'attempts to describe the human situation in purely secular terms'.[8] The spirit pervading *Cain* represents an extreme in the Byronic canon, not of the 'Satanic' viewpoint, but of a Job-like rebellion and silence in the face of divine mystery.

NOTES

1. Elledge, *Byron and the Dynamics of Metaphor*, pp. 141–42. In his article 'Byron: Troubled Stream', p. 629, Leslie Brisman makes a subtle point: 'In a terrible irony, even the soil is alienated from Cain when it absorbs Abel's blood; as a vagabond, Cain will be estranged from the earth he thought most truly his own.'

2. Sewall, *The Vision of Tragedy*, p. 5.

3. To this day perhaps the best defence of the play against irreligion is '"Harroviensis", A Letter'. The argument of this pamphlet was 'conclusive' for Byron, who intended to append it to the drama in the next edition. See *The Works of Lord Byron: Letters and Journals,* ed. Rowland E. Prothero (London: John Murray, 1898–1901), VI, 49, 54, 60–61, hereafter cited as *LJ*.

4. Marchand, *Byron's Poetry*, p. 86.

5. Prior, *The Language of Tragedy*, p. 258.

6. Cooke, *The Blind Man Traces the Circle*, p. 77.

7. Roston, *Biblical Drama*, p. 203; cf. Thorslev, *The Byronic Hero*, pp. 92, 98, 178.

8. Leigh, *'Infelix Culpa'*, p. 132.

'In Caines Cynne':
Byron and the Mark of Cain

DANIEL M. McVEIGH

The dedicatory letter to John Cam Hobhouse which introduces Canto IV of *Childe Harold's Pilgrimage* explains that
the Childe has finally become almost indistinguishable from
the poet he made famous, because Byron 'had become weary
of drawing a line which every one seemed determined not to
perceive'.[1] It was not the last line so ignored. Byron's work
has always given his readers the *impression* of autobiography.
Has any other writer created characters—Harold, the Giaour,
Conrad, Manfred and the rest—so quickly assumed to be
authorial alter egos? [...]

Now, Byron clearly *did* inject a good deal of himself into his
'heroes'. Yet the image of ego projection perpetuates a
tendency to see those heroes in isolation from their context—
as *his* 'voice' set against opposing, non-Byronic 'voices'. This
weakening of the usual critical assumption of distance
between writer and work has resulted in a depressing tendency
to reduce Byron's elusive vision to the far simpler amalgam of
attitudes identifiable as 'heroes'. *Cain: A Mystery* strikes me
not as one of Byron's best works but—given both the now-
amusing furor at its publication[2] and the modern tendency to
convert it into an ideology—as one of the clearest instances of
critical oversimplification of the complex, ironic world of his
dramatic poetry. For the disparity between the Byronic hero's
assertion of ego and the vision self-enclosed in the dramatic
world he inhabits—the gap between part and whole—manifests itself in irony. Byron's Chamois Hunters and Abbots, his

273

Adams and Abels, have dramatic lives (though small ones) of their own, and they perform the healthy function of framing Romantic assertion in such a way as to draw attention to its limitations. Manfred's people were, after all, happier under Manfred's father.

In 1821 Byron was entering late into Cain mythology. At most important stages of the tradition neither ambiguity nor irony has played much part. The Yahwist himself appears to have had in mind the fruits of Adam's sin, imbuing an ancient tale of farmer-nomad hostility with a vague sense of what was later called original sin. To the early church fathers, Abel symbolized Christ, and Cain us. The Cains of medieval mysteries would be surly, almost laughable brutes. Folk mythology through the ages made Cain the progenitor of *Beowulf*'s 'eotenas ond ylfe ond orcneas',[3] and later of the slaves of pious plantation owners. The Romantics, Peter L. Thorslev, Jr, tells us, linked Cain with noble outlaws like Faust, Satan, and Prometheus—and the ancient fratricide, after twenty-eight unappreciative centuries, had finally been promoted to rebel. Jorge Luis Borges, an heir to this vision in our age, has wondered which of the two—Cain or Abel—was the good brother.[4]

Yet Byron's Cain fits snugly into no single part of this tradition. Here is how his drama portrays the startling moment at the heart of the Cain mythology—the crushing of his brother's skull before a smoking altar. After God's whirlwind scatters Cain's fruit offering, Abel urges his brother to sacrifice again, 'before/ It is too late':

> *Cain.*   I will build no more altars,
>   Nor suffer any—
> *Abel* [*rising*].   Cain! what meanest thou?
> *Cain.* To cast down yon vile flatt'rer of the clouds,
>   The smoky harbinger of thy dull prayers—
>   Thine altar, with its blood of lambs and kids,
>   Which fed on milk, to be destroy'd in blood.

Abel [*opposing him*]. Thou shalt not:—add not
    impious works to impious
    Words! let that altar stand—'tis hallow'd now
    By the immortal pleasure of Jehovah,
    In his acceptance of the victims.
Cain.   *His!*
    His pleasure! what was his pleasure in
    The fumes of scorching flesh and smoking
        blood,
    To the pain of the bleating mothers, which
    Still yearn for their dead offspring?
                         (III.i.288–301)

Confused and outraged, Cain presses to throw over Abel's
offering, and the tragedy is at hand.

Cain.   Give—
    Give way!—thy God loves blood!—then look
        to it:—
    Give way, ere he hath *more!*
Abel.   In *his* great name,
    I stand between thee and the shrine which hath
    Had his acceptance.
Cain.   If thou lov'st thyself,
    Stand back till I have strew'd this turf along
    Its native soil:—else—
Abel [*opposing him*].   I love God far more
    Than life.
Cain [*striking him with a brand, on the temples,*
    which he snatches from the altar]. Then take
        thy life unto thy God,
    Since he loves lives.
Abel [*falls*].   What hast thou done, my
        brother?
Cain. Brother!

Abel.   Oh, God! receive thy servant, and
          Forgive his slayer, for he knew not what
          He did....   (III.i.309–20)

What are we to make of this? Are we dealing with a climax,
or an anticlimax? We might assume that Cain's blow is not
aimed against Abel, but against an unjust life and a tyrant
God. Byron, writing to John Murray on 3 November 1821,
commented that Cain strikes 'rather against Life—and the
author of Life—than the mere living'.[5] W. Paul Elledge accordingly tells us that the murder is 'a vicarious assault on God
Himself'. Taken in this sense, Cain's lashing out at a God who
demands blood sacrifice (Byron loved animals, as G. Wilson
Knight reminds us) is the resistance of a rebel—a Romantic
Prometheus or Faust, assaulting an archaic, oppressive
Christianity. If such critics as Thorslev and Elledge are right
about *Cain*, then (in a sense) so was the 'Devout Stockade', as
Truman Guy Steffan calls the nervous voices of orthodoxy in
Byron's time.[6]

Still, this approach brings problems. Cain does *not*, after all,
kill God, but his own brother—and not inadvertently. Lines
308–11, 314–15 and 316–17 imply a threat against Abel's life.
No Billy Budd, Cain assaults Abel in a murderous fit of rage.
He repents frenzy rather than accident. To make matters
worse, Abel's last words of forgiveness echo, not Christ
Pantocrator, but Christ martyred. So even devoted fans of the
Byronic hero tend to have troubles with Cain. Edward E.
Bostetter, adding a twist to the hero theory, writes:

> Ironically, Cain is led into the very violence he has
> opposed, into adopting the tactics of the tyranny
> he has defied. Broken and defeated, he is driven
> into exile as much by his parents, self-righteous
> supporters like Abel of the tyrant God, as by the
> Angel. And, at least momentarily, he abandons his
> right of reason, repudiates his trip with Lucifer as a
> 'dreary dream,' and intellectually submits to the

values of the victor. Cain suffers the tragic fate of the enlightened man who openly challenges the anachronistic ruling dogmas of society.[7]

Yet this, too, is peculiar. Did God kill Abel? Or tell Cain to? Did Eve, or Adam? Is Abel's mother 'self-righteous' in being more than merely aggravated at her son's killer? Besides, Byron himself told Murray (3 November 1821) that Lucifer deceives Cain into slaying his brother.[8] If so, Cain, in bludgeoning Abel, turns towards Lucifer, not away from him. Outside the dramatic context, Lucifer's speeches make fine rhetoric, but within it they lead Cain, like Manfred, only to his 'proper Hell' (*Manfred*, I.i.251). In fact, throughout the drama Cain often seems less like Prometheus or Faust than like a naïve boy, with a surly streak. To G. Wilson Knight he has 'many virtues of Christian tone'.[9] Yet he ends as mankind's first murderer, not as Christ but as Christ's killer. Is it not Cain's pathetic *weakness* rather than his strength that Lucifer has played on—and in this case, what is heroic (never mind titanic) about poor Cain at all?

Still, the aspects of the drama which have led critics like Elledge, Thorslev and Bostetter—as well as the parsons of Byron's own time—to see *Cain* as a theodicy-in-reverse cannot be ignored. Cain complains powerfully against God's order; the play explores the conundrum of evil in the world with brutal frankness; and, as contemporary critics were quick to note, Lucifer's opinions about the deity are never refuted. Lucifer's God is Blake's Nobodaddy, a God of holocausts and death. Satan assails Milton's God in similar fashion, of course, but *Paradise Lost* leaves Satan chewing ashes. In contrast, *Cain* keeps a suspicious silence about Satan's aspersions. Was Byron then of the devil's party, knowing it? But if so, why choose Cain—especially *this* Cain—to carry the burden of his protest? Like a true devil, Byron seems everywhere, and nowhere.

Perhaps it is *Cain*'s fundamental ambiguity that has made

good critics look like so many blind men, stroking Byron's ears and trunk and legs. Voices revealing a certain strain have tended to mutter about his lordship's 'poverty of religious ideas' and his 'sophomoric and bland philosophizing'.[10] Calvert sees the poet as 'unconsciously' putting strong arguments in his devil's mouth (p. 176), while Steffan concedes that Lucifer's arguments are weak because Byron himself was no good at that sort of thing (p. 459). More aggressively, Leonard Michaels sees *Cain* as so muddled philosophically as to constitute an attack on the aspirations of intellect itself.[11] Now, Byron's gift was not for metaphysics, but too much apologizing would doubtless be unfair to his quicksilver genius. No Augustine or Dante, he asked, not answered, questions. In addition, his characters speak for themselves, and not necessarily for him. Contradiction, I think, lies at the heart of *Cain* itself—and as much as any work this 'mystery' is tossed about on the edge of certain conflicting currents in the Byronic sea.

Like 'The Rime of the Ancient Mariner', 'Christabel', and *The Borderers*, *Cain* is a Romantic exploration of the spiritual fracture which Western tradition has long termed 'evil'. Any interpretation that makes the first murderer a hero in any but an ironic sense risks improbability. Still, Byron portrays Cain sympathetically; he felt deeply ambivalent towards his own ego projection. Cain finds himself (in the poet's own ambiguous term) in 'The Land without Paradise', trapped between desire and reality. Wanting—needing—life, happiness, freedom, he faces death, misery, entrapment:

> Cain [*solus*].   And this is
>   Life!—Toil! and wherefore should I toil?—
>   because
>   My father could not keep his place in Eden.
>   What had *I* done in this?—I was unborn:
>   I sought not to be born: not love the state
>   To which that birth has brought me. Why did he

Yield to the serpent and the woman? or,
Yielding, why suffer? What was there in this?
The tree was planted, and why not for him?
If not, why place him near it, where it grew,
The fairest in the centre? They have but
One answer to all questions, "Twas *his* will,
And *he* is good.' How know I that? Because
He is all-powerful, must all-good, too, follow?
I judge but by the fruits—and they are bitter—
Which I must feed on for a fault not mine.

(I.i.64–79)

Unlike his parents, and like us, Cain has not *lost* paradise. His Eden is a paradise of the mind, defining itself by negation, forever out of reach, like the fruit of Tantalus. The members of his family, all 'as pious as the Catechism', as Byron described them to Murray (*BLJ*, IX, 53), accept the idea that, since they themselves have fallen, their place is a fallen world. But Cain—a Romantic—sees the original sin as 'a fault not mine', and Eden as his 'just inheritance' (I.i.87). An Everyman, he is torn existentially between ultramundane imaginings and the cold reality of the senses.

So Lucifer enters.[12] His early appearance suggests what even in Byron's time a critic like Francis Jeffrey saw: that Lucifer is 'little more than the personified demon of [Cain's] imagination' (quoted by Steffan, p. 365). The demon shapes inchoate doubts and ambiguities in Cain's own mind: 'Thou speak'st to me of things which long have swum/ In visions through my thought ...' (I.i.164–65). Lucifer exploits the traditional devil's advantage by holding out what Cain already secretly wants. As Steffan notes (pp. 50–60), tension arises between the two. Lucifer is the voice of one part—but only one—of Cain's soul. Against it other parts, like those given symbolic voice by Adah and Abel, will struggle.

With Lucifer begins the central irony which energizes the drama as it dances between the appearance of Cain's strength and the reality of his inner weakness. Dramatically, Lucifer draws out the implications of this ironic disparity to their logical conclusion in the slaying of Abel, weakening Cain by means of ostensibly encouraging words and actions. This counterplay between Cain's apparent 'enlightenment' and his real fragmentation is progressively revealed and the disparity widened until it climaxes in fratricide—an exercise of brute force urged by a consciousness of absolute powerlessness.

Lucifer confuses in order to seduce. The seduction involves three interdependent movements:

(1) He convinces Cain that the universe is a curtain rent to the bottom. God's tyranny can never be secure; the world is volleyed between him and Lucifer—the 'great double mysteries! the *two Principles!*' (II.ii.404), in one of Byron's less immortal lines. Lucifer's vision only superficially resembles Manichaeanism, since neither principle embodies good, a binding as opposed to destructive force. Both principles struggle only for power. Byron was not Shelley, and his Lucifer is no Prometheus. Lucifer himself admits the amorality of his shoving match with the Creator. 'Dost thou love nothing?' Cain asks. And Lucifer responds, 'What does thy God love?' (II.ii.310). *Cain* often answers one such question with another. But the implication is clear: neither of Lucifer's '*two Principles*' is love. The universe blindly struggles for power; it creates only to destroy, its law a perverse Darwinism, the survival of the weakest, the devolution of species. Lucifer is not a Manichaean, but a nihilist.

(2) This belief in a primal fault in the universe, in its movement towards the *tōhū wā bhōhū* of Genesis or the χάος of Hesiod, hastens Cain's own tendency towards emotional disorder. Lucifer widens the divide between Cain's aspiration and reality; he gouges deeper Cain's gulf of purposelessness. He praises his spirit:

> *Lucifer.*   I know the thoughts
> Of dust, and feel for it, and with you.

Cain.   How!
   You know my thoughts?
Lucifer.   They are the thoughts
      of all
   Worthy of thought;—'tis your immortal part
   Which speaks within you.   (I.i.100–04)

He urges spiritual independence: 'Nothing can/ Quench the
mind, if the mind will be itself/ And centre of surrounding
things—'tis made/ To sway' (I.i.210–13). Yet these rallying
cries alternate with a Mephistophelian scorn for the 'Poor
clay!' (I.i.123) that is man. Cain's tour through time and space
to Hades stretches unbearably this disparity between ambition and hopelessness. His sense of self-worth plunges; his
aspiration soars:

   Oh God! Oh Gods! or whatsoe'er ye are!
   How beautiful ye are! how beautiful
   Your works, or accidents, or whatsoe'er
   They may be! Let me die, as atoms die
   (If that they die), or know ye in your might
   And knowledge! My thoughts are not in this hour
   Unworthy what I see, though my dust is;
   Spirit! let me expire, or see them nearer.
                                   (II.i.110–17)

Yet Lucifer convinces him that the distance between earth and
heaven can never be bridged, the walls of Eden can never be
scaled. Finally, Cain's 'enlightenment' amounts to this:

Cain.   Alas! I seem
      Nothing.
Lucifer. And this should be the human sum
      Of knowledge, to know mortal nature's
         nothingness;
      Bequeath that science to thy children, and
      'Twill spare them many tortures.
                                   (II.ii.420–24)

(3) The increasing fragmentation of Cain's ego widens the rift between him and his family. In drawing away from the rest of the human race, Cain shies away from a part of himself. Lucifer sets about quickly to further Cain's estrangement from the others (I.i.319–31), and he succeeds. Like most of us, Cain wants to believe that love and knowledge are co-operative forces. Lucifer argues that they are irreconcilable antagonists (I.i.426–27). To follow Lucifer, Cain must leave Adah. In Lucifer's world, sexual love is 'a sweet degradation,/ A most enervating and filthy cheat' which procreates misery (II.i.55–60), and Cain's debt to Adam and his family amounts to a mutual curse (II.ii.22–26). Finally (and climactically), Lucifer cleverly introduces the subject of Abel:

> *Lucifer.* I pity thee who lovest what must perish,
> *Cain.* And I thee who lov'st nothing.
> *Lucifer.*   And thy brother—
>   Sits he not near thy heart?
> *Cain.*   Why should he not?
> *Lucifer.* Thy father loves him well—so does thy God.
> *Cain.* And so do I.
> *Lucifer.*   'Tis well and meekly done.
> *Cain.* Meekly!
> *Lucifer.*   He is the second born of flesh,
>   And is his mother's favourite.
> *Cain.*   Let him keep
>   Her favour, since the serpent was the first
>   To win it.
> *Lucifer.*   And his father's?
> *Cain.*   What is that
>   To me? should I not love that which all love?
> *Lucifer.* And the Jehovah—the indulgent Lord,
>   And bounteous planter of barr'd Paradise—
>   He, too, looks smilingly on Abel.
> *Cain.*   I
>   Ne'er saw him, and I know not if he smiles.

Lucifer. But you have seen his angels.

Cain. Rarely.

Lucifer. But
Sufficiently to see they love your brother:
His sacrifices are acceptable.

Cain. So be they! wherefore speak to me of this?

Lucifer. Because thou hast thought of this ere now.

(II.ii.337–55)

As might be expected, Lucifer is a subtle devil.[13] He aims, after all, at getting blood on Cain's hands.

Lucifer's boasts, arguments, and evasions combine to accomplish two things: they make Cain admire Lucifer (and thus his own spiritual aspiration) more, and himself and his humanity less. The erosion of Cain's self-image undermines the wholeness of personality needed to keep ego assertion within non-destructive bounds. One aspect of Cain's personality—not evil in itself—gains a destructive ascendance over his gentler social tendencies. Cain carries this Fall within him. His spiritual fracture becomes symbolically externalized in the irrevocable sundering of the human family at the end of the play. As Cain's sister and epipsyche (resembling in this, perhaps, Manfred's Astarte), Adah symbolizes the gentler half of a divided personality. Yet even in her pious heart the devil's temptations find a disturbing echo (I.i.403–10). The three suggest in their dramatic configuration a psychic fracture the symbolic outcome of which will be Abel's murder. The fratricide destroys a part of Cain himself: 'I/ Have dried the fountain of a gentle race,/ Which might have graced his recent marriage couch,/ And might have temper'd this stern blood of mine ...' (III.i.556–59). Cain's descendants will inherit his spiritual fracture. This recapitulated Fall is the culminating irony of a profoundly ironic drama. Bitter at death, Cains brings it violently into the world; a hater of sacrifice, he spills Abel's blood; seeking the divine, he finds a curse.

Though Byron, writing to Douglas Kinnaird on 4

November 1821, disingenuously claimed that *Cain* was 'as orthodox as the thirty nine articles' (*BLJ*, IX, 56), the work is far from an orthodox Christian statement because it raises and never dispels the disturbing possibility that Lucifer's vision of the universe—no matter how destructive its implications— may be accurate. Lucifer *may* oppose God in an eternal duel with no one the winner, and everyone the loser. If so, perhaps man *should* despise his mortal part, and retain the dignity of his immortal spirit through an act of heroic self-isolation. Byron was not a nihilist, I think, but he knew before Nietzsche what nihilism was, and its spectre haunted him. On the other hand, what if Lucifer only blusters? His strength may be weakness; his knowledge, ignorance. Even Cain's cosmic tour may be deception, a diabolical magic-lantern show accompanied by the sales pitch of a charlatan. Byron never tells us if or when his devil lies; he leaves the reader, too, without Paradise, with no way to scale its walls, or even peep over them.

Lucifer and Cain apparently give voice to an important part of Byron's own personality, one of which the poet himself was highly suspicious. Byron's is not a world of ideology, but of ironies and uncertainties. As Byron insisted to Murray (8 February 1822), 'Cain is nothing more than a drama—not a piece of argument' (*BLJ*, IX, 103). Byron is far larger than any of the human characters in *Cain*, and his sympathies are with all of them, making their way in a hard world. Leonard Michaels, indeed, claims that Abel's murder 'makes him no different essentially than he was alive—uncritically pious, mentally dead—and it leaves us with no sense of loss' (p. 75). But I find it hard to believe that Byron feels this way. Though he himself was not one of the Abels of this world, he did not hate, or even despise, them.[14] The image of his ventriloquizing through an assemblage of heroic alter egos obscures the real truth that *none* of his characters speaks unqualifiedly for him. No master of Negative Capability, Byron could nonetheless find in himself both Imogen and Iago. Thus his portrait of the apparently very un-Byronic Abel is in its own way as

sympathetic as his portrait of Cain. Cain ends up, after all, not
a tragic but rather a pathetic hero. His pursuit of truth makes
piety impossible for him, and he rises above the Adams and
Abels around him. But to follow Lucifer is to leave Adah. A
Byronic hero—an ironic hero—he gains stature, but loses that
fellow feeling with suffering man felt by less imaginative and
less daring characters. In terms of knowledge, the Harolds and
Manfreds and Cains of Byron's world become more human; in
terms of love, they become less so. [...]

Such an ironic context as *Cain*'s scarcely offers a metaphysical doctrine. Yet many critics today seem as unable as the
clerics of Byron's age to spy the double edge of his vision.
Byron is a poet, not of despair, but of existential uncertainty.
On one level *Cain* is an early birth of that agonized stage of
Christianity in which scientific philosophy first called into
question the literal truth of biblical symbols. Drawn to the
spirit of Christianity, Byron could not accept its letter, or the
dogmas of a Scripture whose meaning is restricted within the
bounds set by the mimetic understanding. His own Cain-like
disequilibrium between the pull of the senses and that of the
spirit gave rise to such marvellously enigmatic statements as
this, to an apprehensive Thomas Moore (8 March 1822):

> This war of 'Church and State' has astonished me
> more than it disturbs; for I really thought 'Cain' a
> speculative and hardy, but still a harmless produc-
> tion. As I said before, I am really a great admirer of
> tangible religion; and am breeding one of my daugh-
> ters a Catholic, that she may have her hands full. It
> is by far the most elegant worship, hardly excepting
> the Greek mythology. What with incense, pictures,
> statues, altars, shrines, relics, and the real presence,
> confession, absolution,—there is something sensible
> to grasp at. Besides, it leaves no possibility of doubt;
> for those who swallow their Deity, really and truly,

in transubstantiation, can hardly find anything else otherwise than easy of digestion.

I am afraid that this sounds flippant, but I don't mean it to be so; only my turn of mind is so given to taking things in the absurd point of view, that it breaks out in spite of me every now and then. Still, I do assure you that I am a very good Christian. Whether you will believe me in this, I do not know.... (*BLJ*, IX, 123)

Has any other English writer had such a voice, or entangled his meanings in such Gordian knots? Satire and sincerity are so delicately intertwined that to seize on one threatens to tear the other. Alexander's ancient recourse may tempt us, but it sunders Byron along with the knot. His side glances are not just habitual; they are compulsive. Writing to Douglas Kinnaird on 11 September 1821, he could describe *Cain* as 'full of poesy—& pastime.... It is in my very fiercest Metaphysical manner—Like "Manfred" and all that' (*BLJ*, VIII, 205).[15] Byron's startling capacity for self-distancing from his own posturings makes much of his work enormously difficult to reduce to the usual critical categories, since criticism itself tends to use the very different language of analysis and logic. How many critics have seen 'pastime' in *Cain*? Byron often wore Turkish uniforms and Albanian uniforms— but can we doubt that he knew better than those who gawked at him what he was doing in them? *Cain* moves in many different directions at once, some of the more pugnacious of them, doubtless, for 'pastime'. Intellectually Deist, emotionally Catholic, Byron understood the void that might underlie both ways of looking at the world. Faith did not come easily to him—but neither did disbelief. As William P. Fitzpatrick writes,

> Byron's mysteries preclude resolution on any 'philosophical' level—they defy the facile assignment of delineated motives to either God or His

mortal antagonists. Byron's vision is paradoxically dual, and although beyond logic, ultimately honest. Because of his devotion to the real human condition the plays defy synthesis with any abstract system, whether it be Deism, Calvinism, or Catholicism.[16]

So Byron's spiritual homelessness poetically resulted in the kind of ironic indirection we find in *Cain*, where critics have so often bobbed for dogmas like children for Halloween apples, with less success. Byron always slips away from us. Lucifer is both rebel and demon; Cain, both Faust and brute. Adam and Eve are puny sticks of figures—but not murderers. God permits evil in the world, but often those who fight him accomplish it. This kind of ironic indirection, I think, typifies Byron's struggle with the paradoxes of reality, with what Thomas McFarland has analysed in his study of Wordsworth and Coleridge as the 'chorismos' in Romantic vision between the world of the senses and the 'hyperouranic' world of the imagination.[17] If the Romantic quest was marked by an often desperate combat against the age's tendency towards fragmentation, then Blake charged his enemy, and Wordsworth and Coleridge ultimately withdrew behind Tory fortifications. Byron fought as a guerrilla. A visionary, he saw the limitations of all vision; a revolutionary, he rebelled against his own Augustan sense of order. So *Cain* is neither theodicy nor manifesto; it is a wandering in those desert regions without Paradise, looking back at Eden with bitterness, and with longing. In a sense, then, *Cain*'s wanderings are those of Christianity itself for the past two centuries—and Byron, as much as Blake and Coleridge, was its prophet. [...]

NOTES

1. *The Works of Lord Byron: Poetry*, rev. edn, ed. E. H. Coleridge (London: John Murray, 1898–1904; rpt. New York: Octagon Books, 1966), II, 323. All quotations from Byron's poetry are from this edition.

2. [Ed. note: For the fullest account of this furor see Steffan, *Lord Byron's 'Cain'*, pp. 309–426.]

3. *Beowulf*, l. 112. For the phrase 'in Caines cynne', see l. 107.

4. Thorslev, *The Byronic Hero*, pp. 92–98, 176–84; Stabb, *Jorge Luis Borges*, p. 99.

5. *Byron's Letters and Journals*, ed. Leslie A. Marchand (Cambridge: Harvard University Press, 1973–82), IX, 54, hereafter cited as *BLJ* plus vol. and page.

6. Elledge, 'Imagery and Theme', p. 51; Thorslev, *Lord Byron*, pp. 3–15; Steffan, *Lord Byron's 'Cain'*, pp. 26–34.

7. Bostetter, *The Romantic Ventriloquists*, p. 288.

8. 'Cain is a proud man—if Lucifer promised him kingdoms &c.—it would *elate* him—the object of the demon is to *depress* him still further in his own estimation than he was before—by showing him infinite things—& his own abasement—till he falls into the frame of mind—that leads to the Catastrophe ...' (*BLJ*, IX, 53).

9. Knight, *Byron and Shakespeare*, p. 178.

10. Rutherford, *Byron: A Critical Study*, p. 91; Elledge, 'Imagery and Theme', p. 50.

11. Calvert, *Byron: Romantic Paradox*, p. 176; Steffan, *Lord Byron's 'Cain'*, p. 459; Michaels, 'Byron's Cain', pp. 71–78.

12. Lucifer is 'A shape like to the angels,/ Yet of a sterner and a sadder aspect/ Of spiritual essence' (I.i.80–82). We might compare him to Manfred's last tempter, that 'dusk and awful figure' who symbolizes Manfred's curse (*Manfred*, III.iv.62). Lucifer is the spirit of Cain's curse. But Cain's guilt, unlike Manfred's, lies in the future.

13. Intermittently, one might note, the mask of Lucifer, existential rebel, slips slightly, and just for a moment Byron lets the red mask of the traditional folk devil peep out; see, for example, II.ii.209–14, 397–99. Perhaps these are among the moments of 'pastime' in the play of which Byron spoke; see *BLJ*, VIII, 205.

14. By 'Abels' I do not mean political Christians like Robert Southey, whom Byron both hated and despised. A contemporary 'Abel' might have been a certain John Sheppard, an obscure author of devotional works who wrote to Byron saying that before his wife's recent death she had composed a prayer that the poet would turn from evil to good. Byron's gently diplomatic response (8 December 1821; *BLJ*, IX, 75–77) reveals a side of his

personality which might surprise those most familiar with the haughty poet of legend.

15. In a letter to Murray (12 September 1821), Byron also spoke of *Cain* as being in his 'gay metaphysical style' (*BLJ*, VIII, 206).

16. Fitzpatrick, 'Byron's Mysteries', p. 624.

17. McFarland, *Romanticism and the Forms of Ruin*, pp. 401, 393–418.

EDITORS' BIBLIOGRAPHICAL NOTE

Criticism on *Cain* is extraordinarily plentiful, extending quite literally from Byron's own day (and the pamphlet and reviewers' outcry that the play provoked) to ours, the former generously sampled by Steffan in his *Lord Byron's 'Cain'*, pp. 330–422), which includes, in addition to over 100 pages of commentary, a substantial bibliography of critical work on *Cain* since Byron's time to about 1966. 'To assemble the complex literature on this disputatious drama', Steffan writes, 'would require several large reverberant volumes', and in any case even a cursory examination of this mass of material reveals a steady 'tradition' of repetitious ideas and insights which unfortunately (though perhaps inevitably) continues to this day. In light of Steffan's invaluable work, still an indispensable starting point for any serious study of *Cain*, we exclude from our own bibliographical listings below any article or book that is listed in *Lord Byron's 'Cain'*.

Bauer, 'Byron's Doubting Cain', pp. 80–88.
Blackstone, *Byron: A Survey*, pp. 244–50.
Butler, 'Romantic Manichaeanism', pp. 13–37.
Cantor, 'Byron's *Cain*', pp. 50–71.
Cooke, *The Blind Man Traces the Circle*, pp. 74–79.
Corbett, *Byron and Tragedy*, pp. 143–74.
Cox, *In the Shadows of Romance*, pp. 128–33.
Farrell, *Revolution as Tragedy*, pp. 174–84.
Fisch, 'Byron's Cain as Sacred Executioner', pp. 25–38.
Franklin, 'Adah [in *Cain*]', in her *Byron's Heroines*, pp. 232–46.
Gleckner, *Byron and the Ruins of Paradise*, pp. 321–27.
Goldstein, 'Byron's Cain and the Painites', pp. 391–410.
Hirst, 'Byron's Lapse into Orthodoxy', pp. 151–72, and his '"The Politics of Paradise"', pp. 243–64.
Hoagwood, *Byron's Dialectic*, pp. 90–151.
Jump, *Byron*, pp. 166–75.

Knight, *Byron and Shakespeare*, pp. 81–84, 177–79, 305–11.

Manning, *Byron and His Fictions*, pp. 146–56.

Martin, 'Cain, the Reviewers, and Byron's New Form of Old Fashioned Mischief', in his *Byron: A Poet Before His Public*, Chapter 7.

McGann, *Fiery Dust*, pp. 255–62.

Merchant, 'Lord Byron: *Cain: A Mystery*', pp. 73–80.

Michaels, 'Byron's *Cain*', pp. 71–78.

Otten, *After Innocence*, pp. 19–31; and *The Deserted Stage*, pp. 41–75.

Quinones, 'Byron's *Cain*', pp. 36–57.

Reisner, '*Cain*: Two Romantic Interpretations', pp. 124–43.

Richardson, 'Seduction and Repetition in *Cain*', in his *A Mental Theater*, pp. 59–83.

Ryan, 'Byron's *Cain*', pp. 41–45.

Thorslev, 'Byron and Bayle', pp. 58–76.

Other useful shorter analyses may be found in Fitzpatrick's 'Byron's Mysteries', pp. 615–25; and Roston, *Biblical Drama*, pp. 198–212.

Orthodoxy and Unorthodoxy in *Heaven and Earth*

MURRAY ROSTON AND JEROME J. McGANN

I

If the blasphemies of *Cain* formed, at least ostensibly, an indictment of Christianity, *Heaven and Earth* was, despite Murray's rejection of it as 'another Cain', an almost innocuous defence. Byron himself described it as 'less spectacular than *Cain* and very pious' and perhaps as a result of his experiences with its predecessor, he expressed a readiness to soften any hints of impiety to which readers might object.[1] Erected on an even flimsier biblical foundation than *Cain* (which, though not contradicting the text, was largely an elaboration),[2] it took as its hero Japhet, the righteous son of Noah, suffering the pangs of unrequited love for a maiden consorting against divine commandment with a celestial creature. The allegorical representation of divine justice is here not the expulsion from Eden but the Flood which, as Wilson Knight has pointed out,[3] had a special significance for Byron, fascinated by the enormous power of the ocean. But it goes further than that; for the ocean symbolized to him the immanence of God in nature and man's insignificance before such might. He described it in *Childe Harold* as:

> Thou glorious mirror, where the Almighty's form
> Glasses itself in tempests ...
> ... boundless, endless and sublime,

> The image of eternity, the throne
> Of the Invisible. (IV, clxxxiii)

And there is in this Hebraic sense of wonder before the divine presence in the natural world a recognition of the hand of the Creator holding its might in check and directing its course.[4]

In *Heaven and Earth* man is not seduced by Lucifer but dismisses his arguments as specious. The rebellious spirit, cynically asking Japhet whether man will be good after the Flood, is answered with calm conviction:

> The eternal will
> Shall deign to expound this dream
> Of good and evil; and redeem
>   Unto himself all times, all things;
>   And gather'd under his almighty wings,
>   Abolish Hell!
> And to expiated Earth
> Restore the beauty of her birth,
>   Her Eden in an endless paradise. (I.iii.193–210)

Similarly, the fallen angels, although portrayed as creatures of dignity and grandeur, are outshone by the radiance of Raphael, the loyal servant of God. True, Japhet is a questioner like Cain, unable to comprehend the need for divine wrath in the world, but where Cain's intelligent thrusts are left unparried, Japhet's are gently but firmly dismissed by a merciful Raphael:

> Patriarch, be still a father! smooth thy brow:
> Thy son, despite his folly, shall not sink:
> He knows not what he says. (I.iii.764–66)

Again the allusion to the forgiveness of Christ on the cross. Moreover, Noah, the representative of that unthinking, doctrinaire spirit so distasteful to Byron, is reproved for the abruptness of his reply to Japhet's outburst, with the effect that the rigidity of Calvinism is condemned and true Christianity portrayed as kindly, understanding and just.

Yet Byron had not turned pious overnight, and the defiance which marked the figure of Cain finds its counterpart in Aholibamah—scornful of authority, vigorously independent and penetrating in her religious cynicism. Her pride in her descent from Cain leaves no doubt of her function in the drama. Yet here again the sharpness of her attack is blunted by the presence of Anah, who, as the object of Japhet's love, timorously attempts to restrain her sister's impiety but proves the weaker of the two. That polarity of religious belief which distinguished Byron's character was reflected in the close of this fragmentary play. The rebellious angels, instead of drowning in the Flood, are permitted to fly with their loves to another star, and, whatever the author may have planned for them in the unwritten sequel, those 'sons of God' and 'daughters of men' who, according to Genesis, had been the prime cause of the retributive Flood, were spared, at least temporarily, the watery death of mankind. Similarly, a mother's pathetic plea that Japhet should take her innocent babe aboard again challenges heavenly justice:

> Why was he born?
> What hath he done—
> My unwean'd son—
> To move Jehovah's wrath or scorn?   (I.iii.836–39)

But these challenges are offset by the calm faith of an anonymous drowning mortal speaking with Jobian echoes for all mankind:

> And though the waters be o'er earth outspread,
>> Yet, as *his* word,
>> Be the decree adored!
> He gave me life—he taketh but
> The breath which is his own.   (I.iii.885–89)

Heaven and Earth is by no means a theodicy but, like *Cain*, it constitutes an examination of divine justice, counterbalancing the scepticism of the earlier work by its more generous appraisal of divine benevolence. And like *Cain* it too is unmistakably concerned with the Fall of man, although the Fall is presented in an even more camouflaged form. The image of the serpent seducing mankind is prominent in the opening scene, the colloquy between Raphael and the rebellious angels is patently reminiscent of Satan's speeches in *Paradise Lost*, the sin of Anah and Aholibamah is their transgression of divine prohibition, and the Flood itself parallels the expulsion from Eden. The criticism that greeted Byron's plays, particularly his *Cain*, showed that the parallels they afforded to Milton's work had not been overlooked, despite Byron's hesitant disclaimer in the Preface: 'Since I was twenty I have never read Milton; but I had read him so frequently before, that this may make little difference.'[5] But the parallels were less in the literary techniques employed than in the two poets' projection of their own religious searchings into the theme of the Fall.

II

[...] Byron had an impulse to write upon the theme of the fall of the seraphim as early as 1814, and he told Annabella several times that he sometimes believed he was himself a fallen angel.[6] He clearly saw himself in the rôle of fallen cherub many times, but on these particular occasions his mind took a seraphic turn: he was one of those 'sons of God' who left heaven and the love of God for earth and the love of a woman. (He often suggested that the exchange, if not exactly a bad one, was certainly troublesome.)

Running through all of *Heaven and Earth* is the image of the 'All beauteous world' that is this earth. Japhet is particularly eloquent on the subject (I.iii.1ff.), but Anah and the seraphim defectors also attest to it. The beauty of the two women, especially Anah, is an analogous phenomenon, as it is in most of Byron's works. Japhet is in agony that the earth and Anah are both to be destroyed by the Deluge.

> All beauteous world! ...
> I cannot save thee, cannot save even her
> Whose love had made me love thee more....
>
> (I.iii.47, 51–52)

Byron told Medwin that, in the sequel, he had 'once thought of conveying the lovers to the moon, or one of the planets; but it is not easy for the imagination to make any unknown world more beautiful than this....'[7] Thus speaks one fallen angel, and his attitude carries over into Samiasa and Azaziel. 'Stung', as Raphael says, 'with strange passions, and debased/ By mortal feelings for a mortal maid' (I.iii.543–44), the errant seraphim choose to give up immortality rather than their love for the earth and its beautiful creatures. As angels they 'should be, passionless and pure' (I.iii.715), but they prefer the 'strange' and mysterious world of corporeal desires and Byron clearly sanctions their inclinations. The angels propose to bridge the gap between earth and heaven, and their aim is matched by that of their lovers. The godlike angels long to 'become as mortals' (*Childe Harold*, IV, 52), and mortality aspires to a state of divinity.

But Noah sets out the inhibiting force in the play when he says:

> Woe, woe, woe to such communion!
> Has not God made a barrier between earth
> And heaven, and limited each, kind to kind?
>
> (I.iii.473–75)

Japhet is much too orthodox to reject such a decree outright, but he protests constantly against the evident evil which it produces. His protests generally take the form of requests for mercy, baffled questions about the nature of his god, or declamations that he will share the fate of the sinful lovers. He cannot secure mercy or share their doom, however, nor can he solve the riddle of Jehovah. He is left at the end 'condemn'd' to ponder the significance of it all. This is what he must 'remain' for (I.iii.929–30). As such, Japhet stands for the well-intentioned, relatively liberal Christian of Byron's day. Reading Byron's play, such a man will be led to question the fundamentals of his orthodoxy as Japhet does.

Much of *Heaven and Earth* is superficial, and the allegory is flimsy compared with the richness of *Cain*. But the play helps us to understand what *Cain* is about. The importance of the earth in any 'divine' scheme is clearly stated, as is the idea that the upper and the lower worlds in some way need each other, and that each constantly gravitates towards the other despite Jehovah's decree. As Raphael says of the angelic hosts:

> oh! why
> Cannot this earth be made, or be destroy'd
> Without involving ever some vast void
> In the immortal ranks?   (I.iii.562–65)

They cannot because the earth is as beautiful as the love of a woman (who is, in so many of Byron's works, the *genius loci* in the world of nature): 'but she will draw/ A second host from heaven, to break heaven's law' (I.iii.592–93).

Further, the play sets out, more clearly than *Cain*, a redemptive programme. Japhet represents the first stage in that process. Early in the play a chorus of Luciferian spirits chants to Japhet a hymn about the future doom of man. In the midst of it he interrupts them to say that a time will come when all the evils they have prophesied will cease: hell will be abolished, earth transfigured, and all creatures will live in peace.

> *Spirits.* And when shall take effect this wondrous
>   spell?
> *Japhet.* When the Redeemer cometh; first in pain,
>   And then in glory.

Spirit. Meantime still struggle in the mortal chain,
  Till earth wax hoary;
  War with yourselves, and hell, and heaven,
    in vain,
  Until the clouds look gory
  With the blood reeking from each battle-plain.
  New times, new climes, new arts, new men;
    but still,
  The same old tears, old crimes, and oldest ill....
                                        (I.iii.204–13)

At first it seems as if Byron (through Japhet) were being perfectly orthodox in his Christianity: the millennium will be established after Christ's second coming, and man will suffer as usual in the meantime. But the gloomy prospect which the play appears to hold out for man in the 'meantime' suggests Byron's unorthodox attitudes. From a traditional point of view, Christ's first coming ('in pain') reconstituted the moral world. He saved man by that coming, by that atonement. But the spirit echoes Byron's own pessimism when he prophesies the general persistence of evil, a fact which we all (with Byron) recognize even after the coming of Jesus. The Christian redeemer seems not to have succeeded in saving man from sin by His death.

As I mentioned earlier, however, Byron did not believe in the atonement. What he is doing in this passage is analogous to what he does in *Childe Harold's Pilgrimage IV*, and elsewhere, when he eulogizes 'Spirits which soar from ruin' (*Childe Harold*, IV, 55); or what Foscolo does in 'De' Sepolcri', a poem which may have influenced Byron's Italian canto. Both poets resurrect and praise the heroic spirits of the past because their particular examples can inspire men now. Jesus is not *the* redeemer to Byron but *a* redeemer, or an embodiment of the meaning of redemption. Shelley's *Defence* is written from a similar vantage. Byron's Jesus is a specific man who represented the larger humanistic ideal.

Pragmatically, what Jesus achieved for himself all men have also to achieve for themselves; and the time that this takes to be effected is the time of 'pain'. Byron suggests much the same thing in an early letter to his friend Francis Hodgson, who was trying to lead him back to an orthodox Christianity:

> I won't dispute with you on the Arcana of your new calling; they are Bagatelles like the King of Poland's rosary. One remark, and I have done; the basis of your religion is *injustice*; the *Son* of *God*, the *pure*, the *immaculate*, the *innocent*, is sacrificed for the *Guilty*. This proved *His* heroism; but no more does away *man's* guilt than a schoolboy's volunteering to be flogged for another would exculpate the dunce from negligence, or preserve him from the Rod.[8]

In this view, Jesus becomes the example of the man who *consciously* suffered all this life's 'pain' and achieved 'glory' as a result. Byron's redeemed earth will be a communion of such saints. To Byron, Jesus is significant in a classical (and pagan) sense: he is a model for others, more sublime, perhaps, than men like Sylla, Tasso or Alexander, but not essentially different. Similarly, the convulsions in human history are for him images of the redemptive agonies which each particular man has to undergo. In other words, Byron is always primarily interested in the individual rather than the collective man. Man as 'humanity' is inconceivable except as a diverse group of specific persons; and humanity is not redeemable as a whole but only (so to speak) piece by piece. Thus, the St Peter's stanzas do not simply lay out the fundamental Byronic *aesthetic* at the end of *Childe Harold's Pilgrimage*. They intimate his pluralistic ethic as well when they urge a 'piecemeal' salvation, an advance to a univocal end through 'mighty graduations, part by part' (*Childe Harold*, IV, 157).

Given the terms of his analogy in the *Heaven and Earth* passage, however, Byron had to postulate an eventual millennium in order to assert the possibility of individual fulfilment.

He fought shy of all optimistic evolutionary theories of history, and his sceptical mind naturally found Cuvier's ideas most congenial. In the mystery plays Byron chose to use Cuvier as a guide to more ancient patterns of historical thought, and he sets out a regressive theory of history to usher in the necessary millennial event. Cuvier's theories appealed to Byron because they asserted a series of cataclysms in which the earth proceeded from her Golden Age, her youth, to her less and less splendid periods. His own was the Age of Bronze, or worse, and the future certainly seemed a bleak one. But in terms of the theory of redemption set out above (and the book of Revelation would support Byron), such increasing horrors and advancing age were the means to the return of paradise. The regressive myth of history is ancient and quite classical, of course, and Shelley's Count Maddalo (Byron) indicates the psychological aspect of it when he tells Julian:

> Most wretched men
> Are cradled into poetry by wrong,
> They learn in suffering what they teach in song.
> (*Julian and Maddalo*, ll. 544–46)

For Byron, this myth is epitomized in the repeated 'falls' which centre in the book of Genesis particularly, and which Byron (with some help from the book of Enoch) reiterates in his two mystery plays. In Byron's view, every 'fall' occasions a convulsion of some sort and though the event seems to signal a recession in one sense, its truest function is to provide an occasion for further blessedness. Falls are evil only if they are not capitalized upon. More surely they are the gifts of life, for, as Byron told Augusta during his great fall, 'not in vain,/ Even for its own sake do we purchase pain'. Samiasa and Azaziel fall away from heaven, but in so doing they become more admirable, indeed, more capable morally than the God whom they desert. Their 'lower' state of being is presented as really more full. Similarly, Japhet defects from his father's orthodoxy in the end and the play clearly argues that his retrograde behaviour is actually a gain.

NOTES

1.   *The Works of Lord Byron: Letters and Journals*, ed. Rowland E. Prothero (London: John Murray, 1898–1901), VI, 31, 47, hereafter referred to as *LJ*.

2.   Apart from the verses from Genesis prefixed to the work, Byron was indebted also to the apocryphal book of Enoch, but even this debt is very general. See Eimer, 'Das apokryphe buch Henoch', p. 18.

3.   Knight, *Lord Byron, Christian Virtues*, pp. 111–12.

4.   *Childe Harold's Pilgrimage* IV, clxxxiii. Cf. Psalm 104:6: 'The waters stood above the mountains. At thy rebuke they fled: at the voice of thy thunder they hasted away.... Thou hast set a bound that they may not pass over; that they turn not again to cover the earth.'

5.   For details of the pamphlet warfare arising out of the publication of *Cain*, see Chew, *Byron in England*, pp. 80 f., and especially Steffan, *Lord Byron's 'Cain'*, Part III.

6.   Elwin, *Lord Byron's Wife*, pp. 263, 271.

7.   *Medwin's 'Conversations'*, p. 157.

8.   *LJ*, II, 35.

On the Borders of
Heaven and Earth

ALAN RICHARDSON

The Deluge is read, in traditional Christian typology, as an antetype of the Apocalypse: the earth's first destruction by water foreshadows its ultimate purgation by burning, as the sacrament of baptism prefigures the spirit's baptism by fire.[1] Such associations underlie the image of the Deluge in most English poetry before the Romantic period; Donne, for example, brings all of them to bear in Holy Sonnet 5, 'I am a little world made cunningly':

> Pour new seas in my eyes, that so I might
> Drown my world with my weeping earnestly,
> Or wash it if it must be drowned no more.
> But O, it must be burnt! Alas the fire
> Of lust and envy have burnt it heretofore,
> And made it fouler; let their flames retire,
> And burn me, O Lord, with a fiery zeal
> Of thee and of Thy house, which doth in eating heal.

Byron's mystery of the Flood is written against this tradition. Byron reads the Flood backwards rather than forwards; he presents it as a shadow of the Fall of Man and evokes apocalyptic connotations only to reject them. As in *Cain*, he portrays humankind suffering the remembrance of one fall—

> the flaming sword
> Which chased the first-born out of Paradise
> Still flashes in the angelic hands   (I.iii.785–87)

—even as a repetition of the Fall takes place. The God of *Heaven and Earth* is not the judge of revelation but the incomprehensible creator and destroyer of Job, which inspires the drama's sublime imagery as Genesis inspires its action.

The contemporary reception of *Heaven and Earth* leads one to question the twentieth-century tradition of dismissal and neglect. Hazlitt called it, in *The Spirit of the Age,* the 'best' of Byron's dramas: while *Manfred* was too much a projection of Byron's personality, in his last mystery 'the space between Heaven and Earth ... seems to fill his Lordship's imagination; and the Deluge, which he has so finely described, may be said to have drowned all his own idle humours'. Goethe was deeply impressed with *Heaven and Earth* and, according to Crabb Robinson, preferred it above any other of Byron's 'serious poems'. And two contemporary reviewers, Francis Jeffrey and John Wilson, described the mystery in terms that attest to its power while suggesting a critical approach which does that power justice.

Wilson reviewed *Heaven and Earth* in *Blackwoods* in January 1823, a few months after its publication, and characterized it as 'dark and massy, like a block of marble'. The simile encapsulates Wilson's appreciation of Byron's ability to compress violently mingling contraries in dramatic form: 'passion seen blending in vain union between the spirits of mortal and immortal, love shrieking on the wild shore of death, and all the thoughts that ever agitated human hearts dashed and distracted beneath the blackness and amidst the howling of commingled earth and heaven'.[2] Jeffrey, writing a month later in the *Edinburgh Review*, found in Byron's mystery 'more poetry and music ... than in any of his dramatic writings since Manfred'. Like Wilson, Jeffrey was impressed by the dialectical intensity of the drama's thematic movement.

> It is truly, in every sense of the word, a meeting of 'Heaven and Earth': angels are seen ascending and descending, and the windows of the sky are opened

to deluge the face of nature. We have an impassioned picture of the strong and devoted attachment inspired in the daughters of men by angel forms.... There is a like conflict of the passions as of the elements—all wild, chaotic, uncontrollable, fatal— but there is a discordant harmony in all this—.[3]

The reactions of Wilson and Jeffrey, however impressionistic they sound to modern ears, capture as no later criticism has the principal thematic concern of Byron's last work of mental theatre: the complex violation of spatial, metaphysical and psychic borders. Border violation figures in Wordsworth's *The Borderers* and in Byron's *Manfred* and *Cain* as the thematic accompaniment to a drama of seduction; in *Heaven and Earth* it becomes a dramatic subject in itself. The mystery portrays effects rather than causes, and withholds even the retrospective glimpses of past actions that underlie the characterization of Manfred. The past is equally omnipresent in *Heaven and Earth*, but as a collective past shared by all the characters, a succession of prior falls—Satan's, Eve's, Adam's, Cain's—that leads inexorably towards the latest and most cataclysmic of all.

Heaven and Earth is concerned not with action so much as with reaction—the reaction of mankind to the Fall, the reactions of its characters to their fallen predicament. Byron appropriately described it as a 'lyrical drama ... *choral* and mystical—and a sort of Oratorio on a sacred subject'.[4] Perhaps inspired by *Prometheus Unbound*, Byron revives the chorus—a conventional device for commenting on dramatic action—with brilliant effect, and the central characters most often adopt the lyric voice, crying out at events which they cannot alter. But the drama does not founder, as later would Arnold's lyrical monodrama, *Empedocles*, in closed subjectivity. Byron brings dramatic intensity to the internal debate of Japhet, Noah's divinely chosen but unregenerate son, and to the clashes of his beliefs with those of the angels and their mortal lovers, the 'offspring of Cain'. The inexorable approach of the Deluge adds immediate relevance to the ideological conflict and underscores its dramatic progression with a steadily building suspense. In another respect, however, the 'lyrical' aspect of the drama is less successful, as Byron varies the strong and eclectic blank-verse measure of *Cain* with a great deal of lyrical verse which, again, seems directly inspired by *Prometheus Unbound* but which rarely captures the sureness or the beauty of Shelley's lyrical style.

Heaven and Earth is also a departure in that Byron no longer grounds his poetic argument on allusions to Shakespeare and Milton, but draws instead on his own works of mental theatre. The subject of *Heaven and Earth* can itself be found in germ in Manfred's apostrophe, on the eve of his death, to the setting sun:

> the idol
> Of early nature, and the vigorous race
> Of undiseased mankind, the giant sons
> Of the embrace of angels with a sex
> More beautiful than they, which did draw down
> The erring spirits who can ne'er return.
>
> (III.ii.174–79)

Like Manfred, the angels and their mortal lovers in *Heaven and Earth* are doomed through engaging in forbidden sexual union, and like Cain, the mortals (who are, moreover, his direct descendants) fall through choosing to consort with spirits rather than with humankind. Interwoven with the story of the angels and their consorts is that of Japhet, who shares Manfred's haunted and brooding consciousness, and who struggles like Manfred against an irrevocable destiny, though Japhet is fated, paradoxically, not to be damned but to be saved.

Heaven and Earth opens, as does *Manfred*, with a midnight 'invocation' of spirits as Anah and Aholibamah, Cain's granddaughters, call to their seraphic lovers. Anah's name underscores the family resemblance in her gentle, loving nature to that of Adah in *Cain*, while she inherits her desire to consort with a spiritual being rather than with 'dust' (I.i.18) from Cain himself. Although Anah settles for sensual rather than intellectual companionship—'With me thou canst not sympathize,/ Except in love' (I.i.52–53)—her dilemma is Cain's, the inner conflict aroused in a mortal by traffic with immortal spirits:

> Great is their love who love in sin and fear;
> And such, I feel, are waging in my heart,
>   A war unworthy.   (I.i.67–69)

She feels compelled to hide a love that, again like her fore-father's relation with Lucifer, alienates her from God: 'I love our God less since his angel loved me' (I.i.12). She does not resist, however, the attraction of the immortal for the mortal, the unfallen for the 'Adamite' continually aware of the Fall:

> For sorrow is our element;
>   Delight
> An Eden kept afar from sight,
> Though sometimes with our visions blent.
>   (I.i.71–74)

In union with the angel Anah finds forgetfulness, however transient, of her fallen condition, with an intensification of the Edenic feelings 'blent'—one of many terms for interpenetra-tion and mingling used by Byron throughout the work—with her dreams of a deathless world.

Aholibamah has been described, due to her pride and her open defiance of God's commands, as a 'true descendant of Cain',[5] though it would be more accurate to call her a child of Lucifer. Like Byron's devil (and like Milton's before him), she claims an immortal nature that renders her equal to strife with the omnipotent, and worthy of her angel's love:

> Change us he may, but not o'erwhelm; we are

Of as eternal essence, and must war
With him if he will war with us: with *thee*
I can share all things, even immortal sorrow.

(I.i.120–23)

She adopts many of the Satanic gestures characteristic of
Manfred and Lucifer, and the beginning of her invocation,
following Anah's, is marked by the language of mastery and
struggle and by a bitter postlapsarian consciousness:

Wheresoe'er
Thou rulest in the upper air—
Or warring with the spirits who may dare
    Dispute with him
Who made all empires, empire; or recalling
Some wandering star, which shoots through the abyss
    Whose tenants dying, while their world is falling,
    Share the dim destiny of clay in this.   (I.i.82–89)

Anah desires only to escape the pain of mortality through
melting in the embrace of an immortal. Aholibamah, however,
imagines her lover as the embodiment of her own craving for
power, and portrays him as a master of cosmic destinies, not a
servant of God. The preposition in 'warring *with* the spirits' is
intentionally ambiguous, for although Anah believes the
seraphim descend from heaven, Aholibamah (like the Brontë
heroines she in some ways anticipates) prefers to envision her
lover as a fallen angel. However the line is read, she depicts the
war between God and Satan, like Byron's Lucifer, as a dispute
between equally imperialistic antagonists. The 'wandering
star' that mirrors her fallen world draws two related emblems
from Byron's earlier metaphysical dramas into a single,
complex figure. It recalls the 'wandering hell' that ruled
Manfred's destiny and imaged his psychic anguish, as well as
the 'phantasm' of a greater, previously fallen earth with which
Lucifer tormented Cain in their voyage through the 'abyss' of
space. Aholibamah inherits both the apparent strength of

Manfred and Lucifer and the false autonomy that underlies their essential weakness.

After deftly characterizing the sisters through their invocations, Byron renders the angels (named, after the pseudepigraphal book of Enoch, Samiasa and Azaziel) somewhat indistinct, giving them a shadowy, sublime aspect. Their metaphysical allegiance is nebulous as well. Although they do not (as Aholibamah would have it) follow Satan, the angels forsake God without hesitation when forced to choose between their earthly desires and his commands. The verse from Genesis which Byron takes as one of his epigraphs is suitably ambiguous: 'And it came to pass ... that the sons of God saw the daughters of men that they were fair; and they took them wives of all which they chose.' The 'sons of God' can be read two ways. Milton considers them the 'just' sons of Seth in Adam's vision of biblical history in *Paradise Lost* (XI.573–97), but draws elsewhere on the other traditional reading (adopted by Byron) in contrasting the Archangel Raphael's 'unlibidinous' admiration for Eve's nakedness to the licence of the later 'sons of God' who would be 'Enamour'd at that sight' (V.445–50).

As much seduced as seducing, Byron's angels are not demonic tempters like Lucifer but fall instead at the same moment as their lovers. They sin by transgressing the borders between heaven and earth, immortal and mortal, and at the same time they objectify the supernatural cravings of Cain's fated descendants. Byron's second epigraph, 'And woman wailing for her demon lover', belongs to Coleridge's 'Kubla Khan', a poem that expresses the Romantic desire to weld contrary states together through an erotically charged vision of earthly paradise. But Coleridge's vision of a pleasure dome mingling nature and 'device', hedonism and 'ancestral voices prophesying war', proves untenable, like the mismatch of woman and demon, an image that evokes the related erotic encounters of mortal and immortal in poems such as Coleridge's 'Christabel', Shelley's 'Alastor' and Keats's 'Lamia'.

Such matches prove invariably dangerous, figuring the power of a transient, supernatural vision to ravish the human heart of its attachment to the world 'where', as Wordsworth says, 'in the end/ We find our happiness or not at all' (*Prelude*, XI.143–44). Anah and Aholibamah deny the earth before it is denied them; the angels readily abjure heaven; and both pairs find themselves living out an ungrounded, evanescent fantasy. The immortal no less than the mortal lovers suffer a failure of the imagination to make a home in its native sphere; in the last scene the seraphim are proscribed from heaven even as the Deluge overwhelms the earth.

As the Flood is both a repercussion and a repetition of the Fall of Man, so the fates of the women and the angels are presented as both effects and reflections of previous falls. Repetition does not here, as in *The Borderers* or *Cain*, accompany the successful grafting of a seducer's psychic condition onto the mind of his victim, but signifies instead the ineluctability of the Fall's resonance through successive generations and epochs. The innocence that Anah would recapture is simply not viable in the postlapsarian world, and the sisters find themselves living out instead the Fall they would repeal. Invoking her angel, Aholibamah boasts:

> And shall *I* shrink from thine eternity?
> No! though the serpent's sting should pierce me
>   through
> And thou thyself wert like the serpent, coil
> Around me still!   (I.iii.125–28)

Craving the angels' 'immortal essence', the sisters succumb to an urge similar to Eve's; and just as their grandfather's crime was presented in *Cain* as a version of Eve's, their own inheritance of Cain's legacy is stressed throughout the mystery:

> Too much of the forefather whom thou vauntest
> Has come down in that haughty blood which
>   springs

From him who shed the first, and that a brother's!
(I.iii.397–99)

The fall of Azaziel and Samiasa constitutes a complex act of repetition as well. Beguiled by woman, the angels have 'shared man's sin' (I.iii.619), repeating Adam's fall in following a voice more subtle than the serpent's: 'The snake but vanquish'd dust; but she will draw/ A second host from heaven, to break heaven's law' (I.iii.592–93). As erring angels, Azaziel and Samiasa repeat Lucifer's fall and that of the first heavenly host as well, a parallel which the archangel Raphael will make explicit near the drama's close.

The first scene ends as Anah describes the angels' approach with a passage that exemplifies Byron's reading of the Flood not as a purgation but as another fall.

> On Ararat's late secret crest
> A mild and many-colour'd bow,
> The remnant of the flashing path,
> Now shines! and now, behold! it hath
> Return'd to night, as rippling foam,
>   Which the leviathan hath lash'd
> From his unfathomable home
> When sporting on the face of the calm deep,
>   Subsides soon after he again hath dash'd
> Down, down, to where the ocean's fountains sleep.
> (I.i.149–53)

As the passage begins, Anah's reference to the hidden summit of Ararat seems to herald man's ultimate salvation—although the sisters have yet to hear of the approaching Deluge. The accompanying image of the rainbow would then evoke the covenant that God will soon make with man, an antetype of the union of heaven and earth that follows the Apocalypse. Read only so far, the passage places Byron, as a poet of the Deluge, well within the typological tradition exemplified by Donne. But as the rainbow track of the departing angels—a

wonderfully audacious celestial equivalent of a snail's pris-
matic trail in the dew—subsides, its evanescence causes Anah
to picture a sounding whale, an image resonant with several
layers of dramatic irony. The association of the angels with the
leviathan, a traditional emblem for Satan, prefigures their fall
and the danger they present to the transgressing sisters. As a
central figure in Job for God's awful and inscrutable power,
the leviathan augurs as well the near destruction of mankind;
finally it heralds the form of their destruction in the Flood
later depicted by Japhet as

> When ocean is earth's grave, and, unopposed
> By rock or shallow, the leviathan,
> Lord of the shoreless sea and watery world,
> Shall wonder at his boundlessness of realm.
>
> (I.ii.80–83)

What begins as an intimation of the marriage of heaven and
earth ends by foreshadowing the earth's engulfment through
heaven's wrath.

Japhet, whose story begins in the second scene, is a
complex, though not deep, character. His passionate nature
allies him to Anah and Aholibamah, and Noah condemns his
desires for Anah—the 'daughter of a fated race' (I.ii.94)—as
'forbidden yearnings' (I.ii.100). He resembles Anah more
particularly through his own likeness to Adah in *Cain*: just as
she begs her beloved to 'go not/ Forth with this spirit'
(I.i.372–73), he asks Anah, 'why walk'st thou with this spirit'
(I.iii.331). And like Cain's enduring (but not saving) love for
Adah, Japhet's love for Anah leads him to 'pity' his friend
Irad, who 'lovest not' (I.iii.25), as Cain pities Lucifer, 'who
lov'st nothing' (II.ii.543). But another side of his character
stems from Byron's tragic protagonists, Manfred and the
'abased' Cain. Like them he is restless; although his 'nights
inexorable' to sleep (I.iii.59) initially reflect only erotic disappointment, he grows increasingly torn within by the conflict

of his mortal sympathies with loyalty to his father's intolerant creed.

As Noah's son, Japhet tries at times to justify God's ways, but though singled out for salvation, he can neither unquestioningly accept the divine will nor wholly reject his divine mandate. Noah himself is something of a comic character, as was the henpecked patriarch of the medieval mysteries, though Byron's Noah more resembles the sententious stage Puritan of Jonson's comedies. Not that Noah is a hypocrite, but his tendency to wallow in sanctification reaches Jonsonian dimensions, most memorably when he reproaches the dignified, laconic angels:[6]

> I am
> But man, and was not made to judge mankind,
> Far less the sons of God; but as our God
> Has deign'd to commune with me, and reveal
> *His* judgments, I reply, that the descent
> Of seraphs from their everlasting seat
> Unto a perishable and perishing,
> Even on the very *eve* of *perishing*, world,
> Cannot be good. (I.iii.480–88)

Although Japhet has been placed among the elect, he feels no trace of the confidence of justification; only the burden of surviving the natural and social worlds in which he feels at home. Like Cain, he finds himself trapped by a crudely dichotomized system that allows for no creative resolution, though the principal spokesman for a divided cosmos is in this case not a devil but a saint. The terror of Byron's mystery—felt by his contemporaries if not by his editors—arises from the absence of a middle ground on which to stand. Japhet struggles vainly to reconcile his father and the seed of Cain; the angels must choose between submission and exile; Raphael sadly can provide only ultimatums, despite his wish to mediate between God and his noble, beautiful apostates. In many respects Japhet's dilemma is a study in the limits of

Calvinism. Goethe's perception that in *Cain* 'we see ... how the inadequate dogmas of the church work upon a free mind like Byron's and how by such a piece he struggles to get rid of a doctrine which has been forced upon him' applies equally well to *Heaven and Earth*.[7]

The last scene opens with Japhet at his most Manfred-like. He has departed from Irad to muse alone at the cavern beneath the Caucasus, whose mouth

> opens from the infernal world
> To let the inner spirits of the earth
> Forth when they walk its surface.   (I.ii.42–44)

The description resonates with literary and thematic associations. It recalls the 'deep romantic of chasm' of 'Kubla Khan' and is clearly allied to the chasms and abysses that throughout mental theatre figure psychic disintegration. Its location evokes the Prometheus myth—an association that becomes explicit later in the scene—and the cave not only conjoins earth and hell but 'opens to the heart of Ararat'(I.ii.90)—the locus of heaven's future covenant with man—as well. The spot accordingly marks the convergence of the drama's various worlds and worldviews, represented by Japhet, the demonic 'spirits of the earth', the erring angels and the 'Cainite' women, God's terrestrial representative, Noah, and his heavenly messenger, Raphael. The struggle within Japhet between earthly passions and the divine ethic will give place by the end to the catastrophic mingling of heaven and earth in the Deluge.

Japhet's soliloquy begins as he struggles to understand why an earth 'so varied and so terrible in beauty' (I.iii.3) should be sacrificed to God's anger. His expression of natural piety leads to a loving elegy for his doomed race:

> And man—Oh men! my fellow beings! Who
> Shall weep above your universal grave,
> Save I?   (I.iii.14–16)

Japhet's expression contrasts vividly with Shelley's millennial vision of a redeemed, unified humanity in the fourth act of *Prometheus Unbound*: 'Man, oh, not men! a chain of linked thought.' For Byron, human strife cannot be transcended through a higher, collective consciousness; the pathos of Japhet's fallen, falling world lies instead in Byron's individualization of suffering—not man, but men will perish. Here his father's proto-Calvinism breaks down for Japhet. Far from glorying in self-righteousness, he protests his common humanity—'what am I better than ye are/ That I must live beyond ye' (I.iii.18–19)—and his fundamental kinship with a race 'So young, so mark'd out for destruction' (I.iii.48).

Like Manfred before him, Japhet is mocked in his deep musings by a chorus of infernal spirits, led by a Mephistophelian spokesman, an 'unknown, terrible, and indistinct/ Yet awful Thing of Shadows' (I.iii.63–64) that personifies the abyss, recalling both Milton's Death and Manfred's 'dusk and awful' accuser. The Satanic spirits celebrate the approaching extermination of their replacement and enemy,

> The abhorred race
> Which could not keep in Eden their high place
> But listen'd to the voice
> Of knowledge without power.   (I.iii.76–79)

This last phrase touches on a dilemma felt variously by many of the English Romantics. Wordsworth writes in *The Prelude* of 'knowledge not purchased by the loss of power'; Coleridge, in the 'Logic', 'For that alone is truly knowledge ... which reappears as power'.[8] The protagonists of Byron's metaphysical dramas are betrayed by knowledge that saps, rather than augments, their power: 'The Tree of Knowledge is not that of Life.' Manfred and Cain both founder in a delusive, empty self-knowledge, discovering not an empowering, authentic truth, but the crippling consciousness of guilt and the mocking presence of a misleading, alien voice that disrupts rather than guarantees psychic integrity. The power they give up in order to 'Purchase' such empty knowledge is the power defined by De Quincey, in contrast to merely discursive knowledge, as the 'exercise and expansion' of the 'latent capacity of sympathy'.[9] For Japhet, knowledge of God's will and design proves similarly empty; his consciousness of election only heightens his sense of impotence, and his pre-vision of the Flood torments him in his powerlessness to avert its consequences. The mocking voices of the demons that interrupt his soliloquy—voices that Japhet alone hears—embody the conflict between his sympathies and his inherited ideology.

Japhet struggles with his demons, identifying the 'restless wretchedness' (I.iii.123) that underlies their Satanic irony. They counter with one of Lucifer's stratagems in *Cain*, belittling Japhet and his race by comparing them with the 'glorious giants, who/ Yet walk the world in pride,/ The Sons of Heaven by many a mortal bride' (I.iii.131–33), and endowing them, as the 'giant patriarchs' (I.iii.157), with temporal priority as well. Celebrating the coming holocaust, they herald an anti-Millennium which inverts Isaiah's vision of the peaceable kingdom (Isaiah 11:6):

> even the brutes, in their despair,
> Shall cease to prey on man and on each other,
> And the striped tiger shall lie down to die
> Beside the lamb, as though he were his brother;
> Till all things shall be as they were,
> Silent and uncreated, save the sky. (I.iii.177–82)

Japhet opposes their satiric vision with his own intimations of an apocalypse in which God will 'abolish hell' and restore 'Eden in an—endless paradise/ Where man no more can fall as once he fell' (I.iii.201–02), the final reconciliation of earth and heaven. But the demons have the last word, deriding Japhet's apocalypse as one indefinitely deferred, a mere vision with no effect on the world as it is lived:

The same old tears, old crimes, and oldest ill,
Shall be amongst your race in different forms;
          But the same moral storms
Shall oversweep the future, as the waves
In a few hours the glorious giants' graves.
                                        (I.iii.213–17)

The demonic voices portray the future as a succession of falls
repeating man's 'oldest ill', or original sin, and the Flood as an
antetype not of the fiery apocalypse but of the 'moral storms'
that will continue to assail mankind.

The demons vanish and give place to 'shapes both of earth
and air' (I.iii.310), the two angels and the 'children of Cain'.
Motivated by sexual jealousy as well as orthodox dismay,
Japhet warns that 'unions like to these/ Between a mortal and
an immortal, cannot be happy' (I.iii.369–70), but Aholibamah
dismisses his love and religion together:

          —But the enthusiast dreams
     The worst of dreams, the fantasies engender'd
     By hapless love and heated vigils.   (I.iii.447–49)

Aholibamah reproaches Japhet ironically (but not wholly
inaccurately) with the imaginative failure shared by herself
and Anah, the tendency to palliate mortal despair with erotic
delusions (though the sisters would not characterize their
own misdirected desire as such). Noah then enters the scene
with sterner condemnations: 'Has not God made a barrier
between earth/ And heaven?' (I.iii.475–76). His proclamation
of metaphysical borders, emphasized by the line break, is
undermined, however, by the approaching Flood itself.
Heaven and earth are soon to mingle not in a millennial
consummation but in a catastrophic rain of terror: 'the fountains of the great deep shall be broken/ And heaven set wide
her windows' (I.iii.224–25). The absence in *Heaven and Earth*
of mediation, of a middle ground, finds graphic portrayal as
the heavens open and the sea rises. The boundaries so stoutly

maintained by Noah and so cruelly felt by his son grow mean-ingless as the border area itself yields to God's wrath. Manfred leaped into his abyss, Cain was enticed into Lucifer's; in *Heaven and Earth* the abyss wells up as the 'fountains of the great deep' engulf the entire earth.

The angels are given a final chance to recant and obey by Milton's 'affable angel', Raphael, whose appearance further broadens the variegated metaphysical spectrum of the final scene. As the storm clouds gather above, the language grows crowded with references to prior falls. First Raphael evokes the interdependency of earth's creation and Lucifer's fall as codified in *Paradise Lost*:

>   why
> Cannot this earth be made, or be destroy'd,
> Without involving ever some vast void
> In the immortal ranks?   (I.iii.561–64)

Even from Raphael's perspective, heaven and earth seem less conjoined in a divine plan than confounded in an encom-passing Fall. Like Michael greeting Satan in the 'Vision of Judgment' with 'high, immortal, proud regret' (l. 32), Raphael recalls his infernal opposite with a measure of longing:

> I loved him—beautiful he was: oh heaven!
> Save *his* who made, what beauty and what power
> Was ever like to Satan's! Would the hour
> In which he fell could ever be forgiven!
> The wish is impious.   (I.iii.580–84)

But beauty and power are again crushed by heaven's inalter-able law. The angels embrace their lovers' fate in terms that evoke their ancestor, Cain: 'we have chosen, and will endure' (I.iii.717).

Anah, 'the last and loveliest of Cain's race' (I.iii.386), embraces at the end a Promethean view of Satan, identifying her own dilemma with his fall:

> The first who taught us knowledge hath been hurl'd
> From his once angelic throne
> Into some unknown world.   (I.iii.667–69)

The ensuing fall of man is evoked by Raphael's image of the cherubic sword 'Which chased the first-born out of Paradise' (I.iii.766), and by Japhet's final lament, as impious and as impotent as Raphael's wistful lines on Satan:

> Renew not Adam's fall:
> Mankind were then but twain,
> But they are numerous now as are the waves
> And the tremendous rain,
> Whose drops shall be less thick than would their
> graves,
> Were graves permitted to the seed of Cain.
> (I.iii.706–11)

Compassion, however, is not an Old Testament virtue. At last a pathetic 'chorus of Mortals', fleeing the rising waters, dismally bewails that 'The heavens and earth are mingling' (I.iii.795).

One should not read too much bitterness, however, into the final tableau. Byron does not, as a younger Byron might have, dismiss Genesis with Voltairean satire. Instead, he leads the reader into Japhet's dilemma: neither the Cainites' escapism nor God's final solution seems acceptable. One of the last speeches is given to a nameless, doomed mortal who echoes Job's heroic incomprehension:

> Time—space—eternity—life—death—
> The vast known and the immeasurable unknown.
> He made and can unmake;
> And shall I, for a little gasp of breath,
> Blaspheme and groan?   (I.iii.898–902)

Heaven and Earth ends, as does *Cain*, with questions rather than with answers. It is no accident that Byron left this work fragmentary. The text we have is subtitled 'Part I', but Byron seems hardly to have toyed with a sequel; Medwin reports him as saying that he had 'talked of writing a second part of it; but it was only as Coleridge promised a second part to "Christabel"'.[10] One remembers as well that an epigraph to *Heaven and Earth* comes from another unfinished work by Coleridge, and that the 'poet of great and deserved celebrity' who induced him to publish 'Kubla Khan' in its fragmentary form was Byron himself. Like Coleridge, he found in the fragment a device for remaining in uncertainties, mysteries, doubts, without reaching after a conclusion, and for plunging the reader into a similar dilemma, teasing us (again to paraphrase Keats) out of habitual patterns of thought.[11]

Heaven and Earth is the last of Byron's works that can be called mental theatre. The two dramatic works that followed —*Werner* (1822) and the sketch *The Deformed Transformed* (publ. 1824)—bring thematic elements from the metaphysical dramas into forms more suited to conventional nineteenth-century stagecraft, but in neither does Byron return to his themes with any depth. Based on a youthful play that he wrote while associated with the Drury Lane, *Werner* clearly aspires to the contemporary stage, and is in fact his only drama to have succeeded in the theatre. Its subtitle, 'The Inheritance', underscores the plot's indebtedness to Gothic conventions, although it touches at the same time on the presence of a theme developed in *Heaven and Earth*—the inheritance of an ancestral fall. The transference of crime and fall from Werner to his son, however, is a matter of simple imitation, involving neither the elaborate pattern of seduction and repetition developed in *Cain* nor the pervasive postlapsarian dilemma of *Heaven and Earth*. *The Deformed Transformed* similarly fails to bear out the promise of its *Faust*-like plot, the encounter of Arnold, a dejected hunchback, with a Mephistophelian tempter who takes on the name 'Caesar' promising a Satanic psychic imperialism that the action fails to develop. Although the plot might have taken an interesting turn had Byron lived to complete the drama,[12] the extant scenes recall in their sentimentality, bluster, and melodrama less *Cain* than *Otho the Great*.

The anticlimax of Byron's dramatic career should not blind us, however, any more than should his static historical plays, to the importance of his three works of mental theatre. The portrayals of psychic agony in *Manfred* and psychic agony in *Cain*, with the brief but intense drama of parallel and intertwining ideological struggles in *Heaven and Earth*, establish Byron as an innovative and profound master of the dramatic poem. Read on their own terms as addressed not to a deserted stage but to the reader's mind, Byron's three works of mental theatre constitute a major Romantic achievement, rivalled in their genre only by Shelley's dramatic poems of 1819.

NOTES

1.   This interpretive tradition begins in the New Testament with 2 Peter 3:6–7: 'Whereby the world that then was, being overflowed with water, perished; but the heavens and earth, which are now, by the same word are kept in store, reserved unto fire against the day of judgment and perdition of ungodly men.'

2.   Wilson, 'Byron's "Heaven and Earth"'.

3.   Francis Jeffrey, review of *Heaven and Earth* and Thomas Moore's 'Loves of the Angels', *Edinburgh Review*, XXXVIII (February 1823); rpt. in Reiman, II, 945.

4.   Letter to Kinnaird, 14 December 1821, *Byron's Letters and Journals*, ed. Leslie A. Marchand (Cambridge, MA: Harvard University Press, 1973–82), IX, 81. [Ed. note: In *The Death of Tragedy* George Steiner, as if taking up Byron's claim, called *Heaven and Earth* 'a kind of dramatic cantata, rather in the manner of Berlioz' (p. 209).]

5.   Chew, *The Dramas of Lord Byron*, p. 141.

6.   E. H. Coleridge remarks on this passage that 'Byron said that it was difficult to make Lucifer talk "like a clergyman." He contrived to make Noah talk like a street-preacher.' *The Works of Lord Byron: Poetry*, V, 309.

7.   Cited by Rutherford, *Byron: The Critical Heritage*, p. 218.

8. Wordsworth, *The Prelude* (1850) XI.143–44; Coleridge, 'Logic', p. 42.

9. De Quincey, 'The Literature of Knowledge', p. 331.

10. *Medwin's 'Conversations'*, p. 156. [Ed. note: But see George Steiner's quotation of Medwin's transcription of Byron's idea for an ending, *The Death of Tragedy*, p. 210.]

11. Thomas McFarland gives a brilliant overview of the significance of the Romantic fragment in *Romanticism and the Forms of Ruin*, pp. 3–55.

12. See George Steiner's remarks on Byron's sketch for completing *The Deformed Transformed* in *The Death of Tragedy*, pp. 211–12.

EDITORS' BIBLIOGRAPHICAL NOTE

Although very recently *Heaven and Earth* has received some major critical attention, prior to that time substantial commentary or analysis is relatively scarce. The three recent considerations are Richardson's (reprinted above), Corbett's *Byron and Tragedy*, pp. 174–88, and Franklin's *Byron's Heroines*, pp. 246–60, focused sharply (but hardly exclusively) on Anah and Aholibamah. While there are very brief comments on the play in a number of the many omnibus studies of Byron's *oeuvre*, most of them adjudge it, in one way or another, as 'in the main, a traditional theology ... accepted without apparent examination' (Joseph, *Byron the Poet*, p. 124). Other somewhat less brief, and more valuable, commentary may be found in the following:

Blackstone, *Byron: A Survey*, pp. 250–52.

Butler, 'Romantic Manichaeanism', pp. 13–37, which, with respect to *Heaven and Earth*, argues its establishment of 'Byron's heterodox but not altogether irreverent attitude to religion'.

Foot, *The Politics of Paradise*.

Knight, *The Burning Oracle*, pp. 224–25.

Manning, *Byron and His Fictions*, pp. 156–59.

Marchand, *Byron's Poetry*.

Marshall, *Byron's Major Poems*, Chapter 7 (on *Cain* and *Heaven and Earth*).

Taylor, *Magic and English Romanticism*, pp. 221–40.

In addition, there are these few specifically devoted to *Heaven and Earth*:

Barsky, 'Byron and Catastrophism', pp. 109–25.

Stevens, 'Scripture and the Literary Imagination', pp. 118–35.

Watkins, 'Politics and Religion', pp. 30–39.

The Devil as Doppelgänger in *The Deformed Transformed*: the Sources and Meaning of Byron's Unfinished Drama

CHARLES E. ROBINSON

Byron's *The Deformed Transformed* is a complex, fragmentary and uneven drama which has received little critical attention and less praise since its publication in 1824; yet the potential effect of this drama prompted Montague Summers in an unguarded moment to express 'infinite regret' that Byron 'did not finish the piece, which has an eerie and perhaps unhallowed fascination all its own'.[1] Summers undoubtedly praised this drama because of its unorthodox plot containing a pact with the devil, its perplexing incompleteness, its autobiographical revelations and its indebtedness to Byron's acknowledged sources: Joshua Pickersgill's unbridled Gothic novel, *The Three Brothers* (1803), and Goethe's *Faust, Part I* (1808). But the 'fascination' attending *The Deformed Transformed* is manifestly increased when one realizes that Byron's drama was conceived and written and would have been completed under the indirect influence of Percy Bysshe Shelley, that it is a central document for a literary motif transcending continents and centuries, and that it is in fact the 'Unwritten Drama of Lord Byron' publicized by Thomas Medwin and Washington Irving in 1835.

Of the three parts of the incomplete *Deformed Transformed*, the first scene of Part I is by far the most imaginative and intense. [...] In this first scene, Arnold, the deformed hero, was rejected by his mother and reminded of his hunchback and lame, cloven foot by his reflection in a fountain. Hated and hating himself, Arnold despaired and attempted suicide, but was deterred by a Mephistophelean 'Stranger' who miraculously appeared from the fountain and offered Arnold a new body in order that he could successfully love and be beloved by others. After engaging a compact with the Stranger, who then raised the bodily forms of Julius Caesar, Alcibiades, Socrates, Antony, Demetrius Poliorcetes, and Achilles from antiquity, Arnold chose the form of Achilles and was transformed into the 'unshorn boy of Peleus' and and 'Beautiful shadow/ Of Thetis's boy' (I.i.268, 381–82).[2] But then the Stranger, transforming himself, cleverly assumed Arnold's rejected and deformed 'form', consequently became the 'shadow' (I.i.449) or second self of Arnold, and chose to be called Caesar. The protagonist and antagonist in new forms then mounted their coal-black horses and raced to 'where the World/ Is thickest', to 'where there is War/ And Woman in activity' (I.i.494–97).

The remainder of the unfinished drama presents Arnold's and Caesar's exploits with 'War' and 'Woman'. [...] Part III of *The Deformed Transformed* includes only a 67-line choral song which offers virtually no suggestion concerning the future adventures of Arnold, Caesar, and Olimpia. The setting had been changed to a castle in the Apennines, but the plot is advanced no further than 'The wars are over,/ The spring is come;/ The bride and her lover/ Have sought their home' (III.i.1–4). But in 1901 E. H. Coleridge published from Byron's manuscript a second scene for Part III in which Arnold expressed his jealousy and regret that Olimpia could not love him as he loved her. Noting that the new Achilles would become 'jealous of himself under his former figure', Byron was prepared to increase the conflict between Arnold and Caesar, his 'former figure'.

Of these three parts, the first scene of Part I reveals an

emotional intensity that rivals *Manfred* and *Cain*. This intensity is manifest in Byron's sympathetic portrait of the unloved hunchback, in the Faustian pact between Arnold and Caesar, and in Arnold's glorious transformation, for each of which Byron acknowledged his indebtedness to external influences. But significantly more important for the meaning of *The Deformed Transformed* is what Byron did not acknowledge: his indebtedness to the doppelgänger tradition for his apparently unique portrayal of the Stranger's assumption of Arnold's deformed body. It is this second transformation that not only intensifies the action of the first scene but also imposes a unity on the drama, in that Caesar inseparably accompanied Arnold as a reflection of his former self, that is, as his metamorphic doppelgänger. That Byron was consciously working within the tradition of the double may be demonstrated, but it is first necessary to consider the sources he acknowledged for his unfinished drama.

Byron once confessed to Lady Blessington that *The Deformed Transformed* was 'suggested' by his own lameness and by the 'rage and mortification' he experienced when his mother ridiculed his 'personal deformity'.[3] But if Byron sought to purge these feelings of rage and mortification by empathically portraying Arnold's deformities, he also welcomed other reproaches. Shortly after concluding the fragmentary *Deformed Transformed*, Byron offered the following comparison between his own lameness and that of his friend, Henry Fox: 'but there is this difference, that *he* appears a halting angel, who has tripped against a star; whilst I am *Le Diable Boiteux*,—a soubriquet, which I marvel that, amongst their various *nominis umbrae*, the Orthodox have not hit upon'.[4] Byron, by portraying the diabolical Stranger's assumption of Arnold's deformed body (with both hunchback and cloven foot), was evidently provoking the Orthodox to compare him with the cynical and deformed devil in Le Sage's *Le Diable Boiteux*.

Byron did not mention his own lameness in the prefixed

advertisement to *The Deformed Transformed*, but he did acknowledge two literary sources for his drama: 'This production is founded partly on the story of a novel called "The Three Brothers," published many years ago [1803], from which M. G. Lewis's "Wood Demon" [*sic*] was also taken; and partly on the "Faust" of the great Goethe.'[5] *The Three Brothers* was written by Joshua Pickersgill, an author who in 1804 was unknown by his reviewer, and who in 1826 was mistakenly 'supposed to have been the late M. G. Lewis'.[6] Byron, who may have been introduced to this novel in 1816, borrowed incidents chiefly from its fourth volume, in which the diabolical villain, Julian, recounted the miseries of his former life as Arnaud. Like Byron's Arnold, Pickersgill's Arnaud was a hunchback (he had been wounded and deformed by the banditti at the age of eight) whose parents had rejected him. Unsuccessful in love, depraved in character yet proud in spirit, ('I! I! I! being the utterance everlastingly on his tongue'[7]), Arnaud despaired. Just as Arnold attempted suicide when he saw his reflected ugliness in the fountain or 'Nature's mirror' (I.i.47), so also had Arnaud twice attempted to hurl himself from a precipice after a polished broken blade had mirrored his deformity. Unsuccessful in these attempts, Arnaud conjured up Satan who offered the deformed hero a new body. [...]

The power of this scene was not wasted on Byron, for he adopted the substance of it, even to the similar choice of forms offered by the tempter. Yet the character of the Demon was not developed beyond this point, although he was twice seen as an infernal spirit attending Arnaud (called Julian after the transformation). And there is no suggestion in the four volumes that Arnaud was shadowed by his former self. In fact, Arnaud's rejected and deformed body had been preserved in a grotto in the Forest of the Pines.

Since Byron mentioned in his advertisement that Monk Lewis's unpublished drama, 'The Wood Daemon' (1807), was also influenced by *The Three Brothers*, he may have read this drama in its published and revised form, a 'Grand Musical Romance' with the title *One O'Clock! or, The Knight and the Wood Daemon* (1811). Lewis acknowledged his indebtedness to Pickersgill's novel in his advertisement to the first edition, and the parallels between the two works are quite obvious. Hardyknute, Lord of Holstein and villain of the drama, was 'born deformed' (like Byron's Arnold, but unlike Pickersgill's Arnaud) and engaged 'a dreadful compact with the Wood Daemon', Sangrida, by which he was transformed: 'She chained success to my footsteps; she rendered me invulnerable in battle; she endowed me with perpetual youth and health; and she cast over my person a magic charm to dazzle all female eyes, and seduce all female hearts. I was rich, potent, beloved, and wretched! for, oh! to that fatal bond was annexed a penalty.'[8] This fatal 'penalty' was Monk Lewis's adaptation of Arnaud's desire for a second transformation in *The Three Brothers*: seeking a new form to elude detection on the first anniversary of his initial transformation, Arnaud promised Satan to kill the first person he saw; similarly, Hardyknute had sacrificed for eight years a young child on the anniversary of his transformation (the 'seventh of each revolving August' at one o'clock) in order to maintain his transformed body. In the climax of Lewis's drama, Hardyknute failed to fulfil the bargain the ninth time and forfeited his soul to Sangrida, the Wood Daemon. Yet, like the Demon in *The Three Brothers*, Sangrida was virtually undeveloped, did not assume Hardyknute's body and did not influence Byron's characterization of Caesar in *The Deformed Transformed*.

The final influence Byron acknowledged for his drama was Goethe's *Faust*, translations of which he read in January 1822, just before he began *The Deformed Transformed*. [...] He had written part, if not all, of the first scene 'some days after' 6 February 1822, [...] [but] Byron was preoccupied in February 1822 with the adverse critical reception of *Cain* and with Southey's attacks on him; and the Dragoon affair in March, the death of Allegra in April, the writing of Cantos VI and VII of *Don Juan* from April to June, and Shelley's death in July were more than enough to prevent his continuation of *The Deformed Transformed*, which he attempted to finish in Genoa even as late as January 1823.[9]

Yet it was in Pisa, shortly after he had finished *Werner* on 20 January 1822, that Byron began *The Deformed Transformed*, and he had access to at least two translations of *Faust* at this time.[10] [...] Byron's avowed interest in *Faust* before and during his writing of the first scene for *The Deformed Transformed* significantly affected the structure of his drama. The long temptation scene between Arnold and Caesar and their companionship for the remainder of the drama undoubtedly reflect the similar pattern between Faust and Mephistopheles in Goethe's drama, a pattern not present in either *The Three Brothers* or 'The Wood Daemon'. Goethe himself remarked on Byron's indebtedness to *Faust* for the characterization of Caesar, at one point egotistically asserting that 'Lord Byron's transformed Devil is a continuation [with no originality] of Mephistophiles.'[11] [...] Furthermore, as will be demonstrated below, Byron saw Mephistopheles as Faust's symbolic doppelgänger, and he imitated their psychological identity in his characterizations of Caesar and Arnold. But since Mephistopheles did not assume Faust's body, Goethe's drama did not, in itself, provide Byron the idea to use the transformed Caesar as Arnold's physical double.

I do not mean to propose that Byron's conception of the transformed Caesar as Arnold's physical double was his unique creation; quite the contrary. Byron owed a manifest debt to the doppelgänger tradition in literature, extending to such diverse works as Dryden's *Amphitryon*, Monk Lewis's *The Bravo of Venice*, and Le Sage's *Le Diable Boiteux*.[12] Neither *Amphitryon* nor *The Bravo of Venice* employs the devil as double, but both emphasize a schizophrenia that is thematically central to *The Deformed Transformed*. In Dryden's *Amphitryon* (as in Plautus' and Molière's dramas by the same title), Jupiter and Mercury assumed the forms of Amphitryon and his slave, Sosias, in order that Jupiter might easily seduce Amphitryon's wife, Alcmena. Having fulfilled his desires with Alcmena, Jupiter (still impersonating Amphitryon) concluded an ironic argument on the difference between the husband and the lover in this fashion:

> To please my niceness you must separate
> The Lover from his Mortal Foe, the Husband.
> Give to the yawning Husband your cold Vertue,
> But all your vigorous Warmth, your melting Sighs,
> Your amorous Murmurs, be your Lovers part.
> (II.ii.92–96)

Although Alcmena later accused Jupiter of speciousness ('How vainly wou'd the Sophister divide,/ And make the Husband and the Lover, two!'), the husband (Amphitryon) and the lover (Jupiter) in Dryden's comedy are psychologically and symbolically reflections of one personality.

Byron had also discovered a different and a more intense double personality, without intervention of god or devil, in Monk Lewis's adapted translation of J. D. D. Zschokke's *Aböllino, der grosse Bandit*, first published as *The Bravo of Venice* in 1805. The Neapolitan hero, Rosalvo, requiring a disguise, symbiotically projected for himself two distinct personalities: Abellino, the extremely ugly bravo of Venice whose dissembling ultimately freed the Doge from the threat of the banditti; and the extremely handsome Florentine nobleman, Flodoardo, who ultimately won the love of the Doge's daughter, Rosabella. [...] This physical antagonism between two personalities manufactured by one self in *The Bravo of Venice* contrasts with [...] Arnold's extraordinary pact with the devil in *The Deformed Transformed*, Rosalvo's transformations [being] self-initiated and selflessly directed to preserving the Venetians and the Doge from the banditti. Notwithstanding these differences, *The Bravo of Venice*, which Byron had read, provided an entertaining characterization of dual personality and revealed the potential of subtle variations on the doppelgänger motif. [...]

Byron's discovery of the devil as doppelgänger in *Faust* was occasioned by his receipt, by 12 January 1822, of *Retsch's Series of Outlines* which contained, in an anonymous introduction, the following interpretation of Goethe's drama: 'that the easiest clue to the moral part of this didactic action is, to consider Faust and Mephistopheles as *one* person, represented symbolically, only in a two-fold shape'.[13] Encountering this highly sophisticated interpretation of *Faust*, Byron was led to recognize the potential of devil as doppelgänger in Goethe's drama and to realize this potential in *The Deformed Transformed*. Consequently, the companionship of Faust and Mephistopheles in *Faust* takes on new meaning in relation to Byron's drama, for if Mephistopheles and Faust, though distinct dramatis personae, were symbolically one personality, then the devils Mephistopheles and Caesar merely embodied Faust's and Arnold's moral imperfections (compare, for example, each protagonist's suicide attempt before the devil appeared). Furthermore, Byron made explicit what was but implicit in *Faust* by having Caesar, through transformation, embody not only Arnold's moral imperfections but also his physical deformities.

That Byron encountered and adopted this interpretation of *Faust* appearing in the Retsch volume would be highly speculative were it not for Byron and Shelley's discussions of the doppelgänger in January 1822. Shelley, having read at least part of *Le Diable Boiteux*,[14] having understood the symbolic relationship between Frankenstein and his monster in Mary Shelley's novel, having employed Demogorgon to represent a union of Prometheus (head) and Asia (heart) in *Prometheus Unbound*, and having completed by February 1821 'Epipsychidion' which, like *Alastor*, employed the epipsyche as the idealized double of one's self, was no novice in the tradition of the doppelgänger. And by January 1822 Shelley was translating for Byron not only episodes from Goethe's *Faust* but also scenes from Calderón's *El Mágico Prodigioso*, a drama depicting a relationship between demon and hero similar to that between Mephistopheles and Faust, [and] another Calderón drama, most often entitled 'El Embozado', containing a bizarre plot in which the protagonist was pursued by his 'second self'. Since Byron, who had already experimented with the double in *Manfred* and *Cain*, intended to adapt the plot of 'El Embozado' for his own dramatic purposes, there can be no question that he and Shelley discussed the dramatic possibilities and function of the doppelgänger. [...]

Having discovered the symbolic doubling within *Faust*, Shelley, and consequently Byron, proceeded to compare Goethe's drama with Calderón's *El Mágico Prodigioso*, based on the legend of St Cyprian's pact with the devil in Antioch. [...] And when Byron discussed *Faust* with Medwin in January, he repeated Shelley's earlier and more extensive comparison of the two plays: 'You tell me the plot [of *Faust*] is almost entirely Calderón's. The fête, the scholar, the argument about the *Logos*, the selling himself to the fiend, and afterwards denying his power; his disguise of the plumed cavalier; the enchanted mirror,—are all from Cyprian. That *Mágico Prodigioso* must be worth reading, and nobody seems to know any thing about it but you and Shelley.'[15] The demon or fiend in this drama has been interpreted as a 'projection, as it were, of processes that go on within Cyprian's mind, imagination, and sensibility';[16] by comparing Calderón's demon to Goethe's Mephistopheles, Byron and Shelley undoubtedly made the same judgement.

The demon of *El Mágico Prodigioso*, like Mephistopheles in *Faust* and Caesar in *The Deformed Transformed*, is a Protean figure who frequently transformed himself. Disguised *'as a fine Gentleman'* searching for Antioch in Act I, the demon initially engaged the pagan Cyprian in a theological debate. Having lost this debate, the demon then manipulated Cyprian's involvement with the fair Justina, and in Act II, after Cyprian offered his soul to Hell's 'most detested spirit' in exchange for Justina's love, the demon reappeared in an 'unknown form' as a shipwreck victim to claim Cyprian's soul. Preceding the symbolic embrace between Cyprian and his magical tempter, the demon quite clearly explained that he would become Cyprian's shadow or second self: 'so firm an amity/ 'Twixt thee and me be, that neither Fortune ... nor Time ... nor/ Heaven itself ... can ever make/ The least division between thee and me,—/ Since now I find a refuge in thy favour.' This symbolic unity between devil and hero was eventually destroyed when Cyprian realized he had been duped by the demon who was powerless in comparison with the Christian God.[17] [...]

If the anonymous editor of *Retsch's Outlines* provided the formal cause [...] for *The Deformed Transformed*, then Shelley provided the efficient cause by acquainting Byron in January 1822 with a bizarre doppelgänger in another Calderón drama, which Byron acknowledged as the source for a drama he intended to write. Mistakenly entitled either 'El Embozado' or 'El Encapotado', this was actually Calderón's *El Purgatorio de San Patricio*.

The evidence for Byron's interest in this Calderón drama was offered by Thomas Medwin to Washington Irving in 1825 in the form of an 'unpublished note' which recorded Byron's summary of 'El Embozado' or 'El Encapotado' together with Byron's expressed design to adapt Calderón's plot of the doppelgänger for his own projected drama. Medwin's alternate titles (neither of which was correct) resulted from his 'scanty' record of Byron's conversations in Pisa on this subject. [...] Irving retained these misconceptions when he rewrote Medwin's 'unpublished note' for publication as 'An Unwritten Drama of Lord Byron' in *The Knickerbocker: New York Monthly Magazine*. [...] Horace E. Thorner, in 1934, satisfactorily identified the plot of 'El Embozado' as but a scene from Calderón's *El Purgatorio de San Patricio*, in which Ludovico Enio vainly attempted to kill a mantled figure ('un Hombre Embozado') who finally revealed himself as Enio's skeletal 'second self'.[18] That Byron's projected drama was 'unwritten' has been accepted as fact, for no one has recognized that Byron adapted Calderón's bizarre plot in the unfinished *Deformed Transformed*.

Although Irving's 'An Unwritten Drama of Lord Byron' has been reprinted often since its publication in August 1835, Irving's transcription of Medwin's 'unpublished note' in his 1835 journal has never been published. [...]

> The hero of the piece is a nobleman (whom I call Alfonzo) just making his debut on the stage of life. His passions from early and unrestrained indulgence are impetuous and ungovernable and he follows their dictates with a wild and thoughtless disregard of consequences. These consequences are obvious enough. Such a moral would be a very common place one but with Calderón [i.e. following Calderón's example] I should take a new and different way of enforcing it and a truly dramatic one it might be made if treated in the genuine spirit of Goethe. Soon after our Spaniards entrance into the world a person in a masque or cloak, that prevents his features or figure from being recognized (for the titles of the play leave us in doubt as to the express nature of the disguise) becomes as it were his shadow—his second self.
>
> This mysterious being Alfonzo is unable to identify with any of his acquaintances; his real name—or country—or place of abode are a mystery—and he is equally at a loss to form even a conjecture as to the peculiar observations and interest of the stranger. This curiosity at first scarcely noticed, or only considered as idle impertinence, daily becomes more irksome. Not only his most-private actions pass under the scrutiny of this officious monitor, but his most secret thoughts are known to him. Speak of

him, he stands by his side—think of him—though invisible he feels his presence oppress and weigh upon his spirits like a troubled atmosphere. Waking or asleep he is ever with him or before him—he crosses his path, at every turn he intrudes like the demon in Faust in his solitude—he follows him in the crowded street, in the brilliant saloon, he sees him winding through the assembly & the honied words of seduction that he is addressing to his fair partner in the dance die unfinished on his lips. One voice like the voice of his own soul whispers in his ears and silences the music—Who can he be [?]

Is it the false embodying of his fantasy—a shape his melancholy spirits have engendered out of the atoms of the day? No! It is something more than an apparition that haunts him. Like the Schedoni of The Italian † († vide. romance by Mrs Radcliff) his evil genius counteracts all his projects, thwarts him in all his deep laid schemes of ambition and fame, unwinds through all their intricacies and shapes, the webs of his intrigues, developes [*sic*] the hidden motives of his conduct and betrays that those actions which he wishes to make appear the most disinterested are only based in self.

The Hero of the drama is become abstracted and gloomy. Youth, health, wealth, power all that promised to give life its zest in the outset have lost their charm. The sweetest cup to others is poison to him. Existence becomes a burthen, and to put a [? trouble] to his misery & drive him to a state bordering on frenzy he suspects that the guilty object of his affections has fallen a prey to his tormentor. Alonzo now thirsts only for vengeance but the unknown eludes his pursuit and his emissaries endeavour in vain to discover his retreat; at length he succeeds in tracing him into the house of

his mistress & attacking him with all the fury which
jealous rage inspires, taxes him with his wrongs and
demands *satisfaction.* His rival scarcely defends
himself and the sword of Alonzo at the first thrust
pierces the breast of his enemy, who in falling utters
'are you satisfied!' his mantle drops off and
discovers—his own image the spectre of himself—
his self—He dies with horror!

    The spectre is an alegorical [*sic*] being—the
personification of conscience or of the passions.[19]

    When Washington Irving rewrote this 'unpublished note'
by Medwin in 'An Unwritten Drama of Lord Byron', he
correctly observed that the plot summary was 'somewhat
vague and immature, and would doubtless have undergone
many modifications' in Byron's projected adaptation. But
because Joshua Pickersgill's *The Three Brothers* and Goethe's
Faust provided these 'modifications', Irving (as well as
Medwin and subsequent Byron scholars) failed to recognize
the fundamental similarity between 'El Embozado' and
Byron's written, not 'unwritten', *The Deformed Transformed.*
The conflict between Alonzo and his 'double' and that
between Arnold and Caesar are essentially identical, but
Byron disguised his indebtedness by altering the character of
Alonzo. Influenced by his own lameness and borrowing from
Pickersgill's *The Three Brothers*, Byron created a hunchbacked
Arnold whose physical deformities symbolically embodied
Alonzo's 'impetuous and ungovernable' passions. The consequences of Arnold's deformity, his Faustian pact with Caesar
and his transformation into Achilles, were significant structural additions to the frame of 'El Embozado', but Byron did
not change the function of the doppelgänger in his adaptation,
even though Caesar became the double of Arnold's *former*
self. The 'stranger' in Calderón's drama was Alonzo's uneludable 'shadow—his second self'; in nearly identical fashion,
Byron's 'Stranger', before he took the name of Caesar and

became Arnold's 'second self', revealed Arnold's destiny: 'In a few moments/ I will be as you were, and you shall see/ Yourself for ever by you, as your shadow' (I.i.447–49). Just as Calderón's 'stranger', a 'personification of conscience or of the passions', shadowed Alonzo as a reflection of his moral weaknesses, Caesar, who assumed the rejected and hunchbacked body, accompanied Arnold as a reminder of his former physical deformities and of his diabolical transformation.

Byron's adaptation of the physical doubles in 'El Embozado' was also influenced by his awareness of the symbolic doubles in Goethe's *Faust*. Byron recognized the parallels between the two works and told Medwin that his modification of 'El Embozado' would be 'in the genuine spirit of Goethe' and that Alonzo's double intruded 'like the demon in Faust'. In other words, Arnold and Caesar in *The Deformed Transformed* were a product of Alonzo and the 'stranger' interpreted as Faust and Mephistopheles. This accounts for the difference between Alonzo's ignorance of his pursuing double and Arnold's knowledge of his accompanying double: having altered the structure of his source by introducing the Satanic pact and Arnold's physical transformation, Byron could not retain the unrecognized physical double in 'El Embozado'; instead, like Goethe, Byron had the Mephistophelean Caesar accompany Arnold as a symbolic representation of his moral and mortal inadequacies. However, since he assumed Arnold's hunchbacked body, Caesar, like Alonzo's 'second self', was Arnold's physical double. Thus, the doppelgänger in *The Deformed Transformed* was a unique and imaginative fusion of 'El Embozado' and *Faust*: Byron not only retained the bizarre physical doubling in Calderón's drama; he also made explicit what Goethe but implied in the characterization of Faust and Mephistopheles.

Having fused these two plots, Byron could not recreate the actual suspense of self pursuing self in 'El Embozado', but he did intend to use the climactic scene between Alonzo and his second self in order to resolve the conflict between Arnold and Caesar. Because Byron's indebtedness to this Calderón drama has never been recognized, no reader of *The Deformed Transformed* has satisfactorily projected the conclusion of this unfinished drama. Mary Shelley, who copied what Byron wrote, acknowledged that she did 'not know how he meant to finish it' but reported that Byron had 'the whole conduct of the story ... already conceived'.[20] [...] When E. H. Coleridge first published the 'fragment' of Part III which contained not only Byron's memorandum on jealousy ('Jealous—Arnold of Caesar. Olympia [sic] at first not liking Caesar—then?—Arnold jealous of himself under his former figure, owing to the power of intellect, etc., etc., etc.'), but also Arnold and Caesar's dialogue on jealousy, he cautiously, but correctly, stated that 'Byron intended to make Olimpia bestow her affections, not on the glorious Achilles, but the witty and interesting Hunchback'.[21] [...] The text suggests that Arnold would kill Olimpia, but this action would not forfeit his soul but only formalize the bond between tempter and tempted. It is generally overlooked that Arnold had not signed any compact with Caesar in *The Deformed Transformed*, but Byron did indicate the nature of this 'signature' in Caesar's veiled threat to Arnold: 'You shall have no bond/ But your own will, no contract save your deeds' (I.i.151–52). But this 'deed' of contract does not appear in the finished portion of Byron's drama: the transformed Arnold does not join the devil's party by any ignoble action; quite the contrary, as Samuel C. Chew objected, 'all that Caesar incites him to do [in the siege of Rome and after] it would occur to any high-minded man to undertake'.[22] Most probably, the 'deed' was to be Arnold's shedding of Olimpia's blood. Arnold, through his own wilful act, would assume the spiritual depravity of Caesar just as Caesar had assumed Arnold's physical deformities.

Byron's introduction of Arnold's jealousy 'of himself under his former figure' was merely an imitation of Alonzo's jealousy of his double, the mantled figure in 'El Embozado'.

Arnold's destruction of Olimpia would have bound him to
Caesar, but it would not have provided Byron the means to
resolve the conflict between Arnold and his double. Rather,
Byron, who had 'already conceived' the climax and 'transformed' Calderón's doubles into Arnold and Caesar, intended
that Arnold would forfeit his soul by a symbolic 'suicide': just
as Alonzo died when he killed his own physical double,
Arnold, motivated by a similar jealousy, would have shed 'all'
of his own blood by killing his diabolical rival and double.
Byron's intentions are clear not only from his expressed
'design' to imitate Calderón's plot but also from his explicit
preparation for this climax in the finished portions of *The
Deformed Transformed*. [...] When Caesar asked Arnold for 'a
little of [his] blood' to make the transformation effective,
Arnold offered 'it all'. Caesar's answer indicates that Arnold's
body would later be slain: 'Not now. A few drops will suffice
for this' (I.i.157). Byron further prepared for Arnold's fate by
consciously paralleling the fundamental destructive conflict
between Arnold and Caesar to that between other mutually
antagonistic doubles: Romulus and Remus; Gore and Glory;
Lucifer and Venus; Eros and Anteros; and even Huon and
Memnon. The most significant doubles in this series are the
twins, Romulus and Remus, and Byron twice referred to
Romulus' destruction of Remus: Caesar informed Arnold that
he had seen 'Romulus .../ Slay his own twin', and the Chorus
of Spirits bemoaned Romulus' 'Awful ... crime' and 'inexpiable
sin' (I.i.80–81, II.i.38, 76). Metaphorically, the foundation for
the 'Glory' of Romulus' Rome was the 'Gore' of Remus'
blood; thus Caesar's description of Arnold's coming 'Hand in
hand with the mild twins—Gore and Glory' (II.ii.12) and his
allusions to Romulus and Remus do more than provide a
historical perspective to the Bourbon's pillage of Rome—they
actually prepare for Arnold's slaying of his own twin.[23] Thus
the 'deed' of *forfeiture*, Byron's climax for *The Deformed
Transformed*, was to be Arnold's suicide, symbolically repre-

sented by his wilful murder of his double, Caesar in the form of Arnold's hunchbacked body.

Once Byron's intended imitation of the climax in 'El Embozado' is recognized as the only logical resolution between Arnold and his diabolical double, the function of the doppelgänger in this drama becomes more apparent. Like *Manfred* and *Cain*, Byron's only finished 'speculative' dramas, *The Deformed Transformed* dramatized man's self-destruction whereby his immortal aspirations were annihilated by his own mortality. Unlike the heroes in Byron's Oriental Tales and unlike Prometheus, Childe Harold and even the narrator of *Don Juan*, the protagonist in the 'speculative' drama was engaged not in a constructive conflict whereby the self triumphed, sometimes even in death, through its independence and defiance of the 'other' (whether man, nature, society, government, religion, or 'metaphysics'); rather, with a 'chaos of thought and passion, all confused', this protagonist precipitated a destructive conflict within his own nature in which mortal self destroyed immortal self. Byron's introduction to the plot of 'El Embozado' was actually fortuitous, because it provided him the artistic means to give final form to the idea of self-alienation and self-destruction which had been dramatized in *Manfred* and *Cain*.

In *Manfred*, his first 'speculative' drama, Byron created an introspective hero whose 'half dust, half deity' (I.ii.40) engendered a conflict between his mortally limiting body and his immortally aspiring mind. Byron externalized this internal conflict by juxtaposing to Manfred 'The Lady Astarte, his [physical double and psychological counterpart]' (III.iii.47), as I interpret and complete Manuel's interrupted description of her. Manfred himself described his resemblance to Astarte: 'She was like me in lineaments—her eyes—/ Her hair—her features—all, to the very tone/ Even of her voice ... were like to mine' (II.ii.105–07). Yet with 'gentler powers', 'humility', and 'virtues', Astarte possessed a heart which had psychologically complemented Manfred's Faustian pursuit of knowledge. Manfred confessed to the Chamois Hunter that he and Astarte formerly possessed 'one heart' (II.i.26), but he told the Abbot that this heart was now 'withered, or ... broken' (III.i.145). Because Astarte, representing Manfred's heart, had died, the zealous Abbot sensed the futility of appealing to the half-destroyed Manfred: 'my humble zeal ... May light upon your head—could I say *heart*—/ Could I touch *that*, with words or prayers, I should/ Recall a noble spirit' (III.iv.47, 50–52). Even the Chamois Hunter unwittingly recognized this 'noble spirit's' divided nature when he cautioned Manfred, 'Thy mind and body are alike unfit/ To trust each other' (II.i.2–3) and when he prayed for Manfred, 'Heaven give thee rest!/ And Penitence restore *thee* to *thyself*' (II.i.87–88, my italics). In other words, the 'thee' (Manfred's heart or mortality as represented by Astarte) had been severed from the 'thyself' (Manfred's mind with its immortal aspirations).

Because Manfred had destroyed his own heart, his gentler self in the person of Astarte, he should have died; yet it was his 'fatality to live' (I.ii.24). Protesting too much for 'self-oblivion' and 'forgetfulness' (I.i.144, 136) of Astarte, whose uneludable 'shadow' (I.i.219) reminded him of his divided self, Manfred really quested for self-integration. The Witch of the Alps best understood Manfred's quest for Astarte:

> And for this—
> A being of the race thou dost despise—
> The order, which thine own would rise above,
> Mingling with us and ours,—thou dost forego
> The gifts of our great *knowledge*, and shrink'st back
> To recreant *mortality*.   (II.ii.121–26, my italics)

Manfred's head or knowledge could not transcend his heart or mortality. His self-sufficient claim to be 'self-condemned' in Act III (i.177) misrepresented the truth: he was his 'own destroyer' (III.iv.139) only because he had 'loved her, and destroyed her [Astarte, his double]' (II.ii.117).

That Byron was artistically prepared for the development of the doppelgänger in *The Deformed Transformed* is also manifested by his second 'speculative' drama, *Cain*, whose hero, like Manfred and Arnold, was self-destructive. But this time Byron externalized man's internal conflict by using not just one, but two doubles: Lucifer, the Mephistophelean spirit, represented Cain's Faustian quest for knowledge and immortality; and Adah, Cain's twin sister, represented his emotional need for mortal love. Although Cain could judge the differences between his two companions—he said that Adah 'understands not' (I.i.188) and that Lucifer 'lov'st nothing' (II.ii.338)—he did not recognize their symbolic functions. Rather, only Adah sensed that Lucifer represented Cain's 'own/ Dissatisfied and curious thoughts' for immortality (I.i.402–03), and only Lucifer judged Adah to represent Cain's enfeebling love for 'frail mortality' (II.ii.269). Thus when Lucifer and Adah debated the relative merits of knowledge and love in Act I, Cain did not know that this external debate represented his internal conflict. But finally choosing knowledge over love, Cain separated himself from Adah, his heart, and entered the abyss of space with Lucifer. As Adah informed Lucifer in Act I, 'thou ... steppest between heart and heart' (I.i.349).

In Act II, Cain attempted to unify his divided nature. Declaring '*I* must be/ Immortal in despite of *me*' (II.i.90–91, my italics), he requested knowledge not only of his 'I', his 'immortal part' (I.i.104), but also of his 'me', his mortal limitation or death. What Cain discovered, in Byron's slightly altered phrase, was the 'inadequacy of his [mortal] state to his [immortal] conceptions' (*LJ*, V, 470). The incompatibility of Cain's two natures is suggested by his dialogue with Lucifer at the end of Act II:

> *Lucifer.*   Didst thou not require
>   Knowledge? And have I not, in what I showed,
>   Taught thee to know thyself?
> *Cain.*   Alas! I seem
>   Nothing.
> *Lucifer.*   And this should be the human sum
>   Of knowledge, to know mortal nature's
>   nothingness.   (II.ii.418–22)

Cain, like Manfred, learned that the 'Tree of Knowledge is not that of Life': self-knowledge revealed a disintegrated personality in conflict with itself.

The final act of this drama is but a phenomenal representation of Cain's noumenal experience in Act II. Still alienated from his gentler self—'leave me' (III.i.94), he says to Adah—Cain, according to Byron, 'falls into the *frame* of *mind* that leads to the Catastrophe' (*LJ*, V, 470): he murdered Abel, brought death into the world, and confirmed 'mortal nature's nothingness'. Ironically, Cain finally recognized Abel, not Adah or Lucifer, as his double: ''Tis blood—my blood—/ My brother's and my own! and shed by me!/ ... I have taken life from my own flesh' (III.i.345–48). [...] Cain's destruction of Abel, who had 'sprung from the same womb ... drained/ The same breast', and Cain's consequent expulsion 'Eastward from Eden' (III.i.535–36, 552), phenomenally represented the destruction of his own immortal aspirations and his self-alienation.

Having already used the double to dramatize the divided self in *Manfred* and *Cain*, and having used the devil as doppelgänger in *Cain* (according to Samuel Chew, the 'tempter and tempted are absolutely at one'[24]), Byron in January 1822 adopted the doppelgänger in 'El Embozado' to once more portray man's self-alienation. Even before the transformations of Arnold and Caesar, Arnold revealed his double identity by damning his mortal form which limited not his mental conceptions, as in *Cain*, but his emotional desire for love:

'[oh] that the Devil, to whom they liken me,/ Would aid his likeness! If I must partake/ His *form*, why not his *power*' (I.i.40–42, my italics). Like Narcissus, Arnold gazed into the fountain, hoped for the devil's power to complement his form, but was mocked by his 'horrid shadow' (I.i.51)—a reminder that his devil's likeness determined the barrenness of his mortality since he could neither be loved nor love himself. Hated by others and hating himself, Arnold despaired and attempted suicide, but was prevented by the stirring of the fountain, the source of his double or reflected image. 'Nature's mirror' not only revealed a disintegrated personality but actually separated the opposing principles within Arnold: the diabolical 'form' reflected in the fountain was miraculously transformed into the diabolical 'power' in the person of the Stranger who emerged from the waters. Thus the Stranger, like Faust's Mephistopheles and Cain's Lucifer, appeared not as an incarnation of the power of abstract evil in the universe; rather, he was an embodiment of Arnold's idealization of power—a double who reflected Arnold's potential for disintegration and self-destruction.

Because the tempter and tempted are symbolic representations of one disintegrated personality, the remainder of *The Deformed Transformed* is a phenomenal representation of Arnold's internal conflict. Naïvely idealistic and risking his soul for the love he lacked, Arnold chose to be transformed into the glorious Achilles. Thinking that he had transcended his mortal limitations, the new Achilles believed he had the power to realize his desires: 'I love, and I shall be beloved' (I.i.421). That Arnold was only deluding himself and could not transcend his mortality was symbolically represented by the Stranger's transformation into the deformed Arnold. Thus the Mephistophelean Stranger, who had represented Arnold's idealization of power, remained Arnold's double by regressing into the hunchbacked form initially mirrored by the fountain. Power and form were not integrated; they merely changed places. Ever by his side as his shadow, Caesar reminded

Arnold of his eternally conflicting double nature, and Arnold discovered that neither esteem in war nor possession of Olimpia, the 'Essence of all Beauty' (II.iii.143), could reintegrate the divided self.

Arnold's desire for self-integration through love was, then, limited by his mortality. In Part I, Caesar rose from the fountain as Anteros (the negation of love) to confront Arnold's desire for Eros. And in the 'fragment' of Part III, Caesar (still representing Anteros in the form of Arnold's mortally limiting body) accurately diagnosed the source of Arnold's frustrations:

> you would be *loved*—what you call loved—
> *Self-loved*—loved for *yourself*—for neither health,
> Nor wealth, nor youth, nor power, nor rank, nor
>   beauty—
> For these you may be stript of—but *beloved*
> As an abstraction.   (III.61–65)

But the power and the form of one personality were not united by the ideal of self-love. As Cain discovered from Lucifer (I.i.420–31), knowledge destroyed love. Similarly, Arnold's ideal of self-love was an illusion and would be destroyed by his final knowledge of his divided self: 'owing to the power of intellect', Arnold was to become 'jealous of himself under his former figure' (Byron's memorandum to this 'fragment'). The disintegrating reality of jealousy rather than the integrating ideal of love was to seal Arnold's fate. Caesar warned Arnold that he would become jealous of his mortal self, and he metaphorically explained the nature of this jealousy: 'Now Love in you is as the Sun—a thing/ Beyond you—and your Jealousy's of Earth—/ A cloud of your own raising' (III.80–82). Thus Arnold would have attributed his inability 'to be [Olimpia's] heart as she is [his]' (III.101) to the presence of Caesar, confirmed his mortality by being jealous of his own hunchbacked form, and consequently increased his self-alienation. As in *Othello* (which Byron and Shelley talked of 'getting up' in February 1822[25]), Arnold, motivated by jealousy, was destined to yield up love to tyrannous hate, to destroy Olimpia (an object of his love), to recognize his self-delusions, and finally to destroy himself. But since the doppelgänger modified this tragic action, Arnold, finally recognizing the source of his self-delusions, would destroy that which he wanted to love—himself, mortally represented in the form of Caesar. Thus the suicide which the self-alienated Arnold had prevented by self-hypnosis in the fountain was to be symbolically re-enacted at the end of the drama by his murder of Caesar: ironically, Arnold's final triumph over his mortally limiting body would have confirmed his mortality; he would have destroyed himself.

Having demonstrated the subtleties of *The Deformed Transformed*, I propose that it contains something more significant than what G. Wilson Knight calls 'Byron's "Richard" complex'.[26] Whether Byron could have artistically completed this representation of the destructive conflict within man is doubtful, not only because the disproportionately detailed account of the Siege of Rome violates the drama's integrity, but also because its bitter portrayal of 'mortal nature's nothingness' demanded a total cynicism that is not readily compatible with the increasing mellowness of the last few cantos of *Don Juan*. Yet if Byron had completed *The Deformed Transformed*, it would have been a major document in the Byron canon and among other literary treatments of the doppelgänger. As it is, Byron's development of Arnold and his summary of 'El Embozado' as reported by Medwin and Irving influenced such diverse works as Irving's abortive 'El Embozado' (1825), Mary Shelley's short story, 'Transformation' (1831), Hawthorne's 'Howe's Masquerade' (1838), Poe's 'William Wilson' (1839), Irving's 'Don Juan: A Spectral Research' (1841), and even Yeats's *A Vision* (1925).[27]

NOTES

1. Summers, *The Gothic Quest*, p. 276.
2. *The Works of Lord Byron: Poetry*, ed. Ernest Hartley Coleridge (London, 1898–1904), V, 487, 491. All subsequent quotations from Byron's poetry will be from this edition (hereafter cited as *Poetry*), followed by line numbers.
3. *Lady Blessington's Conversations*, pp. 80–81.
4. *The Works of Lord Byron: Letters and Journals*, ed. Rowland E. Prothero (London: John Murray, 1898–1901), VI, 178–79. Hereafter cited as *LJ*.
5. *Poetry*, V, 473–74.
6. *The Gentleman's Magazine*, LXXIV (1804), p. 1047; Clinton, *Memoirs of Lord Byron*, p. 666.
7. Pickersgill, *The Three Brothers*, IV, 273–74.
8. These and other quotations from *One O'Clock! or, The Knight and the Wood Daemon* are taken from Act III of the Oxberry edition (London: Pub. for the Proprietors by W. Simpkin and R. Marshall, 1824). For the play's complex history see Summers, *The Gothic Quest*, pp. 274–76.
9. Byron had Mary Shelley copy at least the first scene of *The Deformed Transformed* by November 1822, at which time she quizzed Byron about the transformed Caesar: 'I have copied your MSS. The "Eternal Scoffer" seems a favourite of yours. The Critics, as they used to make you a Childe Harold, Giaour, & Lara all in one, will now make a compound of Satan & Caesar to [? serve as *(MS torn)*] your prototype' (*The Letters of Mary W. Shelley*, I, 202). But Byron had apparently not finished Part II of the drama by that time, for he sent Mary Shelley a 'few scenes more' for transcription on 25 January 1823 (*LJ*, VI, 165). For Mary Shelley's continued praise of this drama, see *Letters*, I, 213.
10. See *LJ*, V, 488 and *The Letters of Percy Bysshe Shelley*, ed. Frederick L. Jones (Oxford, 1964), II, 376, 368–69 n., hereafter cited parenthetically as *LPBS*, volume and page.
11. Goethe, *Conversations*, p. 108.
12. Byron's references to *Amphytrion* and *The Bravo of Venice* (*Medwin's 'Conversations'*, pp. 178, 191) and to *Le Diable Boiteux* (*LJ*, VI, 178–79) demonstrate his knowledge of these works.
13. *Retsch's Series of Twenty-Six Outlines*, p. 2.
14. *Mary Shelley's Journal*, p. 42.
15. *LPBS*, II, 407; *Medwin's 'Conversations'*, pp. 142, 143n.
16. Parker, 'The Devil in the Drama of Calderón', pp. 19–20. For a similar interpretation of the devil as doppelgänger in *El Mágico Prodigioso*, see Hesse, *Calderón de la Barca*, p. 92.

17. Shelley's translation of *El Mágico Prodigioso* in *The Complete Works of Percy Bysshe Shelley*, IV, 299–320. After failing to pervert Justina, the demon intended to impersonate and defame her through his actions. But it was the Christian God who sent a phantom-figure of Justina in skeletal form to intimidate Cyprian and effect his conversion. Note then the tradition of the angelic as well as the diabolical doppelgänger.

18. Thorner, 'Hawthorne, Poe, and a Literary Ghost', pp. 146–54. Thorner was indebted to Mac-Carthy, *Calderón's Dramas*.

19. Quoted from Washington Irving's 'Note book containing extracts of poetry and prose; hint for a tale or farce; and miscellany [1824–26]' with the permission of the Manuscript Division, The New York Public Library. In subsequent references to this plot summary, the hero will be called Alonzo. Irving (or Medwin) called the hero both 'Alfonzo' and 'Alonzo'.

20. *Poetry*, V, 474n.

21. *Poetry*, V, 532–33n.

22. Chew, *The Dramas of Lord Byron*, p. 148.

23. For the reference to Lucifer and Venus, see II.iii.189, and for the possible allusion to Eros and Anteros, see *Poetry*, V, 480n. That Arnold as Achilles would slay Caesar is also indicated by the names given to the two pages at the end of the first scene. Although they are not twins and are not mentioned again in the drama, Huon (with the 'golden horn' and the 'bright/ And blooming aspect') and Memnon (the 'darker' one 'who smiles not') reflect the antagonistic countenances of the transformed Arnold and Caesar. [...] Byron certainly recognized that the Ethiopian, Memnon, a son of Eos and brother of Phosphor or 'Lucifer', was slain by Achilles in the Trojan war. Thus this allusion to Memnon (an oblique reflection of the diabolical Caesar with the 'swart face') who had been slain by Achilles prepares for the destruction of Caesar (and consequently Arnold) by the new Achilles, Arnold himself.

24. Chew, *The Dramas of Lord Byron*, p. 131.

25. See *Mary Shelley's Journal*, p. 167n.

26. Knight, *Byron and Shakespeare*, p. 155.

27. For Irving's proposed 'El Embozado', see *The Journals of Washington Irving*, II, 171–74; for the influence of 'El Embozado' on 'Howe's Masquerade' and 'William Wilson', see Thorner, 'Hawthorne, Poe, and a Literary Ghost'; for its influence on 'Don Juan: A Spectral Research', see Lovell, *Captain Medwin*, p. 149 and Williams, *The Life of Washington Irving*, I, 466–67; and for Yeats' use of *The Deformed Transformed* see Melchiori, *The Whole Mystery of Art*, pp. 277–79.

The Ideological Dimensions of Byron's *The Deformed Transformed*

DANIEL P. WATKINS

Byron's interest in radical politics developed with increasing intensity from 1818 until his departure for Greece in 1823. By late 1821 he had come to believe that 'There is nothing left for Mankind but a Republic', and his enthusiastic (if brief) involvement with the Italian Carbonari reflects his eagerness to help move society to this end.[1] The scope and character of his mature political vision are documented fully in his prose and poetry of this period; he wrote energetically (and sometimes recklessly) on social questions that he felt were central in politics. In 1821 alone he not only began reassessing his political and social past in the *Detached Thoughts* but he also wrote or began writing no fewer than five plays, each of which was aimed at illuminating some aspect of social reality: history, religion, war, violence, class. If in these works he did not develop a clear political programme, he did discover and define some of the prevailing social attitudes governing political thought and conduct, thus establishing a groundwork for informed political involvement. By late 1822 when he left Pisa he had worked through many of the difficult problems that heretofore had discouraged action and was ready to take a political stand.

The importance of *The Deformed Transformed* to Byron's social and political thought during these years has never been fully considered. This of course is partly Byron's fault. He wrote the drama with even less patience and precision than usual, allowing his ego and impulse towards autobiography to obscure other interests. Consequently readers unanimously have brought an exclusive psychological perspective to the play, stressing Byron's deformity, his relationship to his mother, and his long-standing fascination with the doppelgänger theory.[2] These psychological imperatives notwithstanding, *The Deformed Transformed* is most fully understood in terms of its radical critique of social order. The play presents an array of ostensibly isolated topics from alienation to violence, from religion to art, affirming their essential 'connectedness' in society. Moreover, it articulates the complex relation between abstract ideas and these social properties, thus demystifying the powerful ideological processes that both reflect and shape human perceptions of individual and social life. These concerns illuminate Byron's quarrel with conventional contemporary assessments of society (as found, for example, in Burke) and help to explain his belief that political action can be successful only when it understands and is able to change the concealed structures at society's core.

In its treatment of what Jerome McGann calls the Romantic belief in 'a final solution to the recurrent problems of human change and suffering',[3] *The Deformed Transformed* clarifies Byron's aesthetic and political differences with the generally acknowledged 'Romantic' position. Romanticism derives its intellectual cohesiveness at least partly from belief in a transcendental redemptive power: Coleridge saw power as the main objective of philosophic inquiry; Wordsworth deified it; Shelley extolled it as the one goal worthy of human pursuit. And the apocalyptic fervour that M. H. Abrams sketches comes from a definite view of spiritual power.[4] Although writers and thinkers described it differently—as imagination, vision, philosophy—they shared a common belief that this consummate power was to be equated with deep truth, that it was the culminating reality subsuming and reconciling all other discordant qualities.[5]

According to Byron, this abstract controlling belief produces an isolating, spiralling effect because it rests upon the unspoken motivating assumption that material reality is ultimately insufficient. Intentionally or not, it relegates history and society to a subordinate position, and concentrates systems of values into narrow, private contexts (all this despite the many serious Romantic expressions of liberalism, comprehension of historical process, and even—in Shelley's case—political radicalism). The insistence upon a universal redemptive power that continually recedes the more vehemently it is pursued requires the construction of ever new and more abstract value systems to replace the old ones that become unsatisfactory as their relation to material life is made manifest. And, in turn, as value systems become more selective, limited and abstract, they lose meaning because they are increasingly sensitive and vulnerable to the unavoidable presence of material life. As so much of the poetry of Keats and Shelley firmly attests, the inevitable result of this nondialectical view of things is despair.

The deformed Arnold convincingly illustrates the Romantic dilemma as Byron understands it, for his appearance, his temperament, even his simple-mindedness represent the distortions inherent in power ideally conceived. Like the stereotypical Romantic hero he displays a 'natural' attraction to the noblest qualities in life: 'Beauty' (I.i.191), 'peace' (I.ii.21), 'honour' (II.iii.80), 'mercy' (II.iii.93–94), and 'forgiveness' (II.iii.111); and he sincerely wishes to be loved (I.i.29–31, 421–22). But these noble abstractions emphatically elude him, never becoming part of his ordinary everyday experience. His mother looks on him as an 'incubus' (I.i.2), a 'nightmare' (I.i.2), an 'abortion' (I.i.3), a 'monstrous sport of Nature' (I.i.15); and when he reflects upon his situation he reluctantly agrees that he is despicable (I.i.46),[6] fit only for slave labour despite his desperate and sincere longing for something better.

Arnold's unfortunate predicament of course traces immediately to his deformity, but this is only the physical manifestation of a deeply ingrained and unquestioned set of beliefs. The

scorn for his ugliness rests upon the prevailing assumption—
which even he accepts—that he (like Caliban) is too ugly and
weak to deserve better than what he has, that his situation is
his fault alone. Or, put bluntly, he is despised because he is
unable to be anything other than what he is; he cannot attain
full integration into the mainstream of life because of his own
limitations. This view makes human life fundamentally individual, without essential historical and social character, and it
denies that real value abides in the very texture of material
existence. Further, it makes circumstance a fixed, static,
unyielding arena that does little more than test one's private
strength and serve as a measure of one's success or failure. In
short, it sets up an absolute dichotomy between private character and overriding 'real' value, without admitting the active,
shaping role of history and society. In this view, to be loved
and appreciated, to experience freedom and meaning, Arnold
would need first the strength to overcome the severe limitations that presently make him worthless; and, second, he
would need somehow to embody the ideals held up to him as
sacred.

The consequences of the ethic he has inherited and fully
embodied are exemplified in his transformation into Achilles.
His transformation (he thinks) marks his first step towards
acceptance and love; it gives him near-perfect beauty and
bestows on him unsurpassed physical skills as well, enabling
him to overcome those individual deficiencies that limit him.
That he understands his acquisitions in purely moral rather
than selfish terms is evidenced in his initial exclamation as
Achilles: 'I love, and I shall be beloved! Oh, life!/ At last I feel
thee! Glorious spirit' (I.i.421–22). Yet once he has actually
achieved his idealized vision of himself his desire for love
modulates rapidly into a wish to go 'Where the World/ Is
thickest' (I.i.494–95), or as the Stranger realistically states it,
where 'the whole race are just now/ Tugging as usual at each
other's hearts' (I.i.500–01). In his new form he displays the
grossest selfishness and inhumanity: not only does he insist

on preceding his commander Bourbon into battle, but he also fights with savage disdain of bodily injury and even skirmishes bitterly with his own soldiers when they beat him to the spoils of war. He proceeds relentlessly until he becomes the single greatest living man, blatantly superior to his fellow soldiers and in complete possession not only of fallen Rome but also of Olimpia, Rome's most beautiful and distinguished survivor.

Although he confesses that his path 'Has been o'er carcasses' (I.ii.2), he never realizes that there has been a radical change in his thinking. Worse, he never realizes that from the start his actions produce the exact reverse of what he most desires. His inability to evaluate experience accurately and discriminate such significant shifts of thought illuminates the true object of his desire. His consuming effort to free himself from all restraints and thereby confirm his real virtue translates into his strong need to embody an image of himself that always stands just outside experience as he knows it; *he envies what he might be*, and this of course precludes satisfaction with what he is (even if he is Achilles and the conqueror of Rome). In the final incomplete section of the play the Stranger makes this point explicit:

> *The Stranger.* You are jealous.
> *Arnold.*   And of whom?
> *The Stranger.* It may be of yourself, for Jealousy
>   Is as a shadow of the Sun. The Orb
>   Is mighty—as you mortals deem—and to
>   Your little Universe seems universal;
>   But, great as He appears, and is to you,
>   The smallest cloud—the slightest vapour of
>   Your humid earth enables you to look
>   Upon a Sky which you revile as dull;
>   Though your eyes dare not gaze on it when
>   cloudless.
>   Nothing can blind a mortal like to light.
>   Now Love in you is as the Sun—a thing

Beyond you—and your Jealousy's of Earth—
A cloud of your own raising.   (III.i.69–82)

This view of his character explains why he sees his persistent campaign to make himself 'the superior of the rest' (I.i.317) both as moral and as consistent with his original desires, and why at the same time he becomes increasingly frustrated with every achievement. His on-going search for his elusive and ever-changing self steadily destroys his public or social awareness, and necessitates the continual re-definition of values in progressively narrow terms. Like Mary Shelley's *Frankenstein* or Blake's Urizen his motives and goals are honest but sadly misguided and thus doom him to confusion and despair.

Byron's belief that the Romantic ideology of culmination is in fact a mirroring of self-idealization is expressed elsewhere in his poetry. In his poems 'From the French', written shortly after the Battle of Waterloo, he studies closely Napoleon's rise to greatness and subsequent demise, recognizing that the powerful general's downfall was due at least partly to the diminishing understanding that accompanied his successful military exploits. Though beginning with a sincere desire to secure France's liberty and building a broad power base from popular support, Napoleon gradually became consumed by his lust for ever greater control over those he was fighting to defend; and once 'goaded by Ambition's sting,/ The Hero sunk into the King' ('Ode from the French', ll.32–33). This transformation from noble hero into despised conqueror involved a steadily narrowing vision to the point of private desire only, and Byron would have Napoleon realize this: 'I [Napoleon] have warred with a World which vanquished me only/ When the meteor of conquest allured me too far' ('Napoleon's Farewell', ll.5–6). He is depicted similarly in *Childe Harold* III. To achieve his increasingly private vision of greatness he was compelled to ignore public concerns; he became obsessed with his own accomplishments, losing touch with the masses of people who were the ultimate source of his greatness. And finally when he became 'A God unto thyself' (*Childe Harold*, III, xxxvii), he became vulnerable.

In *The Deformed Transformed* Byron attempts to expand and to substantiate this perspective by depicting in greater detail the social implications of abstract thinking. It is in this regard that the mysterious, misunderstood Stranger is so important.[7] With bitterness and cynicism unrivalled even by the narrator of *Don Juan*, the Stranger assails those abstractions which pass for truth and which deny the social quality of our most cherished values. He makes the play more than a psychological curiosity, more than a study in the disparity between ideals and actions, by insisting that every facet of human life is vitally connected with every other, that every act has both public motive and consequence, and that the pervasive violence around him traces directly to ignorance of these facts.

The Stranger's rôle is established from the beginning. His initial appearance as a black man emerging from a smoke screen immediately causes Arnold to suspect him of being a diabolical figure (I.i.85). Conventional occultish descriptions associate him both with soul-selling (I.i.144) and with the standard devilish blood-compact (I.i.154). But this entire scene is farcical, a devil–man encounter only because Arnold insists on making it one. It is Arnold, after all, who labels the Stranger a devil, a term, incidentally, applied earlier to Arnold himself (I.i.40ff.); and it is Arnold who introduces the issue of soul-selling, as well as the blood-compact. The Stranger simply plays along good humouredly with Arnold's wild surmisings and accusations, occasionally providing revealing glimpses into Arnold's shallowness. (For example, without Arnold's even realizing it, the Stranger lambasts conventional notions of devil–man agreements by accepting blood from an accidental rather than self-inflicted wound.) He is not so easily made into the devil Arnold perceives in him; and if he is a tempter, he is so in the same way Lucifer is a tempter in *Cain*: 'I tempt none,/ Save with the truth' (*Cain*, I.i.196–97).

He functions mainly as a satirical practical consciousness, remaining throughout essentially a truth-representing force who sees through the assumptions, motives, and goals that bind Arnold's character and society at large, and who offers a sometimes bitter, sometimes humorous commentary on the limited views that perpetuate strife and injustice.

The Stranger criticizes Arnold's purely private ethic and establishes his own opposing perspective by transforming himself into Arnold's old deformed shape. By confidently embracing the body which Arnold disdainfully rejects as 'horrible' (I.i.482), the Stranger of course condemns Arnold's belief that his difficulties are entirely physical, but more importantly he asserts the unavoidable truth of historical context. Although Arnold prefers to forget his past, even to deny it, the Stranger insists upon its continuing influence. According to the Stranger, Arnold's deformity is biological fact and thus cannot be refused or ignored, despite Arnold's total commitment to beauty and truth. In this view, the Stranger's transformation is much more than cynicism in action: it is positive criticism that places a supposed individual matter in its proper historical perspective. It is a corrective, a bitterly realistic statement of what Arnold must understand if he hopes to survive. As the play bears out, only at his own peril can Arnold ignore the Stranger's wisdom.

Central to the Stranger's philosophy—and in contrast to Arnold's thinking—is the assumption that the social relation is the basic principle of human life, and that failure to understand its truth and absolute priority produces man's alienation. This view develops with increasing poignance as the Stranger witnesses the impact of Arnold's self-absorption. The Stranger maintains that Arnold is discontented even after his transformation because he 'know[s] no better than the dull/ And dubious notice of your eyes and ears' (I.ii.14–15). And what is true for Arnold is true in general; mankind 'thinks chaotically' (I.ii.318) about social relations. Society, the Stranger emphatically states, is all-embracing, created by man, and connected by human thoughts and actions on every level; the many elements of social life—language, religion, art, law, morals—are a single, unified *human* creation. Any system of values (such as the one to which Arnold subscribes) that divides social properties from one another and from basic individual concerns must ultimately collapse:

> [Men] have built
> More Babels, without new dispersion, than
> The stammering young ones of the flood's dull
>   ooze,
> Who fail'd and fled each other. Why? why, marry,
> *Because no man could understand his neighbours.*
>   (I.ii.108–12; my italics)

Byron develops this focus and establishes Arnold's thinking as part of a set of social relations by moving the play's action to Rome, which manifests socially those issues heretofore manifested personally in Arnold's character. The city shows how extreme individualism and abstract thinking can both control life and breed pestilence through an entire culture. Built from the most extreme selfishness—'Rome's earliest cement/ Was brother's blood' (I.ii.83–84)—the city symbolizes in both its art and religion Western man's most basic values. Byron understands this biting irony and in the Stranger's running commentary he presents in gory detail the vile contradictions imbedded in Roman culture. He does not merely lament the sack of the ancient city at the hands of Charles of Bourbon, but rather explains it as an inevitable result of a system of values that has actually sanctioned and caused strife through the course of Western history (see II.i.1–122).

In his description of Rome, Byron concentrates on art and religion to express the Roman experience. But he stresses that these are not simply passive reflections of Rome's character. While they do indeed powerfully articulate a set of values, they also operate as rigid controls, holding those values in place by reacting back on every facet of actual human life.

This point comes out in the play's brief but telling depiction of Benvenuto Cellini, one of the most representative of Italian Renaissance sculptors. In fewer than fifteen lines Byron introduces and dismisses Cellini, as though the artist were an afterthought or a minor concern. But the brief treatment accomplishes several very significant tasks. First, it allows Byron to mention an otherwise unacknowledged major source for the play: his description of the sack of Rome is taken directly from Cellini's *Autobiography*.[8] But more significantly Byron uses Cellini to present a compelling analysis of art. By having the sculptor simply appear and disappear without forewarning or comment, Byron creates the impression that there is no need to question the artist's actions. Cellini's noble, even ethereal sculpture speaks for itself, attesting to his belief in the values and ideals of Roman culture; in common with his fellow Romans, he would naturally defend this culture against siege.

But as a source for the play, the *Autobiography* provides a behind-the-scenes look at Cellini and a gloss on the real significance of his art. Cellini's defence of Rome was not exactly what we commonly regard as natural and noble. His involvement was vigorous, to be sure, but not because he was inspired by high purpose and spiritual passion; according to his own account he was motivated by his love for bloodshed and physical violence. Three passages from the *Autobiography* illustrate his character:

> ... directing my arquebuse where I saw the thickest and most serried troop of fighting men, I aimed exactly at one whom I remarked to be higher than the rest.... When we had fired two rounds apiece, I crept cautiously up to the wall, and observing among the enemy a most extraordinary confusion, I discovered afterwards that one of our shots had

killed the Constable of Bourbon; and from what I subsequently learned, he was the man whom I had first noticed above the heads of the rest.

I fired, and hit my man exactly in the middle. He had trussed his sword in front, for swagger, after a way those Spaniards have; and my ball when it struck him, broke upon the blade, and one could see the fellow cut in two fair halves. The Pope, who was expecting nothing of this kind, derived great pleasure and amazement from the sight.

I was perhaps more inclined by nature to the profession of arms than to the one [sculpture] I had adopted, and *I took such pleasure in its duties that I discharged them better than those of my own art.* (my italics)[9]

Cellini's art stands in direct contrast to this savage mockery of human life. His best work—the *Nymph of Fontainebleau*, the *Apollo and Hyacinth*, even the violent *Perseus*—is ornate, intricate and sensitive, and enthusiastically celebrates the beauty of the nude human figure. Defective as much of the sculpture is, it displays the impassioned vision of unchanging beauty and truth (the very ideals that Arnold early in the play had admired) that is characteristic of so much Italian Renaissance art.[10] In relying on the *Autobiography*, however, Byron is not simply depicting the grave disparity between Cellini's personal character and art in order to call attention to a psychological curiosity; rather he is focusing the ideological function of art. Cellini's sculpture in all its grandeur embodies the abstract system of belief at the centre of Roman culture. The eternal laws it insists upon mystify actual experience—including the violence to which Cellini is partner—and thus mask the ugly machinations of the culture from which it grew. In this way it actually shapes and controls individual expectations, preventing a true knowledge of society.[11]

Byron's handling of Cellini does not dismiss all art out of hand as deceptive or useless; nor does it suggest that biography is the determining property of the value of art. Rather it deplores the prevalent tendency of ignoring the contextual nature of art, suggesting that to do so is to reduce artistic expression to a largely ideological function of endorsing existing power structures (if only tacitly by throwing obstacles in the way of social and political awareness). Viewed as the sacred preserver of ahistorical, timeless ideals, art relegates to virtual insignificance complex social relations, thus radically limiting man's social power. If it is to realize its full human potential, art must be understood as a social product within a full network of social exchange. By presenting Cellini as a momentary, almost intrusive element in the play, Byron punctuates our persistent ignorance of this social dimension, and implies that outside its true social and historical context Cellini's art is mere abstraction, an illusion that ever further alienates man from his true social self.

Religion serves essentially the same ideological function as art. It is a structurally coherent system that both mirrors society's noblest principles and at the same time creates social attitudes. The play captures this vital connection between religious belief and social reality, and traces the pervasive trouble and discord that plague Western culture to a set of values protected by Christian religion. This radical position is evidenced in the Stranger's sporadic jibes at Christianity (for instance, II.i.137ff. and 161–62), but Byron makes the point vivid by moving the play's climactic and goriest scene into the interior of St Peter's Church; this scene magnifies the gross contradictions that society allows to go unquestioned and that somehow are upheld and even sanctified by prevailing attitudes.

The Stranger has carefully guided Arnold to the very centre of his culture, and now exposes him to 'the two great professions' (II.iii.30)—of priest and soldier—which are its most powerful representatives. It becomes evident in St Peter's that

Arnold's character cannot be understood in purely psychological terms; he is shown to be merely one participant in an unwell culture. Ignorance, violence and noble rhetoric are pervasive and presented indiscriminately, constituting an uncamouflaged savage critique of the motivating values that have stood behind Arnold's character from the beginning. The cries for 'eternal glory' (II.iii.22) and the pleas 'In the holy name of Christ' (II.iii.6) justify murder and plunder; the altar becomes both a place of death and a vantage point for killing (see, for instance, the various stage directions in this scene); and even the crucifix is used as a murder weapon (II.iii.63ff.). This scene represents the play's most extreme and inclusive statement about the power and pervasiveness of ideology. The events in St Peter's bring to a head the Stranger's contention that alienation and social strife trace directly to the comprehensive system of values that determine human actions and hopes. From the very start of the play he has maintained that abstract thinking is destructive and that deeds are the only true measure of virtue (I.i.151–52).[12] And here his point is made convincingly, as the desperate struggle for love, honour, glory, beauty—for a permanently ennobling ideal—totally deadens Arnold and the warring soldiers to genuine human feeling (see, for instance, the exchange between Arnold and Olimpia, II.iii.105ff.), and makes them contributors to public chaos and madness.

In the play's final fragmentary section Byron restates in simpler terms the issues that have been presented heretofore, namely that Arnold's unhappiness results from his obsessive search for 'the Philosopher's stone' (III.i.57), that his desire in fact is for self-idealization (III.i.69–82), and that social relations alone are redemptive and truly meaningful (III.i.99–101). But he was unable to develop his views beyond what he had already accomplished, and perhaps felt that the introduction of Olimpia threatened to reduce his major interests to a simple love relationship, so he discontinued the play.

Still, even in its fragmentary state *The Deformed Transformed* stands as a radical and compelling analysis of social order. The play bitterly records the fundamental contradictions at the core of Western culture that are concealed by the ideological structures of society. These contradictions produce man's alienation; they derive from abstract thinking that reduces human value to a purely individual or private context and that hence perpetuates a social system of human sacrifice. Despite contentions of noble purpose, both Arnold and Rome graphically illustrate the complex workings of this process.

Approached in terms of its political and social content the play appears clearly to be coherent and incisive rather than planless as several critics have complained; it is a convincing example of Byron's refusal to submit to institutionalized aesthetic conventions that, as he explains in the Cellini episode, can prevent true social awareness.[13] *The Deformed Transformed* follows the direction of Byron's other dramas, examining the underpinnings of society to discover its controlling system of values. The play rejects completely the ideological assumptions of Romantic art and society as unjust, immoral and dangerous. It denies the possibility of a transcendental redemptive power and offers instead a purely human vision grounded firmly upon the priority of social reality. This focus illuminates Byron's politics and suggests as well the extent to which he had parted company with his fellow Romantics.

NOTES

1. *Byron's Letters and Journals*, ed. Leslie A. Marchand (Cambridge, MA: Harvard University Press, 1973–82), X, 49.

2. See, for example, Chew, *The Dramas of Lord Byron*, p. 147; Robinson, 'The Devil as Doppelgänger', pp. 177–202; Manning, *Byron and His Fictions*, pp. 170–74; Blackstone, *Byron III*, p. 32; Marchand, *Byron's Poetry*, p. 94.

3. McGann, 'The Anachronism of George Crabbe', p. 568.

4. Abrams, 'English Romanticism', pp. 26–72.

5. I am relying here on John Kinnaird's remarks in *William Hazlitt: Critic of Power*, pp. 88–89. See also Rajan, *Dark Interpreter*.

6. All quotations from Byron's poetry are taken from Coleridge, *The Works of Lord Byron: Poetry* (rpt 1966), and references are cited in the text.

7. For the standard critical attitude towards the Stranger see, for example, Marchand, *Byron's Poetry*, p. 94 or Manning, *Byron and His Fictions*, p. 170.

8. E. H. Coleridge mentions that 'it is evident that he [Byron] was familiar with Cellini's story' (V, 471), but he does not pursue Cellini's influence; and Robinson's definitive source study of the play fails altogether to mention Cellini.

9. Cellini, *The Life of Benvenuto Cellini*, pp. 117–24.

10. See Chase and Post, *A History of Sculpture*, pp. 343–45, and Read, *The Art of Sculpture*, pp. 62–63, 82.

11. I am relying here especially on the arguments of Berger, *Ways of Seeing, passim*, and Eagleton, *Marxism and Literary Criticism*, pp. 16–19.

12. Marchand's comment that Byron fails to pursue the issue of deeds indicates the extent to which psychological approaches can obscure the play's meaning. See Marchand, *Byron's Poetry*, p. 95.

13. I do not think it an overstatement to say that conventional assessments of the play actually tell us more about criticism than about *The Deformed Transformed*. An excellent, if not entirely related, consideration of the ideological dimensions of criticism can be found in Hawkes, *Structuralism and Semiotics*, pp. 151–60.

EDITORS' BIBLIOGRAPHICAL NOTE

There is not a great deal to add beyond Robinson's and Watkins' footnotes to the critical literature on *The Deformed Transformed*, a situation no doubt bred of its fragmentary state as well as its daunting internal confusions. Indeed the only other work of substance is Corbett's *Byron and Tragedy*, pp. 206–16, which postdates the Robinson and Watkins essays. Despite its central concern, for example, Kelsall's *Byron's Politics* ignores both the play and Watkins' analysis. On the other hand, G. Wilson Knight piques our interest by saying he would have liked to 'give detailed notice' to the play, which he regards as having 'an importance in conception perhaps not quite borne out in execution: involving realization of a power-dream, consequent desecration by war of Church and heroine, with a suggested resurrection after apparent death ... of the lady concerned' (*The Burning Oracle*, p. 286). George Steiner, in *The Death of Tragedy*, also has a few words to say about the play: it 'shows a tiring of invention' and, apropos Robinson's essay, 'there is in it too much of Goethe's *Faust* and of an obscure Gothic romance, *The Three Brothers*'. More provocatively, he concludes that the play's 'mixture of lyric fantasy, wit, and melodrama points directly to *Don Juan*' and hence 'marks a transition in Byron's work from the dramatic to the mock-epic'; it is, though, but a 'queer fragment' (pp. 211–12).

More substantial are G. Wilson Knight's comments in *Byron and Shakespeare*, pp. 155-59, all built around what he regards as Byron's Richard III 'complex' set sharply against the play's character of Achilles as a 'self-reflection of Byron's best'. Knight's conclusion is that the play is 'a disturbing fragment' but also 'a brilliant clarification of the Byronic complex', its 'inter-knotted meanings' precisely related to those which are 'constituent to such Satan works as *Richard III* and *Macbeth*' and 'to the instinct and love of bloodshed which seems to be rooted, from age to age, in the human psyche'. Equally substantive, though quirky, are Bernard Blackstone's comments in *Byron: A Survey*, pp. 259–62, where the play is regarded as moving 'around the poles of man and his masks—transformation, renewal, the formidable allurements of illusion and power', all caught up 'into a crazy, slap-stick scarcely viable mélange of "sick" comedy, history, and psychodelic mythology which leaves us gasping'. Yet somehow it is also 'a true Apocalypse', rounding off the sequence of Scripture-slanted dramas 'begun in *Manfred* and continued through the biblical plays to the "Pauline theology" of *Werner*'. Gasping is right!

More recently, other than Corbett, *The Deformed Transformed* is usually referred to only dismissively, as, for example, in Richardson's *A Mental Theater*, pp. 98–99: the play is not mental theatre at all but rather an effort, as in *Werner*, to 'bring thematic elements from the metaphysical dramas into forms more suited to conventional nineteenth-century stagecraft', an effort that fails to bear out the promise of its *Faust*-like plot in a pot-pourri of 'sentimentality, bluster, and melodrama' more like Keats' *Otho the Great* than Byron's *Cain*. But see also Taylor, *Magic and English Romanticism*, pp. 232–38.

With respect to Watkins' essay, see also his 'Violence, Class Consciousness, and Ideology', pp. 799–816 and his recently published 'summa', *A Materialist Critique*, as well as McGann's *The Romantic Ideology* and 'The Book of Byron', pp. 255–93, Woodring's chapter on Byron in *Politics in English Romantic Poetry* and Barton's '*Don Juan* Transformed', pp. 199–220. See also the Editors' Bibliographical Note appended to the essays on *Marino Faliero* above.

The Sins of the Fathers: *Werner*

PETER J. MANNING

Werner is at once the first and the last of Byron's finished plays, and so offers a microcosm of his dramatic universe. It is based on 'Kruitzner, or The German's Tale', which is contained in Volume IV of *The Canterbury Tales* by Harriet Lee and her sister Sophia. Byron read the novel shortly after its appearance in 1801, and at thirteen was inspired to attempt a dramatization that, as he later recalled, he 'had sense enough to burn'. The impression made by the tale was lasting, however: in 1815 while on the Drury Lane committee Byron again tried to turn the story into a play 'for the house', and had written several hundred lines when interrupted by the scandalous separation from Annabella. The stubborn fascination exerted by the novel persisted during the succeeding busy years; on 9 October 1821, the day he began *Heaven and Earth*, Byron wrote to Murray for the materials of a fresh start:

> Don't forget to send me my first act of *Werner* (if Hobhouse can find it amongst my papers)—send it by post (to Pisa); and also cut out Sophia Lee's 'German's tale', from the *Canterbury Tales*, and send it in a letter also. (*LJ*, V, 390)

Reacquaintance did not disappoint Byron, and he told Medwin subsequently: 'There is no tale of Scott's finer.... I admired it when I was a boy, and have continued to like what I did then. This tale, I remember, particularly affected me.'[1] The MS of the 1815 effort could not then be located, but Byron was undeterred; he set about writing on 18 December and finished all five acts within a month, discovering as he proceeded that he 'perfectly' remembered many lines from his earliest adolescent version.[2]

Two impulses are discernible in Byron's renewed endeavour to transform Miss Lee's clumsily handled story into an effective drama. His resumption of a work begun before his disillusionment with Drury Lane and admittedly designed for production seems a deliberate bid for the theatrical success refused *Marino Faliero*. As was his custom, Byron announced in the Preface that 'the whole is neither intended, nor in any shape adapted, for the stage', but its harmony with popular taste was obvious and earned *Werner* a substantial record of performance.[3] The enigmatic, guilt-ridden protagonist, hinting at his sins to a priest and flaring up in histrionic confrontations with all around him, is a rôle tailored for a star wanting to score 'points'. Byron compellingly unfolds the murder mystery plot, embellishes it with duels, and gives scope to the scenic elaboration cherished by nineteenth-century audiences in the contrasted settings of the action, a decaying provincial palace complete with secret passage and a 'large and magnificent Gothic Hall in the Castle of Siegendorf, decorated with Trophies, Banners, and Arms of that Family'. The Gothic elements Byron had abjured in recent years recall *Manfred*, begun not long after his previous effort to dramatize 'Kruitzner'. In both instances the emotional excess encouraged by the genre seems to have provided a conventional outlet for very personal expression. He wrestled with Miss Lee's mediocre tale off and on for twenty years, and this prolonged engagement points to an involvement more intricate than the desire for recognition as a playwright which is the immediate cause of *Werner*. The tenacious hold upon his imagination enjoyed by 'Kruitzner' is explained by its moral: the sins of the fathers shall be visited upon the sons. If it is understood that a confirmation of his own psychodynamics might easily appear to Byron as an external cause, his statement in the Preface to *Werner* that the tale 'may, indeed, be said to contain the germ of much that I have since written' is the conclusive evidence for the oedipal themes at the core of Byron's work.

The themes of *Werner* are characteristic, but the colouring shows some new lights. Siegendorf is a penurious Bohemian aristocrat disinherited long since by an unforgiving father for the rash acts of his youth, chief among them his match with a beautiful but poor foreigner, Josephine. This blocking figure has just died when the play opens, and Siegendorf hopes at last to claim his position. He has never ceased to lament the loss of his 'wealth, and rank, and power' (I.i.78), what his wife perceptively describes as 'these phantoms of thy feudal fathers' (I.i.137), and there are traces in his conduct towards her in the first scene of a resentment that his love cannot wholly eradicate. His wishes are frustrated anew by a powerful cousin, Baron Stralenheim, who covets the lands and vacated title for himself, and to that end misuses his authority, persecuting Siegendorf and forcing him to hide under the pseudonym of Werner. Stralenheim's intervention merely repeats the exclusion originally imposed by the elder Siegendorf; in the 1815 draft Werner laments: 'My father's wrath extends beyond the grave,/ And haunts me in the shape of Stralenheim!' (I.i.18–19). Thus doubly barred from his rightful legacy and bereft even of his name, Werner is a type of the son too weak to establish his identity while his father lives.

Werner is not the only son in the play, and significant perspectives are added by the already noticed phenomenon of duplication. Werner and Josephine, fleeing from the representative of parental opposition, are themselves parents in search of missing offspring. They have a child, Ulric, whom the elder Siegendorf relented so far as to raise as his own, but the boy, re-enacting his father's wildness, vanished shortly before the old man's death. Ulric and Werner are son and father, but to the head of the clan they stand in the same filial relationship, and it is the complex modulation of their rôles that energizes the drama.

To the decrepit manor where Werner has taken refuge

circumstances bring Stralenheim, rescued from drowning in
the upset of his carriage at a river-crossing by two passing
strangers, Gabor the Hungarian and, as Act II discloses after
suspenseful delay, the sought-for Ulric. The coincidence
strains credulity, and its very improbability prompts a question of its function. A well-known passage of Freud brilliantly
illuminates its significance, especially when the place filled by
Stralenheim is remembered:

> In actual fact the 'rescue-*motif*' has a meaning and
> history of its own, and is an independent derivative
> of the mother-complex, or more accurately, of the
> parental complex. When a child hears that he *owes
> his life* to his parents, or that his mother *gave him
> life*, his feelings of tenderness unite with impulses
> which strive at power and independence, and they
> generate the wish to return this gift to the parents
> and to repay them with one of equal value. It is as
> though the boy's defiance were to make him say:
> 'I want nothing from my father; I will give him back
> all I have cost him.' He then forms the phantasy of
> *rescuing his father from danger and saving his life*; in
> this way he puts his account square with him. This
> phantasy is commonly enough displaced on to the
> emperor, king or some other great man; after being
> thus distorted it becomes admissible to conscious-
> ness, and may even be made use of by creative
> writers. In its application to a boy's father it is the
> defiant meaning in the idea of rescuing which is
> by far the most important; where his mother is
> concerned it is usually its tender meaning.[4]

These insights permit the connection of Ulric's gesture to the
struggles of other Byronic heroes to achieve autonomy, and
are corroborated as the hostile motives Freud hypothesized
beneath a surface benevolence gradually manifest themselves
in the drama.

By his familiarity with the secret passage Werner gains access to the room where the exhausted Stralenheim is sleeping, and though tempted to murder his enemy he only steals a rouleau of gold to pay for his journey to safety. The following morning Ulric arrives, and, his lineage unknown to the baron as the baron's pursuit of his father is unknown to him, is commissioned to investigate the robbery. Ulric thus unwittingly becomes the hunter of his father, producing a situation that literally renders the deepest level of the drama. The happiness of their subsequent surprise reunion after twelve years of separation is destroyed when, still ignorant of who has committed it, Ulric denounces the theft. Werner confesses and eloquently defends himself against his son:

> Ulric, before you dare despise your father,
> Learn to divine and judge his actions. Young,
> Rash, new to life, and reared in Luxury's lap,
> Is it for you to measure Passion's force,
> Or misery's temptation? Wait—(not long,
> It cometh like the night, and quickly)—Wait!—
> Wait till, like me, your hopes are blighted, till
> Sorrow and Shame are handmaids of your cabin—
> Famine and Poverty your guests at table;
> Despair your bed-fellow—then rise, but not
> From sleep, and judge!   (II.ii.100–10)

He concludes:

> ... there are crimes
> Made venial by the occasion, and temptations
> Which nature cannot master or forbear.
>   (II.ii.147–49)

By depicting him as a sensitive soul driven to dishonesty this speech is calculated to win the audience's sympathy for Werner, and Ulric, now apprised of Stralenheim's machinations, vows to aid his escape. Once more he figures as saviour, this time directly of his parents. He gives Werner a diamond formerly his grandfather's to bribe the guards and obtain transportation; his possessing the stone emphasizes that his grandfather's power has passed to him. Despite the assistance Werner fears that his son condemns him, and he implores Ulric not to despise him:

> *Werner.* Oh, do not hate me!
> *Ulric.*   Hate my father!
> *Werner.*   Aye,
>   My father hated me. Why not my son?
> *Ulric.* Your father knew you not as I do.
> *Werner.*   Scorpions
>   Are in thy words! Thou know me? in this guise
>   Thou canst not know me, I am not myself;
>   Yet (hate me not) I will be soon.
> *Ulric.*   *I'll wait!*
>   In the meantime be sure that all a son
>   Can do for parents shall be done for mine.
>   (III.i.228–35)

This pathetic colloquy replays Werner's subjection to the elder Siegendorf and attests to the complete reversal of the positions of Werner and Ulric: by saving Werner, Ulric accomplishes the son's desire to surpass and dominate the father. An instructive comparison with *Manfred*, which suggests itself at this point, measures the changes in Byron since the shattering events of 1816. His earlier protagonist owes his life to the Chamois Hunter and is humiliated by the rescue; his only compensation is to condescend to the hunter. When the Abbot, his spiritual father, offers divine salvation, Manfred's need to prove his self-sufficiency requires that he reject him too. In the last scene of the revised version Manfred demonstrates a kind of equality with the impressively solid Abbot, but it is at the price of his life, and there is no vision before 1822 of a son victorious like Ulric.

The relations between father and son are disrupted again at the instant of flight. Ulric excitedly informs Werner that

Stralenheim has been killed and demands to know whether he is the assassin. The second aspersion of his rectitude angers Werner, but Byron subtly interweaves a tacit admission of his repressed desires into his plea of innocence:

> If I e'er, in heart or mind,
> Conceived deliberately such a thought,
> But rather strove to trample back to hell
> Such thoughts—if e'er they glared a moment
> through
> The irritations of my oppressed spirit—
> May Heaven be shut for ever from my hopes,
> As from mine eyes!   (III.iv.43–49)

Ulric withdraws the imputation and Werner's suspicions fall on Gabor the Hungarian, whom Stralenheim had accused of the robbery. Werner, knowing that the other was maligned, had sheltered him in the concealed passageway, but with such heavy-handed warnings not to explore its turnings—'who knows it might not/ Lead even into the chamber of your foe?'—as to reveal a half-conscious wish to provoke Gabor to the murder he did not have the daring to attempt himself (III.i.96–97). The pervasiveness of filial resentment in every part of the drama is illustrated by lines that Byron singled out to recite to Medwin from Gabor's soliloquy: as he counts the hours in darkness Gabor meditates that each clang of Time's clock 'takes something from enjoyment' but 'the knell/ Of long-lived parents finds a jovial echo/ To triple time in the son's ear' (III.iii.1–12).[5] Gabor proceeds towards Stralenheim's room, but the scene closes before he reaches it, and as he has fled the palace when Ulric discovers Stralenheim's corpse, Byron neatly tantalizes the reader's curiosity about the culprit. Ulric urges Werner to depart and profit from the removal of his enemy, and by promising to settle everything quiets his objection that flight at this juncture will stain his reputation. The act ends on his pious proclamation that 'To save a father is a child's chief honour' (III.iv.168).

By the beginning of Act IV Byron has thus fulfilled the expectations aroused by his creaky plot: parents and child have been reunited, Ulric has proved himself a model son, and as if by providence the trappings on which the inwardly insecure Werner relies for his identity have been restored to him, making him at last Count Siegendorf. But Byron prepares the happy outcome only to snatch it away, and in so doing he first engages sympathies and then forces an examination of the assumptions on which they are based.

The mythical dramas allowed Byron little scope for social criticism, but that concern returns with the realistic, historical mode of *Werner*. The aristocratic status Werner hungers for allies him with a class which the drama repeatedly characterizes as cruel or fatuous. In a long soliloquy in the first act Josephine decries the oppression 'Of feudal tyranny o'er petty victims' and regrets her husband's yearning to take his place among the 'despots of the north' (I.i.697–730); her words are immediately followed by Werner's entry with the gold he has stolen, a perfect example of the moral ambiguity of his pride in birth. Gabor laments the degeneration of the 'brave chivalry ... of the good old times' (II.i.324–25) and protests the 'trampling on the poor' by the nobility (I.i.656). The grand assembly of the aristocracy that Werner rapturously describes in the last act is no more to Josephine than a tedious ritual— 'Well, Heaven be praised! the show is over' (V.i.14)—and to the servants who are required to march in it nothing seems worse than forming 'the train of a great man,/ In these dull pageantries' (V.i.12–13).

The later acts of the play further ask the reader to consider Werner's complicity in the death that has brought his good fortune. He attempts to expiate the robbery by giving the coins he purloined to a monastery, but his heavy sense of guilt is out of all proportion to the sole criminal act for which he is strictly responsible. The obscure feeling of accountability that haunts him grows rather from the correspondence of Stralenheim's murder with his own wishes; his plan to marry Ulric to the slain man's daughter, Ida, is evidently an effort to atone the wrong he unconsciously blames on himself. Ida is the one major addition Byron made to Miss Lee's tale, and she is yet another variation of the motif of the redemptive daughter.

Whatever uncertainty may remain about the nature of the motives for which Werner punishes himself is dispelled when Gabor reappears amid the festivities. In an effective *coup de théâtre* he clears his name by convincingly demonstrating that Ulric is the murderer; aghast, Werner exclaims 'God of fathers!' (V.i.335), and then, in the most pregnant speech in the play, reveals that at the moment of the assassination he had 'horrid dreams': 'I dreamt of my father—/ And now my dream is out!' (V.i.357–60). Byron could hardly declare more emphatically that the killing of Stralenheim is a displaced realization of Werner's repressed filial rage, carried out essentially by his double, since Ulric occupies a position identical to his in respect to the elder Siegendorf. Without remorse Ulric avows his culpability; his only emotion is wonder that his father had not deduced it long before. Werner's ignorance is easily explained by the speeches quoted above, and witnesses the fine consistency of Byron's characterization. Werner's glorification of the aristocracy is symptomatic of his general psychic strategy of coping with oppression by identifying with his oppressor, instead of fighting him as Ulric does. Werner's meagre self-respect depends on not admitting to consciousness the hostility the murder expresses, and what he denies in himself he is precluded from observing in others. 'Parricide!' he cries out as Ulric coolly schemes the disposal of Gabor (V.i.423), and the stigma is symbolically if not literally true: it correctly describes the motives of the crime already committed, and indicates that in consequence of his identification with paternal authority Werner has made himself their next object. His reunion with Ulric is a deadly confrontation with his own buried self, who inexorably rises to terrify him when he ceases to be a son and becomes Count Siegendorf.

The repressed returns with primitive starkness as Ulric vindicates himself by exactly repeating his father's words:

> *Who* proclaimed to me
> That *there were crimes* made venial by the occasion?
> That passion was our nature? that the goods
> Of Heaven waited on the goods of fortune?
> *Who* showed me his humanity secured
> By his *nerves* only? ...
>   The man who is
> At once both warm and weak invites to deeds
> He longs to do, but dare not. Is it strange
> That I should *act* what you could *think?* We have
>   done
> With right and wrong; and now must only ponder
> Upon effects, not causes.   (V.i.441–55)

'Ida *falls senseless*—Josephine *stands speechless with horror*'
reads Byron's last stage direction, and the play closes with
Ulric's flight to the outlaw bands he clandestinely leads and
Werner's despairing recognition that his dynastic aspirations
are blasted: 'Now open wide, my sire, thy grave;/ Thy curse
hath dug it deeper for thy son/ In mine!— The race of
Siegendorf is past' (V.ii.64–66). Werner's collapse at Ulric's
revelation is only the outward completion of the psychic
suicide he chose in disowning his aggressive energies, reducing
himself to a passive, querulous victim, but like all Byron's
protagonists he is blind to the inner source of his misfortunes.
His ascription of them to a father's curse even as Ulric
charges his crimes to his father makes up a double portrait of
the figure of the blighted son that obsessed Byron.

This ending requires attentive consideration, however,
especially in the ways it diverges from the original. In Miss
Lee's novel Kruitzner retains power and his fugitive son is
inadvertently killed in a skirmish with hussars whom he has
sent to police his borders. The freedom Byron accords Ulric is
a remarkable contrast to this crude poetic justice, and it

appears still more surprising when compared with the severely constricted fates allotted the sons in the preceding dramas. It would be foolish to seek a particular cause for the relative enlargement Ulric enjoys, but Byron's life had become happier in the months since *Heaven and Earth*. In November he had moved to Pisa, joining the Shelleys and their friends there and renewing his intimacy with Teresa after the weeks of separation resulting from the exile of the Gambas from Ravenna. Comfortably settled for the first time with his mistress, who had quit her much older husband for him and gained the sanction of *il Papa* to do so, Byron was living in circumstances that suggestively parallel the fantasies detectable in his works. Wherever the explanation lies, Ulric achieves an ambivalent success beyond the reach of his fellow alienated Titans: in the final scenes of the play he undoes his father and establishes his independence. He drops the pose of the dutiful son and like Selim and Hugo steps forth in his true rebelliousness to witness more potently than they could to the suppressed resentments Byron invariably discovers beneath filial obedience. The motives Freud observes in the rescue motif fully emerge in Ulric's justification for the murder of Stralenheim: 'As stranger I preserved him, and he *owed me/ His life*: when due, I but resumed the debt' (V.i.462–63). This hostility, vented initially on a surrogate, now finds its real target and Ulric contemptuously abandons his beseeching father:

> *Siegendorf.* Stop! I command—entreat—implore!
>   Oh, Ulric!
>   Will you then leave me?
> *Ulric.*   What! remain to be
>   Denounced—dragged, it may be, in chains;
>   and all
>   By your inherent weakness, half-humanity,
>   Selfish remorse, and temporizing pity ...

          No, Count,
     Henceforth you have no son!
Siegendorf.   I never had one;
     And would you ne'er had borne the useless
       name!
     Where will you go? I would not send you forth
     Without protection.
Ulric.   Leave that unto me.
     I am not alone; nor merely the vain heir
     Of your domains; a thousand, aye, ten
       thousand
     Swords, hearts, and hands are mine.
                           (V.ii.33–46)

'Henceforth you have no son!': Ulric's words express the inverse of his meaning, which is that after this rejection of his heritage for an authority based on his own accomplishments he will have no father. Werner's well-meaning offer of protection reflects once again the parental imago from whom he has never been able to emancipate himself, but Ulric, in Freud's phrase, strives to become the father of himself. It may be speculated that his bleak triumph accounts for much of Byron's attraction to 'Kruitzner'.

    Ulric's wilful exile to his private army comes full circle to the stern warrior-outcasts of the Oriental Tales, but Byron now provides an aetiology of his hero that impressively deepens the characterization. The oedipal conflicts that motivate his protagonist are visible only obliquely and imperfectly in early works like *The Giaour* and *Lara*; there are many reasons for his having adopted the discontinuous narrative mode of the tales, but part of its appeal to Byron may have lain in his discovery that through it he might simultaneously confront and conceal the psychological stresses that generated the poems. The results are largely artistically successful, but at a price: the reader responds to the spectacular events he relates but can only guess at their springs. Time seems to have brought Byron sufficient composure to explore his situation: in *Werner*, years after he had reshaped his own childhood and marriage in the opening cantos of *Don Juan*, he presents his hero in the environment that moulds him. Ulric's predecessors loom large because they stand in isolation, but what they gain in awesomeness they lose in credibility; Ulric, in contrast, forms part of a complexly realized picture of family psychodynamics, and the ampler context conduces to better understanding.

The increased comprehension is effectively illustrated by one respect in which Ulric is more alone than his forerunners, his departure without a woman to solace him. Like them he is diffident towards the woman who adores him, but *Werner* furnishes the materials to uncover the roots of this typical pattern. Ida has been all but adopted by Josephine's maternal love (V.i.14–74) and she is the bride selected by his father. This close association with the parents from whom he is trying to break free makes it impossible that Ulric should reciprocate her affection, and her rôle thus brings into sharper focus a threatening aspect possessed in common by Byron's women. The extensively depicted family relationships of *Werner* repeatedly illuminate Byron's other works in this fashion, and give a richly detailed picture of the habitual workings of his imagination. Ulric, though he defeats his father, remains entrapped in the futile conflicts that for Byron symbolize the world of men. As Stralenheim says in Act II, recognizing his affinity with Ulric and hoping to engage him in his service, war is the natural condition of this world: 'peace/ Is but a petty war..../ War will reclaim his own' (II.i.169–72). Ulric makes war 'for himself' (IV.i.37), pursuing it with complete indifference to cause, as if it were simply a more exciting chase. His murder of the man he has just rescued displays his utter amorality, and indeed the forces that drive him rise from depths of the personality untouchable by the persuasions of morality. His declaration to Werner that 'we have done with right and wrong' casts as a psychological imperative Lucifer's proclamation of the end of metaphysical absolutes: 'Were I the victor, *his* works would be deemed/ The only evil ones' (*Cain*, II.ii.445–46). The full analysis of *Werner* brings greater knowledge to the reader but no remission of strife for Byron's characters.

It is through its effect on the reader that Ulric's escape is especially provocative. Punishment of the villain permits an audience to distinguish itself from him and thus flatters its moral superiority, and Byron's refusal to meet our expectations should direct us rather to recognize ourselves in Ulric's hostility. The conclusion rebounds against us by asking that we admit the probable presence in our own minds of the desires for which we want Ulric punished. 'In the crowd,' the comic steward Idenstein has already joked,

> your thief looks
> Exactly like the rest, or rather better:
> 'Tis only at the bar and in the dungeon,
> That wise men know your felon by his features; ...
>   (II.i.206–10)

The challenge to complacent assumptions runs throughout the play and is social as well as personal. Stralenheim's servant Fritz equates the 'soldiers and desperadoes' of the black bands Ulric leads in their ravages to a list of celebrated generals:

> After all,
> Your Wallenstein, your Tilly and Gustavus,
> Your Bannier, and your Torstenson and Weimar,
> Were but the same thing upon a grand scale; ...
>   (II.i.138–41)

The insistence that society's outlaws and its heroes are identical is a colloquial, satiric counterpart to the statements of Lucifer and Ulric, and reveals the filiation of attitudes and techniques between *Werner* and *Don Juan*. 'Had Buonaparte won at Waterloo,' the narrator of Byron's epic comments in Canto XIV,

It had been firmness; now 'tis pertinacity;
Must the event decide between the two?
I leave it to your people of sagacity
To draw the line between the false and true,
If such can e'er be drawn by Man's capacity: ...
(XIV. 90)

Beneath the surface differences the dramas and *Don Juan* are continuous, and Byron's adaptation of melodrama shows its beholders not monsters and saints, but themselves.

NOTES

1. *Medwin's 'Conversations'*, p. 258.
2. *Medwin's 'Conversations'*, p. 258. The 1815 draft is printed in Coleridge, *The Works of Lord Byron: Poetry*, V, 453–66.
3. The stage history was first presented by Motter, 'Byron's *Werner* Re-estimated'. Macready gave the first performance of *Werner* in England on 25 January 1830, and it remained a prominent feature of his repertory until his retirement in 1851. It was his fifth most frequently performed rôle in London, and in the provinces where his spectacular Shakespearian productions were unfeasible the proportion was probably higher. Dickens and G. H. Lewes thought Werner the foremost of his interpretations, and in 1850 the *Theatrical Journal* placed it at the head of his rôles listed 'in order of excellence'. Macready, however, damagingly expanded the lachrymose elements of the drama in order to capitalize on his forte—the expression of domestic tenderness. The *Examiner* neatly and approvingly epitomized his emphasis, which was scarcely the author's: 'Byron makes us think only of the *theft of a purse*; Macready of the *love of a father*.' Alan Downer discusses this sentimental interpretation in *The Eminent Tragedian*. Samuel Phelps also played *Werner* in the provinces at the outset of his career, and produced it during eleven of his eighteen seasons as manager at Sadler's Wells. One is intrigued to discover, considering the themes of the drama, that Phelps chose it to introduce his son Edmund to London audiences in 1860 as Ulric to his own Werner. Phelps' career is considered by Allen, *Samuel Phelps*. The last actor to take up the drama was Henry Irving, who appeared once as Werner on 1 June 1887, in a benefit for Westland Marston. Irving employed

a four-act redaction by Frank Marshall, retaining the mawkish interpolations of Macready and destroying the suspense by depicting Ulric's murder of Stralenheim.

    4.   Freud, *The Complete Psychological Works*, II, pp. 172–73.

    5.   *Medwin's 'Conversations'*, p. 260.

EDITORS' BIBLIOGRAPHICAL NOTE

As Thomas J. Corr notes at the outset of his essay (see below), *Werner* has received virtually no considered critical attention, and what there is is almost universally negative (the exceptions to the negativity being Ehrstine's *The Metaphysics of Byron* and Peter Manning's essay reprinted above). But there is a handful of other commentaries that are generally positive and contribute to the play's interest, including a few on its stage performances:

Barker, 'The First English Performance', pp. 342–44.

Blackstone, *Byron: A Survey*, pp. 252–57.

Bone, 'Political Choices', pp. 152–65.

Corbett, *Byron and Tragedy*, pp. 189–206.

Corr, 'Byron's *Werner*', pp. 375–98.

Damico, 'The Stage History of *Werner*', pp. 63–81.

Knight, *Byron and Shakespeare*, pp. 179–84.

Lansdown, *Byron's Historical Dramas*, pp. 50–54.

Otten, 'Byron's *Cain* and *Werner*', in his *The Deserted Stage*, pp. 41–75.

Bibliography

BLJ: *Byron's Letters and Journals*, ed. Leslie A. Marchand, 12 vols (Cambridge, MA: Harvard University Press, 1973–82; London: John Murray, 1977).

Correspondence: *Lord Byron's Correspondence*, ed. John Murray (London: John Murray, 1922).

CPW: *Lord Byron: The Complete Poetical Works*, ed. Jerome J. McGann (Oxford: Clarendon Press, 1986).

LJ: *The Works of Lord Byron: Letters and Journals*, ed. Rowland E. Prothero (London: John Murray, 1898–1901).

LPBS: *The Letters of Percy Bysshe Shelley*, ed. Frederick L. Jones (Oxford: Clarendon Press, 1964).

Medwin: Thomas Medwin, *Conversations of Lord Byron* (London: Henry Colburn, 1824).

Poetry: *The Works of Lord Byron: Poetry*, ed. Ernest Hartley Coleridge (London, 1898–1904).

M. H. Abrams, 'English Romanticism: The Spirit of the Age', in *Romanticism Reconsidered: Selected Papers from the English Institute*, ed. Northrop Frye (New York and London: Columbia University Press, 1963).

Alfred Adler, *The Practice and Theory of Individual Psychology* (New York: Harcourt, Brace and Co., 1924).

Shirley Seifried Allen, *Samuel Phelps and Sadler's Wells Theatre* (Middletown, CT: Wesleyan University Press, 1971).

William Archer and Robert W. Lowe (eds), *Dramatic Essays by John Forster and George Henry Lewes* (London: Walter Scott, 1896).

Thomas L. Ashton, 'The Censorship of Byron's *Marino Faliero*', *Huntington Library Quarterly*, XXXVI (1972).

——'*Marino Faliero*: Byron's "Poetry of Politics"', *Studies in Romanticism*, XIII (1974).

Patricia M. Ball, *The Central Self: A Study in Romantic and Victorian Imagination* (London: Athlone Press, 1968).

Samuel Bamford, *Passages in the Life of a Radical* (London: Simkin, Marsh, 1844).

Kathleen M. D. Barker, 'The First English Performance of Byron's *Werner*', *Modern Philology*, LXVI (1969).

John Barrell, *English Literature in History 1730–80: An Equal Wide Survey* (London: Hutchinson, 1983).

Robert Barsky, 'Byron and Catastrophism: A Reading of *Heaven and Earth*', *Discours Social/Social Discourse*, I (1988).

Anne Barton, '"A Light to Lesson Ages": Byron's Political Plays', in *Byron: A Symposium*, ed. John D. Jump (London: Macmillan, 1975).

———'*Don Juan* Transformed', in *Byron: Augustan and Romantic*, ed. Andrew Rutherford (New York: St Martin's Press, 1990).

N. Stephen Bauer, 'Byron's Doubting Cain', *South Atlantic Bulletin*, XXXIX (1974).

W. G. Bebbington, '*The Two Foscari*', *English*, IX (1953).

Beowulf and the Fight at Finnsburg, ed. Fr. Klaeber, 3rd edn (Lexington: D. C. Heath, 1950).

John Berger, *Ways of Seeing* (London: BBC and Penguin, 1972).

Murray Biggs, 'Notes on Performing *Sardanapalus*', *Studies in Romanticism*, XXXI (1992).

Bernard Blackstone, *Byron III. Social Satires, Drama and Epic* (London: Longman, 1971).

———*Byron: A Survey* (London: Longman, 1975).

J. Drummond Bone, 'Political Choices: *The Prophecy of Dante* and *Werner*', in *Byron: Poetry and Politics*, ed. E. A. Stürzl and J. Hogg (Salzburg: University of Salzburg, 1981).

Edward Bostetter, *The Romantic Ventriloquists* (Seattle: University of Washington Press, 1963).

James T. Boulton, *The Language of Politics* (London: Routledge & Kegan Paul, 1963).

Gamaliel Bradford, 'The Glory of Sin: Byron', *Saints and Sinners* (Boston, MA: Houghton Mifflin, 1932).

C. P. Brand, *Italy and the English Romantics* (Cambridge: Cambridge University Press, 1957).

William D. Brewer, 'Byron's *Sardanapalus*: The Shelley Hero Transformed', in his *The Shelley–Byron Conversation* (Gainsville, FL: University of Florida Press, 1994).

Leslie Brisman, 'Byron: Troubled Stream from a Pure Source', *English Literary History*, XLII (1975).

David Bromwich, *Hazlitt: The Mind of a Critic* (Oxford: Oxford University Press, 1983).

Marilyn Butler, 'Romantic Manichaeanism: Shelley's "On the Devil, and Devils" and Byron's Mythological Dramas', in *The Sun is God: Painting, Literature and Mythology in the Nineteenth Century*, ed. J. B. Bullen (Oxford: Clarendon Press, 1989).

———'John Bull's Other Kingdom: Byron's Intellectual Comedy', *Studies in Romanticism*, XXXI (1992).

Byron, *The Complete Works of Lord Byron: With his Letters and Journals and his Life by Thomas Moore*, ed. John Wright, 17 vols (London: Murray, 1832–33).

William J. Calvert, *Byron: Romantic Paradox* (Chapel Hill: University of North Carolina Press, 1935).

Paul Cantor, 'Byron's *Cain*: A Romantic Version of the Fall', *Kenyon Review*, n.s. II (1980).

Richard A. Cardwell, 'Byron: Text and Counter-Text', *Renaissance and Modern Studies*, XXXII (1988).

Julie A. Carlson, 'A Theatre of Remorse', in *On the Theatre of Romanticism*, ed. Julie A. Carlson (Cambridge: Cambridge University Press, 1994).

Richard A. Cave, 'Romantic Drama in Performance', in *The Romantic Theatre: an International Symposium*, ed. Richard A. Cave (Gerrards Cross: Smythe, 1986).

Benvenuto Cellini, *The Life of Benvenuto Cellini, by Himself*, trans. John Addington Symonds (New York: Liveright, 1931).

George Henry Chase and Chandler Rathfon Post, *A History of Sculpture* (New York and London: Harper and Brothers, 1925).

Samuel C. Chew, *The Dramas of Lord Byron* (Göttingen: Vendenhoeck Ruprecht, 1915; Baltimore: The Johns Hopkins Press, 1915; rpt. New York: Russell & Russell, 1964).

———*Byron in England* (London: John Murray, 1924).

Jerome Christensen, 'Byron's Career: The Speculative Stage', *English Literary History* (Spring 1985).

———'*Marino Faliero* and the Fault of Byron's Satire', *Studies in Romanticism*, XXIV (1985).

———'Byron's *Sardanapalus* and the Triumph of Liberalism', *Studies in Romanticism*, XXXI (1992).

———*Lord Byron's Strength: Romantic Writing and Commercial Society* (Baltimore: Johns Hopkins University Press, 1992).

C. J. Clancy, 'Death and Love in Byron's *Sardanapalus*', *Byron Journal*, X (1982).

George Clinton, *Memoirs of the Life and Writings of Lord Byron* (London: James Robins, 1825).

Ernest Hartley Coleridge (ed.), *The Works of Lord Byron: Poetry*, rev. edn

(London: John Murray, 1898–1904; rpt. New York: Octagon Books, 1966).

Samuel Taylor Coleridge, 'Logic', ed. J. R. de J. Jackson (Princeton: Princeton University Press, 1981).

——*The Collected Works of Samuel Taylor Coleridge: Biographia Literaria*, ed. James Engell and W. Jackson Bate (Princeton: Princeton University Press, 1983).

Michael G. Cooke, *The Blind Man Traces the Circle: On the Patterns and Philosophy of Byron's Poetry* (Princeton: Princeton University Press, 1969).

——'The Restoration Ethos of Byron's Classical Plays', *Publications of the Modern Language Association*, LXXIX (1974).

Martyn Corbett, *Byron and Tragedy* (New York: St Martin's Press, 1988).

——'Lugging Byron Out of the Library', *Studies in Romanticism*, XXXI (1992).

Thomas J. Corr, 'Byron's *Werner*: The Burden of Knowledge', *Studies in Romanticism*, XXIV (1985).

Jeffrey N. Cox, *In the Shadows of Romance: Romantic Tragic Drama in Germany, England, and France* (Athens, GA: University of Georgia Press, 1987).

David A. Crocker, *Praxis and Democratic Socialism: The Critical Social Theory of Markovic and Stojanovic* (Totowa, NJ: Humanities Press, 1983).

Helen Damico, 'The Stage History of *Werner*', *Nineteenth-Century Theatre Research*, III (1975).

De Quincey, 'The Literature of Knowledge and the Literature of Power', in *Confessions of an Opium Eater and Other Writings*, ed. Aileen Ward (New York: Signet, 1966).

D. M. DeSilva, 'Byron's Politics and the History Plays', in *Byron: Poetry and Politics*, ed. E. Stürzl and J. Hogg (Salzburg: University of Salzburg, 1981).

Madame de Staël, *Considerations on the French Revolution*, 3 vols (London: Baldwin, 1818).

Diodorus Siculus, trans. C. H. Oldfather, 10 vols (London: William Heinemann, 1946).

Bonamy Dobrée, *Byron's Dramas* (Nottingham: Byron Foundation Lecture, University of Nottingham, 1962).

Alan Downer, *The Eminent Tragedian* (Cambridge, MA: Harvard University Press, 1966).

Charles du Bos, *Byron and the Need of Fatality*, trans. Ethel C. Mayne (1932; New York: Haskell, 1970).

Terry Eagleton, *Marxism and Literary Criticism* (Berkeley and Los Angeles: University of California Press, 1976).

John Ehrstine, *The Metaphysics of Byron: A Reading of the Plays* (The Hague: Mouton, 1976).

M. Eimer, 'Das apokryphe buch Henoch und Byrons mysterien', *Englische Studien*, XLIV (1912).

T. S. Eliot, 'Byron', *On Poetry and Poets* (London: Faber and Faber, 1957).

W. Paul Elledge, 'Imagery and Theme in Byron's *Cain*', *Keats–Shelley Journal*, XV (1966).

————*Byron and the Dynamics of Metaphor* (Nashville: Vanderbilt University Press, 1968).

Malcolm Elwin, *Lord Byron's Wife* (London: Macdonald, 1962).

David Erdman, 'Byron's Stage Fright: The History of his Ambition and Fear of Writing for the Stage', *English Literary History* (September 1939).

John P. Farrell, *Revolution as Tragedy: The Dilemmas of the Moderate from Scott to Arnold* (Ithaca and London: Cornell University Press, 1980).

K. G. Feiling, *The Second Tory Party 1714–1832* (London: Macmillan, 1938).

Harold Fisch, 'Byron's Cain as Sacred Executioner', in *Byron, the Bible, and Religion*, ed. Wolf Z. Hirst (Newark, DE: University of Delaware Press, 1991).

William P. Fitzpatrick, 'Byron's Mysteries: The Paradoxical Drive Toward Eden', *Studies in English Literature*, XV (1975).

Michael Foot, *The Politics of Paradise: A Vindication of Byron* (London: Collins, 1988).

Caroline Franklin, *Byron's Heroines* (Oxford, Clarendon Press, 1992).

Sigmund Freud, *The Standard Edition of the Complete Psychological Works of Sigmund Freud*, ed. James Strachey (London: Hogarth Press, 1957).

Frederick Garber, *The Autonomy of the Self from Richardson to Huysmans* (Princeton: Princeton University Press, 1983).

John S. Gatton, '"Put into Scenery": Theatrical Space in Byron's Closet Historical Dramas', *Themes in Drama IX: The Theatrical Space* (Cambridge: Cambridge University Press, 1987).

————'"Pretensions to Accuracy": Byron's Manipulation of History in the Venetian Dramas', in *Byron e la cultura veneziana*, ed. Giulio Marra et al. (Mira, 1989).

René Girard, *Violence and the Sacred*, trans. Patrick Gregory (Baltimore: Johns Hopkins University Press, 1977).

Robert F. Gleckner, *Byron and the Ruins of Paradise* (Baltimore: Johns Hopkins University Press, 1967).

Johan Goethe, *Conversations of Goethe with Eckermann and Soret*, trans. John Oxenford, rev. edn (London: Bell, 1909).

Stephen L. Goldstein, 'Byron's Cain and the Painites', *Studies in Romanticism*, XIV (1975).

'Harroviensis', *A Letter to Sir Walter Scott* (London: Rodwell and Martin, 1822).

Donald M. Hassler, '*Marino Faliero*, the Byronic Hero, and *Don Juan*', *Keats–Shelley Journal*, XIV (1965).

Terence Hawkes, *Structuralism and Semiotics* (Berkeley and Los Angeles: University of California Press, 1977).

William Hazlitt, *Table Talk; or, Original Essays*, 2 vols (London: Henry Colburn, 1822); reprinted in *The Complete Works of William Hazlitt*, ed. P. P. Howe, 21 vols (London: J. M. Dent, 1931).

Bishop Heber, 'Lord Byron's Dramas', *Quarterly Review*, XXVII (1822).

Everett W. Hesse, *Calderón de la Barca* (New York: Twayne, 1967).

E. D. Hirsch, Jr, 'Byron and the Terrestrial Paradise', in *From Sensibility to Romanticism*, ed. Frederick W. Hilles and Harold Bloom (New York: Oxford University Press, 1965).

Wolf Z. Hirst, 'Byron's Lapse into Orthodoxy: An Unorthodox Reading of *Cain*', *Keats–Shelley Journal*, XXXIX (1980).

————'"The Politics of Paradise", "Transcendental Cosmopolitics", and Plain Politics in Byron's *Cain* and Keats's *Hyperion*', in *Byron: Poetry and Politics*, ed. Erwin A. Stürzl and James Hogg (Salzburg: University of Salzburg, 1981).

Terence A. Hoagwood, *Byron's Dialectic: Skepticism and the Critique of Culture* (Lewisburg: Bucknell University Press, 1993).

Margaret J. Howell, '*Sardanapalus*', *Byron Journal*, II (1974).

————*Byron Tonight: A Poet's Plays on the Nineteenth-Century Stage* (Windlesham, Surrey: Springwood Books, 1982).

Washington Irving, *The Journals of Washington Irving*, ed. William P. Trent and George S. Hellman (Boston: The Bibliophile Society, 1919).

F. Jeffrey, 'Lord Byron's Tragedies', *Edinburgh Review*, XXXVI (1822).

E. D. H. Johnson, 'A Political Interpretation of Byron's *Marino Faliero*', *Modern Language Quarterly*, III (1942).

M. K. Joseph, *Byron the Poet* (London: Gollancz, 1964).

John D. Jump, *Byron* (London: Routledge & Kegan Paul, 1972).

Malcolm Kelsall, *Byron's Politics* (Brighton: The Harvester Press, 1987).

——'The Slave-Woman in the Harem', *Studies in Romanticism*, XXXI (1992).

Katherine Kernberger, 'The Semiotics of Space in Byron's *Marino Faliero*', in *Byron e la cultura veneziana*, ed. Giulio Marra *et al.* (Mira, 1989).

Lucille King, 'The Influence of Shakespeare on Byron's *Marino Faliero*', *University of Texas Studies in English*, II (1931).

John Kinnaird, *William Hazlitt: Critic of Power* (New York and London: Columbia University Press, 1978).

G. Wilson Knight, *The Burning Oracle: Studies in the Poetry of Action* (London and New York: Oxford University Press, 1939).

——*Lord Byron, Christian Virtues* (London: Routledge & Kegan Paul, 1952).

——*The Golden Labyrinth* (London: Phoenix House, 1962).

——*Byron and Shakespeare* (New York: Barnes & Noble; London: Routledge & Kegan Paul, 1966).

Lady Blessington's Conversations of Lord Byron, ed. Ernest J. Lovell, Jr (Princeton: Princeton University Press, 1969).

Richard Lansdown, *Byron's Historical Dramas* (Oxford: Clarendon Press, 1992).

Thomas W. Laqueur, 'The Queen Caroline Affair: Politics as Art in the Reign of George IV', *Journal of Medieval History*, LIV (1982).

David Leigh, '*Infelix Culpa*: Poetry and the Skeptic's Faith in *Don Juan*', *Keats–Shelley Journal*, XXVIII (1979).

J. Lemprière, *A Classical Dictionary* (1788), 8th edn (London: T. Cadell and W. Davies, 1812); 'Fifth American Edition, Corrected and Improved by Charles Anthon' (New York: Evert Duyckink *et al.*, 1825).

Ernest J. Lovell, *Captain Medwin, Friend of Byron and Shelley* (London: Macdonald, 1963).

Denis Florence Mac-Carthy (trans.), *Calderón's Dramas* (London: H. S. King, 1873).

David Magarshack, *Stanislavsky: A Life* (London: McGibbon & Kee, 1950).

Peter J. Manning, 'Edmund Kean and Byron's Plays', *Keats–Shelley Journal*, XXI–XXII (1972–73).

——*Byron and His Fictions* (Detroit: Wayne State University Press, 1978).

Leslie A. Marchand, *Byron: A Biography* (New York: Knopf, 1957).

——*Byron's Poetry: A Critical Introduction* (Cambridge, MA: Harvard University Press, 1968).

——*Byron: A Portrait* (Chicago: University of Chicago Press, 1970).

Roderick Marshal, *Italy in English Literature 1755–1815* (New York: Columbia University Press, 1934).

L. E. Marshall, "'*Words* are *Things*": Byron and the Prophetic Efficacy of Language', *Studies in English Literature*, XXV (1985).

William H. Marshall, *The Structure of Byron's Major Poems* (Philadelphia: University of Pennsylvania Press, 1962).

Philip W. Martin, *Byron: A Poet Before his Public* (Cambridge: Cambridge University Press, 1982).

Thomas McFarland, *Romanticism and the Forms of Ruin: Wordsworth, Coleridge, and Modalities of Fragmentation* (Princeton: Princeton University Press, 1981).

Jerome J. McGann, *Fiery Dust: Byron's Poetic Development* (Chicago and London: University of Chicago Press, 1968).

———'The Anachronism of George Crabbe', *English Literary History*, XLVIII (1981).

———*The Romantic Ideology* (Chicago: University of Chicago Press, 1983).

———'The Book of Byron and the Book of a World', *The Beauty of Inflections: Literary Investigations in Historical Method and Theory* (Oxford, Clarendon Press, 1988).

———'Hero With a Thousand Faces: The Rhetoric of Byronism', *Studies in Romanticism*, XXXI (1992).

Thomas Medwin, *Conversations of Lord Byron* (London: Henry Colburn, 1824).

Medwin's 'Conversations of Lord Byron', ed. Ernest J. Lovell, Jr (Princeton: Princeton University Press, 1966).

Giorgio Melchiori, *The Whole Mystery of Art* (London: Routledge & Kegan Paul, 1960).

William M. Merchant, 'Lord Byron: *Cain: A Mystery*', in his *Creed and Drama: An Essay on Religious Drama* (London: S.P.C.K., 1965).

Leonard Michaels, 'Byron's Cain', *Publications of the Modern Language Association*, LXXXIV (1969).

Ellen Moers, *The Dandy: Brummell to Beerbohm* (London: Secker & Warburg, 1960).

Thomas Moore, *Memoirs of the Life of the Right Honourable Richard Brinsley Sheridan*, 3rd edn (London: Longman, Hurst, Rees, Orme, Brown and Green, 1825).

Thomas Moore, 'Loves of the Angels', *Edinburgh Review*, XXXVIII (February 1823); rpt. in Reiman, *The Romantics Reviewed*, II, 945.

T. H. Vail Motter, 'Byron's *Werner* Re-estimated', *Essays in Dramatic Literature*, ed. Hardin Craid (Princeton: Princeton University Press, 1935).

Chester W. New, *Life of Brougham* (Oxford: Clarendon Press, 1961).

Terry Otten, *The Deserted Stage: The Search for Dramatic Form in Nineteenth-Century England* (Athens, GA: University of Georgia Press, 1972).

———*After Innocence: Visions of the Fall in Modern Literature* (Pittsburgh: University of Pittsburgh Press, 1982).

Dorinda Outram, *The Body and the French Revolution: Sex, Class, and Political Culture* (New Haven: Yale University Press, 1989).

A. A. Parker, 'The Devil in the Drama of Calderón', *Critical Essays on the Theatre of Calderón*, ed. Bruce W. Wardropper (New York: New York University Press, 1965).

Ronald Paulson, *Representations of Revolution (1789–1820)* (New Haven: Yale University Press, 1983).

J. Pickersgill, *The Three Brothers: A Romance* (London: printed for John Stockdale, 1803).

J. B. Priestley, *The Prince of Pleasure and his Regency: 1811–20* (New York: Harper & Row, 1969).

Moody E. Prior, *The Language of Tragedy* (New York: Columbia University Press, 1947).

Peter Quennell, *Byron: The Years of Fame* (New York: The Viking Press, 1935; London: Faber & Faber, 1935).

Ricardo J. Quinones, 'Byron's *Cain*: Between History and Theology', in *Byron, the Bible, and Religion*, ed. Wolf Z. Hirst (Newark, DE: University of Delaware Press, 1991).

Tilottama Rajan, *Dark Interpreter: The Discourse of Romanticism* (Ithaca and London: Cornell University Press, 1980).

Herbert Read, *The Art Of Sculpture*, 2nd edn (Princeton: Princeton University Press, 1961).

Donald Reiman (ed.), *The Romantics Reviewed* (New York: Garland, 1972).

Thomas A. Reisner, '*Cain*: Two Romantic Interpretations', *Culture*, XXXI (1970).

Retsch's Series of Twenty-Six Outlines, Illustrative of Goethe's Tragedy of Faust, Engraved from the Originals by Henry Moses, and an Analysis of the Tragedy (London, 1820).

Kenneth Richards and Peter Thomson (eds), *Essays on Nineteenth-Century British Theatre* (London: Methuen, 1971).

Alan Richardson, *A Mental Theater: Poetic Drama and Consciousness in the Romantic Age* (University Park: Pennsylvania State University Press, 1988).

George Ridenour, *The Style of 'Don Juan'* (New Haven: Yale University Press, 1960).

Charles E. Robinson, 'The Devil as Doppelganger in *The Deformed Transformed*: The Sources and Meaning of Byron's Unfinished Drama', *Bulletin of the New York Public Library*, LXXIV (1970).

——*Shelley and Byron: The Snake and the Eagle Wreathed in Flight* (Baltimore and London: Johns Hopkins University Press, 1976).

Murray Roston, *Biblical Drama in England from the Middle Ages to the Present* (London: Faber, 1968; Evanston: Northwestern University Press, 1968).

William Ruddick, 'Lord Byron's Historical Tragedies', in *Essays on Nineteenth-Century British Theatre*, ed. Kenneth Richards and Peter Thomson (London: Methuen, 1971).

Lord John Russell, *Life of William Lord Russell*, 4th edn (London: Longman, 1853).

Andrew Rutherford, *Byron: A Critical Study* (Stanford: Stanford University Press, 1961).

Andrew Rutherford (ed.), *Byron: The Critical Heritage* (New York: Barnes and Noble, 1970).

Robert Ryan, 'Byron's *Cain*: The Ironies of Belief', *The Wordsworth Circle*, XXI (1990).

Roger Sales, *English Literature in History 1780–1830, Pastoral and Politics* (London: Hutchinson, 1983).

Richard Sennett, *The Fall of Public Man: On the Social Psychology of Capitalism* (Cambridge: Cambridge University Press, 1977; rpt. New York: Vintage Books, 1978).

Richard B. Sewall, *The Vision of Tragedy* (New Haven and London: Yale University Press, 1959).

Mary W. Shelley, *The Letters of Mary W. Shelley*, ed. Frederick L. Jones (Norman, OK, 1944).

Mary Shelley's Journal, ed. Frederick L. Jones (Norman, OK: University of Oklahoma Press, 1947).

Percy Bysshe Shelley, *The Complete Works of Percy Bysshe Shelley*, ed. Roger Ingpen and Walter E. Peck (New York: Gordian Press, 1965).

Frederick W. Shilstone, 'Byron's "Mental Theatre" and the German Classical Precedent', *Comparative Drama*, X (Autumn 1976).

Philip J. Skerry, 'Concentric Structures in *Marino Faliero*', *Keats–Shelley Journal*, XXXII (1983).

Gordon Spence, 'The Moral Ambiguity of *Marino Faliero*', *Journal of the Australasian Universities' Modern Language Association*, XLI (1974).

———'Moral and Sexual Ambivalence in *Sardanapalus*', *Byron Journal*, XII (1984).

Martin S. Stabb, *Jorge Luis Borges* (New York: Twayne, 1970).

Truman Guy Steffan, *Lord Byron's 'Cain': Twelve Essays and a Text with Variants and Annotations* (Austin and London: University of Texas Press, 1968).

George Steiner, *The Death of Tragedy* (New York: Knopf, 1961).

Ray Stevens, 'Scripture and the Literary Imagination: Biblical Allusions in Byron's *Heaven and Earth*', in *Byron, the Bible, and Religion*, ed. Wolf Z. Hirst (Newark, DE: University of Delaware Press, 1991).

Montague Summers, *The Gothic Quest: A History of the Gothic Novel* (London: Fortune Press, 1938).

Boleslaw Taborski, *Byron and the Theatre* (Salzburg: University of Salzburg, 1972).

———'Byron's Theatre: Private Spleen, or Cosmic Revolt: Theatrical Solutions—Stanislavsky to Grotowski' in *Byron: Poetry and Politics*, ed. E. A. Stürzl and J. Hogg (Salzburg: University of Salzburg, 1981).

Anya Taylor, *Magic and English Romanticism* (Athens, GA: University of Georgia Press, 1979).

Horace E. Thorner, 'Hawthorne, Poe, and a Literary Ghost', *The New England Quarterly*, VII (1934).

Peter L. Thorslev, Jr, *Lord Byron: Christian Virtues* (London: Routledge & Kegan Paul, 1952).

———*The Byronic Hero: Types and Prototypes* (Minneapolis: University of Minnesota Press, 1962).

———*Romantic Contraries: Freedom versus Destiny* (New Haven and London: Yale University Press, 1984).

———'Byron and Bayle: Biblical Skepticism and Romantic Irony', in *Byron, the Bible, and Religion*, ed. Wolf Z. Hirst (Newark, DE: University of Delaware Press, 1991).

Charles Chenevix Trench, *Portrait of a Patriot* (Edinburgh: Blackwood, 1962).

Voltaire, *The Works of Voltaire*, trans. William F. Fleming, 42 vols (Paris: E. R. Dumont, 1748).

Daniel P. Watkins, 'Violence, Class Consciousness, and Ideology in Byron's History Plays', *English Literary History*, XLVIII (1981).

———'Politics and Religion in Byron's *Heaven and Earth*', *Byron Journal*, XI (1983).

——*Social Relations in Byron's Eastern Tales* (London and Toronto: Associated University Presses, 1987).

——*A Materialist Critique of English Romantic Drama* (Gainesville: University of Florida Press, 1993).

Elizabeth P. Watson, 'Mental Theatre: Some Aspects of Byron's Dramatic Imagination', *Renaissance and Modern Studies*, XXXII (1988).

Edwin Wexberg, *The Psychology of Sex* (New York: Farrar & Rinehart, 1931).

Allen Whitmore, *The Major Characters of Lord Byron's Drama* (Salzburg: University of Salzburg, 1974).

Stanley T. Williams, *The Life of Washington Irving* (New York: Oxford University Press, 1935).

John Wilson, 'Byron's "Heaven and Earth"', *Blackwood's Edinburgh Magazine*, XIII (January 1823); rpt. in Reiman (ed.), *The Romantics Reviewed*, Part B: *Byron and Regency Society Poets*, I, 196.

Susan J. Wolfson, '"Their She Condition": Cross-dressing and the Politics of Gender in *Don Juan*', *English Literary History*, LIV (1987).

Carl R. Woodring, *Politics in English Romantic Poetry* (Cambridge, MA: Harvard University Press, 1970).

Index of Proper Names and Works